THE NATIVE AMERICANS

THE INDIGENOUS PEOPLE OF NORTH AMERICA

THE NATIVE
AMERICANS

THE INDIGENOUS PEOPLE OF NORTH AMERICA

EDITORIAL CONSULTANT
COLIN F. TAYLOR

TECHNICAL CONSULTANT
WILLIAM C. STURTEVANT
CURATOR OF NORTH AMERICAN ETHNOLOGY
SMITHSONIAN INSTITUTION

SMITHMARK

A SALAMANDER BOOK

This edition published in 1991 by SMITHMARK Publishers, a division of U.S. Media Holdings, Inc., 16 East 32nd Street, New York, NY 10016

10 9 8

SMITHMARK books are available for bulk purchase for sales promotion and premium use. For details write or call the manager of special sales, SMITHMARK Publishers, 16 East 32nd Street, New York, NY 10016; (212) 532-6600.

© Salamander Books Ltd 1991

ISBN 0-7651-9927-0

All correspondence concerning the content of this volume should be addressed to Salamander Books Ltd, 129-137 York Way, London N7 9LG, England

CREDITS

Editor: Richard Collins
Designer: John Heritage
Color photography: Don Eiler, Richmond, Virginia (© Salamander Books Ltd)
Color artwork (figures): Lois Sloan, Washington, D.C. (© Lois Sloan)
Additional color artwork: Jeffrey Burn (© Salamander Books Ltd)
Maps: Janos Marffy (© Salamander Books Ltd)
Filmset: SX Composing DTP, England
Color reproduction: Magnum Graphics Ltd, England
Printed in Italy

TECHNICAL CONSULTANT

William C. Sturtevant is Curator of North American Ethnology, Department of Anthropology, National Museum of Natural History, Smithsonian Institution in Washington, D.C., and General Editor of the *Handbook of North American Indians*. In his capacity as Technical Consultant, Dr Sturtevant has been responsible for the selection and identification of all the objects in the artifact spreads, as well as providing explanations for each piece and writing introductions to Indian tribes and groups represented in the spreads. On the figure artworks by Lois Sloan, he selected the figures to be represented, provided sources of models, advised on the clothing and ornaments they wore, the objects they carried and the activities they were engaged in. He also wrote captions for each illustration. In working so closely with the artist, he was in a unique position to be able to ensure accuracy and veracity. Dr Sturtevant also helped with the original selection of black and white photographs from the National Anthropological Archives and other institutions, although final selection was made by Salamander Books.

ACKNOWLEDGMENTS

Artifacts
This book could not have been published without the assistance of staff at the American Museum of Natural History, New York, and the Smithsonian Institution, Washington, who made their outstanding collections available to Salamander for photography. In New York: Dr Stanley Freed (Curator of Anthropology), Laila Williamson (Scientific Assistant), Anibal Rodriguez (Technical Assistant), Dr Lisa Whittall (Keeper of Textiles) and Amy Rudnick (Guest Services) gave their time and expertise most willingly. In Washington: Linda Eisenhart (former Acting Collections Manager), Margaret Waddell (Technician) and Dr Sturtevant gave outstanding support. For the artifact spreads, figure artworks, initial photograph selection and in the preparation of all but three captions in the California chapter, Sally McLendon provided technical consultation, and her role is gratefully acknowledged.

Photographs, color plates
Grateful thanks go to the following for assistance provided in obtaining illustrations and for granting permission to publish them in this book:
National Anthropological Archives, Washington, especially Paula Richardson Fleming (Photo Archivist), who was unstinting in her efforts to obtain photographs from the archives; to the SI Office of Printing and Photographic Services, especially Jim Wallace (Director), Joyce Goulait, Alan Hart and Nicholas Parella, all of whom provided a substantial number of prints of excellent quality.
All black and white photographs, with the exception of those mentioned below, are published with the permission of the NAA, Smithsonian Institution. Lack of space precludes the inclusion of negative numbers of NAA photographs included in this book, but these numbers may be obtained from Salamander Books on behalf of the NAA. The publishers are grateful to the following individuals and institutions for permission to publish black and white photographs and color illustrations:
Joslyn Art Museum, Omaha, Nebraska: pp i, iii, 15, 33 (left), 66 (left and right), 76, 94 (above), 237 (above), 249 (above), (all watercolors by Karl Bodmer. The title page illustration is of Mató-Tópe [Four Bears], a Mandan Chief.)
Stark Museum of Art, Orange, Texas: pp 102 (above), 176 (above), 180, 192, 236 (oils on paper and watercolors by Paul Kane)
Pitt Rivers Museum, Oxford: pp 63, 225, 231 (top)
Courtesy of the Royal Ontario Museum, Toronto, Canada: 102 (below), 103, 240 (below)
Courtesy Bancroft Library, University of California, Berkeley: 130 (above)
Courtesy Peter Palmquist: 136
Mendocino Cty Historical Society, Robert J. Lee Collection: 130 (below)
Courtesy Department Library Services, American Museum of Natural History: pp 188 (below) (neg. no. 283, 779), 189 (neg. no. 283, 786), both photographs by P.E. Goddard, 193 (neg. no. 105479), 196 (neg. no. 19851), 205 (neg. no. 34915), photograph by H.D. Chichester, 220 (above) (neg. no. 15231), photograph by V. Stefansson, 221 (below) (neg. no. 26173), photograph by George Comer.
The Anchorage Museum of History and Art: pp 206 (81.68.7), 207 (above) (81.68.4 and B90.13.5), 210 (both, above) (81.68.4 and B90.18.1) (all watercolors by Louis Choris).

Additional acknowledgments
To the Federal Writers' Project, for permission to publish the quote on page 128, from *California: A Guide to the Golden State.*
To Colin and Betty Taylor for their outstanding contributions. Much of the clothing and equipment featured in the six illustrations by Jeffrey Burn, as well as in the jacket artwork, were based on items in the C.F. Taylor collection, Hastings, England. The jacket artwork depicts a Crow buffalo hunt of the early 1870s and was prepared with Mr Taylor's assistance.
To Valérie Chaussonnet, Washington D.C., for providing consultation on the St Lawrence Island Eskimo artwork (page 211).
To Nigel Duffield and Mark Holt, for their inspired laying out of artifacts in New York and Washington.
Figure artworks by Lois Sloan appear on the following pages: 26, 40, 51, 84, 117, 125, 144, 149, 174, 198, 211, 230, 238.

Editor's note
The final selection and captioning of all illustrations in this book have been the responsibility of Salamander Books Ltd and not of the individual contributors.

CONTENTS

INTRODUCTION 6
Natalie Tobert, Horniman Museum, London

THE SOUTHEAST 12
William Sturtevant, Smithsonian Institution, Washington, D.C.

THE SOUTHWEST 36
Nancy Parezo, Arizona State Museum, Tucson

THE PLAINS 62
Colin Taylor, Hastings College of Art and Technology, Hastings

PLATEAU AND BASIN 100
Colin Taylor

CALIFORNIA 128
John Langellier, Gene Autry Western Heritage Museum, Los Angeles

THE NORTHWEST COAST 154
Victoria Wyatt, University of Victoria, Victoria

THE SUBARCTIC 182
Colin Taylor

THE ARCTIC 204
Susan Rowley, University of Alberta, Edmonton

THE NORTHEAST 224
Colin Taylor

BIBLIOGRAPHY AND CATALOG 250

INDEX 253

INTRODUCTION

A HUNDRED thousand years ago the world was suffering from the last part of the Ice Age: great ice sheets covered much of North America, and sea levels fell dramatically revealing land corridors. During this time Neanderthal man developed fire for warmth and cooking. *Homo sapiens sapiens* evolved around 35,000 years ago, a big game hunter with a sophisticated tool kit and great intellectual capacity. Though less robust physically than Neanderthal man, he was more adaptable to climatic variations. Families lived in substantial dwellings and buried their dead with grave goods. Evidence for *homo sapiens sapiens* first occurred in Africa, Asia and the Near East, where they absorbed and replaced the Neanderthal populations. Several millennia later they appeared in Australia and Siberia. At the time when Europe was under glaciation, Northern Asia was cold, dry and free of glaciers.

The date of man's arrival in America is open to discussion, though archeological evidence from sites suggests a date after 14,000 years ago. *Homo sapiens sapiens* (fully modern man) was the first to inhabit the Americas during the latter part of the Ice Age. Anyone living in the region needed to have the right technology: warm clothes and shelter, strategies for food storage, a means of traveling over snow and ice and a mobile way of life.

Geologists agree that for two long periods between 75,000-45,000 and 25,000-14,000 years ago, the Bering land bridge was exposed. The first Americans migrated from Siberia over the Bering Strait. Research has shown that common linguistic and cultural traditions survive to this day on both sides of the Bering Strait, and fauna and flora are almost identical in these land masses.

Central Beringia was dry land for several thousand years. It was a cold place, with strong winds and thin snow cover, believed to be treeless, but with enough vegetation and grasslands to support the late Ice Age mammals (mammoth, bison, wild horse, and caribou). The study of fossil pollen grains has indicated that the vegetation may have been areas of steppe or tundra where reindeer roamed. Beringia may have been a refuge for animals and humans during the cold intervals of the last glaciation, and when conditions changed the animals moved on followed by the humans.

Around Beringia 11,000 years ago the inhabitants had adapted to a variety of different environments: maritime, tundra, river valley and mountain. Thus during the Ice Age there were several cultural groups living in northeast Asia, with diverse lifestyles under different environmental conditions. Of those groups, some scholars say it was only the big game hunters who crossed over on the land passage between the ice masses following the animals south into America, and later evolved according to the landscape, climate and available resources.

The sea levels rose about 14,000 years ago and by 9,000 years ago the land bridge had vanished. It is generally accepted that the American Indians migrated from Siberia.

At Paleo-Arctic sites by the Yukon and in Alaska, there is evidence of post-glacial occupation around 11-12,000 years ago. Artifacts (small cores and microblades and bladelets) have been discovered similar to those found near Lake Baikal in Siberia. At such settlements people stayed in tent-like houses and lived by hunting, fishing and gathering wild fruits.

The skulls of Indians found by the great mounds were examined and compared with modern recent Indian and Mongolian crania. It was claimed that they were the same peoples, and that the first Americans were descended from Asian origins. Biologists have discovered that there is a relationship between the teeth of humans from North China and those from North America. Apparently there was a single early migration of hunter-gatherers who evolved by cultural differentiation. Two further migrations took place later, and gave rise to the Athapaskans and the Eskimo-Aleut populations.

According to Christy Turner (1984), an expert on the physical characteristics of prehistoric

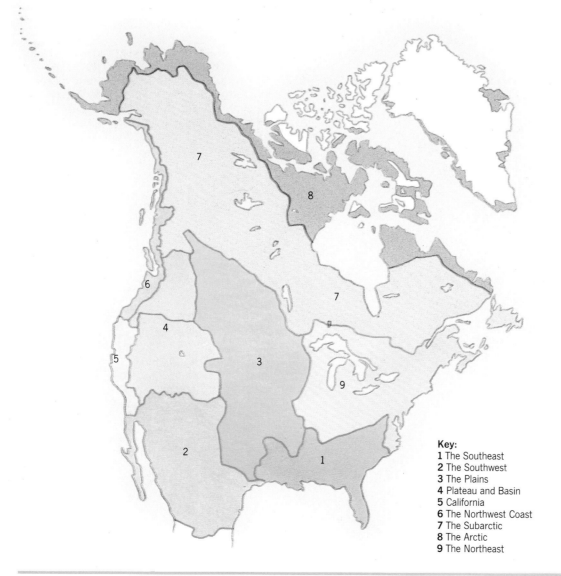

Key:
1 The Southeast
2 The Southwest
3 The Plains
4 Plateau and Basin
5 California
6 The Northwest Coast
7 The Subarctic
8 The Arctic
9 The Northeast

This map shows the ten geographic areas of Native North America (the Plateau and Basin appearing together in this book) within each of which the aboriginal cultures were broadly similar. Color-coded in the map are the nine cultural areas into which chapters in the book are divided. More detailed keys to tribes and their tribal lands are shown on maps which appear on the first pages of each chapter.

Above: *Seminole – 'The unconquered' – man of the Southeast. A Muskogean tribe, the Seminole split off from the more northern Creeks and mixed with the remnants of Florida's original Indians, before 1600 consisting of more than twenty-five separate tribes.*

Above: *Face of the Southwest. A Quechan man, more popularly known as Yuman who lived on both sides of the Colorado River in SW Arizona and eastern California. They were linguistic members of the Yuman subfamily of the Hokan family.*

Above: *A Cheyenne warrior of the Plains. The Cheyenne belonged to the Algonquian linguistic stock. They migrated from Minnesota c.1750 and finally settled on the central Plains, becoming a typical nomadic Plains tribe.*

man's teeth, the earliest penetration of Alaska by Asians took place over 14,000 years ago. They were followed a few thousand years later by two waves of immigrants from Siberia: the ancestors of modern Athapaskan Indians and northwest coast peoples; and the ancient Eskimo-Aleut.

Various bodies of research have divided the American peoples into three distinct pre-European groupings: the Paleo-Indians (Puebloans, Pimas, Pai); the Athapaskan speakers (Apache and Navajo); and the Eskimo-Aleut. Neither the Athapaskans nor the Eskimo-Aleut penetrated deep into the Americas: the Central and South American Indians were Paleo-Indians (Fagan, 1987). All three peoples came from North East Siberia, but there were three language groups: Amerindian (most North American and all South American languages were part of one Amerind family); Na-Dene; and Eskimo-Aleut. According to certain scholars these three linguistic groups correspond to the three waves of migration. The Amerindian group arrived before 11,000 years, the Na-Dene around 9,000 years ago and the Eskimo-Aleut around 4,000 years ago.

There is more linguistic diversity in extreme northwest America where there are more contrasting environments than in the recently deglaciated northeast. It is suggested that the Eskimo-Aleut, Na-Dene and Algonquian languages spread from the periphery of the ice sheets into the newly unglaciated lands. The later two migrations limited their settlements to the north and northwest coast without penetrating further into the interior of the Americas.

The period between the first proposed crossing by man approximately 14,000 years ago, and the arrival of the so-called Clovis peoples around 11,500 years ago, is a subject

fiercely discussed by archeologists. There are widely accepted and precise dates for 'Clovis' artifact sites throughout the Americas from around 11,500 years ago.

The following passages set out a few of the sites around which this controversy rages.

In the western United States, there may have been settlement of the US Pacific coastal and inland regions in the very early post glacial period, 14-13,000 years ago, for humanly made stone fragments have been found. In California, on Santa Rosa Island, there were temporary encampments where hunter-gatherers butchered mammoths and settled for a few days during their seasonal migrations. This site is firmly dated around 7,500 years ago, though claims have been made for much earlier settlement. Pre-Clovis man may have occupied China Lake sites in California, but the stratigraphy is questioned by scholars. Other sites on the high plains of Colorado and in Texas may have been visited by pre-Clovis man but scholars have put

Left: *America 11,500 years ago, showing the migration of the Paleo-Indians through North and South America. The first Americans migrated from Siberia across the Bering Strait; research shows that common linguistic and cultural traditions still survive on both sides of the Strait.*

Ice sheet cover, 9500 BC. Area later settled by early Athapaskan and Eskimo–Aleut peoples.

Passage used by Paleo-Indians during first wave of migration.

Migration path through America over the first thousand years.

forward a plethora of arguments against this.

In the eastern United States, Meadowcroft Rockshelter on Cross Creek by the Ohio River was one of the earliest occupied sites in North America, from which were found 45 species of mammal, 68 birds and 30,000 plant fragments. The environment there was stable for 11,000 years, and the rockshelter is known to have been used from 12,000 to 700 years ago, though archeologists claim it was used much earlier.

In southern Florida, the area was cooler and drier than it is today; Paleo-Indian sites at sinkholes are today submerged below sea level, but may date from before 11,500 years ago. There the peoples camped for short periods while hunting game and may have exploited huge territories using pre-Clovis artifacts.

Although not directly relevant to this book, it is interesting too to note archeological evidence of human occupation in Central and South America. In Central America archeologists such as MacNeish (1986) are convinced that human occupation in Mexico can be dated back to 20,000 years ago, though the most reliable record begins 11,000 years ago, when the hunting groups are found to the south of the Rio Grande with Clovis-type points. In South America very early settlement dates of 14,000 years ago have been given for Pikimachay Cave in Peru, but these are highly controversial. In Brazil beautifully painted rockshelters have

been found, mostly dating to between 7,600 and 8,000 years ago.

Evidence from artifacts for humans inhabiting the Americas prior to 14,000 years ago is open to debate. Scholars argue that the 'early' artifacts are intrusive, accumulations are natural, the association between mammoth bones and flakes is tenuous, or that dating materials are excavated from earlier levels and radiocarbon readings are inaccurate. It is agreed that after 12,000 years ago Paleo-Indians settled in South America, bringing with them their stone technology from the North.

Clovis peoples were hunters who followed the migratory paths of the larger mammals. They camped by rivers and streams where big game came to drink, and in the winter they stayed in rock shelters. People collected wild foods including fruits, berries, vegetables and nuts, to supplement their diet. They also ate the meat of both large and small mammals as is indicated by the discovery of these bones from their occupation sites. They were expert stone workers and artisans, renowned for producing beautiful translucent stone points with

Below: *People of the in-between land: Umatilla and Palus of the Columbia Plateau. Such eastern groups as these were heavily influenced by the Plains tribes after what might be called 'The Equestrian Revolution', which occurred c.1750.*

fluted bifaces, known as Clovis points.

These Paleo-Indians arrived approximately 11,500 years ago and within a few centuries spread to the North American coasts and as far south as Mexico. On the Great Plains of America Clovis culture stone artifacts have been found, in direct association with bones of large extinct Ice Age mammals.

While it is generally accepted that Clovis people came from north of the ice sheets and migrated south as the glaciers melted, the problem for archeologists is to trace their origins. The mystery exists because they appeared at sites with their fine, highly-developed stone tools, for which there appears to be no precedent. Scholars believe that the Clovis point was developed on the Plains and not in the Arctic (Alaskan points are different). Clovis points have been found in the Canadian Provinces, throughout the United States, on the Great Plains, in North America, Mexico and South America.

The Clovis people (the big game hunters) flourished on the Plains for about 500 years, then around 11,000 years ago abruptly vanished. They were replaced by a multitude of different hunting and gathering peoples. Various reasons have been put forward to explain their disappearance. It was suggested that the climate had changed resulting in reduced water availability. Consequently animals clustered around the remaining springs, were easy prey and were over-hunted.

However, Paul Martin (1974) claimed that when the first Americans arrived they found themselves in an extremely favorable environment, with large herds of mammoth and other mammals who were not wary of hunters. As a result the human population exploded, and the rapidly expanding human population quickly depleted the slower breeding mammal groups. As big game became scarce the hunters moved on across America, and once the big game became extinct a population crash followed. Martin developed a computer projection that suggested that Paleo-Indians arrived in Panama by 10,930 years ago, and at Tierra del Fuego by 10,500 years ago. He suggested that the population of the entire continent south of the ice sheets took a mere 1,000 years.

After the disappearance of the Ice Age mammoth, the people who had preyed on them turned to bison (buffalo) hunting, and for over 10,000 years the successors of Clovis pursued bison on the Plains. By 10,500 years ago, bison were the most dominant species found at all

Below: *Faces of the living past: Ute Indians of the Great Basin region. The Utes were the most southerly of the Basin culture which was essentially unchanged and isolated for thousands of years, with few rivers seeking the sea.*

Above: *Face of a land of migrants and wanderers: a Yurok woman of northern California. This was an area of great contrast with perhaps the highest population density in North America and at least six different linguistic stocks.*

Above: *Faces of the Northwest Coast: Tillamook of northwest Oregon. Early 19th century they were a prominent Salishan-speaking tribe occupying some eight villages, with a population of about 2,200. By the 1850s that had been reduced to around 300.*

archeological sites in the region. Bison survived because they adapted to feed on grass land in post-glacial times.

Mass bison drives took place: in Colorado the Olsen-Chubbock site held 152 carcasses in a canyon into which bison had been stampeded 8,500 years ago. Such bison hunts were communal affairs that may have been conducted once annually. When the bow and arrow reached the plains in AD 500, communal bison hunting reached its greatest prehistoric intensity. In 1547 horses were introduced by the Spanish, and their use brought about dramatic change: bison herds were further reduced, the nomadic population grew and placed greater demands on the farm produce of sedentary populations. Tensions surfaced, different cultural values took hold and raids were prevalent. During the nineteenth century, Europeans with their muskets joined the bison hunt and herds were decimated. In the twentieth century great efforts have been made to save the bison, which were largely successful, and there are now herds on the Plains again, although not in the large numbers there used to be.

In the far north, the environment could only support a small population, so people moved regularly depending on the season. Na-Dene speakers came first. They were forest hunter-gatherers and spread south and west and into the interior, where they became known as Athapaskan. Later some split off, moved south and became the modern Navajo and Apache. The Eskimo-Aleut came after the Paleo-Indians, before the land bridge was severed (though some say that they arrived by boat). They are the most Asian of North Americans, and their language has Siberian roots.

The Eskimo spread over thousands of miles of mainland and probably split away from the Aleut about 4,000 years ago. Ties weakened as each group adapted to different environmental conditions. The Eskimo hunted using skin kayaks, traveled by dog sled and occupied land from the Bering Strait to Greenland between the tenth and eleventh centuries AD. Their predecessors hunted caribou and musk oxen on land, walrus and whale in the sea. They dug their houses into the ground to protect them against the arctic winter, with trap doors to shield them against the cold. The Aleut were maritime hunters and fishermen, excellent boatmen, hunting seal, sea lion and otter on the open seas.

The first wave of settlement to the newly exposed northwest coastal regions were forest hunter-gatherers from Alaska, distinct from the Eskimo-Aleut. The climate and sea levels stabilised 5,000 years ago: there was a predictable supply of maritime food and more elaborate hunting and foraging societies developed in which wealth and social status assumed a vital importance. Powerful individuals came to the fore, and it was they who regulated ceremonial life and controlled commodities.

People lived in villages all year round in substantial log houses, and used canoes to move between settlements such as early sites on the Queen Charlotte Islands. Another coastal site was excavated at Ozette in Washington State where a mud slide buried a whaling village 500 years ago, and all household artifacts were preserved in mud. Baskets, nets, fish hooks and looms were found in cedar longhouses which had been divided into small rooms using low walls and hanging mats.

The Native American Indians occupied the entire American continent whether rain forest, desert, plains or arctic by the time Europeans arrived on the scene. In the desert and woodland areas, the first inhabitants had been dispersed bands living in seasonal camps, though more intensive foraging developed from 9,000 to 4,500 years ago, with people returning to the same location year after year. Maize cultivation developed 1,500 years ago: the cycle of planting and harvesting reduced people's mobility and greater storage was needed. Trade networks also developed.

The Eskimo-Aleut had settled on the islands and coasts of the central Canadian Arctic by the twelfth and thirteenth centuries, and the climate had warmed. Norsemen traded in the area in AD 1000 and remained until a new wave of Westerners penetrated the land in the sixteenth century.

In the eastern woodlands, the farmers of 4,000 years ago developed a preoccupation with burial: Adena people built earthworks and ceremonial compounds. The Hopewell burial mounds were even more elaborate than those of the Adena, and a flowering of artistic tradition came about. The Mississippian Culture emerged around AD 700, with both farmers and hunter-gatherers. The population grew to around 10,000 peoples and powerful chieftains ruled the valleys. This was contemporary with Mexican civilization when heavily fortified

Left: Faces of the great Subarctic: Ahtna of the Copper River Valley, Alaska. Typical of many Subarctic tribes, they spoke the Athapaskan language and practiced a semi-nomadic way of life; hunters of small game, their main subsistence was fishing.

Below: Regalia of the Northeast: early Chippewa (Ojibwa) costume worn by the son of a Mississaugi leader. Typical of the region, it is of buckskin embellished extensively with bead- and quillwork.

communities with temple mounds and plazas were built. These were seen by the Spanish in the mid-sixteenth century.

In the Pacific coastal regions most societies lived by hunting and foraging up until European contact. In seventeenth century Mississippi the Cherokee were living in the north, with 100 settlements of around 60,000 people. In California people lived off the land and sea, and with rich resources large, permanent villages grew up ruled by local chiefs, and the population grew.

In Arizona in the southwest around 2,000 years ago the Hohokam people began planting their crops to coincide with the rainfall patterns: they dug terraces, canals and dams to control water flow. By AD 900 the Anasazi (ancestors of the Hopi, Zuni and other Pueblo Indians) were farmers living in multi-room structures in New Mexico.

Today ethnologists generally divide North America into nine culture groups, mostly based on geographical location, for the early peoples adapted their skills to suit environmental conditions. This book offers the following breakdown: Southeast; Southwest; Plains; Plateau and Basin; California; Northwest Coast; Subarctic; Arctic, and Northeast.

The arrival of the Europeans changed the face of the entire continent and the lives of its indigenous peoples irredeemably. Vikings,

Below: Faces of a resourceful race: Eskimos of the Bering Strait region. Modern-day Eskimos refer to themselves as Inuit, meaning 'humans', the word Eskimo deriving from the Algonquian meaning 'raw meat eaters'. In common with other groups of this vast region, they displayed a wide variety of subsistence patterns but a good proportion of their raw materials were obtained from the caribou and from sea mammals. These people have moved rapidly with the times; by 1982 many of the young had completed technical and professional courses in high school and local colleges.

English, French and Spanish explored the coasts of America and then settled there permanently. Colonists, missionaries, and explorers arrived, spreading disease, destruction and disruption which affected the traditional Indian way of life. Within a few mere centuries the old Indian way of life had been swept away forever.

Change came slowly. After World War II, increased awareness of the multi-cultural nature of society came about. Popular interest in the country's various ethnic groups surged, and the market for Indian arts and crafts soared, a market partly kept buoyant by the poor economic situation in the reservations and the Indians' ability to adapt their work to the preferences of their customers. Today Native American Indian artifacts and the people who produce them receive world-wide acclaim. The artifacts and the importance of their original function within Indian society are now more widely appreciated than ever.

'My people are scattered and gone; when I shout, I hear my voice in the depths of the forest, but no answering voice comes back to me – all is silent around me.'

COLONEL COBB OF THE CHOCTAW

THE SOUTHEAST

THE INDIAN cultures of the Southeast in the nineteenth century and the first half of the twentieth century were the products of a long period of change, disruption, and destruction – almost genocide, although the destruction was not the direct result of conscious state policies. Thousands of years of cultural development in this region were rudely diverted and truncated by the arrival of Euro-peans in the early sixteenth century. Little can now be known about what the lives of the southern Indian people were like when the invaders arrived, for the first literate observers left few records, and none for most of the region, and the archeological evidence cannot answer many important questions. Native traditions cannot help, for the details of an old way of life cannot be preserved by word of mouth alone over 400 years in a society undergoing very rapid social and cultural change. However, the scale of the cultural and biological disaster that was visited on the Southeastern Indians has recently become clearer from advances in archeological interpretations, filled out by scraps of information from the thin documentary record left by the first Europeans.

Certainly this was a naturally favored region.

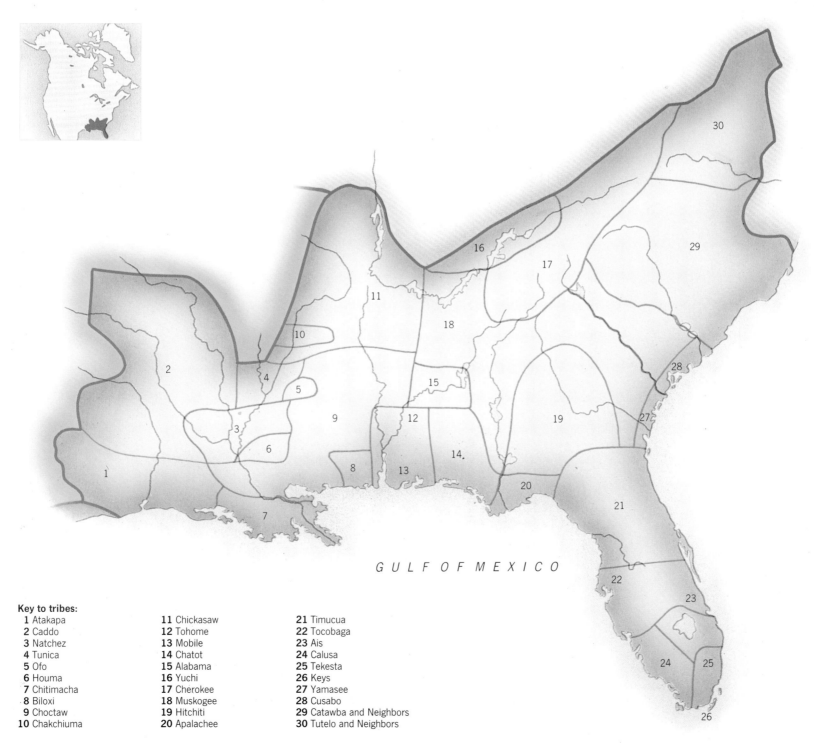

GULF OF MEXICO

Key to tribes:

1 Atakapa	11 Chickasaw	21 Timucua
2 Caddo	12 Tohome	22 Tocobaga
3 Natchez	13 Mobile	23 Ais
4 Tunica	14 Chatot	24 Calusa
5 Ofo	15 Alabama	25 Tekesta
6 Houma	16 Yuchi	26 Keys
7 Chitimacha	17 Cherokee	27 Yamasee
8 Biloxi	18 Muskogee	28 Cusabo
9 Choctaw	19 Hitchiti	29 Catawba and Neighbors
10 Chakchiuma	20 Apalachee	30 Tutelo and Neighbors

It is in the warmest part of the northern temperate zone, and south Florida is actually subtropical in climate. Most of the Southeast falls within the broad coastal plain bordering the Atlantic and the Gulf of Mexico. In this low-lying area the rivers meander and deposit fertile alluvial soils. In the broad valleys were many oxbow lakes and vast swamps of cypress and cane. Fields were easily cleared in the bottom lands along the rivers, and their productivity was rapidly renewed by the silt from seasonal floods. Fish were plentiful especially in the river backwaters, and migratory water fowl were easily taken. In some areas such as along the lower Mississippi River fish and water fowl provided at least half the protein in the Indian diet. Other animal food came from white-tailed deer, raccoons, and other mammals. Wild plant foods – nuts, fruits, berries – were a very important resource. Cultivated corn, beans, squash, sunflowers, and gourds were a major source of food everywhere except in south Florida, where, at least on the southwest coast, fish and shellfish were so plentiful that they allowed the Calusa to develop a complex sedentary society of a sort that normally depends on agriculture. The northeastern part

This map shows approximate territories of tribes and tribal groupings at about 1600 in Florida and along the Atlantic coast, and about 1700 in the rest of the region. After that, all tribes lost territory, many disappeared, many moved west, some new tribes arose.

Above: *Ben P. Harris, a prominent Catawba man, c.1899, in the traditional accoutrements of a participant in a 'medicine show': non-Catawba turkey-feather headdress, fringed cloth jacket and trousers, Plains-style beaded vest, bow and arrows.*

of the area includes the piedmont above the fall-line, and the low mountains of the Appalachian highlands. The environment here was different but also favorable. The valleys are narrower, but still fertile, and fish abounded in the river shoals. The economic cycle in general depended on growing crops and fishing during the warm season, then hunting deer during the cooler season.

What one sees now in the region is far different from the aboriginal situation. The forests and cane brakes are gone, many rivers are dammed and swamps drained, and the soil is much degraded and eroded from exploitative commercial farming of first indigo, then tobacco, cotton, and corn. The passenger pigeons are extinct, and other birds, fish, and most wild animals are far less plentiful than they were even at the beginning of the nineteenth century.

The radical, disastrous changes in Indian life occurred before most of the environmental degradation. In the early period precipitous depopulation was the result of the introduction of European diseases, such as smallpox, to which the Indians at first lacked immunity. In many communities half or more of the inhabitants died within a period of weeks. The social and psychological effects of this disaster can scarcely be imagined, in general and in the loss of the bearers of knowledge and tradition. Later, after immunities to the new diseases had been established, the Indian societies were

SOUTHEASTERN TRIBES

Ais. A small tribe on the east coast of south Florida, numbering perhaps 1,000 in 1650 and extinct by the 1720s. They grew no crops, being mainly dependent on fish. There is no evidence whatsoever on the Ais language.

Alabama. Their language, belonging to the Muskogean family, is very close to Koasati, the two being perhaps dialects of a single language. The Alabama population was less than 1,000 in 1704; after 1763 they were dispersed, some joining the Seminoles and Creeks and most going to Texas with the Koasatis. By 1910, there were only about 300 Alabamas in addition to those among the Creeks.

Apalachee. Speakers of a Muskogean language, missionized by the Spanish, their population was perhaps 5,000 in 1676. They were destroyed in the eighteenth century by English and Creek raids, a few survivors joining the Creeks.

Atakapa. The population was about 1,000 in the early eighteenth century, and the group was extinct by 1900. The Atakapa language was an isolate, that is, without demonstrable relationship to any other language.

Biloxi. Amounting to perhaps 1,000 people in 1650, the Biloxi spoke a language belonging to the Siouan family. By the end of the nineteenth century there were very few identifiable survivors, in Louisiana, Oklahoma, and eastern Texas.

Caddo. This term includes several tribes, mostly in three confederacies, all speaking the Caddo language which is the southern branch of the Caddoan language family of which the other languages were spoken on the Plains. The Caddo population may have been 8,000 in 1700; by 1910 there were only about 550 Caddos, in Oklahoma.

Calusa. This was a non-agricultural chiefdom in south Florida, which may have included as many as 10,000 people in the 1560s. By 1750 there were none left. So little of the Calusa language was recorded that its affiliations are unknown.

Catawba. This tribe of the South Carolina piedmont is the descendant of several small tribes that joined together in the seventeenth and eighteenth centuries. Speakers of several different languages were probably involved, but only Catawba, a language of the Siouan family, survived into the twentieth century.

Chakchiuma. A small tribe, now extinct, probably speakers of a Muskogean language (perhaps actually Choctaw).

Chatot. Another small tribe, also probably speakers of a

Muskogean language, driven by the Creeks to Mobile and then Louisiana. They probably merged with the Choctaws in Indian Territory (Oklahoma).

Cherokee. The largest Southeastern tribe from the eighteenth century until the present, speakers of an Iroquoian language. Some survive in their Appalachian homeland in western North Carolina, while most today live in Oklahoma.

Chickasaw. Numbering about 8,000 in 1650, they were removed to Oklahoma where they live today. The language is a variety of Choctaw, although the two groups have always been politically different.

Chitimacha. The population may have been 4,000 in 1700, while less than 100 survived in 1930. The language is an isolate, not known to be related to any other.

Choctaw. Speakers of a Muskogean language, they numbered about 15,000 in 1650. In 1930 there were about 18,000, mostly in Oklahoma but some in Mississippi and Louisiana, their original homeland.

Creek. This is the English name for the political Confederacy centered on the Muskogee and including the Hitchiti and others.

Cusabo. A small tribe, totalling 535 in a 1715 census and now extinct, whose language is entirely unknown.

Hitchiti. A Muskogean language, spoken by seven or so large towns incorporated into the Creek Confederacy.

Houma. A small tribe in Louisiana, numbering 600-700 in 1700 and about the same in 1930. The language, now extinct, perhaps belonged to the Muskogean family.

Keys. The inhabitants of the Florida Keys seem to have been politically independent of their larger neighbors. Nothing of the language they spoke was ever recorded. They were extinct by the end of Spanish Florida in 1763.

Koasati. A Muskogean tribe numbering perhaps 250 in 1750, of whom in 1910 there were about 100 in Texas and one town among the Creeks in Oklahoma. The language is very close to that of the Alabamas, perhaps even the same.

Lumbee. Now one of the largest Southeastern tribes, numbering about 30,000 in 1970, the Lumbee are descended from the Cheraw and other Indian neighbors of the Catawba, as well as from Black and White refugees from the European frontiers. By the eighteenth century no Indian language survived among them. In most respects they are culturally the same as their White and Black neighbors,

although socially and politically they are definitely Indian.

Mikasuki. About two-thirds of the Florida Seminoles speak Mikasuki, which is the same language as Hitchiti, as did many Seminoles in Oklahoma formerly.

Muskogee. This is the dominant element in the Creek Confederacy. The language, in the Muskogean family, is also spoken by about one-third of the Seminoles in Florida, and by most of the Oklahoma Seminoles.

Natchez. Numbering about 4,500 in 1650, the survivors were eventually amalgamated with the Creeks and Cherokees. The language is an isolate, not known to be related to any other.

Ofo. Speakers of a Siouan language, they were driven south from the Ohio River region by the expanding Iroquois.

Seminole. This tribe originated in the eighteenth century, when settlers from the Creek Confederacy moved into Florida. The Seminole Wars of the 1830s and 1850s resulted in most being deported to Oklahoma, while a minority survived in southern Florida.

Tekesta. A small, non-agricultural tribe inhabiting the Miami region, they became extinct in the eighteenth century. Their language is entirely unknown.

Timucua. A large group of northern Florida tribes, they numbered some 13,000 in 1650 (and many more a century earlier). The language, well recorded by Spanish missionaries, is not known to be related to any other. The last few Timucuas left Florida when the Spanish withdrew in 1763.

Tocobaga. A small tribe, nearly totally unknown, of the Tampa Bay region in Florida.

Tohome and **Mobile.** Two groups that evidently spoke a variety of Choctaw.

Tunica. Numbering perhaps 2,500 in 1650, less than 50 survived in 1910. Their language, although well recorded, is not related to any other.

Tutelo. Speaking a Siouan language, they numbered some 2,700 in 1600, but by 1800 the descendants had joined the Iroquois in Canada.

Yamasee. Perhaps speakers of a Muskogean language, they numbered about 1,200 in 1715, but soon fled to Spanish Florida where they had disappeared by 1763.

Yuchi. A tribe originally in the Appalachian highlands, they numbered about 1,500 in 1650, and by 1930 only about 200 among the Creeks in Oklahoma. The Yuchi language is an isolate, unrelated to any other.

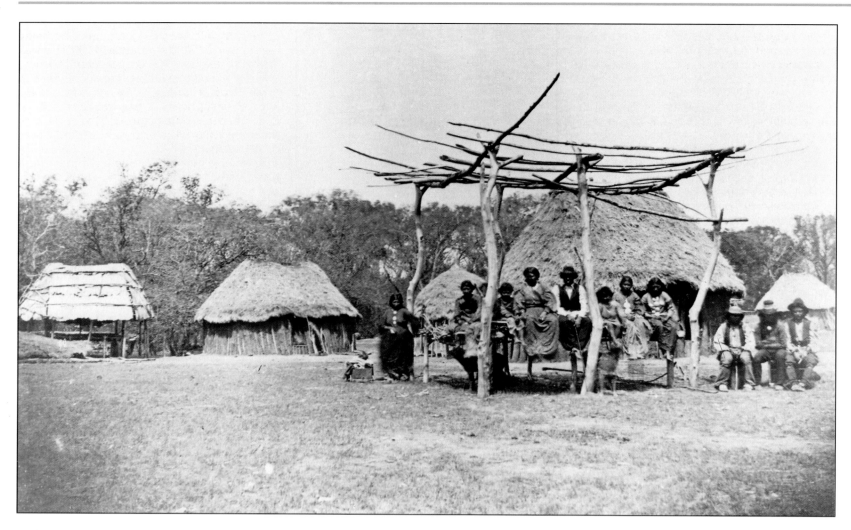

further disrupted by the complex effects of European and Euro-American intrusion: trade, new kinds of warfare, enslavement, the usurpation of food supplies, of goods, and then of land, epidemics of new diseases, and finally actual replacement of the Indian populations by people of European and African origins.

A good deal is known about southern Indian cultures over the last 100 to 150 years, but probably less than in any other region of the continent can this knowledge be taken as indicative of the ways of life before European influence was felt. The first shocks came in the middle of the sixteenth century. The first good written descriptions of Southeastern Indians date from more than 200 years later at the end of the eighteenth and the beginning of the nineteenth century, after massive realignments and restructuring of the societies had taken place. Really thorough records (and representative museum collections, and extensive series of photographs) begin still another century later, at the end of the nineteenth century and the beginning of the twentieth after most of the surviving Indians in the Southeast had been deported to quite different cultural and natural surroundings in Indian Territory west of the Mississippi (present Oklahoma).

The table above includes all the tribes on the map (p.12), as well as those mentioned in the text and captions but not on the map.

The first contacts of Europeans with southeastern Indians are unknown. The first recorded visit was by Ponce de Leon, who landed in Florida, probably in the Calusa area, in 1513. But the hostile reception the Indians gave him strongly suggests that they had previous experience with some Europeans who 'left no

Below: *Benjamin Paul, a Chitimacha chief, c.1910. This small tribe lived on the Mississippi delta of Louisiana. Mr Paul was J.R. Swanton's principal authority on traditional culture of his people. Photographed by Swanton in his home in Louisiana.*

Above: *A Caddo camp, probably near the Washita River, Oklahoma, c.1869. The Caddo occupied parts of what is now Arkansas and Louisiana. This scene is traditional Caddo, with conical-shaped dwellings thatched with grass or bark (as left).*

other record. Other brief contacts followed, in Florida and along the Atlantic coast, which left very scanty records although they probably had serious effects on the Indians: European diseases were probably introduced, and more Indians learned how dangerous the strangers could be. Finally, in 1539-43 came Hernando de Soto's long incursion far into the Southeast. He arrived at Tampa Bay with some 700 men, 200 horses, a herd of hogs, and a huge quantity of weapons and supplies, and proceeded inland north across what is now Georgia and South Carolina, into Tennessee, then down through Alabama, back north again and across northern Mississippi, across Arkansas, then south again to the lower Mississippi River in Louisiana. This expedition was a disaster for de Soto and his men, and even more a disaster for the Indians he met, hundreds of whom he and his men killed and kidnapped, and for many others, surely many thousands, who died from the diseases introduced.

The several contemporary written descriptions of the de Soto expedition are sufficient to give us a narrow window on the aboriginal societies of the Southeast, but these records are frustratingly brief and imprecise. Archeological research provides more information, but of rather different sorts, and there are many problems in identifying specific archeological remains with the poorly localized descriptions in the de Soto accounts. In recent years archeological theory has suggested reasonable integrations of these two kinds of data, in part by looking at much later societies in the Southeast and by considering comparable societies in other parts of the world.

A reasonable reconstruction of the aboriginal Southeast when Europeans first arrived shows many chiefdoms spread all across the interior and reaching the coast in several places. These were complex societies, each with a capital town containing massive earthworks in the form of mounds supporting temples and council houses, often surrounded by large canals and usually stockaded. Each chiefdom normally included several smaller towns with only one or two mounds, subordinate to the principal town. The largest of these chiefdom capitals was at Cahokia, in present Illinois across the Mississippi River from St Louis. This is well outside the historic Southeast, for one of the consequences of early contacts with Europeans was a retraction of the area covered by chiefdoms. Cahokia seems to have reached its height by about 1250 AD, after which its population declined. At its maximum Cahokia

Right: *Johnnie, a Choctaw man visiting New Orleans, by Karl Bodmer (1833). At the time of Bodmer's visit, many Choctaw had been 'removed', but some survived in Louisiana and Mississippi.*

Below: *Temporary Choctaw camp on the Mississippi River, near Natchez, by Karl Bodmer (1833). These travelers are cooking in metal vessels with typical canepack baskets near one lean-to.*

JOSLYN ART MUSEUM, OMAHA, NEBRASKA

covered more than five square miles and may have had a population of some 10,000. This was surely the largest town north of central Mexico, and in it was the largest artificial structure in North America. The central earth mound here rose in four terraces to a height of 100ft (30m.), where a large building was built on the flat top, while the base of the mound measured about 700 × 1000ft (215 × 305m.) and covered sixteen acres. More than a hundred other mounds were grouped around plazas. Most were platform mounds supporting public buildings and perhaps the houses of leading people. There were also conical burial mounds. The central 200 acres of the town were surrounded by a large wall of upright logs set in a deep trench, with watchtowers and gates spaced along it.

Another chiefdom had its capital at Moundville, about sixty miles southwest of present Birmingham, Alabama, on the northeastern edge of the territory of the Muskogees in later times (whose ancestral capital it may have been). Moundville covers 300 acres on a bluff on the Black Warrior River. Here are twenty major mounds on two sides of a rectangular plaza covering some eighty acres. These mounds are more or less pyramidal, although with flat tops, and the largest rises almost 60ft (18m.) above the level of the plaza. On the tops of these mounds were buildings, probably both temples or ceremonial structures, and houses for the rulers. A wall divided the plaza from a nearby settlement area, and the whole was surrounded by a palisade. High ranking individuals, probably especially the holders of ritual

JOSLYN ART MUSEUM, OMAHA, NEBRASKA

offices, were buried in about half the mounds along the edges of the plaza. These burials were often accompanied by those of infants and of skulls or heads without bodies. Houses were built outside the plaza but within the surrounding palisade. Controlled from Moundville were about twenty smaller settlements, most of them with one small mound apiece, which were located within the valley for a few miles north and south of Moundville. In addition, the Moundville center dominated hundreds of small residential hamlets. It has been estimated that Moundville drew labor from as far as forty-five miles away, and much tribute especially from the secondary centers within ten miles or so.

Another, smaller archeological site represents a chiefdom in what was later Cherokee country; it may itself have been subordinate to a larger site well to the south. Toqua, on the Little Tennessee River about thirty miles southwest of Knoxville, contains two flat-topped mounds, one 24ft (7m.) high resulting from eight enlargements after it was first raised, and the other, about 300ft (90m.) distant, only 6ft (1.8m.) high and built in two construction stages. Both served as burial mounds as well as supporting structures. The village, consisting of some forty households, covered about fifty acres.

Construction of such large sites must have required well-organized labor. There is other evidence that these were heirarchical societies, each under a high chief ruling in a large town, which was surrounded by smaller towns and villages headed by subordinate chiefs. The chief and his relatives were considered to be descendants of the sun. The chiefs had great power and prestige, with many perquisites in the form of special insignia and possessions. They were surrounded by retainers, offered tribute, and deferred to by their subordinates. Each chiefdom was expansionist, fighting with its neighbors. There were graded ranks within the nobility, while most of the populace were commoners. Everyone belonged to one of a set of clans, each of which included both nobles and commoners. These were totemic in that each was associated with a tutelary spirit, usually an animal, and members were considered to share character and behavior with this totem. The clans were matrilineal – each person's membership in the mother's clan was acquired at birth. The clans were exogamous, that is, marriage within the clan was prohibited. But the clans were not organized groups, and every clan was spread through many villages,

Below: Joe Silestine (Toshkachito), Choctaw, of Bayou Lacombe, La., 1909, demonstrating a cane blowgun. The wooden dart used, feathered with thistle down, had a range of 25ft.

with each village inhabited by members of several clans.

Although each clan was quite egalitarian – most members were equals – the clan as a whole was ranked. There were two sets or sides or moieties, the clans in each in a ranked series. Furthermore, one side seems to have been considered superior to the other. The chiefly offices were hereditary, certainly matrilineally, and offices of lesser rank were also hereditary, probably most of them matrilineally but perhaps another set inherited patrilineally, from father to son. However, nobles seemingly could only marry commoners, and the children in each generation were of lesser rank than the noble parent, becoming commoners after four or five generations.

The political and social systems surely varied from chiefdom to chiefdom, they were quite complex, and the few literate Europeans who were in a position to observe them in action certainly did not understand them very well. One striking example that was quite thoroughly investigated by a Jesuit missionary in the 1560s was that of the Calusa in southwest Florida. Here the high-chief was differentiated from the rest of the society by an exception to the incest rules: he was required to marry his full sister (to the distress of the missionary). This custom is known from only a few other societies anywhere in the world, all of them with high social

Above: *Choctaw ballgame, 1925, near Philadelphia, Miss. At far right is David Jim. This is the Choctaw form, still popular among them in the state, of the widespread SE Indian team game.*

Below: *Haylaema, a Choctaw woman in Louisiana, in 1909. Her sturdy pack basket is of split river cane, woven in a twilled technique, with a supporting buckskin tumpline across her chest.*

belongings were taken out of the house and packed to be buried with him. A special red-painted pole was hung with forty-six cane rings representing the number of enemies he had killed.

The first day the mourners fasted (this was a means for gaining spiritual strength among most southeastern Indians). Those who were to accompany him into the afterworld were prepared. There were eight of them; the Great Sun himself would have joined them but was dissuaded, with difficulty, by the French. These eight people were the Tattooed Serpent's principal wife and his second wife, five officials or servants (one called by the French the First Warrior or Chancellor; a Noble woman who was a doctor and a special friend; the deceased's Head Servant, perhaps the same as his Pipe Bearer, and his wife; and the warclub maker); and a woman who would have been sacrificed at the death of an earlier Sun had she not then been a hostage of the French. Another man who had escaped a previous sacrifice but whose French protector had left was brought forth by thirty warriors, but since he was still reluctant to die he was dismissed by the Tattooed Serpent's principal wife as unworthy to accompany her and the rest to the other world. This was described to the French as a place without hunger, death, or war, where the weather was always fine. For two or three days there were

and political stratification and all very concerned with inherited rank. Royal full-sibling marriage is especially appropriate where the nobility is exogamous and no child can inherit the full rank of the noble parent.

For a late expression of the social stratification once typical of much of the Southeast, we may summarize French reports of the death and funeral of a high ranking Natchez chief.[1] The Natchez had two social classes, nobility and commoners. Within the nobility there were three ranks, Suns, Nobles, and Honored People. These were exogamous: all could only marry commoners. Class membership and noble rank were acquired from the mother at birth, except that the children of fathers of Sun and Noble rank belonged to the next lower rank rather than inheriting their mothers' commoner rank. While rank in general was hereditary, some commoner men and their wives could achieve Honored rank through special merit. The king or highest ranking chief was known as the Great Sun, and he was succeeded in office by the son of his sister. There is much evidence for the deference and special privileges afforded to this man. The other high civil, military, and probably religious offices were also filled by Suns. When any Sun died, his or her spouse was willingly sacrificed – one could say committed suicide – to accompany the spirit of the dead to the afterworld.

In 1725 a man named Tattooed Serpent died. He was the Great War Chief and a much-beloved brother of the Great Sun. As soon as he died, the news was relayed by death cries from village to village. His body was laid out on a cane bed in his house, probably on a small mound near the town plaza, dressed in his finest and with his face painted vermilion. His weapons were tied to his bed and around it were arrayed all the calumets (peace pipes) he had received during his career. All his other

Yuchi

From at least the early 18th century the Yuchi were part of the Creek Confederacy, and they were removed with the Creeks in 1836 from their ancestral lands in Georgia to Indian Territory, in present-day Oklahoma. Their long association with the Creeks resulted in much cultural similarity, although they retain a distinct identity and until the mid-20th century they preserved their distinctive language. In 1904 and 1905 the ethnologist

Frank G. Speck conducted research among the Yuchi, finding them engaged in agriculture and cattle raising and living in widely dispersed households in three settlement areas, although politically they formed a single town in the organized Creek Nation. Speck's research and the monograph on Yuchi culture that he published in 1909 described many aspects of Yuchi life as it then was; Speck paid particular attention to their medicine and rituals. The items illustrated here were all collected by Speck in 1904 and 1905.

1 Man's hunting jacket, of green cotton cloth with red calico borders.
2 Man's shirt, black cotton cloth decorated with appliqué bands.
3 Man's breechclout of red flannel, edges bound with blue cotton cloth.
4 Man's leggings of strouding, ribbons along inner seams of flaps.
5 Scratcher; six pins in turkey quill frame with leaf of button snakeroot attached.

6 Cane tube used by medicine man to impart curing power by blowing into medicine.
7 Flageolet of cedar wood, used by young men during courting.
8 Dance wand with heron feathers; pair carried by leader of Feather Dance during Green Corn Dance.
9 White heron feather attached to spring, worn in hat by men during Green Corn Dance.
10 Cloth for medicine man's

18

turban.
11 Medicine man's hat band.
12 Man's beaded neck band.
13 Bow of bois d'arc with twisted rawhide string.
14 Arrows; one with straight point for small game, one blunt bird bunt, one with facetted point for fish.
15 One of a pair of ballsticks for team ballgame.
16 Pounder used by medicine man to prepare ritual emetic taken by men at Green Corn Dance.
17 Pottery vessel, used for

cooking.
18 Twilled cane basket, with decorative band.
19 Twilled cane utility basket.
20 Gourd drinking ladle.
21 Awl for sewing and basket making.
22 Wooden paddle for stirring food while cooking.
23 Crooked knife for wood carving.
24 Girl's dress of calico.
25 Woman's apron.
26 Cloth bag.
27 Model of corn-grinding pestle, made by the father

at the birth of a daughter and kept to ensure proper development.
28 Man's shirt of red cotton cloth, with blue facings.
29 Man's shirt.
30 Woman's belt; design in beads and cloth appliqué said to represent storm clouds breaking up.
31 Pair of man's garters.
32 Man's fingerwoven sash of red wool.
33 Pair of men's leggings of black wool cloth with red edging.

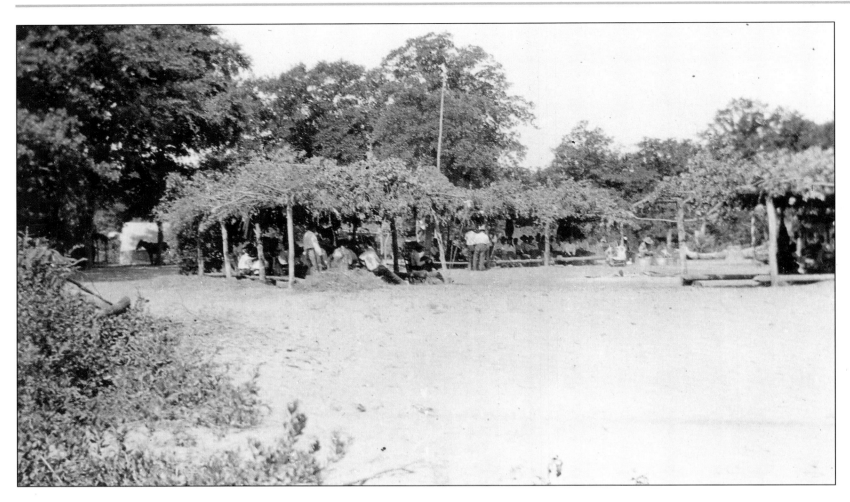

Above: *The square grounds at the Creek town of Asilanapi, Oklahoma, 1912. The busk or Green Corn Festival is in progress, with the ritual medicine being prepared near the central fire.*

dances rehearsing the sacrifices to come on the fourth day after the death. Those who were to die were finely dressed, their hair daubed red, and each carried a large conch shell. Each was escorted by eight male relatives wearing red head feathers: one carried a warclub, one the victim's sitting mat, one the cord to be used for strangling, one the skin for blindfolding, one a clay dish holding six pellets of tobacco (or perhaps it was a stronger narcotic), one a small drinking vessel of water, and finally two men who were to draw the strangling cord tight.

Those who were to die and their attendants paraded from the Tattooed Serpent's house to the front of the temple on a mound at the plaza, issuing death cries. The Chief Priest came out of the temple with a message from the Creator. The celebrants then separated into two bands led by the two wives, and the principals each sat on their mats, giving the death cry in unison, and then danced in place while their attending relatives danced behind them. This dance was repeated in front of the Tattooed Serpent's house, and the War Dance and other dances were also performed.

On the second day the dances were repeated. This time those who were to die each carried a red warclub and a bundle of red cords. Two women relatives of the man who had been dismissed by the principal wife volunteered to die

Right: *George W. Stidham and his family, 1869. Stidham was a leader of the mixed-blood Creek aristocracy in Indian Territory, a slave-owner and supporter of the Confederacy during the Civil War.*

in his place and were accordingly strangled, not only freeing him from the obligation but promoting him to Noble status.

The final day was marked by fasting and smoking tobacco (both to gain strength). The end began when the Master of Ceremonies, his torso painted red and wearing a red feather head ornament and a belt or skirt of red and

black feathers, carrying a red baton with black feathers, entered the Tattooed Serpent's house and raised the death cry, which was repeated by the crowd gathered in the plaza. The body emerged on a litter carried by six men, preceded by the Master of Ceremonies and the oldest War Chief who carried a calumet and the pole with forty-six hoops. The litter was followed by those who were to die, and their attendants. These attendants by this service were raised from commoners to rank as Honored People and were relieved of the obligation to die when another Sun died. After circling the house, the procession slowly looped across the plaza. At each loop, they walked over the body of an infant sacrificed by his parents (by this both releasing them from the duty to be sacrificed at a future Sun's death, and raising them from commoners to status among the nobility).

When the procession reached the temple, the chests containing the possession of the Tattooed Serpent were taken inside, for burial with him. Those to be sacrificed seated themselves on their mats in a semicircle facing the temple. All gave the death cry. They swallowed the tobacco pellets with water, numbing their faculties. The leather blindfolds were placed over their heads, then the cords were looped around their necks. The ends of these were strongly pulled by the relatives assigned this task, quickly strangling them.

One account says that five more were then strangled in the plaza: the 'nurse' of the Tattooed Serpent, a doctor from a nearby town, and three old women.

The Tattooed Serpent and his two wives were buried in a trench inside the temple. The Noble woman doctor and the 'Chancellor' were buried on the mound but outside the temple. The others were carried on litters back to their home villages for burial in the temples there. Finally, the Tattooed Serpent's house was burned.

It is hardly surprising that several eighteenth-century French observers recorded these obsequies in great detail. While they said little about the Natchez beliefs that justified and maintained them, one can hardly doubt that the ideology strongly supported a heirarchical social system. A few years later the Natchez attacked the French, who retaliated and nearly destroyed them. The survivors eventually joined the Creek and Cherokee Indians, and little is heard about them until the end of the nineteenth century and the beginning of the twentieth. The elaborate social system had by then been totally replaced by one much like that of the Creeks.

The economic base which supported the dense populations and their elaborate social and political systems can be envisioned by considering the economic activities of the Choctaws at a later period. An excellent idea of Choctaw subsistence in the late eighteenth century is given by the materials collected in Mississippi in 1823-5 by Gideon Lincecum, a frontier physician who apprenticed himself to a Choctaw medical practitioner and also wrote

Below: *A Mikasuki Seminole single-family village in the Big Cypress Swamp, Florida, c.1920. Canoe trails lead to two docks. The open-ended structure is for cooking.*

down and translated long historical traditions told by an aged Choctaw man named Chahta Imataha.[2]

In the eighteenth century the Choctaws had less territory than their neighbors, and were probably more dependent on agriculture. This was so productive that they were able to export corn. As in all the aboriginal Southeast there were important seasonal differences in Choctaw subsistence. In midwinter the fields were prepared for planting. On new plots, after a ceremony with dances, the underbrush and smaller growth was cut and larger trees were girdled. The dried brush was then no doubt burned, the ashes spread on the field providing the only fertilizer used. Planting was done in the spring, when the soil was turned and holes for planting the seeds were made with a digging stick, which was a short hardwood pole with a point that had been sharpened and hardened by charring in a fire. While the heaviest labor of clearing was done by men, the rest of the work was shared by men, women, and children. In much of the rest of the Southeast, however, agricultural labor after clearing was almost entirely women's work. The most important crop was corn. Also planted in the same plots were beans and squash. Crops of lesser importance elsewhere in the Southeast, and probably for the Choctaw too, were sunflowers, marsh elder, and gourds. By the late eighteenth century the Choctaws had added peas, watermelons, sweet potatoes, and fruit trees.

After the crops were well established, it was still necessary to protect them from squirrels and crows, but most people could scatter to streams and lakes for fishing and turtling and collecting wild fruits, nuts, and berries. These included persimmons, plums, hickory nuts, chestnuts, walnuts, pecans, acorns (probably leached after grinding), cherries, grapes, and mulberries. Fishing methods included a kind of communal fish drive in shallow water, the use of a trap made by sewing a hide cover with a drawstring over a long tube of hoops, muddying the water in a pool of a river (perhaps, although Lincecum does not say so, including the use of buckeye or devil's shoestring as a plant poison to stun the fish), shooting fish with bows and arrows, and finally catching them with metal hooks gotten from the French.

When the corn first ripened in early summer, all gathered for the Green Corn Festival. Fishing, hunting waterfowl, and gathering were then resumed until it was time to return in the fall for harvesting and storing the ripe corn. The men then left for a period of hunting in the fall and early winter, while the women, children, and old people collected nuts and fruits in the woods. In the middle of the winter the hunters returned and the cycle began again with clearing the fields.

For hunting men used bows and arrows, before they acquired guns from Europeans. The most valued game was deer, which were killed in quantities. Decoys made from the skin and antlers of a buck's head were used along with special deer calls. Bear were killed in cane brakes, especially for their fat. Boys as well as men hunted smaller game too, including turtles, alligators, rabbits, raccoons, turkeys, quail, and prairie chickens. A favorite boy's weapon was a cane blowgun, some 7ft (2m.) long, with darts having thistle down at the butt ends. Meat was sun dried and also smoked and dried on racks over fires.

There were many different corn recipes. Green corn was roasted on the cob, and green corn kernels were slowly boiled with meat, with some lye added, to make a popular dish. Ripe corn kernels were pounded into flour in a wooden mortar and pestle. The Choctaw mortar was made of an upright hickory log about 2ft (60cm.) high and 1 to 1½ft (30–45cm.) in diameter, with a hollow up to 1½ft deep charred out of the upper end. The pestle was a hickory

Below: Mikasuki Seminole men, women and children, about 1930, at a cooking fire in the center of their settlement. The radiating logs were gradually pushed in as they burned.

pole about 5ft (1.5m.) long with a weight about 1ft long and 6in. (15cm.) in diameter left on the upper end, and a round shaft about 2in. (5cm.) in diameter narrowing to a point at the bottom. Corn kernels could be ground after parching, or else they were boiled, dried, and parched before grinding. For sifting and cleaning the ground corn there was a set of three baskets made of plaited cane: a shovel-shaped fanner, a shallow squarish sieve, and a large flat container. Hominy was made by pounding dried kernels to remove the husks, then boiling the cracked pieces (the grits) for twelve to eighteen hours in lye water. This was a favorite food called *tanfula* in Choctaw, that was customarily kept in each house ready to serve to all visitors. It was adopted by non-Indians under the name Tom Fuller. There were many kinds of bread made from corn meal, simply baking it, or letting it ferment slightly to make a sour bread, or mixing corn meal with ground sunflower seeds for the dough, or stuffing corn dough in cornhusks and baking them in hot ashes, or wrapping corn dough mixed with beans or hickory nuts in cornhusks and boiling these, or grating green corn and mixing the meal with hot water. A special dish served by the bride's parents at a wedding was made from juice from strained cooked grapes, in which small bits of corn

Above: *Fred Smith, Seminole, with a typical baby's haircut and small boy's dress with patchwork bands and front opening (small girls' dresses opened in the back). Photographed by W.D. Boehmer, 1943.*

Right: *Cow Creek Seminole women, c.1917. Their skirts were of strips of cotton cloth in contrasting colors. Patchwork was just beginning at this time. The central figure has coin silver brooches.*

dough were boiled. A lightweight, nourishing travel food for hunters and warriors (used all over eastern North America) was made from parched kernels ground in the mortar and carfully sifted. This could be eaten as a cold cereal by simply adding water to dampen a handful of the flour. The importance of cornbread in the traditional non-Indian cuisines of the American south is a legacy of the Indians.

Over most of the south documentary records are silent for about 100 years following the mid-sixteenth century, and for much of the area detailed records only begin some hundred years later than that. This was a crucial period of change, when the aboriginal chiefdoms broke up and were replaced by the towns, tribes, and confederacies that can then be followed into modern times. Archeological evidence tends to confirm that this period witnessed massive depopulation, due mainly to the spread of European diseases, with accompanying social and political reorganization, major movements and displacements of populations, and the loss of many elements of culture. The number of populated sites decreased drastically. There were shifts in the tribal balance of power, accompanying demographic changes that proceeded at different rates and to different degrees in various regions. Many sites that had been occupied for centuries were abandoned. The construction of mounds and other major earthworks ceased. The marked differences between settlements in size and, presumably, power and authority, disappeared. In

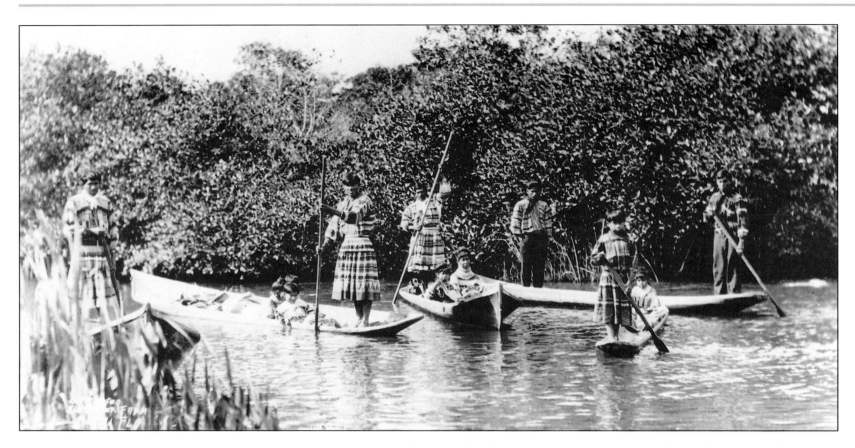

the late seventeeth century the Iroquois wars associated with the fur trade in the north had a domino effect to the south. The introduction of large numbers of firearms by the French, Dutch, and English engaged in the fur trade resulted in Iroquois expansion and the flight of many of their enemies to the south. With the founding of Charleston in 1670 new disruptions entered the area from the east, with English capture

and purchase of Indians for the slave trade in the West Indies, and the development of a massive commerce in deerskins for export to Europe. It was during this period that the Creek Confederacy arose from the broken chiefdoms, in response to these outside pressures. Another result was the total destruction of the aborigines of Spanish Florida, who lacked guns to defend themselves against the Creek and

Above: *A group of Mikasuki Seminole poling canoes, photographed near Miami, c.1920. Flat-bottomed dug-out canoes were commonly used by most SE tribes; both poling and paddling were employed.*

Below: *A Mikasuki Seminole woman grating roots of the coontie plant (Zamia, a wild cycad) from which starch was made, eaten in the Seminole soup known as sofkie.*

English invaders. During the eighteenth century Florida was resettled by Creek colonists, whose descendants became the Seminoles when their connections to the Confederacy ceased.

After a century or so, the southern Indian situation again changed radically. As non-Indian settlement expanded, especially in Georgia and Alabama, the Indians were pushed aside and their lands and fields usurped. Finally in the 1820s and 1830s nearly all were deported to Indian Territory – present-day Oklahoma. Many died during this so-called 'Removal'. A few managed to avoid the deportation: some Seminoles survived in south Florida, some Cherokees in western North Carolina, a few Creeks in far southern Alabama, and many Choctaws in Mississippi. Some tribes entirely escaped Removal: the Catawba in South Carolina, the Tunica and Chitimacha in Louisiana, and the Lumbee and other mestizo populations in the Carolinas.

In Oklahoma the deportees reorganized and established new tribal governments, especially those that became known as the Five Civilized Tribes – Cherokees, Choctaws, Chickasaws, Creeks, and Seminoles. During the Civil War many of these were divided and suffered heavily. Their governments reconstituted afterwards, and then the Five Civilized Tribes lost much land to non-Indians in the 1880s and 1890s. The tribal governments lost most of their remaining sovereignty with the arrival of statehood for Oklahoma in 1907.

Below: *Two Mikasuki Seminole women, c.1895, using wooden mortar and pestles. The corn was ground in a log mortar hollowed by charring. The meal produced was usually used in soup.*

Above: *Billy Smith, a Cow Creek Seminole, 1910, standing in his corn field. Such fields were cleared of undergrowth, large trees cut back and burned off: corn, beans and squash might be grown.*

The Creek Confederacy was (and still is) based on so-called towns. These are social and political units more than residential ones, quite equivalent to what are called tribes elsewhere. Each town was made up of the people affiliated with a ceremonial center, a square grounds (in modern Oklahoma parlance, a stomp grounds). They often lived quite far from the center, in scattered hamlets and homesteads. The number of towns varied over time, as towns could both split, when one faction established a new, separate square grounds, and merge, by two towns agreeing to share a single square grounds. From the middle of the nineteenth century until the 1930s, there were between twenty-five and thirty Creek towns, the total depending partly on how one counted closely associated towns. Most of these were Muskogee-speaking, but some five or ten were Hitchiti-speaking (or had been until recently when they adopted Muskogee for internal as well as external use). There was also at least one town each of other languages: Alabama, Koasati, Natchez, and Yuchi. However, Muskogee was the general language of the Confederacy, through which speakers of other languages communicated with other Creeks and with outsiders.

The towns were divided into two groups, sometimes called 'sides', usually characterized as White and Red. The White or 'peace' towns were preeminent in civil affairs, while the Red or 'war' towns were conceived of as dominant in military matters. The White towns were said to control executive affairs of the Soufederacy, the Red towns legislative and judicial ones. According to Creek traditions, the White towns controlled the Confederacy until the time of the American Revolution. From then through the

Seminole Ballgame, 1895

Players at a ballgame held between men and women at the Green Corn Dance, Pine Island, north of Miami. The ball is aimed at the top of the pole, and score kept by erasing a charcoal mark whenever a goal is made. Women use their hands to throw the ball, while men can use only the ballsticks. On the edge of the dance grounds is the 'bed' or ceremonial seating structure; on the other side is the frame for the ritual sweatbath. In 1895 Seminole women had used sewing machines for about five years, so that machine-sewn patchwork had not yet replaced the older appliqué. The leggings are buckskin. Heavy multiple-strand necklaces were typically worn by women at this time and for some fifty years after. The style of the boy's hairdress was also typical for Seminole men for some decades after 1895.

Civil War period the Creeks were frequently drawn into war so the Red towns ran the Confederacy. After 1865 the White towns again were dominant.

The most important Creek towns around 1900 were the following:

White	Red
Kasihta	Coweta
Hitchiti	Tukabahchee
Abihka	Laplako
Okfuskee	Atasi
Okchai	Kealeychi
Ochiapofa	Chiaha
Tulsa	Osochi
Lochapoka	Alabama
Tuskegee	Eufaula
Koasati	Hilabi
Wiwohka	Hothliwahali
Wiogufki	Talmuchasi
Tokpafka	
Nuyaka	
Okmulgee	
Asilanapi	
Yuchi	
Pakana	

The affiliation of a town as either White or Red was not permanent, however. A town changed sides if it was defeated for four successive times by a town on the other side in the important match ball games. These were the southern Indian form of the team game played between goals that is known as lacrosse in the north. In the southern form, often called 'stick ball' in English, each player used a pair of rackets rather than the single racket used in lacrosse. Like lacrosse, it was a very rough sport. The Creeks conceived it as a substitute for war, sometimes calling it 'the younger brother of war', and explaining that it kept the peace within the Confederacy.

The Creek Confederacy was modelled on the town organization, for the members of each town were also organized into two 'sides'. Here the social units of the dual organization were the clans. Every individual was born into the clan of his or her mother. There were fifty Muskogee clans, of which twenty-three were also Hitchiti clans. Most had animal or bird names, while a few were named for plants, and there were also Wind, Medicine, Salt, and Arrow clans. They were totemic in the sense that the members had a special relationship to the clan species or phenomenon, but they did not trace descent from these totems. The clans had members in various towns, which offered hospitality to visiting clan members. Among the most important functions of clans was punishment for murder, for the victim's clan members took vengeance on the murderer or another member of the murderer's clan. There was no overall clan organization. Rather, within each town the clans filled special functions and provided the incumbents for town offices (not always the same ones in different towns). Each town was an independent, self-governing body headed by its micco or chief, chosen from a specific clan, usually a White clan since his duties were peaceful. Usually there was also a vice-chief or 'twin chief', and a set of assistant chiefs (sometimes from several different clans). There was also a body of sub-chiefs, usually from the micco's clan. Another set of officers directed work in the fields and on public buildings, and ran the Black Drink ceremony. These, the assistant chiefs, and a set of respected elders known as 'beloved men' formed the town council. All of these were, in most towns, from White clans. Each town also had officials from the Red clans – three grades of war officials, who gained their positions from warlike deeds, rather than inheriting them. They dealt with war and the inter-town ball games. The highest grade of warriors also served as town police.

The Creek Confederacy as a whole was governed by a council made up of town chiefs, who met at irregular intervals and not necessarily as a body. It was a loose confederation

Below: *Little Tiger's household, Mikasuki Seminole, on a small island (a 'hammock') in the Big Cypress Swamp, Florida, in 1910. In the foreground is a dock for dugout canoes. A banana plant is at right, and other crops are grown nearby. The structure in the center rear is the cookhouse.*

Seminole

When these things were collected by Alanson Skinner among the Mikasuki Seminoles in south Florida in 1910, they were living quite independent lives in the Everglades and Big Cypress Swamp, traveling by dugout canoe to stores in Miami, Fort Lauderdale, and Fort Myers to exchange alligator hides, feathers, and wages from employment as guides for sport hunters, for the cloth, coffee, salt, tobacco, sewing machines, guns and ammunition, and a few other things needed to supplement the products of their fishing, hunting, and agriculture. They were unaffected by missionaries and by government agents trying to persuade them to move to reservations. Major changes followed, with the rapid increase in the non-Indian population on Florida's lower east coast and the beginning of drainage of the Everglades. Other Seminoles lived near Lake Okeechobee speaking Muskogee, a related but distinct language, and sharing the Mikasuki way of life. Modern Florida Seminoles are descendants of both groups.

1 Woman's blouse of cotton cloth with long cape collar attached, appliqué designs, two rows of coin silver brooches.
2 Long skirt matching the blouse, with ruffles and appliqué stripes.
3 Wooden pestle for grinding corn on upright log mortar; small size, for a girl.
4 Basket for sifting ground corn, made of twilled palmetto leaf stems.
5 Winnowing/storage basket of twilled palmetto stems.
6 Fan of turkey tail feathers sewn to buckskin handle, used to fan log fire.
7, 8 Two wooden spoons used as cups to drink soupy dishes.
9 Cakes of deer brains mixed with fiber and roots, then dried and kept until needed for tanning deerskins.
10 Small girl's dress.
11 Hole-and-slot heddle, for making woven beadwork bands.
12 Man's shirt with waist band and long skirt, design of

appliquéd stripes; worn without trousers.

13 Plume of egret and other feathers tied to stick, worn inserted into man's cloth turban.

14 Woven waist belt of wool and white beads, with long red wool tassels to suspend from each hip.

15, 16 Two pairs of buckskin moccasins, each made of one piece, gathered at seam.

17 Stick wrapped with buckskin, used to buff silver

ornaments by the silversmith Miami John Tiger.

18 Basket with telescoping cover, the type used only to hold medicines.

19 Bracelet of woven beadwork with wool tassels.

20 Double pendant of woven beadwork with wool tassels, worn pinned to a man's turban.

21 Shoulder belt of woven beadwork, design representing rattlesnake, worn over one shoulder and across chest, with long

woollen tassels tied on hip.

22 Man's coat, with open front, large triangular cape collar, complex appliqué designs on skirt.

23 Man's straight shirt, appliqué bands on front yoke.

24 Pair of rackets or ballsticks used by man in single-pole ballgame.

25 Man's breechclout of dark cloth, edges bound with ribbon.

26 Pair of man's leggings, of red-dyed buckskin, fringed buckskin garters attached.

rather than a state-like organization, at least before Removal, and seemingly served mainly to keep the peace between its member towns. It did not, however, unite them in war against any outside power.

The principal ritual of the Creeks was – and for many still is – the annual Green Corn Festival or busk (so-called from its name in Muskogee, *poskitá*). This varied in different towns and changed somewhat over time, but in essentials was the same among all the Creek towns and was very similar among their relatives the Seminoles. Similar festivals were shared by the Cherokees, Choctaws, and probably other southeastern Indians. One of the best accounts we have is by John Howard Payne (actor, playwright, author of *Home Sweet Home*, and supporter of the Cherokees in their failed struggle against Removal). Payne attended the Tukabahchee busk in 1835 in Alabama, just before the Removal. His conclusion to his detailed description indicated real understanding of what he had observed, very unusual for an outsider at that period.

'I never beheld more intense devotion; and the spirit of the forms was a right and religious one. It was beginning the year with fasting, with humility, with purification, with prayer, with gratitude It was burying animosities, while it was strengthening courage. It was pausing to give thanks to Heaven, before daring to partake its beneficence.'[3]

Each town held its busk at a special square grounds, referred to in Muskogee as the 'big house', and evidently serving as a world symbol. The old Tukabahchee square grounds described by Payne were in a secluded location, where there were two adjacent rectangular grounds. The main square had on each side a shelter, called a 'bed', some 40ft (12m.) long, with openings of about 10ft (3m.) at each corner between the beds. Each bed was divided into three compartments, each seating a particular

Below: Jim Osceola's Cow Creek Seminole household, 1910-11. This is the traditional Florida Seminole house type, a chickee, with palm-thatched roof, no sides and so well-ventilated, and an interior platform on which people slept, ate and worked.

clan (or group of linked clans), while in front specific seats were occupied by particular town officials (without regard for their clan affiliations). Outside one corner of this square was a large semi-subterranean council house with a conical roof, on the edge of the second square which contained a ritual tall pole that served as a goal in a ball game played between men (with rackets) and women (without). On two sides of this ball square there were cornfields, on another side was an earth ridge, while the fourth side was formed by the back of one of the beds that faced the other square. In the center was a mound formed from dirt taken from the square grounds each year before a fresh layer was spread to consecrate the grounds in preparation for the busk. Outside one corner of the ball square was another mound, formed from the ashes of the central fire. The square grounds complex with its ritual structures is reminiscent of the massive ritual structures in and around the plazas of the earlier chiefdoms, and it certainly represents a much simplified descendant serving similar functions.

The Creek busk inaugurated the new year, and it was timed to coincide with the first ripening of the town's corn, for it was forbidden to eat the new crop before the busk. The ceremony was a form of renewal, of the people's relations to the spiritual world, as also to the world of plants and animals, and to other people. A feature that repeatedly struck outside observers is the amnesty afforded to those who had committed crimes (except murder) during the previous year. An important part of the ceremony was the ritual lighting of a new fire, which was distributed to all the households to relight the fires that had been extinguished as the houses were swept and cleaned. The same new fire was used to light the ceremonial fire in the center of the square grounds, where the ritual medicines were prepared.

At Tukabahchee the busk lasted eight days, with the pattern of ceremonies on the second four days being similar to the pattern on the corresponding first four days. On the first day the square grounds were cleaned, and participants and visitors gathered there. The second day was a feast day, with dances at night including a woman's dance that much impressed Payne. That night the men (only) slept in the square grounds. The third day was perhaps the

Above: *Margaret Brown, one of the last speakers of Catawba, making pottery in her front yard, 1918. Only among the Catawaba have the ancient Southeastern pottery techniques survived without interruption.*

Below: *A group of distinguished Cherokees visiting Washington in 1866 to negotiate the treaty with the U.S. that was signed on 19 July. Left to right: John Rollin Ridge, Saladin Watie, Richard Fields, Col. Elias C. Boudinot, Col. William P. Adair.*

peak of the busk. The men fasted all day, the new fire was lit with a fire drill, and men took two medicines including the emetic Black Drink. The vomiting in the square that followed was compared by Payne to a libation; it was a form of ritual purification. Young men and boys were scratched with needles on their limbs, to fortify them. The Feather Dance was performed by men carrying poles with feathers attached, signifying peace. Various dances named for animals followed, and social dances filled the whole night. On the fourth day the new corn was eaten for the first time, as part of a feast. The sacred, ancient copper plates, a palladium unique to Tukabahchee, were brought out and reverently displayed. A mock battle known as the Gun Dance was performed, accompanied by women singers. In the evening the town council met. The fifth day was devoted to a ritual deer hunt. On the sixth day there was another feast, when salt was used for the first time in the year (it was felt to be weakening and deleterious). The women danced again, wearing the typical southern box-turtle rattles attached to their calves. At the end the Old Dance was performed, by men alone, to free the feasters from all ritual restrictions. The seventh day was again devoted to fasting. On the eighth day the chief gave a final speech and the people dispersed.

In several ways the busk reflects the Southeastern Indian emphasis on maintaining good health and on curing. Perhaps this is a result of the demographic disaster suffered by their ancestors. In traditional Southeastern cultures there was no sharp distinction between religious and medical beliefs, rituals, and practice. More is known about traditional Cherokee medicine than any other in the region. This is partly because Cherokee doctors made use of Sequoyah's remarkable invention of a syllabary for writing Cherokee. Although he was not literate in English, he was aware of the general nature of writing, or at least of the possibility of representing speech by marks on paper. After several years of experimenting with writing Cherokee, he introduced the results in 1819. He had invented a set of eighty-five symbols, of which five represent vowels, one represents the sound s, and the rest stand for syllables each made up of a consonant plus a vowel. The system was practical, and a great many Cherokees soon could write their own language. Because the system was not introduced by missionaries (as were other writing systems for North American Indian languages), it was readily used for the fundamentally non-Christian purpose of recording the secret magical formulas used for curing. Cherokee doctors made collections of medical charms, prayers, and formulas. These provided an entree for study and description of Cherokee medicine, even though the records themselves are quite abbreviated and allusive in order to keep them secret from competing doctors.

According to Cherokee theory, illness was caused mainly by the spirits of animals, who, according to tradition, had invented diseases in order to take revenge on humans for killing and abusing them. Other diseases were caused by human and animal ghosts, spirits such as

Below: A cabin home on the Cherokee Qualla Reservation, North Carolina, 1888. The cabin belonged to Ayunini, or Swimmer, who stands at the right. He was a key informant to anthropologist James Mooney, being well-versed in Cherokee mythology, history, botany and medicine.

the dwarf-like Little People, and witchcraft. Dreams were sometimes a symptom or omen, and perhaps earlier a direct cause. Diseases were named for their causes, not according to their symptoms. A doctor diagnosed by first inquiring as to the location of the pain. Then the patient was asked whether any prohibitions or taboos had been infringed, and whether the patient had had any indicative dreams or omens, even over the preceding several months or two or three years. The doctor often had to suggest many possibilities that might fit the symptoms, and there were any number of possibilities for the same symptoms. If the interviewing still failed to reveal the cause, the doctor could resort to divination through the movement of beads he held between the thumb and forefinger of each hand. Discovering the cause of the sickness was necessary in order to choose the procedures to effect a cure.

Doctors cured by a combination of herbal remedies and the singing or recitation of magical formulas. Usually the formulas recorded in the Sequoyah syllabary indicate the cause, then often belittle the disease spirit, then threaten it with a rival spirit, who is invoked to drive it away. Frequently the formulas involve color and directional symbolism as well. Several hundred medicinal plants were recognized by skilled Cherokee doctors. Their appropriateness for curing often depended on some similarity in name or appearance to the causative agent of the disease, and sometimes on a perceived similarity between the plant and the symptoms of the disease (according to the ancient folk medical doctrine of signatures). The herbs were collected only as they were needed for a specific case, then usually boiled in water. The medicine might then be rubbed on the patient, sometimes into scratches made on the skin, or alternatively the doctor might blow it over the patient through a cane tube.

The effectiveness of Cherokee medicine is of course impossible to measure, since it depended partly on psychosomatic factors and partly on the pharmacological properties of plants (most of which have never been scientifically tested). However, Cherokee medicine was certainly at least as effective as European and European-American medicine of a century and more ago.

Left: *Tsolocha, a Cherokee man, by Karl Bodmer at Natchez (1833). Bodmer had difficulty in sketching an 'old Cherokee, who didn't want his business at first, but later complied . . . when sketches had been shown to him'. This was almost certainly Tsolocha.*

Below: *Pre-ballgame dance, Cherokee, photographed by James Mooney on the Qualla Reservation, 1888. Seven women dancers stand in a row behind their dance leader, seated with a drum. Note ball sticks hanging on a rack before the women. To the left is the men's dance leader, shaking a gourd rattle.*

JOSLYN ART MUSEUM, OMAHA, NEBRASKA

References

1 These accounts are quoted in translation on pp. 139-57 of John R. Swanton's 'Indian Tribes of the Lower Mississippi Valley and Adjacent Coast of the Gulf of Mexico,' *Smithsonian Institution, Bureau of American Ethnology Bulletin* 43, 1911.
2 T. N. Campbell, 'Choctaw Subsistence: Ethnographic Notes from the Lincecum Manuscript,' *Florida Anthropologist* 12(1): 9-24, 1959.
3 John Howard Payne (introduction by John R. Swanton), 'The Green Corn Dance,' *Chronicles of Oklahoma* 10:170-95, 1932.

Cherokee

The Cherokees have been divided since the Removal of 1838, the Eastern Band living in the mountains of western N. Carolina, and the majority, in eastern Oklahoma, being the descendants of those deported to Indian Territory. Two items shown here are from Indian Territory, the rest from the Eastern Band. Those dated 1868 and 1881 were collected by Edward Palmer. The rest were gathered by James Mooney, the great pioneer ethnographer of the Eastern Cherokee.

1 Water drum for dances, a keg of sassafras wood with groundhog skin head. 1887.
2 Wooden dance stick for dance drum. 1887.
3 Scratcher, seven splinters of turkey leg bone in turkey quill frame, to scratch limbs and chest of ballplayers to cause suppleness. 1886.
4 Eagle Dance wands. 1889.
5 Cane blowgun, about 10 feet long. 1887.
6 Blowgun darts of sharp sticks feathered with thistledown. Before 1913.
7 Bullet mold of local white talc held together with wooden pins. 1886.
8 Pair of box turtle rattles, worn by woman tied on side of legs above ankles.
9 Rattle of gourd holding pebbles, used by lead singer in dance. 1887.
10 Pair of shorts with red appliqué design, worn by ballplayer. 1888.
11 Charm worn on head by ballplayer; eagle feathers and deerhair for speed, snake rattle to frighten opponents. 1889.
12 Two stone pipe bowls carved with pocket knife then greased; with squirrel next to bowl. 1886.
13 Stone bowl pipe, bear next to bowl. 1887.
14 Sourwood pipestem. 1887.
15 Wooden mask worn in Eagle Dance at Big Cove. October 1901.
16 Mask worn in 1901; these impersonate strangers.
17 Mask of buckeye wood. 1887.
18 Ball for team ballgame, made of buckskin stuffed with deer hair. 1881.
19 Pair of ballsticks for team game, of hickory; older long type. 1881.
20 Pair of ballsticks; recent shorter type. Before 1911.
21 Ballsticks with bark wrappings for burning spiral design. Before 1911.

34

22 Toy plow, made by a twelve year old boy. 1889.
23 Awl with antler handle. 1881.
24 Hunter's deer call. 1889.
25 Twilled cane basket. 1881.
26 Muzzle for ox. Before 1913.
27 Pottery drinking cup. 1913.
28 Wooden ladle. 1900.
29 Laurel wood spoon, for hominy gruel. 1910.
30 Clay pot. 1881.
31 Clay pot. 1887.

32 Twilled cane basket. 1881.
33 Fish creel, basketry of hickory splints. 1900.
34 Divination stones, hung from string, used with charms and prayers to locate lost objects. 1888.
35 Two carved wooden combs, worn by women at back of head. 1887.
36 Carved wooden comb. 1881.
37 Pair of ballplayer's shorts. 1888.
38 Pair of ballplayer's shorts, worn in 1888 by Rope

Twister, captain of the Wolftown team.
39 Pair of ballplayer's shorts. 1888.
40 Poplar wood paddle with carved stamp, used to mark pot No. 41. 1887.
41 Round bottomed cooking pot made with paddle marked outside. 1887.
42 Netted woollen scarf from Indian Territory. 1868.
43 Woven woollen shawl from Indian Territory. 1868.
44 Band of woven beadwork. Before 1913.

'There is no climate or soil . . . equal to that of Arizona . . . It is my land, my home, my father's land, to which I now ask to be allowed to return. I want to spend my last days there, and to be buried among those mountains.'

GERONIMO OF THE CHIRICAHUA APACHE

THE SOUTHWEST

THE SOUTHWEST has no specific limits or definite boundaries but can be conceptualized as the states of Arizona and New Mexico in the United States and Sonora and parts of Chihuahua in Mexico. Small parts of Colorado, Texas, Utah and Sinaloa are included in the region. Spanning two modern nation states, this is yet one culture area, characterized by a common arid environment and a multi-cultural present that is the result of a

multi-cultural past. Newcomers to the Southwest of European, African and Asian ancestry meet and mingle with Native Americans to produce a distinctive and rich society. While close to a hundred groups make up the Southwest, it is the Native Americans who give the region its distinctive flavor and who provide its cultural foundations. Unlike other regions of North America, over twenty-five Native American groups have survived the onslaught of Euro-

This map shows approximate territories of tribes and language groups at the earliest periods for which there is reliable evidence: the sixteenth century for the Pueblos (the groups from Hopi to the Piro to N. Tiwa), the seventeenth century for the extreme southwestern part of the area, and the eighteenth century for the Apache, Navajo and groups on the far northwest edge.

After these dates, many tribes lost territory, some disappeared and a few gained territory.

Key to tribes:
1 Cocopa
2 Quechan
3 Halchidhoma
4 Mohave
5 Walapai
6 Havasupai
7 Yavapai
8 Maricopa
9 Papago and Upper Pima
10 Seri
11 Hopi
12 Western Apache
13 Chiricahua Apache
14 Zuni
15 R.Grande Keresans
16 Jemez
17 Navajo
18 Tewa
19 N.Tiwa
20 Tano
21 Pecos
22 S.Tiwa
23 Tompiro
24 Laguna
25 Acoma
26 Piro
27 Jicarilla Apache
28 Mescalero Apache
29 Jocome and Jano
30 Suma
31 Jumano
32 Opata
33 Eudeve
34 Jova
35 Lower Pima
36 Yaqui
37 Guarijio
38 Tarahumara
39 Tubar
40 Mayo
41 Concho
42 Toboso
43 Guasave
44 Acaxee
45 Xixime
46 Tahue
47 Tepehuan
48 Zacatec
49 Pame
50 Karankawa
51 Poorly Known Groups of the Gulf Coastal Plain and Interior
52 Ñakipa
53 Paipai
54 Kiliwa
55 Cochimí
56 Guaycura
57 Pericú

PACIFIC
OCEAN

pean expansion and been able to remain on their traditional homelands with some compliment of their distinctive customs as enclaved cultures. These groups represent almost three-quarters of the Native American cultures that inhabited the region at the time of the first Spanish explorations.

The Southwest as a region is rooted in the land and in ancient traditions. The land is varied – high rugged, snow capped mountains, fruitful river valleys, sweeping grasslands and arid deserts. The vast but often harsh landscape required many ecological adaptations. It also engendered a love of place that is so common among indigenous peoples. This love of place, the feeling of oneness with the land, conceptualized as Mother Earth, permeates Southwest Native American thought and culture as strongly today as it did 300 years ago. The land lives and all peoples respect her. Southwest Native Americans are of the land; they do not exploit it. It is this orientation that helps distinguish them for the descendants of European peoples. This does not mean that all Southwest Native Americans societies are alike, or that they are all homogeneous or never-changing. Each has a distinctive culture, one that is the result of a long historical development. All Southwest Native American cultures are independent, composed of dignified and self-reliant peoples who have wrested their living from local and regional resources. Their cultures today are a legacy of the past, the present and the future. In the Southwest, as nowhere else in North America, all that is vital in life remains as it was and as it will be.

Native Americans came to the Southwest at least 12,000 years ago. In these early times people were hunters and gatherers of wild plants. Following a nomadic way of life, they lived in small family groups and hunted first large game, like mammoths and bison, and later as .the environment changed, small animals such as deer and rabbits. When this transition occurred it signalled a new adaptation and way of life and we have given them a new name, the Archaic or Desert peoples, in recognition of this change. These peoples, whose cultures emerged around 6000 BC, began to experiment with growing food around 2500-3000 BC.

Slowly the peoples of the Southwest developed distinctive cultures; those living in the mountainous regions are called the Mogollon, those on the Colorado Plateau, the Basketmakers and Anasazi, and those in the western and central parts of the region, the Patayan, Sinagua and Salado. (Unfortunately almost nothing is known about the prehistory of northwestern Mexico.) Each group became horticulturists growing corn, beans and squash supplemented by hunting and the gathering of wild foods. Each adapted in different ways to their special environments. Around 300 BC migrations brought new groups into the Southwest from Mexico. These individuals quickly developed a culture, known as Hohokam, that was based on agricultural traditions. Living in central and southern Arizona they built extensive irrigation systems, refined tools and monumental architecture. Each of the four groups centered around a geographical area – desert mountains and plateau. (Unfortunately almost nothing is known about the prehistoric groups living in

Sonora either.) Except for those people who lived in areas that could not support agriculture, all these prehistoric peoples lived in permanent and semi-permanent villages. Some were so large and complex that they resembled small towns with extensive and complex organisations.

The fourteenth and fifteenth centuries were a time of great population movement which has not yet been explained. Following a large drought, old regions were abandoned, the largest trading centers no longer used. Groups aggregated and settlements were frequently abandoned. The main Southwestern groups who developed into the peoples we recognise in the Southwest today – the Puebloans, the O'Odham (Pima) and the Yumans – settled in what is now called their traditional homelands.

Below: *Women from San Ildefonso Pueblo where some of the finest Pueblo pottery was produced and still is. They wear the classic manta adorned with jewelry (turquoise or coral), and hard soled moccasins.*

Heralded in an extensive series of clan or migrations legends, each group has a rich oral history about this period. Other groups moved into the region from the north – the Navajo and the Apaches. From the east came Plains peoples who would trade with the native peoples. Occasionally groups from the Great Basin would meet with the settled peoples in the north and along the rivers. Harassed by drought again and the new roving tribes, groups such as the Anasazi moved on to mesa tops and east to the Rio Grande, but as a region, the Southwest was characterized by much interaction and cultural borrowing.

Finally came the Europeans, first the Spanish and later the English-American. The frontiers of the Spanish and English conquests of the New World met and overlapped in the arid Southwest. When the Spaniards arrived in the mid-sixteenth century, they found the entire region inhabited by numerous groups. Some of these peoples were town-dwelling farmers called Puebloans, others were semi-nomadic hunters and raiders; still others lived in small bands surviving by hunting and gathering. The peoples spoke a bewildering variety of languages and followed numerous ways of life. Yet all were similar in that they differed markedly from the level of political and economic organization the Spanish had encountered in central Mexico. Without the domination of agriculturally based empires like that of the Aztecs, peoples in the Southwest were politically independent and socially and economically self-sufficient farmers; all but a few hundred people on the coast of the Gulf of California and in the northern end of the Sierra Madres Mountains knew how to raise corn, beans and squash. While they differed on the extent to which agriculture was the primary mode of food production or a supplement to hunting and gathering, these peoples were quickly distinguished from the buffalo hunting peoples of the Plains to the east, from the seed-gatherers and rabbit-hunters of the north and the acorn-gatherers of California. Sporadic and small-scale trade in the form of surplus and

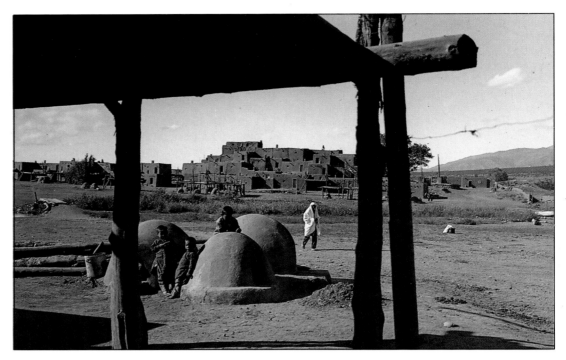

Above: *Children playing around open-air beehive ovens in the northernmost Pueblo of Taos. The present village was built around 1700, a testimony to the enduring qualities of Pueblo architecture.*

Left: *Two women and a child making pottery at Santa Clara Pueblo, famous for its polished black wares. Polished red pottery and red polychrome are also still made in the traditional style.*

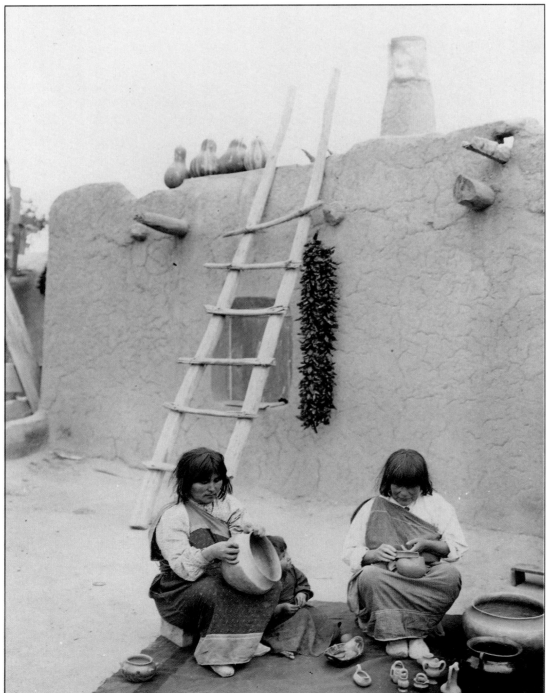

luxury items was mutual rather than a matter of controlled tribute in food staples and people. No society maintained military or political control over another. This did not mean that groups did not form temporary alliances for warfare, but warfare was not conducted for conquest and subjugation. People fought for revenge or to gain new agricultural lands, displacing older inhabitants.

The Spanish quickly began to settle the Southwest but their advance was stopped by the Apache. Wherever they went, the Spanish established a conquest culture with programs designed to 'civilize the savages' and impose a new world view. Backed by military force and identifying civilization with specific Spanish customs, missionaries, soldiers and settlers introduced Castillian (which became the lingua franca of the region), detached houses placed around a central plaza, men's trousers, new concepts of time and work, the notions of empire, politics, and Christianity. They also established a system of forced tribute, forced labor as servants, farm workers and miners, and extensive slave trade with peoples from all over the region sent to the silver mines in Mexico. They introduced some beneficial items as well – new foods and livestock, especially sheep and horses, and silversmithing. The Spanish and later Mexican policies of concentrating the small nomadic bands in Chihuahua led to the consolidation and extinction of many groups. These changes were so drastic in Mexico that some groups, like the Opata, could no longer be distinguished from the Spanish or Mexican population by the mid-1700s. Other groups welcomed these changes. To others they meant nothing; groups that were isolated because of geographical barriers, like the Seri and the

Tarahumara, remained relatively untouched. Others reacted violently. Changes were enforced on the people so brutally that by 1680 the Pueblos were rising in revolt and successfully drove the Spanish from the Rio Grande region. While the Spanish eventually re-conquered the area, they never overcame the Apaches, the Tarahumara, the Upland Yumans or the Yaquis. It was not until the late 1880s that these groups ceased to be military threats and the final Mexican settlements occurred in northwestern Mexico. By this time, the Mexicans were interested in political and economic control, not in religious conversion. Thus groups were not forced to change and it was individuals that assimilated. Many individuals voluntarily left their native communities to find work in Mexican towns.

Anglo-Americans took over the northern half of New Spain from the Mexican government in 1848. With their settlement of the region they, like the Mexican government in the south, erected great obstacles to the retention of the old way of life for Native Americans. The most

important of these was the imposition of the reservation system which isolated groups on sections of their traditional homelands and policies of forced assimilation. Native Americans were provided with agricultural technology and sent to schools far from their families. As dependent nations, these groups were given new forms of government – constitutional tribal governments that exercise inherent and sovereign powers but are limited by treaties, statutes and agreements with the federal and state governments. They were placed in a dependency role, had a set of values superimposed with no consideration of their desires. Paternalism has meant that economic development and self-determinancy were limited, but it has not meant that any groups have died out because of government policies.

Changes in economic possibilities have also

Below: *War captain and chief hunter of the Pueblo of Nambe, New Mexico, 1880. He wears a bear claw necklace, a powder horn and pouch. His blanket of rabbit skin predates the use of woollen blankets.*

meant many changes in Native American life. The destruction of the traditional subsistence strategies and new trading patterns pulled Southwest Native Americans into the nation-state's market economy. Craft objects, formerly created for home use and minor trading of surplus goods by barter, began to be produced as supplemental or major sources of income. Craft production became important in the economic strategies of many families, even though there was a low hourly return for the labor involved. Weaving, basketry, painting, silver-smithing and pottery allowed economic flexibility. People also began working for wages, on farms, on the railroad, in mines as well as in the cities.

While European groups became politically dominant, brought hardship and deprivation, had the force of laws and military might to make the old ways of life impossible, they did not eradicate all cultures. This does not mean that there were not demographic changes; many epidemic diseases raged through the Southwest and took their toll. For example, in 1883 half of the population at Hopi died from smallpox and in the 1918 influenza pandemic over half of the Jicarilla Apache and close to one quarter of the Navajo died. Since the 1920s, however, the populations have slowly and steadily increased. Other Native American groups were destroyed through internal warfare – such as the Halcidoma. But more than any other region in North America, the Native peoples have remained. They have changed, of course. There is a misconception that since Native Americans no longer follow a 'pure' aboriginal culture (i.e. one 'uncontaminated' by Europeans) they no longer exist. This is not true. Native American cultures in the Southwest are vital and vibrant. Native peoples co-exist as part of the culture of the Greater Southwest and as distinctive members with unique ways of life. They are still rooted in the past and in the land. Based on earlier lifestyles, joint ancestry, ecological adaptation, economies and linguistic affiliation we can define four basic groups of Native Americans living in the Southwest. The following pages look at the groups of the Southwest who existed in the 1600s and have survived into the present. For the core has persisted and groups – the Puebloans, the rancheria peoples, the band peoples and the hunters and gatherers – remain distinct.

In northern New Mexico and Arizona, on the Colorado Plateau and along the Rio Grande River and its tributaries, the Puebloan peoples were most in evidence – numbering over 40,000 individuals – living in ninety villages. Today there are only thirty; the others have been abandoned because of drought, disease and warfare. Called Pueblo Indians by the early Spanish explorers because of their distinctive architecture – permanent, compact, multi-chambered houses made of stone and adobe – these peoples were the descendants of the Anasazi and Mogollon peoples. Pueblo means 'village dweller' and this designation accurately reflected Pueblo life. The Pueblo Indians did not constitute a tribe; each Puebloan culture was a village that functioned as an autonomous political entity. This does not mean that these groups lived in a vacuum. They traded with one another, recognized common ances-

Santa Clara Corn Dance, 1950

Two dancers leave the north kiva to enter the plaza at Santa Clara, one of the Tewa pueblos. They are participating in the Corn Dance; the woman has the distinctive tablita headdress for this dance. She wears a woollen manta with a belt woven of wool and cotton, and very high wrapped moccasins. She has turquoise and silver bracelets, and a turquoise and coral necklace. Both hold spruce boughs, and the man also carries a gourd rattle. He has white and black body paint, and wears necklaces of shells and coral, a cotton dance kilt with wool embroidery, a fine woven cotton belt, and a leather belt with bells. His anklets are of skunk fur tied around his white moccasins, while a fox tail hangs behind. A very similar scene inspired a watercolor by the Santa Clara artist Pablita Velarde.

Above: *The Pueblo of Cochiti (1879), which dates from the mid-thirteenth century. Known for its pottery and fine-toned drums, Cochiti is also famous for ceremonies, kachina dances among them.*

Right: *Governor Ahfitche of San Felipe Pueblo using a pump drill to drill holes in shells and flat turquoise (1880). San Felipe lies between the Rio Grande and the foot of the Black Mesa.*

try, occasionally intermarried and shared many similar values and world views.

The Puebloan peoples speak many different languages. The largest language group is *Tanoan*, part of the Kiowa-Tanoan language family. Tanoan consists of three main languages – *Tiwa*, *Tewa* and *Towa*. The people of Taos, Picuris, Sandia and Isleta speak dialects of Tiwa. At San Juan, Santa Clara, San Ildefonso, Pojoaque, Nambe and Tesuque, Tewa is spoken. Tewa is also spoken at Hano in Hopi country because many Tewa families migrated from the Rio Grande valley about 1700 following the re-conquest of the area after the Pueblo Revolt. Jemez is the only pueblo today in which Towa can be heard. In the past the inhabitants of the famous pueblo of Pecos were also Towa speakers but the village was abandoned in the early 1800s.

Living dispersed among the Tanoan speakers are the *Keresans*. Along the Rio Grande and its tributaries are the Keresan villages of Cochiti, Santo Domingo, San Felipe, Santa Ana and Zia; farther west are Laguna and Acoma. Even farther west is the pueblo of Zuni where *Zunian* is spoken. Zuni is part of the Penutian linguistic stock and is unrelated to other languages in the Southwest. (Other Penutian speakers live in California.) Finally there are the Hopi in north central Arizona. Hopi consists of a series of villages located on three mesas on the Colorado Plateau. *Hopi* is a language that belongs to the Shoshonean branch of the Uto-Aztecan lan-

Zuni

Zuni pueblo has been occupied for at least 600 years. Interaction with Spaniards and Mexicans was almost continuous after Coronado arrived in 1540, but Zuni maintained its independence while adopting some European crops, sheep, and burros, and developing a secular governmental structure to deal with the outside world. This still persists, in changed form, alongside the theocratic system that controls internal affairs. The elaborate ceremonial life is organized by six kiva groups, twelve medicine societies, and two sets of priests, interacting with the fourteen matrilineal clans. In the mid-20th century the manufacture of silver and turquoise jewelry and some pottery for sale was a major source of income. However, by the 1970s weaving was extinct at Zuni and basketry nearly so. These crafts were still actively pursued when the items illustrated here were collected by A. L. Kroeber, F. W. Hodge, and H. J. Spinden between 1899 and 1916.

1 Large pottery bowl with four stepped corners with dragonfly designs inside and modelled frogs outside. 1915.
2 Food bowl. 1912.
3 Redware moccasin jars for matches and trinkets, made for sale. 1915.
4 Wooden lightning symbol carried in dance. 1915.
5 Wooden lightning symbol carried in dance. 1915.
6 Breechcloth of cotton cloth, embroidered in wool, worn by dancer.
7 Throwing club for hunting rabbits, of wood painted red and black. 1915.
8 Stone pot containing green paint. 1899.
9 Small redware jar with duck and stepped rainbow designs. 1899.
10 Pump drill for jewelry making, etc.; metal point, stone flywheel. 1915.
11 Wooden tongs for picking cactus fruit. 1915.
12 Shallow openwork twined basket. 1899.

13 Spindle with wooden whorl, spun wool thread. 1915.

14 Small basket of twilled yucca splints. 1916.

15 Pair of boy dancer's moccasins. 1915.

16 Woman's buckskin moccasins with leg wrappings made of buckskin strips. 1915.

17 Cotton dancer's kilt with pattern in wool embroidery. 1915.

18 Large pottery bowl. 1899.

19 Small wooden paddle for making bread. 1915.

20 Stone panther fetish of Hunter society. 1915.

21 Armlets of god impersonator with perforated yellow flaps and leather pendants. 1915.

22 Pair of dance moccasins with quilled heel straps. 1915.

23 Embroidered cotton cape of Shalako dancer. 1915.

24 Ornament of short turkey feathers and long white feather, worn on side of head for Hopi dance. 1915.

25 Large pottery jar with classic rainbird design. 1899.

26 Large pottery bowl. 1899.

27 Wrapped yucca ring stand for hot pot. 1915.

28 White painted naked kachina doll with flower garland. 1916.

29 Twined basket. 1899.

30 Belled flageolet for Society ceremony. 1915.

31 Wooden lightning symbol carried in dance. 1915.

32 Necklace of wooden imitation eagle claws worn in Comanche Dance. 1915.

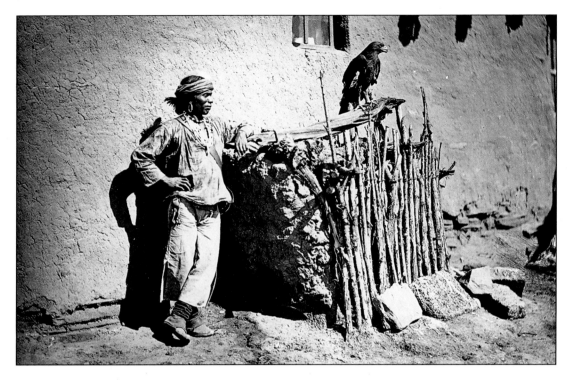

guage family. Thus Hopi is related to Piman, Ute and Paiute in the Southwest and many language groups in central Mexico.

The Pueblos are divided into two main subgroups based on location and ecological adaptation. The Eastern Pueblos (Tanoan and Keresan speakers), who live on the Rio Grande and its tributaries, have a permanent water source enabling them to practice irrigation agriculture. The Western Pueblos (Hopi, Hopi-Tewa, Zuni, Acoma and Laguna), lacking a steady supply of water, rely on dry farming. The difference in water supply affects many aspects of culture from food procurement to religion. Economically all Puebloans are agriculturalists. Many also raise small herds of sheep and cattle, produce art – such as weaving, silversmithing, jewelry, katchina dolls, pottery and baskets. (Most Pueblo Indians, like everyone else in the Southwest, are wage earners today. This means that many must live off their land and move to the large nearby cities of Albuquerque, Santa Fe, Gallup, Flagstaff and Phoenix. All return home for important ceremonies.)

With the Pueblo Indians religion transcends and permeates all aspects of life, including interaction patterns with the land, with other peoples and with the supernaturals. All aspects of Puebloan life – arts, crafts, economics, social structure and the family – are inextricably inte-

Above: *Zuni Pueblo, New Mexico, 1879. The young man stands beside an eagle cage made of adobe and stakes. The eagle was kept for its plumage which was highly valued for ceremonial purposes.*

Below: *The Mesa of Taaiyalone (Corn Mountain) seen from the rooftops of Zuni Pueblo. After conflict with the Franciscans in 1632, the Zunis fled to Taaiyalone, which lies southeast of Zuni.*

woven and integrated under a single world view. From the simple tenet that people must live in harmony with nature, the Pueblo Indians have developed rich cultural traditions that are expressed in poetry, legends, song, dance and art. In this way central values are given outward expression. For example, many of the designs on pottery are derived from motifs connected with ceremonial life. Architecturally the center of a village, both physically and symbolically, is a special chamber called *kivas*. Here private and communal rites are performed daily and at appropriate times throughout the year. Prayers are given for blessing and to insure the germination and maturation of crops and to give thanks for good health. Through religion all else is given significance.

Secular and ecclesiastical authority are sharply delimited in the pueblos. Each village is a tightly and highly structured theocracy, organized around an elaborate ceremonial life. Based on their ancient patterns, this theocracy, whose head is called the *cacique*, is kept secret within the village. To the outside world the secular political structure is more evident. In the eastern Pueblos, the secular organization is in the hands of a *governor* who is appointed or elected each year. These governors were given canes of office by President Lincoln in the 1860s and these have become valued symbols of

office. The governor has several assistants called *principales*, a group of elder statesmen whose lifelong experience enables them to integrate wisely civil and religious matters. In all the pueblos there is a hunt chief and a war chief or war priest.

Tewa pueblos are composed of two social divisions, what anthropologists call moieties.

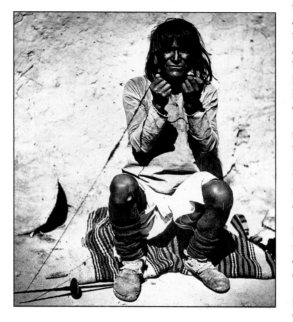

Membership in a moiety is through the father, though a woman may change her moiety affiliation if she marries a man of the opposite group. Each moiety has political officers. During half of the year, the governmental and ceremonial duties of the pueblos are in the hands of the Summer People, while the Winter People (the other moiety) are in charge of obligations for the other half-year. Within each moiety there are certain religious societies, but other societies cross-cut and meld the kinship divisions. Among the Keresan peoples, social organization is more unified. There is but one cacique per village and he is aided by a council composed of the heads of religious societies who all serve for life.

In all the pueblos the family is the cornerstone of life. While in the Tewa communities the extended family of either the father or mother is emphasized, at Zuni and Hopi it is the mother's that serves as the basis for the society. Puebloans, when compared to other groups in the Southwest, are non-individualistic and innovations are accepted or rejected by group decision, by consensus and persuasion. While all Puebloan peoples share many common values, ideas and traditions, each is distinct. A Pueblo village is closely united and highly systematized organization. Each village favors marriage within its own group. There are variations in the ceremonies of each group, and the pottery and stylistic designs are distinctive. (The artifacts on pp. 42–3 offer good examples of just such outstanding pottery and stylistic designs from one Puebloan group – the Zuni.)

Below: *The Hopi Natashka or Bean Planting ceremony at Walpi Pueblo, First Mesa, Arizona (1893). These kachinas are ogres who frighten children into obedience to their parents.*

Above: *A Hopi spinner making a twist in his yarn even by means of a spindle, which is placed under his foot, and by pushing the twist up along the thread (photograph undated).*

At the time of Spanish contact, the rancheria groups – the Cahitans, Tarahumarans, Pimans and Yumans – comprised the largest subgroup in the Southwest, over 150,000 individuals or approximately three-quarters of the peoples in the Southwest. They lived in widely spaced settlements along rivers or in well-watered mountain and desert areas in southern Arizona and northern Mexico. Relying on irrigation and flood waters, rancheria peoples were farmers. The extended family, rather than the village, formed the basic social unit; each family owned a house and fields dispersed along the river as much as half a mile apart. Kinship was generally bilateral or patrilineal. Nevertheless, the members of each settlement still thought of themselves as a community, moved as a unit, and symbolized their unity by placing a community house in the center of each settlement. Rancheria peoples frequently had more than one village, shifting from one settlement to another depending on the season of the year. All rancheria peoples are very interested in social gatherings, disdaining structured situations and displays of wealth, however. They are sensitive to the maintenance of form and custom in social intercourse. While this meant there has been a weak development of religious leadership – the important religious leaders were shamans rather than priests, and political leaders were senior men who were influential speakers – there is a respect for all who have knowledge and wisdom. This has led to a highly developed native literature in myth, song, folk stories and formalized oratory. Among the most famous for these skills are the Huichol.

The rancheria groups belong to two basic linguistic groups – the Uto-Aztecan and the Hokan. The Uto-Aztecans rancheria speakers can be divided into four basic language groups: Pima, Cahita, Opatan and Tarahumaran. The Pimans live in southern Arizona – Upper Piman, Tohono O'Odham, Sobaipuri – and in Mexico – the Pima Bajo and Tepehuan. The Cahitan speakers (the Mayo and Yaqui), the Opatan speakers (the Opata, Eudebe and Jova), and the Tarahumaran speakers (the Tarahumara, Warihio and Concho) live in Mexico in mountainous areas and along major rivers. The Hokan speakers live in Arizona and upper Baja California and are known as the Yumans. The Upper Yumans – the Walapai, Yavapai and Havasupai – live in the upland region of western and northern Arizona while the lowland Yumans – the Mohave, Halchidoma, Yuma, Cocomaricopa, Cocopa and Cochimi – live along the Colorado River and its tributaries. Moving constantly because of intertribal warfare, some Yuman groups all but killed each other off by the early nineteenth century. The Maricopa eventually moved in with the River Pima in the area around Phoenix because they had been displaced from the Colorado River.

In Mexico the mountain-dwelling Tarahumara are well-known. Living in shelters ranging from caves in rugged cliffs to stone masonry houses, they planted small cornfields in mountain valleys in the summer and retreated

Right: Mayo women wove blankets, serapes and sashes from handspun wool on the horizontal loom. Large mats were used for bedding, and also for constructing walls, as shown here, and small baskets were woven from cane.

Above: *Lieta, a Pima woman from the Gila River Reservation, Sacaton, Arizona, 1902. She exhibits a style of face painting obsolete by this time but which was reconstructed for the photograph.*

to the lowlands in the winter. Like other rancheria groups the Tarahumara also utilized wild plant foods. Only recently have the Tarahumara been affected by the outside world: the first railroad into their region did not exist even as recently as ten years ago.

On the plains and lower valleys to the west live groups like the Huichol, the Mayo, and the

Yaqui at the mouth of major river systems, some of the richest farmland in all of Mexico. Favorable agricultural conditions permitted more concentrated settlements than the mountainous and desert regions and the Yaqui and Mayo developed tribal organizations for warfare and defensive purposes. So successful were the Yaqui that they were the only group in the region who were not conquered by the Spanish. Interestingly, the Yaqui were also the only group to request missionaries and voluntarily to become Christians. However, they changed much of the ritual and the meanings and developed what is essentially a new religion, Sonoran Catholicism. This is a mixture of Spanish, Mexican, and traditional beliefs and customs. The central ritual is the Eastern ceremony that lasts for forty days, culminating with the destruction of evil by good in a mock battle the day before Easter Sunday. This ritual, like many others still conducted by Southwestern groups, is done to ensure that the world will continue.

The Yaquis have another distinction in the Southwest. After years of warfare they were finally defeated by the Mexicans who occupied their territory in the late 1880s. At conquest the Mexicans deported most of the people to the Yucatan peninsula to work in forced labor camps. Some of these individuals escaped and came to the United States, building several communities in southern Arizona. The Yaquis sought and were given political refugee status and allowed to stay, even after the Yaqui were allowed to return to their homeland in the mid-1920s. One of the reasons they were given political asylum was because of their distinctive religious ceremonies.

Farther north were the O'Odham (Pima)

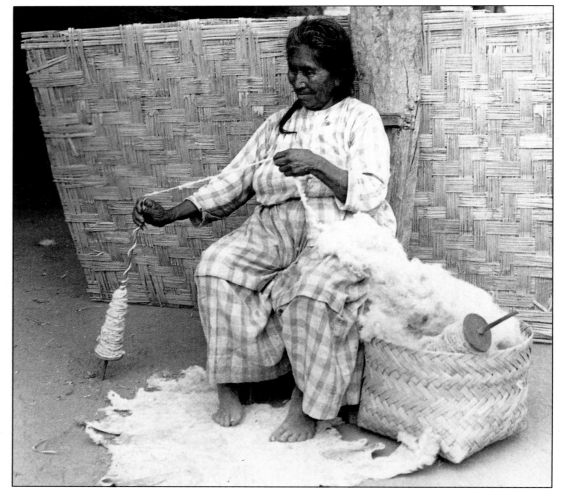

peoples who lived in more compact settlements than the Tarahumara. The Pima have a long history which reaches back into the archeological past of southern Arizona and northern Mexico. The Pima word for themselves is O'Odham', meaning The People. The Pimas can be divided into four basic groups – the River Pima who live along the rivers in central Arizona, the Tohono O'Odham (formerly called the Papago), the Pima Bajo who live in Mexico, and the Sobaipuri who lived in southeastern Arizona and were driven out by the Apache and Spanish. The survivors of this group have intermingled with the other Piman groups. All Piman groups were agriculturalists; in fact, the River Pimans were so successful that they supplied much of the food for the U.S. army during the western campaigns of the Civil War and for Anglo-American settlers moving to California during the Gold Rush of the 1860s. The River Pimans also served in the Civil War as the only Union forces in the Arizona territory; they successfully defeated Confederate troops and kept the lines to California open. After the war they served as scouts in the Apache wars. The River

Pimans remained prosperous until Anglo settlers in the town of Florence, upriver from them, appropriated their water thereby making agriculture no longer possible. The river ran dry at planting time and many people starved. Unfortunately it took the U.S. Congress until 1924 to recognize that their rights have been ignored and allot them water when the Coolidge Dam was built. It took many more years for the Pima to recover economically and socially. The Pima refer to this period as the 'Forty Years of Famine'.

Along the Colorado River lived another group of rancheria peoples, the Yumans. Like the Cahitans they had a permanent water supply and hence could have more densely settled homesteads. They also were organized as a tribe for warfare and had a strong tribal sense of identity. In civil matters, however, the local group made decisions. As groups also they relied more heavily on wild plants for their houses, clothes and food supplements than the Cahitans and their material culture was more like that of the Pimans and their neighbors to the west in California. The River

Below: *Two unidentified Cocopa men – the most southern of the Yuman tribes – on board Admiral Dewey's ship, Narragansett, 1874. Cocopa breechclouts were longer in back than in front.*

Right: *Two unidentified Yuma men, c.1870. Their main weapons were hardwood clubs; the long, weak bows and untipped arrows shown here were rather ineffective and used only for small game and birds.*

Tarahumara

The Tarahumara live in dispersed settlements in southwestern Chihuahua. They are farmers, especially of corn, beans and squash, who raise cattle, sheep, goats, pigs and burros. The first serious study of the Tarahumara was by Carl S. Lumholtz (1902), who collected the objects shown here in the 1890s (except for No. 1, the poncho, which is of more recent origin). Most of these examples have never been published, and none has previously appeared in color. Most of the types of objects shown, however, are also widely used by the present-day Tarahumara.

The wooden cross on the necklace of Jobs-tears beads from Carichí (No.3) indicates that the Tarahumara are nominally Catholics. Pinole, mentioned in No.8, was meal made from parched corn. The spindle and whorl (No.13) were used for preparing wool thread for weaving. The cane-shafted lance (No.16) is notable because it is a rare object. The twilled palm leaves of the basket and cover (No.18) are double woven.

1 Man's poncho, of homespun wool woven on a horizontal loom.
2 Pair of woman's ear ornaments – shell pendants on strings of glass beads.
3 Necklace of Jobs-tear beads, with wooden cross, from Carichi.
4 Fringed leather pouch.
5 Large gourd vessel, from Guajochi.
6 Gourd dipper, from Aboreachi.
7 Wooden ladle.
8 Sun-dried cakes made from ground-up leaves of a wild plant (called *hierba colorado* in Spanish), used as an ingredient in pinole.
9 Rattle of wood, used by matachine dancers.
10 Cane whistle, used to accompany drums played during Easter ceremonies. From the rim of Copper Canyon.
11 Musical rasp – a smooth stick rubbed over the notched stick, over a resonator – used during

Peyote and bakánowa ceremonies. From Barranca de San Carlos.

12 Wooden bowl, used inverted as a resonator for musical rasps. From Guajochi.

13 Spindle and wooden whorl. From Guajochi.

14 Bow for hunting game, of elm or mulberry wood. From Carichí.

15 Quiver of mountain lion skin, and seventeen arrows, most with iron points. From Carichí.

16 Lance with cane shaft and iron point. From Carichí.

17 Gourd rattle, used by ritual chanters and matachine dancers.

18 Basket and cover, of twilled palm leaves.

19 Double-woven twilled basket, containing feathers (probably used in ceremonies).

20 Pottery dish for food, made in coiling technique, sun-dried and then fired. From Aboreachi.

21 Woollen blanket, woven on horizontal loom, used as bedding and also worn by men in cold weather. From Guajochi.

22 Woven wool belt worn by both sexes. From Carichí.

23 Woven wool belt.

24 Woven wool belt, from Narárachi.

25 Woven wool belt, from Carichí.

26 Woven wool belt, from Guajochi.

27 Pair of leather sandals, worn by both sexes, from Guajochi.

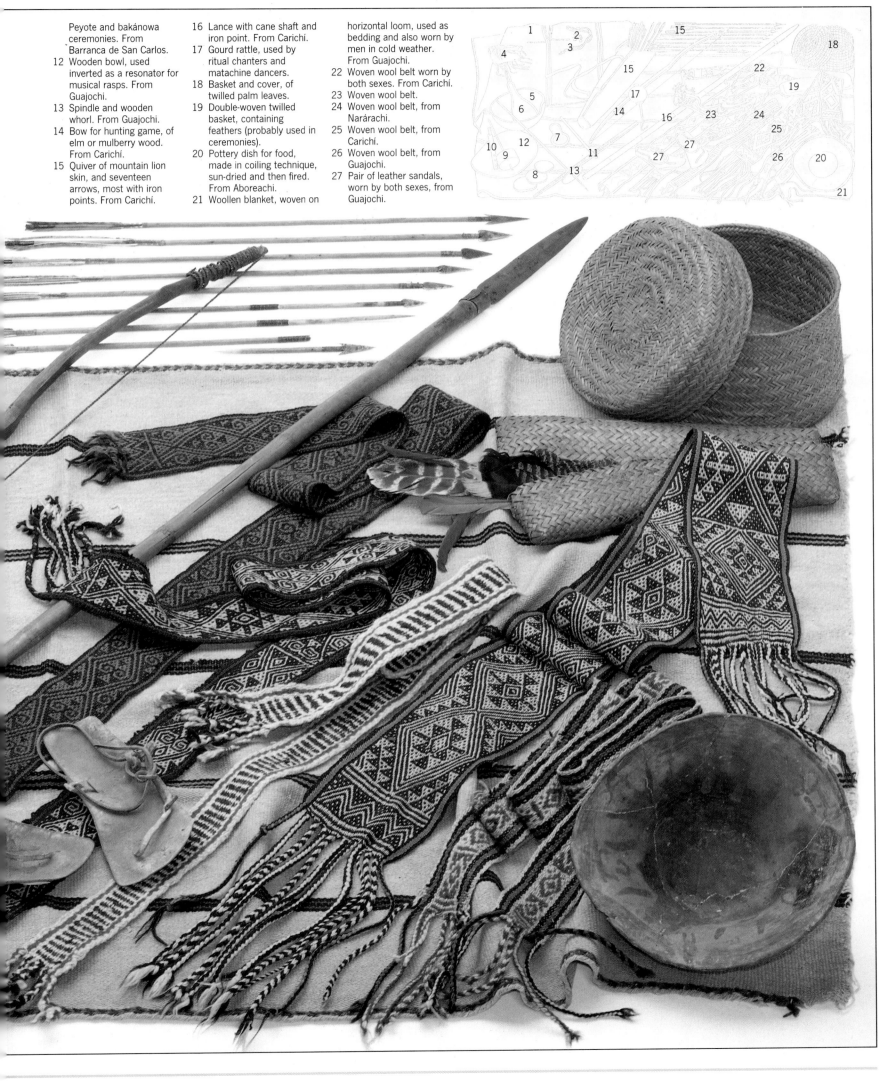

Yumans were tied closely to the annual cycle of river flooding. Since their homes were periodically washed away, they had no cultural incentive for the accumulation of wealth. Even today, the Cocopa, for example, disdain ostentatious displays of wealth. A person's goods are destroyed at his or her death. Even the goods of relatives and friends are placed in the burial fire at death and again in the anniversary festival, the most important religious ceremony. In the

Below: *Juan Chivaria, war leader and shaman, son and niece (Sye-cui-Sall), of the Maricopa, one of the Colorado River tribes. Although in close contact with the Pima, the Maricopa followed a way of life typical of Colorado River Yumans.*

historic period the River Yumans were joined by a group from central California, the Chemuehevi, who have adopted a lifestyle similar to that of the Mohave.

A final group of Yumans, the Upland Yumans, can be placed either with the rancheria peoples or the non-agricultural peoples because their homelands lacked enough water for permanent farming. The Upland Yumans – the Walapai, Yavapai and the Havasupai – lived primarily by hunting and gathering on the upland areas of western and northern Arizona. Living a lifestyle that was similar to other hunting and gathering peoples, the Walapai had a limited technological base and lived in small groups that moved often in an established

round. The Havasupai lived on the Colorado River in Cataract Canyon, next to the Grand Canyon, and have adopted many Hopi traits. The Upland Yumans had little interaction with the Spanish and Mexicans except for meeting an occasional explorer searching for minerals. Today the Yavapai and Walapai live on small reservations and herd cattle or work for wages. Through extensive intermarriage and because of their forced internment on Apache reservations many Yavapai have become intermingled culturally with the Western Apache. By 1900 the Yavapai began to drift off the San Carlos Reservation and return to their traditional homelands in areas that had not been claimed by Anglo-American miners.

Above: *Jodrava, a Havasupai man, drinking from a traditional basket water bottle. Covered inside and out with piñon gum, such bottles are strong, durable and watertight and survive years of use.*

Below: *Havasupai man dehairing a skin stretched over a wooden frame. Finished buckskin was a main item of Havasupai commerce, which they traded for horses, pottery, jewelry with the Hopi and Navajo.*

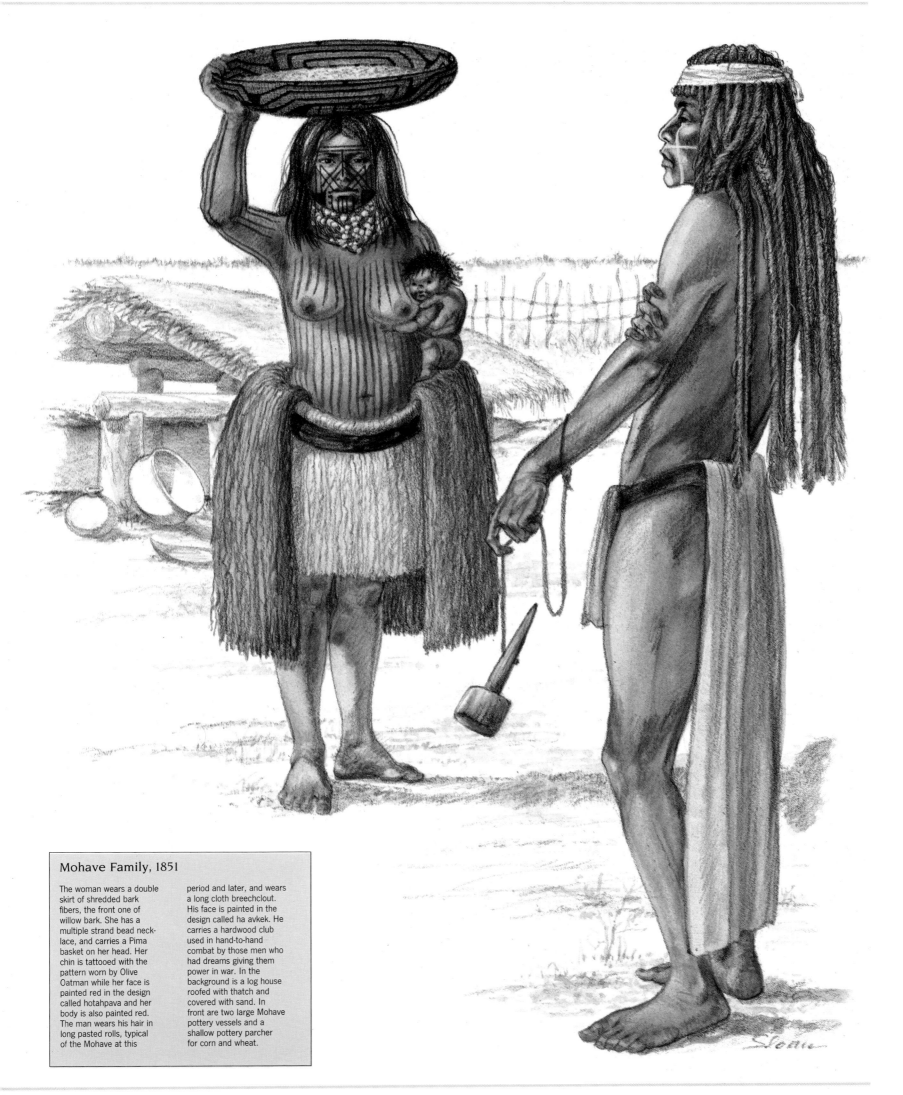

Mohave Family, 1851

The woman wears a double skirt of shredded bark fibers, the front one of willow bark. She has a multiple strand bead necklace, and carries a Pima basket on her head. Her chin is tattooed with the pattern worn by Olive Oatman while her face is painted red in the design called hotahpava and her body is also painted red. The man wears his hair in long pasted rolls, typical of the Mohave at this period and later, and wears a long cloth breechclout. His face is painted in the design called ha avkek. He carries a hardwood club used in hand-to-hand combat by those men who had dreams giving them power in war. In the background is a log house roofed with thatch and covered with sand. In front are two large Mohave pottery vessels and a shallow pottery parcher for corn and wheat.

Pima

When the Spaniards arrived in 1694 the Pimas lived in seven villages on and near the Gila R., where they used river water to raise corn, beans, squash, cotton, and tobacco, gathered wild foods (especially mesquite beans and saguaro cactus fruit), and hunted deer and rabbits. During the 18th century the Pima economy was transformed by the addition of wheat to their crops, which with efficient irrigation allowed a surplus for export. A golden age of Pima agriculture followed, during the first quarter century after American control of S. Arizona began in 1853. Then non-Indians upstream from the Pima diverted the Gila R. water, and Pima economy rapidly declined. When Frank Russell, a Harvard ethnologist, visited in 1901–2 to document Pima history and culture, especially their material world, much of what he collected and later described was obsolete or moribund. A small sample of his collection is shown here; some things collected earlier by others are also shown, with dates.

1 Blanket of homespun cotton, obsolete by 1901. Collected 1877.
2 Headband of cotton and wool; reconstruction of old type.
3 Buckskin jacket. 1877.
4 Mesquite wood war clubs.
5 Models of war club and painted rawhide shield.
6 Pair of rawhide sandals. Collected from Papago in 1895, similar to Pima.
7 Calendar stick with notches and mnemonic symbols for important events of each year from 1833 to 1902.
8 Unfinished mesquite wood ladle.
9 Farmer's spade, Mexican steel blade, Pima oak handle.
10 Stone used as anvil in shaping clay pot.
11 Stone pestle.
12 War bow, old, of mulberry wood with sinew string.
13 Arrow, collected 1885.
14 Arrows, one with stone point, collected 1877.
15 War headdress of

raptorial bird feathers, collected 1885.

16 Glass bead necklace.
17 Wooden tray for mixing bread and other purposes, collected 1885.
18 Mesquite wood ladle, form said to be Mexican, learned by Pima from Papago.
19 Gourd dipper. 1885.
20 Warrior's basket food bowl.
21 Glass bead necklace.
22 Rattle of four tin oyster-can caps set on wires in wood handles;

obtained by Pimas from Papagos or Yaquis.
23 Reed tubes for gambling; all four were filled with sand, then opposing team guessed which one also held a hidden bean.
24 Eagle feathers on short rods, used for ceremonial sprinkling of water.
25, 26 Two shaman's slate tablets.
27 Basket of coiled wheat straw, used for wheat granary.
28 Coiled basket. 1885.

29 Coiled basket.
30 Oak paddle, used with anvil to shape pottery.
31 Twilled basket, for shaman's equipment. 1885.
32 Gourd used to hold seeds. 1885.
33 Sieve of willow rods, for food preparation.
34 Notched and plain sticks – musical rasp.
35 Reed flageolet.
36 Rag doll in cradle improvised from plank.
37 Coccoons strung on cord, worn as leg rattles.

Everyone has heard of the Apaches yet few know much about them except for stereotypes, the 'warlike raiders and marauders' of so many movies. But this is a one-sided view. While the Apacheans were fierce raiders and were feared with good reason, they also had and have rich cultures that have remained unexplored. The Southern Athapascans or Apacheans were newcomers to the Southwest, arriving just before European contact. Related to other Athapascan-speakers in the north, most Apacheans lived in small units based on extended families and followed a semi-nomadic existence; their residences were temporary and seasonal. Local groups composed of several matrifocal extended families formed bands, the largest level of political organization. There were no tribes, as conceptualized by Hollywood producers and writers of pulp fiction. Today each group refers to themselves as a nation, however.

The Apaches can be divided geographically into eastern and western groups. In the east are the Jicarilla, Mescalero, Lipan (forming, in fact, a Southern Plains group), and Chiricahua Apaches; in the west are the White Mountain, Carrizo, San Carlos, Fort Apache, Pinal, Arivaipa, Apache Peaks, Mazatzal, Tonto and Cibecue bands who together are referred to as the Western Apache, and the Navajo. All share a basic world view, religious orientation and mythological cycle. Ceremonies are given to cure illness, to set the world right and to ward off possible evils. All groups are matrilineal and have elaborate and important puberty ceremonies for girls. In the Mescalero ceremony, for example, the family constructs a large, brush tipi or wickiup in which the girls dance to a series of ritual songs. This ceremony is under the direction of a shaman or medicine man, called a singer. In the second part of the ceremony, called the Sun Greeting, the girl is introduced as an adult following a period of fasting and instruction by elders.

The Athapascan-speaking peoples were the last major Native American group to come to the Southwest and the last major groups to be brought under Anglo-American political control. Originally natives of northwest Canada and Alaska, the Athapascans moved into the Southwest during the late 1300s-early 1400s AD, right before the arrival of the Spanish. By 1600 there were probably 15,000 Apaches in the Southwest. When they arrived as small bands of migrating peoples, they were undifferentiated. The groups quickly spread into the areas around the Pueblo villages and claimed areas as their traditional homes with identified sacred locales. Some groups mingled with Plains tribes – the Lipan Apache moved into west Texas and displaced the Comanches; the Mescalero and Chiricahua Apache moved into the area east of the Rio Grande Valley; the Jicarilla and Navajo moved into the northern part of New Mexico while the Western and other Chiricahua Apache moved into the old Western Anasazi and Mogollon homeland.

Apacheans lived by hunting and gathering. When they reached the Southwest they added to this economic base raiding and agriculture. All quickly acquired either Plains, Puebloan or rancheria customs as well as a reputation for fierceness. They also readily took to the horse. Much of the history of the Southwest revolves

Above: *Apache hunters, one in knitted socks probably issued by the army. Note typical Apache costume of headband and high moccasins. Arrows are much longer than those of Plains Indians.*

around Apache raids for goods and Puebloan, Piman, Spanish and Anglo-American retaliation and counter-raiding. By AD 1700 much of the Southwest was an armed camp with fluctuating alliances based on economic expediency. The Jicarilla Apaches were united with the Spaniards in their wars against the French and the Pawnee. Joining the Jicarilla were the

Below: *Eskiminzin and his wife, two Pinal Coyotero Apaches. The Coyotero lived in the vicinity of the Pinal Mountains and were known for their pleasant countenances and for the beauty of their women.*

Utes and the Tewa, especially the people of Taos, to fight the Comanche and Kiowa of the Plains. Other Apaches raided Pueblo villages to such an extent that the Pueblo communities moved to high defensible ground; many Piman communities had stockades and permanent guards. Other Apache groups raided into Mexico to such an extent that entire areas were abandoned. Because of retaliation and these economic patterns, the Apaches, in turn, lived in protected highlands, canyons and mountain valleys. They kept small communities that could be moved quickly and the situation remained thus for over 200 years until the last Apache group was defeated in the mid-1880s.

Apachean raiding was not done by a tribe but by local groups. This pattern can be loosely equated with guerilla warfare. The goal was not to kill; in fact, Apache men gained no status from killing and never took scalps. They gained status from successfully bringing back food and horses to their families. The object was to avoid encounters with the enemy. Those who led raids were men who felt the possessions in the encampment were in short supply. Apache tribes had no recognized leaders; bands and local groups did. These influential men and women had prestige because of their wealth, their abilities and personal influence. The Apacheans made a sharp distinction behaviorally between raids and warfare. A war party was formed to avenge an Apache casuality, led by a relative of the slain individual. In general, Apache attitudes toward warfare contrasted sharply with those of Plains groups; there were no warrior societies and there was no enthusiasm for standing ground in a hopeless situation or counting coup. Legendary figures like Geronimo, Naiche or Cochise became famous because of their ability to elude the U.S. cavalry. The ascendancy of tribal leaders occurred only after Anglo-American political institutions were introduced.

Some Apachean groups practiced very little agriculture and lived almost like Plains groups. The Jicarilla Apache (from the Spanish word for little basket weaver) lived in the northern part of New Mexico and the Mescalero (gatherer of agave) lived in the south central part of the state. Both groups ranged on to the Plains and hence have many cultural traits that reflect contacts with groups in Texas. For example, the Jicarilla and the Mescalero traditionally lived in tipis. (Other Apaches, who lived in forested mountain dells, built shelters of brush, called wickiups.) After a defeat by Kit Carson and the U.S. army in 1868 the Jicarilla were placed on a reservation with the Mescalero, but the two groups constantly fought and the Jicarilla were given their own reservation, in their traditional homeland, in 1887.

The San Carlos Apache, for example, began herding in 1884 when the U.S. government issued live cattle for beef rations. Men became cattlemen while women supplemented the family income by gathering wild foods and producing baskets for sale. As often happened, parts of the reservation held excellent grazing land and Anglo ranchers quickly began to encroach. By the late 1890s the Anglo-owned Chiricahua Cattle Company quietly obtained through its influence with the army permission to graze a herd of 2,000 head at Ash Flats. Other Anglo ranchers encroached illegally on San and raiding and because of this they led a semi-nomadic life.

When the United States government annexed Navajo territory in 1849, the Navajo were feared as a warring, raiding group of bands. They were not organized into a tribe – each community and kin group was independent. For many years the government tried to stop the raids in order to allow settlement by Anglo and Mexican ranchers, but the constant raids on Navajo families by slave traders who wanted to ensure that the territory was in a constant state of flux to make capturing Navajo easier meant that warfare continued.

During the American Civil War, the U.S. government wanted to keep New Mexico and Arizona territories in the Union and ensure that the lines of communication to California remained open. To do this they felt they had to stop Apachean raids, particularly that of the Mescalero Apache and the Navajo. The campaign against the Mescalero lasted five months in 1862. The Mescalero were moved to a new military post on the Pecos River called Fort Sumner (or Bosque Redondo). The location on the edge of the Great Plains lacked firewood, good drinking water and arable land.

In 1863 Colonel Christopher Carson was commissioned by General Carleton to round up The People and move them to the new military reservation in east-central New Mexico. The military sent out peace negotiations to a few bands and local leaders telling them to move; if they refused, the general orders were to remove them forcefully. Most of the Navajo who lived in widely scattered local groups never heard the ultimatum and General Carleton made no attempt to locate them. Instead he sent Carson to destroy the Navajo economic base. Joined by Utes and Pueblos and New Mexican irregulars, Carson undertook a scorched earth policy that destroyed cornfields and orchards, hogans, water holes and livestock. Over a thousand of The People were killed, wounded or captured. The Navajo had nowhere to hide and little to eat; they surrendered in 1864.

Carlos land and shot Apache cattle. By 1900 the situation was critical, a range war was imminent and the army was called in. However, it was not for another ten years that the situation was brought until control.

With the end of their traditional economies based on raiding and hunting, all Apache groups developed a flexible economy in the twentieth century partly based on livestock – cattle and sheep.

The Navajo call themselves the Dineh – 'The People'. The word Navajo is a Tewa term 'Nava-huu' which means cultivated field in an arroyo. The Pueblos and early Spanish chroniclers of the early seventeenth century distinguished the Navajo from other Apaches living west and south of the Rio Grande because they were 'very great farmers'. This success in agriculture

Above: White Mountain Apache women in camp, one with a milling stone. A classic Western Apache twined burden basket can be seen at left; rawhide 'cut-out' saddle bags hang over the line.

was also noted by U.S. army reports 150 years later. Today we think of the Navajo as sheep herders and weavers but this did not happen until after they became agriculturalists. Like other Apacheans the Navajo raided Spanish and Puebloan settlements for sheep and horses. They quickly developed an economy and life that was based on herding, agriculture

Below: A group of Apache scouts in Arizona. Apache scouts were first recruited at Camp Apache, 1871, supplied with rifle, cartridge belt, blanket and canteen, and uniforms too – if they wanted them.

Western Apache

The Western Apaches include five independent divisions speaking slightly different varieties of the same language; one of these is the San Carlos Apaches. Each division consisted of two to five independent bands of some 50 to 700 members each (in 1880). Each of these in turn included several local groups of 35 to 200 people; these were the basic landholding and political units. The Apaches lived in a mountain and canyon country of forests, well-watered valleys, and deserts. They depended mainly on hunting deer and antelope and on gathering wild plants such as mescal tubers, cactus fruits, mesquite beans, and piñon nuts. Farming provided about a quarter of their food, from corn, beans, and squash raised on small irrigated plots in the mountains. During the Spanish-Mexican period Western Apache culture was strongly affected by the adoption of horses and horse equipment, firearms, cloth, and metal tools and implements. Trading and cattle raiding relations were established with their Indian and Spanish neighbors on all sides. For most of the second half of the 19th century the Western Apaches fought the U.S. Army. Hostilities finally ended with the capture and confinement of Geronimo in 1885. By 1909, when all the items shown here were collected among the San Carlos Apaches, many of them were working for wages, some as cowboys on Anglo ranches. Cattle raising became a major Apache industry after 1920, and lumbering became important on the reservations.

1 War club; stone head wrapped in buckskin on wooden handle.
2 Coiled basket to cook and serve food; older style.
3 Knife for trimming leaves off mescal (century plant) tubers used for food.
4 Gourd dipper.
5 Shallow old basket coated with clay for cooking corn with live coals.
6 Small twined water jar, waterproofed inside and out with piñon pitch.
7 Hide scraper, steel blade.
8 Boy's deerskin vest.
9 Awl, probably for basket making, with leather case.
10 Hat with owl feathers.
11 Very large double saddle bag with red flannel behind leather cutwork.
12 Woman's buckskin moccasins, with tops to be folded down.
13 Rope of horsehair.
14 Rope twister; strands tied to notched end of longer stick which revolves on the smaller, to twist rope.
15 Smooth grooved stone for straightening arrows.
16 Woman's beaded moccasins.
17 Coiled basket shaped like an ordinary water basket.
18 Small twined basket water jar.
19 Small twined burden basket, a child's toy.
20 Hairbrush; tied bundle of straw.
21 Coiled shallow basket.
22 Coiled shallow bowl basket.
23 Coiled shallow basket.
24 Seed beater of twined openwork basketry.

By 1864 over 8,000 Navajo had surrendered and begun the Long Walk, one of the bleakest events in Navajo history. Over ten per cent of the captives died on the way to Fort Sumner. The journey was one of hardship and terror. There were no wagons; people walked over 300 miles. People were shot if they complained of being tired or sick; women in labor were killed.

Not all the Navajo went on the Long Walk. Many were sold into slavery or hid in inaccessible locations like the Grand Canyon or moved in with other groups. Those who lived at Fort Sumner recounted their experience as a time of despair and deprivation. Army arrangements were inadequate; there was little food and no blankets. Shelter was inadequate also, epidemic disease rampant. Confined with their traditional enemies the Mescalero Apache, tempers flared and disputes were common. Droughts and poor agricultural land doomed the reservation to failure. The horror of the Long Walk and the imprisonment at Fort Sumner remained pivotal events in the history and consciousness of The People.

When the Navajo were allowed to return to their homeland five years later they quickly re-established their way of life as herders and horticulturalists. They did no more raiding; instead they developed new economic pursuits – craft production and wage labor. In crafts the Navajo are famous as weavers and silversmiths. The tribe prospered and grew so that today they are the most populous group in North America and all cannnot live on the land. Unfortunately, sheep and horses became so prevalent that the fragile land became overgrazed. By the 1930s the land could no longer support the livestock and the federal government ordered the stocks to be reduced, a tragedy for the Navajo.

Navajo ceremonies, like other Apachean ceremonies, are performed not calendrically but when necessary to restore health and secure blessings in order to insure survival. In the Navajo universe there are two classes of people – Earth People (or human beings) and Holy People (supernatural beings who are holy, powerful and mysterious). The Navajo believe that the universe functions according to certain rules that both they and the Holy People must follow. If these rules are followed there will be

Above: A Navajo mother and child wearing silver and turquoise jewelry. The first Navajo to set this stone in silver was reputed to be Atsidi Chon (Ugly Smith) in 1880. The concha belt seen here is typical of Navajo silversmithing, noted for its massive quality and simplicity of design.

safety, plenty and a world that is harmonious and beautiful. If rules are not, if disease and accidental injury affect an individual, ceremonies are held in which the Holy People are asked to restore the delicate balance of the universe. In these ceremonies, which are very complicated and intricate, sandpaintings are made and prayers recited. Sandpaintings are impermanent paintings made of dried pulverized materials that depicted the Holy People and serve as a temporary altar. Over 800 forms of sandpaintings exist, each connected to a specific chant and ceremony. Sandpaintings are made inside the hogan, the center of family life

There are a few tribes who live in extremely marginal environments and on the fringes of the Southwest culture area who never developed agricultural ways of life. In the north, these included isolated groups who lived near the arid Great Basin – the Utes and the Paiutes, in the region – some of the Shoshonean speakers who moved from California to become farmers along the Colorado River, the Upland Yumans (already mentioned), in the south the Chemehuevi and a group of Sand Papago, a subgroup of the Tohono O'Odham already discussed, the Seri, and groups living in Baja California. There were never more than a few thousand people who existed at this level of economic development. The most well-known are the Seri.

Producing none of their own food and following a nomadic and semi-nomadic lifestyle,

Below: Pesh-lakái-ilhini, a Navajo silversmith (left), hammering silver on a steel anvil; his son stands by the bellows, probably learning the trade. The man at right is holding a pump drill. At the rear is a hogan dwelling, here of the oldest style with a forked-pole framework covered with earth.

these groups lived in small bilateral bands. Moving often, they possessed small inventories of material cultures, living off the land for all their needs. For example, the Seri, the smallest group in the Southwest, relied heavily on marine products as did groups in Baja California. They also hunted deer and rabbits, and gathered the abundant cacti fruits, greens and seaweed seeds of the desert coast and adjacent islands. Even today these groups eke out a poverty-level living by fishing and turtle hunting on the desert shores of Baja California.

In anthropology it is usual to discuss the Ute and their relatives the Paiute in the Great Basin and Plains culture areas. Both of these groups speak a Uto-Aztecan language of the Shoshonean stock and were thus in the distant past related to the Hopi.

These groups were so isolated and few in number that they were affected very little by Spanish expansion. It was only in the mid-1800s and later that European incursions changed their ways of life.

These four basic cultural groups of the Greater Southwest can be recognized in modified form today. Even after three hundred years of European contact, three-quarters of the groups have managed to preserve a sense of individual cultural identity, and a feeling for the

Below: A Navajo war captain wearing a war hat of tanned leather and carrying a lance and rawhide shield. In addition, war equipment of the Navajo traditionally included a bow and arrows and frequently a club. This photograph was taken near Keam's Canyon on the Navajo reservation, 1892-3.

land that is recorded in rich oral traditions. Indian groups have not, however, completely retained their pre-contact cultures, nor have they reacted uniformly to the attempts of Hispanic, Mexican and Anglo-American societies to assimilate them. All exist as part of either the Anglo-American or the Mexican socio-economic system and incorporate a mixture of traditional customs and European patterns. Thus, while they are distinct cultures, they are no longer separate societies. They maintain their ethnic identities in various way, such as producing distinctive forms of art and retaining feelings about, and interaction patterns with, their environment. It is this sense of continuity with the land that has helped them survive years of subjugation to conquest cultures. Zunis, for example, say that Anglo-Americans and Mexican Americans have no respect for the land and abuse it rather than work with it.

Southwest Native Americans have retained 'identity systems that have as an important element the symbol of roots in the land – supernaturally sanctioned, ancient roots, regarded as unchangeable', according to noted Southwesternist Edward Spicer. Such a perspective provides these groups with strong mythological sanctions for their residence, their right to live in the Southwest, and their views of the land. The land is not something that can be controlled and changed; it is something of which all human beings are a part.

American Indian thought is integrative and comprehensive. It does not separate intellectual, moral, emotional, aesthetic, economic and other activities, motivations and functions. Beauty is in the nature of things as well as in people, and it is the natural state of affairs. The land is beautiful by definition because the supernatural beings designed it to be a beautiful harmonious, happy and healthy place. For beauty to be maintained the Navajo, for example, feel it must be expressed in actions such as the creation of art or conservation. The land supports life, it is beautiful because of this and must be preserved. Housing and village layout reflect the visions of the land and the universe.

Native Americans face many challenges. They live both on isolated reservations and in cities for they are members of and must survive in two worlds. While European expansion has transformed much of Native American life it has done so unevenly and differentially. But never completely. Native Americans today are struggling for economic and political independence – self-determinancy in a situation where they face poverty facing other rural poor. It is a paradox that once self-sustaining and healthy populations find themselves living under poor conditions in a land of plenty. But Southwest Native Americans will adapt, as they have done in the past for the core of their lives, their relationship to the land has been preserved. No culture is static, even though we tend to portray indigenous peoples as homogeneous and frozen in time and space. But Southwest Native Americans do not regard themselves as deprived members of society. They retain a strong sense of who they are and their special place in the multi-cultural Southwest. They recognize that they have much to offer others if these others will but listen. This rich exchange will continue into the future.

Navajo

The Navajo are the largest North American Indian tribe, in population and in the area of their reservation lands. They are well known for fine rugs and blankets woven by women with wool from their own sheep, and silver jewelry made by men. Other well known features of Navajo culture include the sand paintings associated with curing ceremonies, and the distinctive earth-covered domed houses called hogans. By the late 18th century the Navajo were successful farmers, hunters, and herders, who warred against the Spaniards and Mexicans, and later the Anglo-Americans, to protect their lands, property, and families. Peace finally came with the Long Walk, when nearly all the Navajo were deported to Fort Sumner in 1864. Modern Navajo history dates from their return in 1868 to the newly established reservation within their old territory. The things shown here all exemplify Navajo material culture of a century and more ago; dates indicate when they were collected.

1 Coiled basket. 1870.
2 Woman's wool dress, of two woven rectangles sewn together at sides and shoulders. Probably made between 1850 and 1870.
3 Decorated silver bow guard, called ketoh, worn as a bracelet. 1893.
4 Silver necklace pendant, a crescent ending in hands – form called a naja. 1893.
5 Naja; the shape spread from Moslem North Africa to Spain, then to Mexico, then to the Navajo. 1893.
6–11 Six silver conchas, worn on belts and also bridles. 1893.
12 Silver buckle. 1893.
13, 14 Two silver bracelets, 1893.
15 Silver finger ring. 1884.
16 Silver finger ring with copper inset. 1893.
17, 18 Silver buttons. 1893.
19, 20 Silver brooches. 1893.
21 Hairbrush. 1870.
22 Man's moccasins. 1870.
23 Squirrel skin shirt. 1870.
24 Wool sock-leggings, 1874.

25 Knitted wool cap. 1874.
26 Batten of barberry wood, for beating down the weft while weaving. 1877.
27 Heddle to hold the warp threads on a loom. 1870.
28 Dance drum. Before 1902.
29 Warrior's hat of painted leather, feathers, and dyed hair. Old in 1895.
30 Buckskin belt and pouch. 1893.
31 Small throw used on top of saddle, woven of both Navajo-spun and German-town wool yarn, in 'post-classic' design. 1886.
32 Girth for saddle, warps directly attached to iron rings, then woven between them. 1887.
33 Well-made bow, sinew backed, reinforced with sinew bindings. 1885.
34 Bowcase attached to quiver, of mountain lion skin, fur out on quiver, in on bowcase, wood stiffener inserted in bowcase; contains two arrows. 1893.
35 Four arrows with steel points. 1893.
36 Drinking cup and pouch. Before 1869.
37 Man's shoulder blanket woven in 'chief's blanket' pattern. 1893.
38 War hat of leather, owl feather plume, abalone shells on brow. Not used after 1870; collected in 1887.
39 Cap. 1898.
40 Wool blanket, banded pattern. 1893.
41 Copper powder measure. 1887.

'It is strange that the Americans should complain that the Indians kill buffaloes. We kill buffaloes . . . for food and clothing . . . to keep our lodges warm. Your young men shoot for pleasure . . . What is this! Is it robbery? You call us savages. What are they?'

SITTING BULL OF THE HUNKPAPA SIOUX

THE PLAINS

THE GREAT PLAINS form the very heartland of North America. A land of sun, wind and grass, they stretch north to south more than two thousand miles from the North Saskatchewan River in Canada almost to the Rio Grande in Mexico, while their east-west boundaries are approximately those of the Mississippi-Missouri valleys and the foothills of the Rocky Mountains, in all encompassing an area of some one million square miles.

During the eighteenth and nineteenth centuries, when contact with whites was first made, the Great Plains were largely dominated by Algonquian and Siouan linguistic groups, although others such as Athapaskan and Uto-Aztecan were also represented. The table opposite on page 63 lists the principal tribes on the Plains at this time.

The Northern Plains were largely dominated by Algonquians, the Central Plains by Siouans. These particular linguistic groups were not well represented on the Southern Plains although some Cheyenne and Arapaho formed strong military allegiances with the Kiowa and Comanche who dominated this region. The population was relatively small; in 1780, for example, the Blackfeet (name used in this chapter; also called Blackfoot), one of the largest groups on the Northern Plains, were estimated at fifteen thousand, the Lakota ten thousand and the Cheyenne three and a half thousand, while the semi-sedentary tribes such as the Omaha, Mandan and Arikara on the Missouri River have all been estimated to have been less than four thousand in 1780 (see Kroeber, 1939, and Swanton, 1952).

Climate varies on the Plains; in general the limited rainfall produces a semi-desert type terrain particularly to the west and south, where in places the arid conditions result in so-called 'badlands'. To the east, however, in the Mississippi and Missouri valleys, the rainfall is higher often producing humid conditions and green prairie lands. In these areas the grass is tall and luxuriant; further west in such regions as the present-day states of North and South Dakota, Nebraska, Montana and Kansas this gives way to a short grass; while it is generally referred to as 'buffalo grass', it is in actuality a vital food resource for many Plains animals.

Plains animals exhibit characteristics which are indicative of the nature of the country in which they live. Thus, all can survive without water for extended periods, and all, except the wolf and coyote, are grass-eaters. Most are ultra cautious and extremely difficult to approach and kill, such characteristics being

particularly exemplified by the prong-horned antelope. Its acute sense of sight, great speed and ability to communicate danger by means of the white patch on its rump give it a high survival rating. In the nineteenth century and earlier, the antelope was found in vast herds across the Plains, possibly being even more abundant than the better known buffalo which,

because of its size, first caught the attention of early white explorers.

The antelope was an important resource to both prehistoric and historic man on the Great Plains. When the Cheyenne, for example, first moved out on to the Plains in the late eighteenth century, they found evidence of antelope pounds – converging streams, bush or

Key to tribes:
1 Sarcee
2 Plains Cree
3 Blackfeet
4 Gros Ventre
5 Assiniboin
6 Plains Ojibwa
7 Crow
8 Teton Sioux
9 Hidatsa
10 Mandan
11 Arikara
12 Yanktonai Sioux
13 Santee Sioux
14 Cheyenne
15 Ponca
16 Omaha
17 Yankton Sioux
18 Iowa
19 Oto
20 Pawnee
21 Arapaho
22 Kansa
23 Missouria
24 Kiowa
25 Kiowa-Apache
26 Osage
27 Comanche
28 Wichita
29 Quapaw
30 Lipan Apache
31 Tonkawa
32 Kitsai

This map shows approximate territories of tribes and language groups at about 1800. After that, all tribes lost territory and some moved.

rocks terminating at a deep pit or ditch – which earlier pedestrian inhabitants had employed. The Cheyenne repaired and extended these, realizing that it was the most effective way of capturing such a wily creature. The antelope obviously greatly impressed the Plains tribes; not only were they a nutritious source of meat, but their horns were used in special head-dresses or painted on ceremonial regalia while the skins were fabricated into garments – shirts, leggings and dresses.

The animal which most dominated the Plains, however, was the bison, better known as the buffalo. Although archeological evidence and early explorers' descriptions indicate that this animal was formerly widely distributed in North America, by the mid-nineteenth century it was largely confined to the Plains region where it roamed in immense herds, the total population of which has been conservatively estimated at sixty million. The bull buffalo stood almost 6½ft (2m.) high at the shoulder and weighed 200lb. (about 900kg.); unlike the antelope, buffalo had poor eyesight and although their sense of smell and hearing was well developed they could often be approached downwind by a cautious hunter.

Early pedestrian man on the Great Plains commonly hunted the buffalo in a similar way to the antelope, stampeding the herds in to a V-shaped drive leading over a cliff edge. Evidence of such early drives is noted in the Introduction; one site in southern Alberta was used by Paleo and historic Plains Indians until about 1850, when the buffalo herds began to disappear. Called by the Blackfeet *Estipah-Siki-kini-Kots* – 'Where-he-got-his-head-smashed-in' – it was also a place of great ceremonial and ritual importance, where practical action in the trapping of buffalo was accompanied by appeals to higher powers, evoking the spirits of the mountains, winds, the raven, the latter considered by the Blackfeet to be the wisest of birds.

Thousands of buffalo were killed annually at such sites by stampeding animals, often so many at one time that it was impossible to utilize all the fresh meat and, whilst much was subsequently dried and made into pemmican

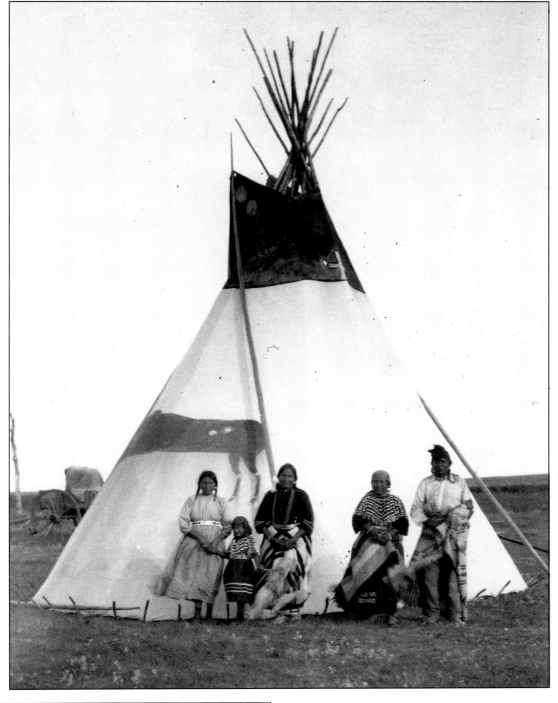

Above: *A Blackfeet (Blood) family and tipi, c.1900. By 1870 canvas, rather than buffalo hides, was widely used. Designs such as the Maltese Cross motif were still painted in the traditional way.*

for winter use and the hides used for tipi covers, there was the inevitable waste. Thus, in December 1809, when the fur trader-explorer Alexander Henry came across a recent pound kill on the Vermilion River (in present-day Alberta), he observed 'The bulls were mostly entire, none but the good cows having been cut up' (Henry and Thompson, Coues ed., 1897:576-7).

Who the *archaic* Plains pedestrians were is conjectural. However, it is almost certain, as was discussed in the chapter on the Plateau and Basin (pp. 100–127) that several tribes such as the Kutenai, Flathead and particularly the Shoshoni commonly travelled on foot to the Plains region to hunt buffalo. Some archeological evidence suggests that several bands may even have lived on the western fringes of the Plains 'for several thousand years' (Hultkrantz, 1968:70).

Location	Tribe	Linguistic group/comment
NORTHERN PLAINS	Blackfeet Plains Cree Plains Ojibwa Gros Ventre	*Algonquian.* Ancient inhabitants of this region. Archeological evidence suggests that there were strong Blackfeet/Cree links and there were similarities in their mythology
	Sarcee	*Athapaskan.* This small tribe, as with the Gros Ventre, allied themselves with the Blackfeet during the nineteenth century
CENTRAL PLAINS	Sioux (Lakota, Nakota, Dakota) Crow Mandan Hidatsa	*Siouan.* The Lakota were the most western of the Sioux tribes. The Dakota, Mandan and Hidatsa were semi-sedentary
	Arikara	*Caddoan.* Sometimes referred to as 'Northern Pawnees'. Semi-sedentary, living south of the Mandan on the Missouri River
SOUTHERN PLAINS	Comanche Kiowa Wichita ⎫ Pawnee ⎭ Kiowa-Apache	*Uto-Aztecan* *Kiowan* *Caddoan.* *Athapaskan*

It was not, however, until the acquisition of the horse from the south and the gun from the east that a full flowering of historic Plains culture emerges; further, whilst the horse gave great mobility and enhanced the general quality of life – the elderly were no longer abandoned, tipis could be larger and more goods and food transported – the gun enabled the pedestrian Blackfeet and Cree to match and finally force the equestrian Shoshoni to abandon the Plains country. A decisive encounter which demonstrated the superiority of the gun, even against an enemy which had horses, was dramatically described by an aged Piegan chief, Saukamappee, to the explorer David Thompson in 1787. The battle, which occurred about 1740 (probably in present-day Saskatchewan), was between the Shoshoni and combined Assiniboin Piegan, the latter considered a frontier tribe of the Blackfeet confederacy who, armed

Above: *Blackfeet (Piegan) Dove Society dance at Heart Butte, Montana, c.1922. The warbonnet of the central figure has hair tipped feathers, a common feature of Blackfeet regalia at this time.*

with a few guns (but no horses), were thrusting their way into the Northern Plains. Saukamappee first briefly explained how conditions had rapidly changed in perhaps just over a decade:

'By this time the affairs of both parties had much changed; we had more guns and iron-headed arrows than before; but our enemies the Snake Indians and their allies had Misstutim (Big Dogs, that is, Horses) on which they rode, swift as the Deer, on which they dashed at the Peeagans, and with their stone Pukamoggan knocked them on the head, and they thus lost several of their best men. This news we did not well comprehend and it alarmed us, for we had no idea of horses and could not make out what they were.'
(Thompson, Tyrell, ed., 1916:330).

Saukamappee then described the formation of the combined Piegan and Assiniboin warparty the preliminary war ceremonials and the tallying of their weaponry by the War Chiefs. In all they had some ten guns with plenty of ammunition and powder between them and those so armed were 'now considered "the strength of the battle"' (Lewis, Hallowell ed., 1942:49) After a few days march they were confronted by a large warparty of Shoshoni; Saukamappee continued:

'When we came to our allies, the great War Tent [was made] with speeches, feasting and dances as before; and when the War Chief had viewed us all it was found between us and the Stone Indians

Left: *Blackfeet warriors, c.1922. Two wear the early traditional straight-up style headdress with eagle feathers and trimmed with ermine. The flared bonnet (middle figure) was adopted from the Sioux.*

Right: *Blackfeet painted tipis, c.1900. Such dwellings were replete with religious symbolism, many of the designs being acquired by their first Blackfeet owners in visions and dreams.*

we had ten guns and each of us about thirty balls, and powder for the war, and we were considered the strength of the battle. After a few days march our scouts brought us word that the enemy was near in a large war party, but had no Horses with them, for at that time they had very few of them. When we came to meet each other, as usual, each displayed their numbers, weapons and shields, in all which they were superior to us, except our guns which were not shown, but kept in their leathern cases, and if we had shown |them|, they would have taken them for long clubs. For a long time they held us in suspense; a tall Chief was forming a strong party to make an attack on our centre, and the others to enter into combat with those opposite to them; We prepared for the battle the best we could. Those of us who had guns stood in the front line, and each of us |had| two balls in his mouth, and a load of powder in his left hand to reload. We noticed they had a great many short stone clubs for close combat, which is a dangerous weapon, and had they made a bold attack on us, we must have been defeated as they were more numerous and better armed than we were, for we could have fired our guns no more than twice; and were at a loss what to do on the wide plain, and each Chief encouraged his men to stand firm. Our eyes were all on the tall Chief and his motions, which appeared to be contrary to the advice of several old Chiefs, all this time we were about the strong flight of an arrow from each other. At length the tall chief retired and they formed their long usual line by placing their shields on the ground to touch each other, the shield having a breadth of full three feet or more. We sat down opposite to them and most of us waited for the night to make a hasty retreat. The War Chief was close to us, anxious to see the effect of our guns. The lines were too far asunder for us to make a sure shot, and we requested him to close the line to about sixty yards, which was gradually done, and lying flat on the ground behind the shields, we watched our opportunity when they drew their bows to shoot at us, their bodies were then exposed and each of us, as opportunity offered, fired with deadly aim, and either killed, or severely wounded, every one we aimed at.

The War Chief was highly pleased, and the Snake Indians finding so many killed and wounded kept themselves behind their shields; the War Chief then desired we could spread ourselves by two's throughout the line, which we did, and our shots caused consternation and dis-

may along their whole line. The battle had begun about Noon, and the Sun was not yet half down, when we perceived some of them had crawled away from their shields, and were taking to flight. The War Chief seeing this went along the line and spoke to every Chief to keep his Men ready for a charge of the whole line of the enemy, of which he would give the signal; this was done by himself stepping in front

with his Spear, and calling on them to follow him as he rushed on their line, and in an instant the whole of us followed him, the greater part of the enemy took to flight, but some fought bravely and we lost more than ten killed and many wounded; Part of us pursued, and killed a few, but the chase had soon to be given over, for at the body of every Snake Indian killed, there were five or six of us trying to

Right: *Blackfeet delegation to Washington, 1916. Seated; Wolf Plume, Curly Bear (with hackle plume, a trade item, on headdress) and Bird Rattler, in costume beaded and fringed with buckskin and ermine.*

Left: *Blackfeet girl in buckskin dress embellished with blue and white pony beads, by Karl Bodmer (1833). Bodmer seldom painted Plains children; this one was living with the Assiniboin.*

Right: *A Cree woman, by Karl Bodmer (1833). Her deerskin dress is of the typical Plains style as are the earrings made of dentalium shells and blue beads. Her chin is tattooed, a common Cree custom.*

get his scalp, or part of his clothing, his weapons, or something as a trophy of the battle. As there were only three of us, and seven of our friends, the Stone Indians, we did not interfere, and got nothing.' (Thompson, Tyrell ed., 1916:330-32).

Under such pressures, the Shoshoni tribes gradually retreated from the Northern Plains, a process which was accelerated as the Blackfeet, Assiniboin and Cree progressively acquired more guns due to the expansion of the fur trade and also changed their warfare tactics, now successfully raiding the Shoshoni for horses.

In contrast, whilst the Shoshoni traded with the Spaniards in New Mexico, obtaining articles of clothing, iron kettles, metal bridles, stirrups and mules, the Spanish policy was not

to trade firearms to Indians. This put the Shoshoni at a decided disadvantage, as one of their distinguished chiefs, Cameahwait, complained to Lewis and Clark, 'But this should not be, . . . if we had guns, instead of hiding ourselves in the mountains and living like the bears on roots and berries, we would then go down and live in the buffalo country in spite of our enemies, whom we never fear when we meet on equal terms' (Lewis and Clark, Coues ed., 1893:559).

Whilst the time-scale and pressures varied, similar patterns were replicated across both the Central and Southern Plains. Thus, into this vast area moved Algonquian and Athapaskan-speaking tribes from the north and east – the Blackfeet Confederacy, Cree, Arapaho, Cheyenne, Sarcee and Kiowa-Apache. From the east and southeast came the Siouan tribes – the Nakota, Lakota and Dakota, Crow, Hidatsa and Mandan and from both west and southeast the Pawnee, Arikara, Comanche and Kiowa. They brought with them a diversity of cultures which, due to the impact of a new environment had, by about 1800, led to a commonality of basic lifestyle enhanced and mixed by trade and warfare, but often retaining much of their former ethos.

On the Northern Plains much, particularly that relating to horse nomadism, was obviously

Below: *Gros Ventre moving camp with a travois. Made by the women entirely of wood and rawhide, the travois had side poles of stout lodge-pole pines generally some 4-5in. in diameter at base.*

adopted from the former dominant occupants, namely the Shoshoni who, as Lewis and Clark observed in 1805, had 'within their own recollection' formerly lived on the Plains, but had been 'driven into the mountains by the Pawkees, [Piegan] or the roving Indians of the Sascatchawain' (ibid:554). Lewis and Clark's descriptions of the Shoshoni fit much of what was to become typical of the nomadic historic Plains Indian: an emphasis on warfare as a means of achieving high social status, a coup-counting hierarchy, scalping, the use of the horse in all aspects of their lives, short bows – typically about 3 ft in length (less than a meter) for effective use on horseback, given high elastic qualities by a backing of sinew – otterskin bow and arrow cases, small circular buffalo hide shields endowed with supernatural powers of protection derived from their ceremonials of fabrication and painting, and the use of highly dangerous stone-headed clubs. Likewise, much of the horse equipment, such as stirrups, saddles and bridles, was clearly similar in style, some of which undoubtedly being strongly inspired by the Spanish. For example, the common pack saddle was modified and given a high flat-topped pommel and cantle and, whilst popular with Shoshoni women at the time of Lewis and Clark's visit, it later emerged as a classic Crow woman's style of saddle. Further, the elaborate horse collar which became such a feature of Crow horse equipment, seemingly had its roots in the Shoshoni custom of suspending 'at the breast of his horse the finest ornaments he possesses' (ibid:563).

One important factor which led to the success in the emergence of historic Plains Indian nomadism was undoubtedly the development of the tipi. It is unclear as to the type of dwelling actually employed by the earlier Plains Shoshoni; possibly it was a small-scale conical shaped dwelling covered with pieces of elk or buffalo skins. However, the true tipi – which consisted of a large semi-circular cover pulled over a conical frame of straight poles and having a facility for regulating the draught of smoke from the central fire generally by the adjustment of the distinctive ears or wings at the top – was observed by Spanish expeditions to the Southern Plains as early as the middle of the sixteenth century. Since dogs were used for transport at that time, it is probable that these dwellings were small, possibly no more than 8ft (2.5m.) in diameter. The inspiration for such habitations may well have been based on the conical wigwam which was found throughout the boreal regions of both the New and Old World for, as one scholar has pointed out, these tipi dwellers observed by the Spanish (probably Athapaskan-speaking Plains Apaches) had only recently migrated from the vicinity of the Northern Plains (Brasser, 1982:312).

The tipi was generally pitched with its back toward the prevailing westerly wind direction, its wide base and sloping sides giving high stability to the sometimes sudden and strong winds which occur on the Plains. Whilst all tipis were similar in appearance, there were some definite tribal variations, classification being broadly based on the number of foundation poles. In the areas where the winds were particularly strong, a three-pole foundation was used, whilst in more protected areas – near the mountains or wooded river valleys – a four-pole foundation was favored. Thus, such widely spaced tribes as the Blackfeet on the Northwestern Plains and the Omaha in the Southeast employed the four-pole base whilst the Assiniboin to the east of the Blackfeet on the windswept Plains of what is now Saskatchewan and Manitoba, and the Kiowa on the Southern Plains, tended to the three-pole type. The Crow favored the use of elegant, unpainted tipis, and the Lakota those which were embellished with both realistic and geometrical paintings, but perhaps the most impressive were some of those belonging to the Blackfeet which, even as early as 1809, were described by the fur trader, Alexander Henry, as heavily embellished with pictographs of animals and birds, both real and mythological.[1]

The designs on tipis were believed to secure for their owners protection against misfortune and sickness, and definite conventions were employed in the painting of symbolic motifs which were clearly understood by the custodians of the particular tribe's religious tradition, but not necessarily by the common man. Thus, for the Blackfeet what might be called the Maltese Cross was traditionally symbolic of the Morning Star – endowed with powers to protect those entitled to employ the motif – and was painted in red at the rear top of the tipi. Ownership of a sacred painted tipi, together with all that it entailed, was an outward display of high social standing within the tribe.

High status, however, also pivoted firmly on success in warfare, the capturing of enemy horses rather than killing being a major objective in the historic period; appeals to higher powers for help in these matters attempted to evoke the spiritual forces which would help

Below: Kill Spotted Horse, an Assiniboin warrior, c.1898. The eagle feather headdress is of quite an unusual style, the feathers being set well back from the brow so as to lie close to the head.

attain the goal. Much of the Plains Indian cosmos centered on observed animal powers – the strength of the buffalo, the speed of the antelope, the bravery of the eagle and weasel, and so on – but there was also a recognition of an intangible power of the universe which manifested itself in varying forms from one linguistic group to the next and was embedded in ancient beliefs which, whilst modified by the Plains environment, can be traced back to the original Woodland homelands of several Plains tribes.

Widespread was the concept of three parallel worlds. Under the surface of the lake on which the earth floated, were powerful spirits which had control over animals and plants on land and in the water, whilst above the earth beyond the dome of the blue sky, lay the realm of the upper world. This world was dominated by spirits which matched those of the underworld, amongst the most powerful of which were the Thunderbirds who, by the flashing of their eyes and flapping of their wings, produced the lightning and thunder. A perpetual state of war existed between the sky and water spirits and whilst the sun was often closely associated with the Thunderbird, it was considered that it, together with the moon, was the energy sources which controlled the day and night and the seasonal 'cycles'. On earth, the spirits of the four winds changed the seasons, their energies both sustaining and perpetrating the life 'cycle'. For hundreds of years, the symbolic and religious artwork of the Woodland tribes gave free expression to these great powers.

These ancient concepts were modified and interpreted in various forms by the historic Plains Indians, environmental factors undoubtedly having considerable influence. Thus, the Eastern Sioux replaced the underwater panther, so important to the Woodland tribes, with symbols of an underwater horned monster which had the ability to emerge from the lakes and live in trees (Carver, Parker ed., 1976:98-9), and further west amongst the Blackfeet the symbol of such powerful underwater spirits was the tadpole, its use on the costume of the owners of the prestigious Beaver Bundle being explained by a Blackfeet myth which associated the frog with the Blackfeet culture hero, Old Man, who defeated the terrible underwater enemies of mankind. The metamorphosis associated with the frog and its ability to move freely from water to land clearly has parallels with Eastern Sioux mythology.

A complex intertribal trade network was anciently developed in the Plains region and whilst there was little incentive for trade between tribes who had similar lifestyles, that between the hunters and horticulturists was beneficial to both sides. Thus, the nomadic tribes could offer dried buffalo meat and other products of the chase such as tanned deer and buffalo hides, numerous articles of apparel and buffalo hide tipis (used by the village tribes on their hunting expeditions), and in exchange the horticulturists offered corn, beans and pumpkins. With the introduction of the horse and European goods, it is probable that the newcomers to the Plains adopted the established trade patterns of those pedestrian nomads who they displaced, and simply extended the activities. Amongst the best documented of these relates to the Cheyenne and Crow, the former trading to Missouri River tribes – the Mandan, Hidatsa and Arikara – the latter mainly with the Hidatsa and Mandan. Such trade expeditions must have been colorful and spectacular affairs. For example, when the fur trader, Charles Mackenzie, travelled to the Hidatsa villages in 1805, he witnessed the arrival of over two thousand Crow Indians on a trading expedition (Mackenzie, in Masson, 1889:360). Dressed in all their finery and subsequently pitching a village of three hundred tipis adjacent to the earth lodges of the Hidatsa, the trade was elevated to the status of an elaborate ceremonial. After smoking the pipe of friendship, the Hidatsa laid before the Crow trade goods which consisted of two hundred guns with one hundred rounds of ammunition for each, a hundred bushels of corn, together with quantities of axes, clothing (probably European) and kettles. In exchange, the Crow gave two hundred and fifty horses, large quantities of buffalo robes, leggings and shirts. The trade was lucrative to both sides. Thus, the Crow sold their horses to the village tribes at double the price that they fetched at the Shoshoni Rendezvous, whilst the village tribes doubled the cost again to the Cree and Assiniboin who brought in European goods from the northeast. Recent research suggests that the rapid movement of trade goods across the Plains appears to have been facilitated by a middle rendezvous between Western and Eastern Crow bands – the so-called Mountain and River Crow (Taylor, 1984:34). This network efficiently distributed guns from the English Hudson's Bay Trading Posts (situated in present-day Manitoba and Ontario), through the Hidatsa/Mandan villages via Assiniboin and Cree, across the Plains via the River and Mountain Crow to be traded to the Nez Perce and Shoshoni for horses and Spanish horse equipment such as saddle blankets and bridles. Whilst the frontier of the gun thus moved west and south, that of the horse rapidly moved to the north and east.

Costume styles were clearly influenced by trade patterns of this sort, well beyond the regions of the Plains, and involved more than just commodities. One ancient and ever ex-

Left: *Star That Travels, an Osage, c.1897. It was the custom among the Osage to tattoo the 'mark of honor' on selected warriors to ensure that they were faithful in keeping the ancient rituals.*

panding network almost certainly introduced cultural influences from the Lower Mississippi Valley via the Mandan and Hidatsa villages on the middle Missouri River. This increasingly led to an integration of early Northern Plains ritual, cosmology and art, with that of the cosmic structure and ceremonialism of the southeast. The spread was undoubtedly via Assiniboin Indians who lived in the region of the Qu'Appelle Souris and Assiniboine Rivers of present-day Manitoba, so that Mississippian cosmology was incorporated in the world-view and rituals of the Plains buffalo hunters. As one observer recently put it, 'The role of Sun and his son, Morningstar, the cosmic struggle between thunderbirds and water monsters, virility derived from the elk spirit, and many other concepts can be traced to the southeast' (Brasser, 1987: 101). Thus, unlike the well documented *trade* of goods across the Plains, the major import from the Lower Mississippi was one of a spiritual nature. Additional evidence for this assumption is provided by petroglyphs painted and etched on cave walls and cliff faces

found in the Plains region which, after about 1730, changed markedly from animal pictures (suggesting spiritual relationships between artist and animal spirits), to scenes of warfare. 'A new way of life emerged, made up of fragments of the old world-view changed to function in new contexts, increasingly motivated by the achieving of war honors and acquiring material wealth, to be ostentatiously displayed in warfare and tribal ceremonies. Much of this colorful paraphernalia and ceremonialism undoubtedly originated in ancient times, but owed its survival to a reinterpretation of

symbolism in terms of warfare' (ibid:106). Coupled with this emphasis, there was also cultural elaboration due to abundance of natural resources and adoption of the horse leading to a shift of regional culture from horticultural villagers to equestrian nomads.

The warlike spirit of many, if not *all*, Plains tribes was clearly motivated by something

Below: *Utse-tah-wah-ti-an-kah, an Osage, c.1880. He wears an otter skin turban and holds a magnificent gun-shaped club, a weapon which tended to be a specialty of the Middle Missouri tribes.*

Below: *An Osage girl wearing a robe decorated with ribbon appliqué. Although the robe is made of trade materials, the style became firmly associated with the Osage. Hands are a common decorative motif on such garments. Note the fine silverwork brooches.*

Osage

These are the regalia and items of special occasion dress of the prominent Osage Tom Baconrind (a mistranslation of his Osage name, Washin-ha), b.1860, d.1932. Elected chief in 1912, he later served several times on the Osage tribal council. Active in both the Peyote religion and the Catholic church, he was the foremost spokesman for the cause of the Osage full-blood traditionalists during the period of greatest Osage wealth in the 1920s.

1 Studio portrait of Chief Baconrind (Washin-ha), taken in 1930, kept by himself.
2 Leather case with eagle and peacock feathers.
3 Bandolier of china tubes and blue glass beads with mink fur pendant.
4 Pair of buckskin leggings with beads and wool tassels.
5 Beaded legging strips.
6 Beaded moccasins, probably Arapaho in origin.
7 Beaded buckskin pouch for pipe.
8 Catlinite pipe bowl and stem.
9 Silk scarf with gold plated brass neckerchief slide lettered with the Osage for 'Baconrind, Osage Chief, 1920'.
10 Breastplate of bone hairpipes and blue and green glass beads.
11 Peacock feather fan, beaded handle, for Peyote ritual.
12 Beaded cloth garters, with wool fringes.
13 Fan of eagle wing feathers, with otter fur pendant.
14 Ceremonial staff of ebony in form of bow stave covered with otter fur and beadwork, with tubular case of Chinese silk.
15 Choker of shell and bone tubes, black glass beads and leather spreaders.
16 Pair of German-silver bracelets, incised eagle and star design.
17 German-silver neckerchief slide with incised design of heart and arrow.
18 Roach headdress of deer and porcupine hair, stored in usual manner on a wooden rod.
19 German-silver spreader worn with roach headdress.
20 German-silver neckerchief slide with incised design of pipe, warclub, eagle, bow, quiver.
21 Tomahawk, the shaft

covered with red felt, with wool pendant with brass bells and eagle feathers.

22 Headband of otter fur lined with blue strouding, beaded edges, and beaded buckskin placque.

23 Necklace made of white and blue beads on buckskin cord, with shell disc.

24 Silver crucifix with wood core, buckskin string.

25 Red velvet shirt with beaded yoke.

26 Leather belt covered with woven beadwork, with brass rivet edging.

27 Pair of garters, woven beadwork, yarn fringes.

28 Pair of buckskin leggings, edged with beads and nickel rivets, blue velvet lining, horsehair tassels.

29 Moccasins, beaded, metal tinklers; perhaps Kiowa in origin.

30 Headband made from fingerwoven wool sash, with sateen lining.

31 Breechclout of dark blue strouding, red silk binding, beaded designs.

32 Peacock feather fan, for Peyote ritual.

33 White feather fan, with beaded handle.

34 Gourd rattle, handle covered with beadwork for use in Peyote ritual.

35 Whistle.

36 Feather fan.

37 Eagle feather fan, with beaded handles, pendant of brass bells.

more than material wealth because a typical Plains Indian family did not require vast herds in order to supply material wants; indeed, considering their nomadic way of life, such apparent wealth could well be a hindrance rather than an asset and, in the main, it is to the Plateau tribes that we must look for individual ownership of several hundred horses. Whilst generosity could enhance a man's status, it was, above all else, the acquisition of *war honors* – an inherited craving for distinction and glory – which seems to have been the basis of Plains warfare. Analysis of the possible nature of cultural ethos input relating to warfare from the southeast shows that here war was considered to be a social institution and that warlike exploits were necessary for social advancement. The essence of much typical Plains warfare, such as counting coup on a live enemy with a harmless stick, was reported on for the Illinois Confederacy in the early 1700s.

Taking a scalp signified more than the death of an enemy[2] and ancient traditions dictated that the deed brought with it several exacting obligations. Thus, in the early eighteenth century, one missionary reported of the 'Nations of Louisiana' that those who for the first time had taken a scalp or made a capture 'do not sleep at their return with their wives, and do not eat any meat; they ought not to partake of anything but fish and thickened milk. This abstinence lasts for six months. If they fail to observe it, they imagine that the soul of him whom they have killed will cause them to die through sorcery, that they will never again obtain any advantage over their enemies, and that the slightest wounds they may receive will prove fatal' (Kenton, 1954:417).

Customs were obviously no less rigid – but with a different emphasis – amongst the pedestrian nomads who occupied the Northern Plains at about the same time. Thus, the Piegan

Right: *Pawnee earth lodge village. Lodges were erected using heavy posts, cross-beams, brush and earth. Such villages disappeared under the plow with the removal of tribes from their homelands.*

Chief, Saukamappee, told of the return of a successful warparty carrying more than fifty enemy scalps.[3] There was much discussion as to the symbolic meaning of those taken from the enemy who were found dead under their shields because no one could say that he had actually slain the enemy whose scalp he held; there was less doubt about the others, the War Chief finally decreeing that those who had taken 'the trophy from the head of an enemy they had killed, said the Souls of the enemy that each of us has slain belongs to us and we have given them to our relations in the other world to be their slaves, and we are contented'[4] (Henry and Thompson, Coues ed., 1897:332-3).

Whilst initial encounters of Plains Indians with the white man were generally friendly, particularly in Canada, the systematic slaughter of

Above: *A Pawnee earth lodge village on the Loup Fork, Nebraska. Such dwellings were typical of the semi-sedentary tribes of the Missouri River; they were generally clustered around a central 'plaza'.*

both beaver and buffalo, brought about by the demands of the fur trade together with the influx of white emigrants into and across the Plains region after about 1840, caused a progressive deterioration in relationships between Red and White. An earlier, unfortunate encounter between two Piegan warriors who were killed by Meriwether Lewis during his epic voyage as Co-leader of the Corps of Discovery after the Louisiana Purchase of 1803, caused relationships to be hostile between Blackfeet and Americans for many years. Further aggravation occurred with the American Fur Company's policy of sending white trappers into Blackfeet country rather than, as in the case of the Hudson's Bay Company, 'depending upon the Indian supply' (Lewis, 1942:27). Not until 1846, when Alexander Culbertson – who was married to the daughter of a Blood chief – established Fort Benton near the junction of the Marias and Missouri Rivers, were relationships stabilized, at least in part, with the fierce Blood, Piegan and Siksika who comprised the Blackfeet nation: thus from that time for some thirty years trading in buffalo hides, a commodity which the Blackfeet could easily supply, was carried on, a commerce which was considered highly beneficial to both sides.[5]

The lucrative returns of the fur trade spelt the death knell of the Plains tribes as the demand for buffalo hides grew. One English observer, William Blackmore, who travelled through the valley of the Platte River in 1868, reported seeing immense herds of buffalo which extended for a distance of over one hundred miles. The Plains were 'blackened with them' and at times the train on which he was travelling was brought to a standstill to let them pass. Some five years later, in the autumn of 1873, Blackmore was to travel over virtually the same ground. This time he was confronted with an entirely different scene, the whole country being whitened with bleaching buffalo bones and in some areas 'there was a continuous line of putrescent carcasses, so that the air was rendered pestilential and offensive to the last degree ... The professional buffalo skinners had moved in.' Subsequent investigations by Blackmore revealed that even as early as 1872 the number of buffalo which were being slaughtered for their hides alone was at least a million per annum. The professional hunters formed lines of camps along the banks of the Arkansas River and *continuously shot buffalo* night and day as they came down to drink (Taylor, 1980:31-2).

The wanton slaughter alarmed and appalled the Plains Indians, as Sitting Bull was said to have observed:

'It is strange that the Americans should complain that the Indians kill buffaloes. We kill buffaloes, as we kill other animals, for food and clothing, and to make our lodges warm. They kill buffaloes – for what? Go through [the] country. See the thousands of carcasses rotting on the Plains. Your young men shoot for pleasure. All they take from dead buffalo is his tail, or his head, or his horns, perhaps, to show they have killed a buffalo. What is this? Is it robbery? You call us savages. What are *they*?'
(*New York Herald*, 16 November 1877)

Not only were the Plains tribes being deprived but, in addition, Blackmore pointed out, the settler who always looked to the buffalo for a winter supply of meat could no longer depend on their appearance and, like the Plains Indian, bitterly opposed the slaughter solely for their hides.

Adding to the decimation of the buffalo was another problem – the emigrant movement to Oregon. By 1845, it was a common sight to see the distinctive covered wagons wending their way along the Oregon Trail, which commenced in Eastern Kansas, followed the Platte River

across Nebraska and on to Fort Laramie in Wyoming. In Western Wyoming it cut through the Continental Divide following the Snake River to Idaho and then into Oregon, terminating at The Dalles on the great Columbia River which led to the Pacific Ocean. Part of the Oregon Trail – in Nebraska and Wyoming – cut across the hunting grounds of the Oglala, one of the largest and most powerful of the Lakota sub-tribes. By the summer of 1850, lured by tales of a land (now called California), where neither snow nor illness existed, and 'the black soil of Oregon was bottomless', thousands of emigrants 'cascaded up the valleys of the Platte and the Sweetwater' (Lavender, 1965:219; Utley, 1967:59).

This large influx of emigrants not only frightened away or destroyed game in the areas through which they passed but, more alarmingly, brought diseases to which the Plains tribes had little or no resistance. Within the

Below: Quanah Parker, Principal Chief of the Comanche, shrewd politician, Peyote religion proselytizer, and his wife Tonasa, c. 1892, *on the front porch of their five-bedroom house.*

space of a few years the Plains Indian and his environment was suddenly and frighteningly subjected to severe pressures, 'even the seemingly limitless bison of the Great Plains, grew suddenly less abundant and in places disappeared from their customary haunts ... Alcohol drained the vitality from those attracted to the settlements and travel routes ... Tribal ranges, ... shifted constantly as groups dispossessed or shouldered aside encroached on others' (Utley, 1967:5). The situation was rapidly getting out of hand. Protection of both emigrants and the indigenous population now became a vital Government concern and to control a potentially explosive situation urgent measures were considered: the outcome was by both Treaty and militarily.

Two major Treaties were drawn up with the Plains tribes in the early 1850s: the Fort Laramie Treaty[6] in September 1851 which led to negotiations with representatives of the Lakota, Cheyenne and Arapaho, Crow, Arikara, Assiniboin, Gros Ventre and Mandan, and the Fort Atkinson Treaty of July 1853 which attempted to stabilize relations with the Southern Plains tribes such as the Comanche, Kiowa

Kiowa

The Kiowa, traditionally among the most warlike of the Plains tribes, lived in the early 18th century around the Black Hills and the upper Yellowstone R., where they were allies of the Crow and enemies of the Cheyenne and Sioux. About 1805 they moved south to present eastern Colorado and western Oklahoma. They made peace permanently with the Comanche about 1790, the Osage in 1834, the Cheyenne and Arapaho about 1840, and were friendly with the Wichita. Their enemies included the Caddo, Tonkawa, Navajo, and Ute tribes, and the frontier settlements in Texas and northern Mexico (down to Durango), and the white overland emigrants from the east. Finally making peace with the U.S. Government at Fort Sill in 1875, they were assigned a reservation nearby that they shared with the Comanche, which they lost in 1901 as a result of the Federal allotment policy. Most Kiowa today live in western Oklahoma in the area of the old reservation. James Mooney conducted studies among the Kiowa in the 1890s, which resulted in a famous monograph that describes Kiowa history on the basis of their oral traditions, especially those correlated with the important pictographic calender histories they kept. He then investigated Kiowa heraldry, the individually owned painted designs on tipis and sacred shields, their origins and the history of their transmission from owner to owner. Part of the documentation of this research consisted of models made for Mooney, and other Kiowa artifacts he collected for the Smithsonian.

1 Hair plates – band of German-silver discs worn suspended from the hair.
2 Model shield, with design belonging to Tsenbo II.
3 Model snake shield, with design belonging to Guitonkagya (Ringboned Wolf) in period 1835-58.
4 Model dragonfly shield, with design belonging to Pa-akanti (Rough Bull), not used after about 1875.
5 Model shield, with design belonging to Setäpeto.
6 Model bird shield, with design belonging to the noted war chief Setängya (Sitting Bear), killed at Fort Sill in 1871.
7 Model shield, with design belonging to Gõtara.
8 Full-size model of shield with design belonging to Padohgai, made by his great grandson Padalti.
9 Eagle-feather warbonnet with long trailer, type worn on horseback.
10 War shirt of Dohasän (Little Bluff) the Younger, who died c.1894. Typically Crow in style (acquired from these Kiowa allies?); hair locks on right shoulder said to be from scalps of Navajo enemy.
11 Pair of man's moccasins.
12 Peyote ritual fan.
13 Metal pipe tomahawk, of Mexican origin (?).
14 Woman's dress.
15 Pair of woman's high-top moccasins, painted leather with beadwork and metal discs.
16 Pair of boy's moccasins.

Above: *A member of the Mandan Buffalo Bull Society, painted by Karl Bodmer (1837). He wears a complete buffalo head mask, marking him as one of the leaders of the Bull dance.*

Left: *Mató-Tópe, or Four Bears, painted by Karl Bodmer (1837). His outfit a symbol of success in warfare, the carved knife in the horned eagle feather headdress represents a battle with a Cheyenne chief.*

and Kiowa-Apache. In the case of the Laramie Treaty, boundaries for the tribes were defined and Head Chiefs appointed, such as Conquering Bear, a Brulé Lakota. Generous presents, with promises of more to come, were an important part of Government policy[7] when encouraging chiefs to become signatories; it caused, together with the appointment of the 'paper chiefs' (as they became known), great discord, particularly with non-Treaty factions. The military build-up in anticipation of potential problems with this latter group, was partially achieved by purchase or garrisoning by the army of the old and established fur trade posts. Thus, Fort Laramie, purchased by the Government from the American Fur Company for $4,000, now became a strategic military post; indeed, even before the 1851 Treaty, it had been garrisoned (in August 1849) by two officers and fifty-three men. A similar pattern was swiftly replicated across the Central and Southern Plains. Whilst the established fur posts took on a military function, others, such as Forts Riley and Larned, were purpose-built by the military for protection of another famous route to the south of the Oregon Trail – the Santa Fe. Additionally, protection of the route from San Antonio to El Paso, and deep in the heart of Comanche, Kiowa, Mescalero Apache

and Tonkawa territory, was achieved by the establishment of military forts, such as Clark (1852), Hudson (1851), Stockton (1852) and Bliss (1849), near or on the Pecos and Rio Grande Rivers. An uneasy peace was established, but it would be less than a decade before, from Mexico to Canada, Comanche, Kiowa, Arapaho, Cheyenne, Sioux and other tribes, would present a formidable opposition to further expansion, which for almost a generation impeded the advance of the frontier.

Dangers and attitudes were succinctly summed up by a popular emigrant camp-fire refrain:

> 'The Injuns will catch you while cross-
> ing the Plains.
> They'll kill you, and scalp you, and beat
> out your brains.
> Uncle Sam ought to throw them all
> over the fence,
> So there'll be no Red Injuns a hundred
> years hence.'
> (Smith,1943:156)

A slow war of suppression of the Plains Indians began with a cow, so thin and emaciated that it had been abandoned by its Mormon emigrant owner. Desiring a piece of rawhide and perhaps a questionable meal in the bargain, High Forehead, a visiting Miniconjou Sioux to Conquering Bear's camp, shot the animal dead on the afternoon of 18 August 1854 'to make restitution or satisfaction for any

wrongs committed . . . by any band or individual . . . on the people of the United States . . .' (McCann, 1956:3-4).

The emigrants demanded compensation and although Conquering Bear immediately offered a horse in payment, Lieutenant Hugh B. Fleming considered the matter so trivial that no decision was reached that night. Probably the matter would have rested there, but next day Lieutenant John Grattan strongly supported the emigrants and claimed the right to command a detachment of infantry to arrest the offending Indian.[8] Reluctantly, Fleming agreed to the proposal, instructing Grattan to receive the offender, and in case of refusal to give him up, to act upon his own discretion, and 'not to hazard an engagement without certainty of success' (ibid:8).

Grattan, along with Sergeant W. Faver, twenty-six infantrymen, two musicians and a terrified interpreter (one Lucien Auguste) rode toward the Lakota encampment. Twice Grattan was forcibly warned of the potentially dangerous situation. Obridge Allen, a professional emigrant guide, rode up and pointed out to Grattan 'that the Oglalas had begun driving in their pony herds – typical Indian preparation for battle'. Shortly after, James Bordeaux, an experienced and shrewd trader at that time trading directly with the Lakota, observed to Grattan, 'Why don't you let the old cow go. It was laying there without food or water and would soon die; it was too lame to walk; its feets [sic] was worn through to the flesh. It was shot by some boys who wanted a piece of skin' (ibid:6). Grattan told Conquering Bear that he had come to take High Forehead back to the Fort. Reported Man-Afraid-Of-His-Horses, 'The Bear said to me, "You are a brave, what do you think of it?" I said to him, "You are the chief. What do you think?".' Then Conquering Bear told Grattan that High Forehead was 'a guest in his village and not subject to his authority.' Although Grattan was made further offers of ponies to

pay for the cow and was urged to delay any action until Major John W. Whitfield, the Indian Agent, arrived, he ordered his troops into the Brulé village announcing that he would 'go himself to High Forehead's lodge' (ibid:13-14). He halted some sixty yards from High Forehead's lodge which stood near that of Conquering Bear's, and then he ordered the howitzers primed and positioned his men on either side of the cannon.

The parley now became increasingly bitter and even the diplomatic Conquering Bear was beginning to lose patience with the arrogant Grattan. Reported Man-Afraid, 'The Bear said it was hard as it was a poor cow and that today the soldiers had made him ashamed that he was made chief by the whites and today you come to my village and plant your big guns . . . For all I tell you you will not hear me. I would strike you were I not a chief. But as I am chief and am made so by the whites will not do it.'(ibid:18).

Within a short time, the frustrated Grattan broke off the parley and, moving toward the

troops, gave a command that the Indians did not understand. Two or three shots were fired and one warrior was hit. Bordeaux then heard the chief's shout to the warriors not to fire, that perhaps this was just a shot to protect the honor of the troops and they would leave. Grattan, however, was now convinced of the need for a further demonstration and ordered the infantry to fire a volley. Arrows began to fly from the bowmen on the flank and Grattan's command, few if any of which had any experience of Plains Indian warfare, suddenly scattered in panic. Grattan himself crashed to the ground struck by arrows; when his body was found later, it had twenty-four arrows in it. One had gone completely through his head and he could only be identified by his pocket watch. Within a short time the entire command, except one, was wiped out. The sole survivor was Private John Cuddy who, although badly wounded, had crawled into the wild rose bushes. Cuddy died two days later without giving any account of the battle.

The clash underlined the vast differences be-

Above: *Oto warriors, c.1880. Of particular note are the superb pipe with a head of red catlinite stone* (*third figure*) *and the fine German silver brooch of the warrior on the right.*

Right: *The Crow generally employed a four-pole basic frame into which other poles were stacked, forming a conical framework for the cover. This arrangement tended to set the smoke flaps farther apart to accommodate the larger number of poles at the top. Unlike the Blackfeet, the Crow used only a limited number of painted tipis, most being a plain off-white.*

Crow Medicine Tipi

Some 20 poles, each 25ft long, needed for the average tipi

Smoke flap poles go through holes in the corners of the flaps

Cover fastened at front with lacing pins

Shield

Willow back rest

Rawhide parfleche

Some 14 buffalo skins of 15ft diameter cut and sewn together to produce semicircular cover (stitching emphasized to show tailoring)

Central fireplace

Lower edge secured with heavy hardwood pegs driven through holes in the hide

Colored cloth streamers invoked powers of the Crow spiritual world

Designs on tipi derive from important dream or vision relating to thunderbird and sky powers tween the two cultures, and it served as a warning to other would-be 'paper-chiefs'. The uneasy peace was over. The Grattan Massacre, as it became known, heralded the beginning of spasmodic and often brutal wars which were only finally and tragically terminated almost forty years later, in December 1890, with the massacre of Big Foot's Lakota on a tiny creek in South Dakota, which the world now knows as Wounded Knee.

As early as 1834, hostility by the Comanches towards white settlers who were moving westwards from Arkansas into the Plains of Kansas and Texas initiated the formation of a Dragoon Expedition led by Colonel Henry Dodge, to lay the foundation for a Peace Treaty. They arrived at the enormous village of some six to eight hundred tipis which was pitched in the vicinity of the confluence of the Washita and Red Rivers (in present-day Texas). Dodge explained to the Comanche the friendly motives of the expedition; that he was sent by the President of the United States and hoped that a system of trade could be established 'that would be beneficial to both' (Catlin, 1926,vol.2:63). The expedition was a success and the following year agreements were ratified.

Problems, however, were looming for the Comanche, as Cheyenne, desirous of trading at Bent's Fort, moved south and joined the Arapaho. Together, these two tribes forced the Comanche, Kiowa and Plains-Apache to accept the Arkansas River as the northern boundary of their domain. Two years later, however, realizing the potential dangers of approaching well-armed eastern Indians and whites into the Southern Plains, *The Great Peace* alliance was formed; not only did it ensure that the Cheyenne and Arapaho now had plenty of horses at their disposal (from the horse-rich Comanche), and the Kiowa and Comanche access to guns and ammunition (via the northern trade), but it also led to a formidable barrier to any further encroachment by whites from the east. The Comanches had every reason to be wary of the whites and even this great alliance did not protect them. In March 1840, for example, twelve Comanche chiefs met with Texas commissioners, hoping to conclude a Peace Treaty; the Texans, however, demanded that the Comanches gave up their white prisoners. On refusing, troops were brought into the council room and in the ensuing fight all twelve chiefs, together with twenty other Comanches, were slaughtered.

After the annexation of Texas to the Union (in 1845), the Federal Government made attempts to develop a consistent and fair policy toward the Southern Plains tribes. In 1847, a tactful and patient agent – one Robert S. Neighbours – was appointed as special agent for the Indians of Texas, and for several years his friendly influence maintained an uneasy peace on the Southern Plains. However, an unratified Treaty made with the Kiowa and Comanche in April 1863 led to further discontent and Comanche, Kiowa, Cheyenne, Arapaho (and some Sioux) caused the routes to Denver and south as far as the Santa Fe Trail to become unsafe: emigration stopped 'and much of the country was depopulated' (Wallace and Hoebel, 1952:306).

Retaliation by Colonel J. M. Chivington, heading a state militia of Colorado Volunteers, led to the massacre and rout of a peaceful Cheyenne village at Sand Creek, some one hundred miles southeast of Denver, under Black Kettle, White Antelope and Left Hand. Whilst the latter two chiefs fell under the hail of bullets, Black Kettle miraculously survived but the barbarity and savagery of the militia – men, women and children were scalped and mutilated in a brutal manner – shocked the nation and the Sand Creek Massacre, as it came to be called, precipitated a policy of continuous harassment by the more militant Cheyenne Dog Soldiers[9] led by Tall Bull and White Horse, whose ranks were swelled by Northern Cheyenne under Roman Nose and Lakotas, under Pawnee Killer. By June 1867, with Denver virtually isolated, the warriors attacked Fort

Left: *Powder Face, an Arapaho chief, 1870. His crooked lance indicates membership of the Arapaho Spear Society — one of the warriors who was expected never to retreat in battle.*

Above: *The so-called Crow Dance of the Arapaho, 1893. Developed in the 1890s by the Southern Cheyenne and Arapaho, it was performed as a preliminary to the Ghost Dance, and modified from the picturesque Omaha dance of the Plains tribes.*

Wallace, just northeast of the now infamous Sand Creek site. An ensuing engagement gave an Englishman, Dr William A. Bell, an insight into the brutality of Plains warfare and made famous forever a fellow countryman, one Sergeant Frederick Wylyams. According to Bell, Wylyams, who was educated at Eton, whilst 'sowing his wild oats had made a fatal alliance in London and gone to grief' (Bell, 1869, vol.1:46, in Taylor, 1975:90-93). Wylyams had then left for America where he enlisted in the U.S. army; he was with Captain Albert Barnitz's G. Troop of the Seventh Cavalry when Bell met him. Wylyams had hoped to gain a commission and thereby get back into the good graces of his family; it was not to be. As the cavalry followed a small band of Indians beyond a ridge, they were suddenly confronted by a large body of warriors. Bell records, 'They halted a few minutes ... then, like a whirlwind, ... they rushed on the little band of fifty soldiers ... Saddles were emptied, and the soldiers forced back over the ground towards the fort ... the Indians pressed heavily cutting off five men, among them Sergeant Frederick Wylyams ... one by one the soldiers fell, selling their lives

Right: *An episode in the Ghost Dance, 1893. Due to white oppression the Arapaho turned to peyotism and the Ghost Dance religion. Repeating the dance regularly would return the earth to the Indians.*

Above: *Arapaho tipis near Camp Supply, Indian Territory, 1870. The entrances to the tipis at the right are all oriented in the same direction – almost certainly east to greet the rising sun.*

Below: *Sun Dance medicine lodge of the Arapaho, 1893. Of major importance was the lodge itself which was situated in the middle of the encampment. The Arapaho dance resembled that of the Kiowa, Dakota and Cheyenne in many features.*

dearly.' The Indians were finally repulsed by Captain Barnitz's better armed cavalry and the bodies of the fallen five discovered. The shocked Dr Bell later recorded, 'I have seen in days gone by sights horrible and gory – death in all its forms of agony and distortion – but never did I feel the sickening sensation, the giddy, fainting feeling that came over me when I saw our dead, dying and wounded after this Indian fight. A handful of men, to be sure, but with

enough wounds upon them to have slain a company, if evenly distributed.' The sergeant's body had been savagely mutilated and, with scientific objectivity, Bell described in detail the different signs which each tribe had left on his body so that their presence in the battle was thus recorded; he felt that there was little difficulty in recognizing the meaning of some of the wounds. 'The muscles of the right arm, hacked to the bone, speak of the Cheyenne, or "Cut

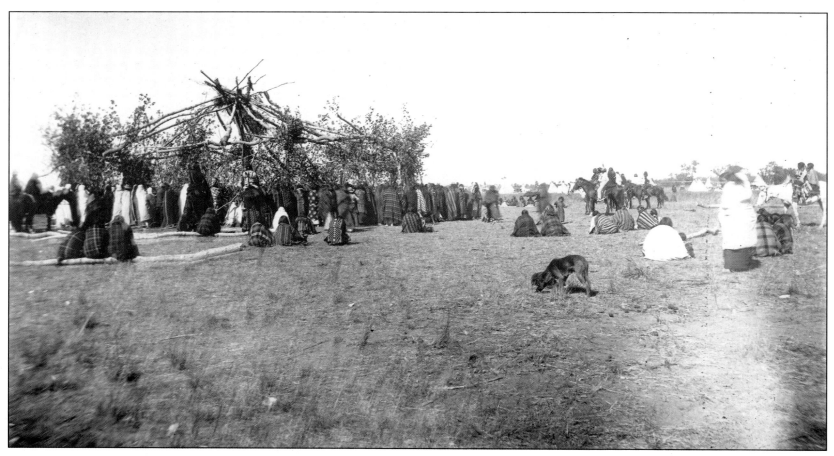

Arms'', the nose slit denotes the ''Smaller tribe'' or Arapaho; and the throat cut bears witness that the Sioux were also present. There were therefore amongst the warriors Cheyenne, Arapaho and Sioux. It was not till some time afterwards that I knew positively what these signs meant, and I have not yet discovered what tribe was indicated by the incisions down the thighs, and the lacerations of the calves of the legs, in oblique parallel gashes. The arrows also varied in make and colour according to the tribe; and it was evident, from the number of different devices, that warriors from several tribes had each purposely left one in the dead mans body.'[10] (ibid:61-4).

A Special Governmental Joint Committee, which published *Condition of the Indian Tribes* in 1867, pointed out that the major problem with these southern tribes was due to extensive white intrusion into their territory. This led to the Medicine Lodge Treaty near Fort Dodge, Kansas, in October 1867; it was a genuine attempt by the Government of the day to reconcile the vast differences which existed between the interests of both Red and White. The great Indian village of some eight hundred and fifty tipis and five thousand Indians – Cheyenne, Arapaho, Comanche, Kiowa and Kiowa-Apache were represented – was finally assembled in the vicinity of Medicine Lodge Creek, so-called because the Kiowa had recently celebrated

their annual Sun-dance nearby and the medicine lodge was still standing at the time of the conference.[11] The some one hundred whites, commissioners, interpreters, clerks and newsmen were escorted by a battalion of the Seventh Cavalry under Major Joel H. Elliott. The assembly has been described as one of the 'largest and most colorful gathering[s] of Indians and officials ever witnessed on the plains' and 'free food and plenty of coffee were provided to ensure that the Indians did not wander away' (Nye, 1968:107).

Although the Treaty was signed by such famous chiefs as Little Raven (Arapaho), Black Kettle and Little Robe (Cheyenne), Satank and Satanta (Kiowa), Wolf Sleeve (Kiowa-Apache) and Ten Bears (Comanche) and the attacks on whites ceased for several months, intertribal warfare continued. Cheyenne and Arapaho raided the Osage and Kaw, whilst the Kiowa and Comanche raided the Navajo, Caddo and Wichita. Later, they began forays to the farms and settlements of the Chickasaw[12] as one of their number wryly observed: 'The wolf will re-

Below: *Arapaho from Fort Washakie, Wyoming, and the Paiute prophet Wovoka. The ethnologist Mooney reported that the Arapaho had great 'faith in the unseen things of the spirit world' and in the early 1890s at least two delegations visited Wovoka at his home in Mason Valley, Nevada.*

spect a treaty as much as Mr Wild Indian' (ibid:113).

The problem stemmed from several misunderstandings and difficulties, a pattern which was to be repeated in later negotiations with tribes on the Central and Northern Plains. The Treaty had stipulated that in return for safe traffic across the Plains, agencies and schools would be built, and farming tools, seeds, doctors, instructors and artisans provided. At the new agencies, rations and annuities were to be regularly distributed and arrangements made so that unscrupulous agents and traders did not cheat the Indians. The Government, however, was slow in meeting the stipulations of the Treaty and it later emerged that many of the Indian signatories did not fully understand their obligations, or if they did, found it difficult to control the younger warriors, particularly those of the Comanche and Kiowa, who still raided into Texas which, since its annexation in 1845, made its people citizens of the United States. Traditionally, raiding south into these areas had been the Kiowa and Comanche warriors' path to wealth and glory and the continued hostile action of the southern tribes led to demands for more effective military protection.

The death of Roman Nose at the Beecher's Island battle in September 1867, and the slaughter of Black Kettle together with over one

Arapaho

These are among many objects collected by A. L. Kroeber in Oklahoma and Wyoming in 1899 and 1900, as part of a famous study of Arapaho symbolism. These things were typical of those made and used by the Arapaho in 1900. Hardly any like them are now made. The meanings of the designs given below are those explained to Kroeber by the original owners or makers of the objects. Color photographs of most of these beautiful things have not been published before.

1 Child's moccasins.
2 Feather bustle worn by a man in the crow dance.
3 Child's moccasins. Green triangles represent horse ears.
4 Moccasins. The design represents clouds and stars in a blue sky, with a tipi at the toe, and a red crayfish in the center.
5 Moccasins. The cross represents the Morning Star, and the bar at the instep is the horizon.
6 Boy's hair ornament worn

during the Ghost Dance, made of cowhair and two brass clock wheels, the larger representing the sun, the other food.
7 Moccasins. The rows of blue triangles represent rocks, the rows of red and blue squares are hills, with three people sitting on each row shown by red squares; a blue path lined by red rocks crosses the center; the two red bars at the top sides are standing people.

8 Woman's leggings attached to moccasins.
9 Pouch for matches and other small things worn by a woman at her belt.
10 Pouch for combs, paint-bags, and other toilet articles. The three crosses represent the Morning Star.
11 Bag for the medicine called 'two babies'.
12 Pouch worn at the belt.
13 Moccasins. The green squares are life symbols, touched by red tipis.

14 Moccasins.
15 Moccasins. The zigzag line represents lightning.
16 Child's moccasins.
17 Moccasins. The green rectangle is a buffalo, standing on a white path.
18 Moccasins. The large triangles represent buffalo horns (red for bare soil, green for grass); zigzag lines are pipes; the tongues are forked, representing rattlesnake tongues, with spotted blue for the snakes' skins and

tin cones representing their rattles.

19 Moccasins. The spotted stripe are buffalo tracks.

20 Moccasins. The blue-striped areas represent fish; the small paired triangles are butterflies.

21 Child's moccasins. All the stripes represent paths.

22 Moccasins. The white background represents snow; blue triangles are tipis, with square doors; the two large triangles on

top are lakes.

23 Moccasins.

24 Rattle of dewclaws.

25 Fan used during Peyote ceremony.

26-31 Six circles of quillworked leather. Each is an ornament attached to the top of a tipi at the back.

32 Ornament of quillwork on leather.

33 Moccasins. The checked red design represents the rought interior of buffalo intestines.

34 Man's beaded vest.

35 Pendant worn attached to the scalplock of a man in the Crow Dance.

36 Eagle bone whistle.

37 Girl's leggings. The triangles represent arrowpoints; those with smaller triangles attached also symbolize tipis.

38 Small girl's leggings with attached moccasins.

39 Woman's moccasins. The large stripe represents the path the wearer travels.

40 Moccasins.

Pawnee War Dance, 1821

In 1821 a delegation of sixteen Pawnees and other western Indians performed a war dance for President Monroe at the White House, which was sketched by the Baroness Hyde de Neuville, wife of the Minister of France to the U.S. An admired member of the delegation was Petalesharo, shown here, who in 1817 had rescued a woman about to be sacrificed to the Morning Star by the Pawnees. His portrait was painted by C.B. King, providing one of the earliest illustrations of the classic eagle feather warbonnet and giving other details of his dress. He wears a James Madison peace medal, silver trade armlets, and multiple silver cones in ear ornaments, and carries a gunstock club decorated with brass tacks. His fingerwoven wool and bead sash and buckskin leggings resemble Pawnee examples in the Smithsonian collections.

hundred men, women and children, by Custer at Washita in November 1867, the progressive decline of the buffalo, superior weapons, the Cavalry's ability to strike the village communities in winter, wore the tribes down. By the early 1870s, the principal Kiowa and Comanche war leaders – Satank, Satanta and Kicking Bird were dead; new leaders – such as Feathered Lance of the Kiowa and the able Quanah Parker of the Comanches – sensing the inevitable, turned to negotiation and many visited the Great Father in Washington.[13]. By 1875, warfare on the Southern Plains was all but over; less so, further north, where smoldering apathy over broken Treaties was being rapidly replaced by open hostility.

The Fort Laramie Treaty, which was finally concluded in November 1868 with Red Cloud's signature together with those of some two hundred leaders of the Lakota – Brulé, Oglala,

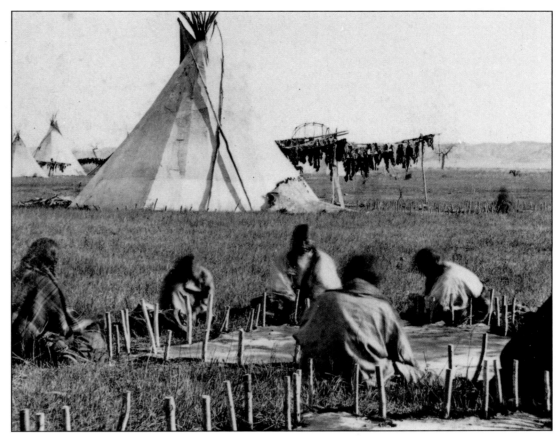

Right: *Cheyenne camp, date not recorded but probably c.1890. The women tan hides staked out on the ground, products of a beef issue rather than the hunt. The tipis appear to be of canvas.*

Below: *Man on a Cloud, Southern Cheyenne, 1892, probably the same Alights on the Cloud who visited Washington in the 1850s. His magnificent warbonnet and scalp shirt denote a high ranking warrior.*

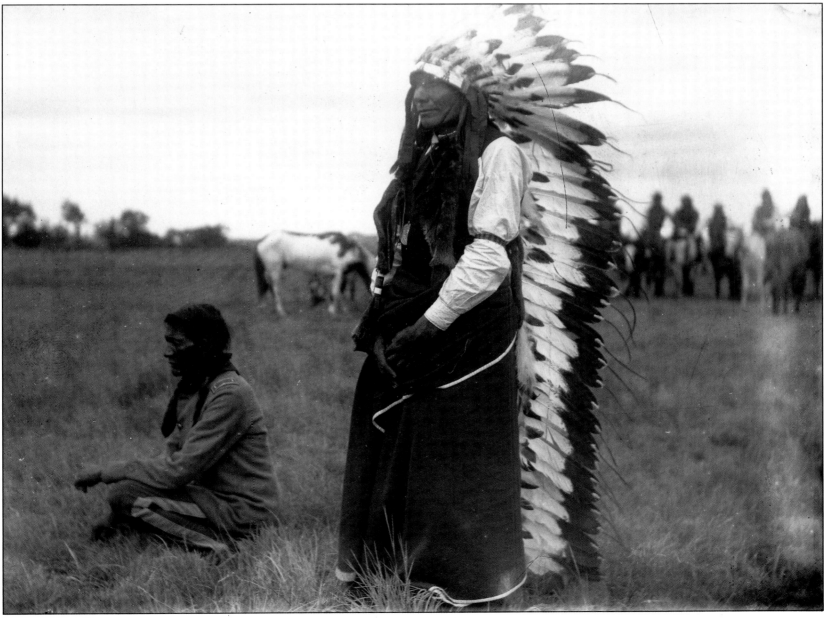

Cheyenne

The Cheyenne are speakers of an Algonquian language whose ancestors moved about 1700 from the wild rice region of the eastern woodlands to establish agricultural and hunting villages on the northern prairies. About a century later they moved farther west on to the high plains where they took on the Plains way of life, living in migratory villages of tipis, hunting buffalo on horseback and engaging in raids and warfare, especially against the Crow, Pawnee, Shoshoni and Ute. By the 1851 Treaty of Fort Laramie the Northern Cheyenne were separated from the Southern Cheyenne who joined the Arapaho. Warfare with the U.S. Army and the Colorado militia broke out as Cheyenne country was invaded by white immigrants, buffalo hunters, and gold miners. The Cheyenne joined their Sioux allies to defeat Gen. Custer in 1876. In 1879 peace was finally established. Most of the items shown here are from the Southern Cheyenne of Indian Territory. The dates indicate when they were collected.

1 Parfleche for clothing. 1868.
2 Medicine man's necklace, with imitation bear claws of carved horn. 1891.
3 One-piece leggings and moccasins, beaded. 1891.
4 Pair of beaded moccasins. 1891.
5 Buckskin pillow with beaded designs. 1891.
6 Buckskin bag for clothing with beaded designs imitating quillwork patterns. 1868.
7 Pair of beaded woman's moccasins. 1891.
8 Saddle-blanket ornament, beaded buckskin strip. 1891.
9 Snake effigy with cord netting, worn as personal war medicine. 1891.
10 Headdress of eagle feathers and buffalo horns, with long trailer. 1881.
11 Wooden medicine bowl. 1891.
12 Pair of woman's leggings. 1891.
13 German-silver arm band.

1916.
14 Paint pouch of turtle skin. 1891.
15 Stone hammer for breaking bones for marrow and mashing wild plums. 1891.
16 Bone hide flesher with metal blade. Northern Cheyenne. 1901.
17 Woman's small parfleche. 1891.
18 Bow obtained from Red Eagle. 1891.
19 Five arrows, iron heads. Northern Cheyenne, 1868.

20 Flageolet. 1891.
21 Powder horn on buckskin pouch with flannel-covered strap. 1891.
22 Pair of woman's moccasins, beaded green-painted leather. 1891.
23 Necklace of bear claws, brass bells. Before 1931.
24 Necklace of dentalium shells and brass studs. 1891.
25 Girl's necklace of bone beads and 14 dimes dated from 1857 to 1888. 1891.
26 Girl's leather belt. 1891.

27 Warrior's quirt, wood with brass tacks. 1877.
28 Drum for curing; with painted design of red-wing blackbird; representing original name of medicine-man owner later called Woman's Heart. Before 1915.
29 Medicine man's cap. Old in 1891.
30 Buckskin shirt bought from Little Chief; painted, decorated with quillwork and tufts of human hair. 1879.

Miniconjou, Hunkpapa, Blackfeet, Sans Arc and Two Kettle – as well as Santee and Yanktonai, conceded all of Red Cloud's demands which 'for the army, it was an unpalatable but not indigestible prescription' (Utley, 1973:134). This was withdrawal of the army from the Bozeman Trail, abandonment of such forts as Fort Phil Kearny and C. F. Smith, and the granting of hunting rights on the Republican River and in Nebraska and Wyoming. It also reserved the Powder River country as 'unceded Indian territory' on which no white might trespass without Indian consent (ibid:135). As with the Medicine Lodge Treaty the previous year, it provided for the building of schools and the issuing of rations and annuities. On several counts the Laramie Treaty was a success; it ended the eponymously named Red Cloud War which had shed so much blood on both sides particularly with the annihilation of Fetterman and more than eighty men on the 21 December 1866 and the later Wagon Box of 2 August 1867 where, although white casualties were not so high, some of the men never fully recovered, mentally or physically, from their ordeal.[14]

The Government-sponsored expeditions to the Black Hills in 1874 and 1875 to investigate mineral wealth led to a largely unfounded rumor of extensive gold deposits. The Treaty of 1868 had defined the Great Sioux Reservation to encompass a vast area west of the Missouri River of what is today the state of South Dakota; this included the Pa Sapa or 'Black Hills', an area considered sacred to the Lakota. By late 1875, a Gold Rush had commenced; encroachment into Lakota territory was a violation of the 1868 Treaty and the army attempted to keep the miners and others out. Inevitably, the task was impossible. 'I say to you there is not power enough in this Government to stop the progress of this [our] conquering race . . . you cannot repress . . . the people of this country . . . there is not power enough to stop the migration of our people' (Senator Hurlbut, Congressional Record, July 1876. See Taylor, 1975:110).

By February 1876, a new war with the Lakota was on, precipitated by Sitting Bull's refusal to leave the Powder River country and register at one of the agencies, the ultimatum being initiated by none other than Ulysses Grant himself, President of the United States: 'If they neglect or refuse so to remove, they will be reported to the War Department as hostile Indians, and that a military force will be sent to compel them to obey the orders of the Indian Office. (Chandler to Belknap, Congressional Record, July 1876).[15]

A winter campaign by Brigadier-General George Crook, who led ten companies of cavalry and two of infantry into Powder River country against Sitting Bull and Cheyenne allies in March 1876 was quickly abandoned due to severe weather conditions. On return, a spring campaign, larger and better organized, was planned by Brigadier-General Alfred H. Terry. On 29 May 1876, Lieutenant-General P. H. Sheridan reported on the projected three-pronged campaign under Terry and Crook. 'Brigadier-General Terry moved out of his command from Fort Abraham Lincoln in the direction of the mouth of Powder River . . . The total strength of his column is about nine hundred men . . . General Crook will move from Fort Fetterman with a column about the same size. Colonel John Gibbon is now moving down north of the Yellowstone and east of the mouth of the Big Horn with a force of about four hundred . . . each column should be able to take care of itself, and to chastise the Indians, should it have the opportunity . . . I presume the following will occur: General Terry will drive the Indians towards the Big Horn valley and General Crook will drive them back towards Terry; Colonel Gibbon moving down on the north side of the Yellowstone, to intercept . . . the result of the movement of these three columns may force many of the hostile Indians back to the agencies . . .' (Lieutenant-General P. H. Sheridan to General W. T. Sherman in Washington, 29 May 1876. See Taylor, 1975:113).

Unknown to these three forces, one of the largest concentrations of Plains Indians ever known in the historic period was rapidly build-

Above: *Crow dancers, date not recorded but probably c.1900. To the left is a man dressed as a clown; during the reservation period, such men wore gunnysacks made into leggings and ponchos. They gave much amusement to their audiences.*

Below: *Crow village, probably near Crow Agency on the Little Big Horn River, Montana, c.1910. Crow tipis are notable for the long lodge-pole pines which were cut in the Big Horn mountains. Note favorite ponies tied by some of the tipis.*

ing up along the valley of the Little Big Horn, drawn by the charismatic Sitting Bull of the Hunkpapa and Crazy Horse, undoubtedly one of the most distinguished war chiefs the Oglala ever produced. A village of some fifteen hundred tipis containing between twelve to fifteen thousand Indians – mainly Sioux and Cheyenne – was strung for three miles along the banks of the Little Big Horn River. Sitting Bull's message had travelled far; a few weeks previously, he had invited the powerful and influential Blackfeet chief, Crowfoot, in Canada 'to join the Sioux in their fight against the Americans . . . after the Americans and Crows had been defeated, the Sioux would come to Canada with the Blackfeet and exterminate the whites' (Dempsey, 1972:88).[16]

The predicted retreat of the Indians from Crook's forces was foiled by Crazy Horse's attack on the morning of 17 June. Crook was camped on the headwaters of the Rosebud with more than one thousand officers and men and some two hundred and sixty Shoshoni and Crow scouts. The Indians struck without warning – Crook was playing a game of cards and his men were having breakfast. The ensuing battle lasted six hours; unhindered by consideration of their women and children who were camped some seventeen miles further north, Crazy Horse's forces employed unusual offensive tac-

Above: *Interior of the Crow Tobacco Society Initiation lodge, showing participants with hand drums in front of them. Tobacco (Nicotiana multivalvis) was an important Crow medicine.*

Below: *A Crow delegation to Washington, 1880. Indians from left to right: Old Crow, Medicine Crow, Two Belly (standing, in beaded shirt), Long Elk, Plenty Coups and Pretty Eagle.*

tics leaving Crook's column severely depleted of ammunition and with nearly one hundred dead and wounded. Most importantly, Crook was eliminated from the three-pronged campaign.

Four days later, on the afternoon of the 21 June, Terry, Gibbon, Custer and Brisbin held a 'council of war on board the *Far West*' (Taunton, 1977:21). Later that day, Mark Kellogg sent what was to be his last despatch to the *New York Herald*; in it he outlined the next step of the campaign. Custer would 'start with his whole command up the Rosebud valley . . . and follow the Indians as long and as far as horse flesh and human endurance could carry his command . . . [he] proposes to live and travel like Indians; in this manner the command will be able to go wherever the Indians can. Gibbon's command has started for the mouth of the Big Horn' (ibid:24). Custer's Seventh Cavalry consisted of some 31 officers, 586 soldiers and in addition 33 Indian scouts and 20 employees and citizens. As Custer bade farewell, Gibbon apparently called out, 'Now Custer, don't be greedy! Wait for us!' Custer made the ambiguous reply 'No, I won't' (ibid:29).

At 12.05 on Sunday 25 June, Custer divided his forces into four columns and prepared to attack. Major Marcus Reno with 131 men was to parallel Custer's movements; Captain Benteen with 113 men to the southwest and Custer with five companies (in all some 215 men), followed a line of hills leading to the lower end of the Indian village. At the Washita battle in November 1868, Custer had divided his forces in a similar way, attacking the village simultaneously from different points and hence maximizing confusion. At 3.15 Reno struck the *southern* portion of the great Sioux-Cheyenne encampment – Sitting Bull's Hunkpapa.

> . . . 'under a towering cloud of dust, they caught the glint of gun barrels, saw the flutter of a guidon, the blue shirts of the troopers . . . Lead whistled overhead, smacking the tipi poles. The soldiers were coming on the gallop straight for the Hunkpapa camp. In that camp all was confusion. Old men were yelling advice, . . . women and children rushing off afoot and on horseback, . . . fleeing from the soldiers . . . grabbed their babies, called their older children, . . . The Hunkpapa stood their ground bravely . . . Every moment reinforcements came up and the firing grew constantly heavier . . .'
> (Vestal, 1948:241-2)

Several weeks earlier, during Sun-dance ceremonials on Rosebud Creek, Sitting Bull had experienced a dramatic vision; it foretold of a great triumph for the Sioux with many dead soldiers falling into camp. Inspired by the promise and imagery, the Hunkpapa stood their ground. 'Instead of running, the Indians ahead multiplied until there was a solid front before the village.' Reno's force was now pushed into a defensive position, the command was being rapidly surrounded by Sioux and Cheyenne warriors and 'the retreat now became a free-for-all' (Taylor, 1975:134). 'The fight was not at all in accordance with my ideas. The so-called charge from the valley was almost a rout. I became sick and dis-heartened with what was going on . . .' (Thomas H. French, 7th Cavalry, in Johnson, 1989:17).

Cut off by a maze of bluffs which caused the timing to be misjudged, 'Custer's luck' had run out; his regiment was fragmented and each potentially exposed to separate defeats before they could again be united. Had Reno's initial charge been sustained, victory may have ensued, but for Reno the odds seemed too great: shortly after ordering his men to dismount, he

Below: *The Hunká-Alowanpi Ceremony, Oglala, 1907. Among the Lakota this was associated with the mythological figure of the White buffalo Maiden. Here the ceremonial pipe is consecrated before a painted buffalo skull lying on a bed of holy sage.*

Crow

These pieces were collected by the anthropologist Robert H. Lowie on the Crow Reservation in Montana between 1910 and 1913. At that time, the Crow had become farmers, whose everyday material culture was largely of non-Indian origin, although moccasins were commonly worn and the old forms, if not the materials, of clothing often remained. Buffalo hunting and warfare had ceased several decades earlier, but what Lowie called the 'war psychology' remained strong, and much of the ancient ritual was still performed, often involving special dress and implements. The Tobacco Society was important to the Crow; the Wolverine chapter (No.6) was a ritual organization of men and women devoted to planting and harvesting a special sacred tobacco. The deerclaw moccasins (No.23) were worn in a Tobacco Society dance. Social and military societies also had their place; the Lumpwoods (see No.8) were one of the two most important of these types of men's societies in about 1910.

1 Parfleche of rawhide, with typically Crow painted design. A container for storage, in earlier times especially for pemmican.
2 Beaded moccasins.
3 Beaded moccasins
4 Rattle, a rawhide circle on a wooden handle, a distinctive type used by a young man belonging to the Crazy Dog Society.
5 A model of the red flannel sash, over 12ft long (3.5m.), of which a pair were worn slipped over the head as emblems of rank by leaders of the Muddy Hands men's social and military society (long extinct by 1910).
6 Wolverine skin emblem of the Wolverine chapter of the Tobacco Society.
7 Horse bridle ornament, cut from an old rawhide parfleche and then covered with beadwork.
8 Otter fur dance ornament, part of the distinctive regalia of the Lumpwoods.
9 Beaded moccasins.

10 Moccasins decorated with red-dyed porcupine quills and light blue beads.

11 Woman's leggings.

12 Shirt with tassels of horsehair, a type worn by young men acting as clowns during rituals.

13 Beaming tool made from the rib of a large animal, used by a woman to soften hides.

14 Wooden bowl used for mixing sacred tobacco.

15 Spoon of mountain sheep horn, used with No.14.

16 Iron flesher, used by a woman in tanning hides.

17 Older flesher, of bone with toothed metal blade.

18 Adze with bone haft and metal blade, used by a woman for scraping skins for tanning.

19 Maul of stone with wooden handle, used to break bones to remove the marrow.

20 Quilled and beaded moccasins.

21 Cover for a rawhide shield, made of buckskin, with painted design revealed in a vision – here evidently a thunderbird (an eagle with zigzag lines).

22 Man's fully-beaded vest.

23 Moccasins with deer dewclaws.

24 Cloth shirt worn in Tobacco Society dance.

25 Beaded mirror case with quilled fringe.

26 Fur wrapper for buffalo medicine.

27 Green flannel sash, emblem of a leader of a men's society:

then gave the command 'Retreat to your horses men!' Confusion reigned: 'I thought that we were to charge headlong through them all, – that was the only chance. To turn one's back on Indians, without being better mounted than they, is throwing away life. When he [Reno] started to that hill he had told me, not one minute before, that he was going to fight – this was in reply to a question of mine' (ibid). Whilst Reno was in retreat, some three and a half miles away Custer attacked the other end of the village. Like Reno, he too was confronted by a mass of Sioux and Cheyenne warriors, this time Hunkpapas under Gall, Oglalas and others under Crazy Horse, and Cheyennes under Lame White Man: they repulsed his charge. Within minutes, Company L under James Calhoun, their horses stampeded by Crow King and his warriors, was annihilated. The other four Companies, C. E, F and I, many soldiers now dismounted, stood their ground on the higher bluffs. Before 5 o'clock, however, Custer and his entire force was completely surrounded and in less than an hour they were all dead. 'Custer's Field' was discovered on the morning of Tuesday 27 June and as Captain Edward S. Godfrey later recorded, it was 'a scene of sickening ghastly horror': Sitting Bull's prophesy had been fulfilled.[17]

The great Indian encampment rapidly dispersed; villages of that size could not be sustained, the grazing was soon exhausted and game driven away. Many returned to the agencies but most of the non-Treaties under

Above: *A Sioux camp, by Karl Bodmer (1833). The buffalo hide tipis are accurately depicted; for example, the details showing the characteristic heavy seams and the lacing at the front with wooden pins.*

Below: *Sitting Bull, the Hunkpapa leader, with William F. Cody (Buffalo Bill), c.1885. He thought highly of Cody, calling him Pahaska (Long Hair) and describing the scout as sincere and genuine.*

Sitting Bull, Crazy Horse, American Horse, Dull Knife and Little Wolf remained in Powder River country; their free life on American soil, however, was rapidly coming to a close.

'One repulse does not give enemies final victory ... the blood of our soldiers demand that these Indians shall be pursued ... [they must] submit themselves to the authority of the nation ...'
(Maginnis, Congressional Record, July 1876)

By late summer 1876 a two-pronged campaign against the Cheyenne and Lakota started to take effect; it extended well into the winter of 1877. At Slim Buttes, 8 September 1876, Mills and Crook attacked American Horse's village; the chief was killed and the village destroyed. At Red Cloud and other Sioux Agencies, Crook subdued the Indians by a display of strength. Crook deposed Red Cloud, whose sympathies with the non-Treaties were all too apparent. Willow Creek, 25 November 1876 (south of the Big Horn Mountains), Ranald S. Mackenzie destroyed Dull Knife's village, thirty Cheyennes were killed and seven hundred ponies captured.[18] Cedar Creek, Yellowstone River, 20 October 1876, Colonel Nelson A. Miles parleys with Sitting Bull who demands peace on the old basis (freedom to roam and hunt). Miles later recorded, Sitting Bull 'spoke like a conqueror and he looked like one' (Miles, 1896:223). Wolf Mountain, Big Horn range, 8

Lakota Headdress

January 1877, Miles attacks the Lakota under Crazy Horse, . . . village destroyed and Crazy Horse withdraws. March 1877, Sitting Bull and some nine hundred followers retreat to Canada. Lame Deer, west of Tongue River, 7 May 1877, Miles attacks and captures Miniconjou village, chiefs Iron Star and Lame Deer killed. Red Cloud Agency, May 1877, Crazy Horse surrenders.[19] Fort Robinson, Nebraska, 7 September 1877, Crazy Horse resists arrest and is bayoneted by a guard: 'My father, I am bad hurt. Tell the people it is no use to depend on me any more now' (Vestal, 1948:272). Fort

Right: This Lakota headdress dates from c.1875. The illustration was inspired by one which belonged to Sinte Maza, or Iron Tail, an Oglala Sioux who was born in the White Clay district of northwest Nebraska in about 1860. It contains some seventy feathers from the tail of an immature golden eagle, each tipped with yellow horsehair and white gypsum. The carefully prepared feathers are laced to a red tradecloth base which is surmounted by a skull-cap supporting a circle of feathers.

White gypsum

Yellow horsehair

Beaded brow band

Skull cap

Ermine fringes and porcupine quill wrapped buckskin thongs

Red tradecloth forms base for single extension reaching to the ground

Fluffed eagle feathers

Selvedge edging

Below: *Members of the Bear, Buffalo and Night societies dance around the sacred cedar and sacred stone, c.1890. The sacred medicine bundle of the society, no longer functional in the tribe, was collected from the son of the last keeper in 1973. The men wear cloth breechclouts, beaded moccasins, fur and feather head ornaments and white body-paint.*

Hidatsa

Between 1906 and 1918 Gilbert L. Wilson worked with several aged Hidatsa men and women on the Fort Berthold Reservation to compile a marvelous, extensive record of daily life as they remembered it when they lived at Like-a-Fishhook Village from about 1840 to 1885. Much had changed by the turn of the century, and even the rich bottom-lands where the Hidatsa lived and farmed have been flooded behind dams since Wilson collected these things among them.

1 Woman's dance dress, of cloth with painted pictographic battle scenes.
2 Quill-decorated carrying case for a man's firemaking materials (flint, steel, and tinder) or a woman's whetstone. Worn tied to the belt or wrist.
3 Quill-decorated carrying case for a flint whetstone, obtained from Owl Woman.
4 Hairbrush made of a porcupine tail with the quills removed. Used by either a man or a woman.
5 Beaded moccasins.
6 Moccasins decorated with quills (probably birds').
7 Beaded and quilled moccasins.
8 Beaded moccasins.
9 Arm band decorated with porcupine quillwork.
10 Man's shirt of tanned elk hide with porcupine quill decoration, with V-shaped neck flap slightly old-fashioned when this was made about 1910. Such shirts were formerly worn only on special occasions or in inclement weather.
11 Dancing cap, probably for a woman.
12 Brush or whip of horsehair used when bathing in a sweat lodge.
13 Rake of ash wood with deer antlers, a model of the kind used about 1860 by a woman preparing her garden. Made by Maxidiwiac (Buffalo Bird Woman).
14 Hoe with elm-wood handle and blade made from the shoulderblade of a buffalo or other large animal. This type was used by a woman to hoe her garden of corn, beans, squash, and sunflowers. This is a model by Maxidiwiac.
15 Arrow point made of sinew from a buffalo's neck. According to Hidatsa tradition, this kind preceded stone points. It was considered to be especially strong, and

good for buffalo hunting. This is a model, for such arrows were evidently last used in the 1830s.

16 Saddle tree, for a woman's saddle.

17 Pipe of a type of black stone found on the Fort Berthold Reservation, inlaid with metal.

18 Box of painted rawhide, used to store clothing and other things.

19 Woman's burden basket, used especially to carry harvested corn, squash,

and beans. Made of dyed and undyed willow and elder bark, woven in diamond and chevron patterns on a bent willow wood frame.

20-23 Three pottery vessels resting on ring stands made of willow twigs and bark. Such pots were used as water vessels and for cooking. They were made of clay tempered with crushed rock, shaped by a paddle and anvil technique, and then fired.

By 1908 when these were made for the collector by a Hidatsa woman named Hides and Eats, no one could make the large vessels with very thin walls that were used before metal pots became common.

23 Bone hoe, as No. 14. The short handle was copied for the later iron hoes to suit the usual Hidatsa woman's method of use.

24 Ladle made of mountain sheep horn.

Robinson, Nebraska, January 1879, Dull Knife's Cheyenne starved into submission, break from army barracks, sixty-four killed and fifty wounded.[20]

There is little doubt that at this time it was Sitting Bull who epitomized the free and independent Plains Indian but the road ahead was to be particularly difficult as game became scarce on the Canadian Plains and gradually hundreds of Lakota crossed back to the United States to join friends and relatives at the agencies. By 1881, Sitting Bull had less than two hundred followers and finally, on 20 July 1881, at the head of his small band, he rode into Fort Buford, Dakota Territory, and surrendered: 'the

Right: *Medicine lodge associated with the Arikara Buffalo Society Medicine Bundle, 1908. Members of the medicine fraternity are seen here just about to enter the lodge; they will then be followed by the Buffalo Society shamans. The ceremonial combined buffalo calling and thanksgiving rites with curing functions.*

Left: *Black Fox, an Arikara warrior. The grizzly bear claws on his magnificent necklace are attached to a collar of otter skin. The turban headdress is likewise of otter and is surmounted by three golden eagle feathers, these undoubtedly symbolic of outstanding deeds performed in battle.*

final surrender of his cherished independence was a hard blow to his pride, and he took it hard. He was much broken' (Vestal, 1957:232).

For two years Sitting Bull was held as a prisoner-of-war, finally returning to his people on the Standing Rock Reservation in 1883; the signs were ominous . . . Sitting Bull's return coincided with the last great Indian buffalo hunt. The immense herds had gone forever.

The continued influx of settlers and the building of the railroads exerted more pressures. The Great Sioux Reservation was increasingly viewed as standing firmly in the way of any further expansion westward and the settlers 'demanded that the Indian move aside' (Utley, 1963:42). In 1889, after much wrangling and questionable promises by the Government, vast areas of the Reservation were signed away, a move bitterly opposed by Sitting Bull.[21] The winter of 1889-90 also heralded epidemics and with frightening suddenness the full realities of Reservation life became starkly apparent: Lakota political organization was shattered, their religious ceremonials were suppressed, the hunting economy abolished and now even their children taken away to distant schools to learn the ways of the white man. Thus, all the old values became meaningless so that the conditions necessary for self-fulfilment and the attainment of happiness no longer existed. The Lakota had reached an *anomic* state, a situation which was common to virtually all other tribes throughout the Plains, and elsewhere, as they were forced to adapt to a new way of life.

Wovoka's message of the *New World* to come was simple and clear. The Son of God would punish the white man for his injustices towards the Indians, he would wipe them from the face of the earth, the dead would be restored to life, the buffalo and other game would return, 'dance four successive nights . . . you must not hurt anybody . . . when the earth shakes [at the coming of the new world] do not be afraid. It will not hurt you' (Mooney, 1896:781).

'They swore that this Messiah came to
                    them in visions sleep
And promised to restore their game
                    and Buffalos a heap.'

The people danced – they called it Ghost or Spirit Dance – and the earth indeed shook for shortly rifles and Hotchkiss guns also thundered.

'They claimed the shirt Messiah gave, no
                    bullet could go through,
But when the Soldiers fired at them
                    they saw this was not true ...

A fight took place, 'twas hand to hand, un-
                    warned by trumpet call,
While the Sioux were dropping man by
                    man – the 7th killed them all ...'
(Extracted from W. H. Prather's (I Company, 9th Cavalry) *The Indian Ghost Dance and War*. See ibid:883)

On 15 December 1890, Sitting Bull crashes dead to the ground, bullets in his head and chest; 29 December, Big Foot together with some one hundred and forty-six men, women and children of the Miniconjou Lakota, dies on the Wounded Knee Field.[22] 'Do not be afraid,' Wovoka had said; 'It will not hurt you.' But the nation's hoop was broken and scattered, there was no longer any center, the sacred tree was

dead – the conquest of the Plains Indian had become a reality. Wovoka's *new* message rang loud and clear, 'My children, today I call upon you to travel a new trail, the only trail now open – the White Man's Road' (Smith, 1975:200).

'A powerful and warlike people, proud, haughty and defiant – well over six feet in height, strong muscular frames and very good horsemen, well dressed, principally in skins and robes; rich in horses and lodges; have a great abundance of meat since buffalo, elk, antelope and deer abound in their country. They say they are *Indians* and do not wish to change their mode of living.'
Samuel N. Latta, Indian Agent, Upper Missouri, circa 1860.

References

1 Blackfeet tipis of this type might use as many as twenty buffalo hides for the cover supported on a foundation of some twenty poles, 25 ft (over 8m.) in length (those of the Crow could be even longer). See Laubin (1957) for the basic study of the Plains tipi.

2 Scalping, however, was *not* necessarily fatal. Several cases have been reported where scalped victims have survived the ordeal. Catlin, for example, sketched an individual 'who had been scalped and recovered from the wound' (Catlin, 1841, vol.1:240). Perhaps the most bizarre episode, however, was that of the brakeman, Edward Thompson, on a Union Pacific Railroad freight train which was travelling across Kansas in 1868. The train was derailed by a combined force of Cheyenne, Arapaho and Lakota warriors. Plunged into the darkness, he was felled by a bullet; later, he reported that although the bullet knocked him down, it 'did not render him unconscious and that his greatest trial in that terrible night was the necessity of shamming dead and not daring to cry out when the Indian was *slowly sawing* at his head covering with a *very* dull knife'. The rescue party later found the scalp and it was put into a bucket of water. On arrival in Omaha, an effort was made by surgeons to sew it back in place, but without success (see Taylor, 1975:93 and Dodge, 1876:400, in ibid, 1980:23).

3 This was related to the explorer, David Thompson, in 1787. It refers to an episode in Saukamappee's youth and took place about 1730.

4 Note also here as with the Louisiana people, the emphasis on the belief that the spirit or soul of the scalped person 'was somehow in and of human hair' – a concept which also prevailed amongst the Sioux (Hassrick, 1964:84).

5 Fort Benton was originally named Fort Clay, founded after the abandonment of Fort McKenzie in 1844 and Lewis in spring 1847. Renamed at Christmas 1850 in honor of Senator Thomas Hart Benton of Missouri who was a strong supporter of the fur trade, the first steamboat arrived a decade later (2 July 1860). River traffic was maintained until the late 1880s when the new railroads took over most of the freight. Although the Missouri was navigatable to St Louis, it had to be continually dredged and cleared of snags.

6 The actual campground for this important Treaty was some thirty-four miles down the North Platte river at Horse Creek in present-day southeast Wyoming.

7 In return for safe emigrant travel up the Platte, west to the mountains, the United States Government agreed to 'make an annual payment to the Sioux in goods valued at $50,000 per year for fifty years, to be delivered in the Fort Laramie area ... should any of the Indian nations, party to this treaty, violate any of the provisions thereof, the United States may withhold the whole or a portion of the annuities mentioned in the preceding Article from the nation so offending, until, in the opinion of the President of the United States, proper satisfaction shall have been made' (McCann, 1956:3-4).

8 The following account of this tragic encounter is based on the superb research of Dr Lloyd E. McCann (1956) of Butler University, Indianapolis, Indiana, being based on data in House and Senate Executive Documents, a narrative of Man-Afraid-Of-His-Horses, now in the National Archives, and an interview with Red Cloud by Judge E. S. Ricker at Pine Ridge, South Dakota, 24 November 1906. It demonstrates so much of the attitudes and prejudices which existed at this time and gives unusual insights into the diplomacy and fair play of mature Plains Indian leaders. Conquering Bear, who emerges as a man of exceptional ability and tact, was mortally wounded in this encounter.

9 The Cheyenne had a legend which told 'how, after a disastrous encounter with some other tribe, they all decided they would become terrible fighters and so become great men'. The formation of the *Hotamĭ itan̄ iu*, 'Dog Men' was a living reminder of that legend. The 'Dog Soldiers', as they became known to the whites, considered that they were the watchdogs of the Cheyenne people. (See Vestal, 1948:63.)

10 Bell and Wylyams had arranged earlier on that fateful day to work together and print some photographs which Bell had taken en route. The shocked Bell later observed 'so I had to print off my negatives alone, and to take a photograph of him, poor fellow, as he lay; a copy of which I sent to Washington that the authorities should see how their soldiers were treated on the Plains' (Bell, 1869:vol.1,64)

11 The town of Medicine Lodge, Barber county, Kansas, now stands on the site.

12 This important tribe of the Muskhogean linguistic stock were originally located on the Mississippi near present-day Memphis, Tennessee. Under White pressure, together with the Choctaw, they began to emigrate west of the Mississippi as early as 1822.

13 Indian delegations were usually treated well and often given the opportunity of publicly presenting their side of the picture. Newspaper reports generally gave sympathetic coverage of such events, pointing out the difficulties confronting both races. Typical was the Cheyenne, Arapaho and Wichita delegation, led by the head chief of the Arapaho, *Ohnastie*, or 'Little Raven', who arrived early in the summer of 1871. As the New York Times expressed it (1 June 1871) 'Their main purpose was to meet the "Great Chief of the American Nation" and to have their reservation boundary lines clearly defined.' They were 'astonished by our cities; such a gathering of men all in one place ... they do not understand our railways, telegraphs, etc. They know such things are done, but they cannot understand by what power, etc ... they have no words in their language to comprehend all they see.' (For further details of this visit and also that of Red Cloud's in 1872 see Taylor, 1975:106-7.)

14 It was, however, a victory paid for dearly by the Lakota whose tactics were to ride down the enemy before they had time to reload. Unknown to Red Cloud, new Springfield breech-loaders had been recently issued to the troopers and more than sixty were killed and one hundred and twenty wounded under the withering fire power during a battle which lasted more than four hours. Such heavy casualties were devastating to small population Plains tribes. Leaders were supposed not to lose any men 'if he could possibly help it' (Pakes, 1989:21). For an excellent up-to-date analysis relating to the nature of Plains Indian warfare, see ibid.

15 After the 1868 Laramie Treaty, the Lakota divided into three main factions: agency Indians wholly dependent on the Government; those who stayed at the agencies in winter and left in spring to live in Powder River country and finally those who permanently shunned the agencies, preferring their own free life in the Yellowstone and Powder River regions. This third group 'was regarded by the army as the principal barrier to white encroachment' (Taunton, 1977:7).

16 Crowfoot refused to join, almost certainly due to the fair-minded and honest treatment which the Canadian Plains tribes received at the hands of the North-West Mounted Police, which was founded in 1873 on the recommendation of Colonel W. F. Butler (Butler, 1891:378-9). Sitting Bull and Crowfoot later became firm friends and Sitting Bull was to name his son in honor of the Blackfeet chief.

17 For a detailed analysis of the aftermath of this historic encounter, see Taunton (1986).

18 This particular battle was graphically documented by Captain John G. Bourke, U.S.A. Third Cavalry. He describes in great detail the complete destruction of the Cheyenne village (which consisted of some two hundred tipis) and hence 'wiping off the face of the earth many products of aboriginal taste and industry which would have been gems in the cabinets of museums ... Never were orders more thoroughly executed ... (Bourke, 1890:29). It was a pattern replicated many times by the United States army in their subjugation of the Plains Indian.

19 Apparently, Crazy Horse and Sitting Bull had discussed surrender on a number of occasions but Sitting Bull said 'I do not wish to die yet' (Vestal, 1957:182).

20 Recent researches by members of the University of South Dakota and the Dull Knife Memorial College, have put a new perspective on the escape route followed by the Cheyennes supporting the oral history of the tribe (see McDonald, McDonald, Tallbull and Risingsun, 1989:265-9).

21 This reduction of the Great Sioux Reservation is considered in great detail by Utley (1963:40-60).

22 A general sentiment amongst those tribes who adopted the Ghost Dance religion was that their domination by the white race would soon end 'and that a beautiful new world was coming in which everyone would live forever' (Smith, 1975:74).

Author's note
In February 1972, a small Catholic church at Wounded Knee became the scene of Wounded Knee II, the headquarters and sanctuary for members of the American Indian Movement who tried to draw attention to the 'Trail of Broken Treaties', a cry of impatience and despair with human waste so commonplace on the Reservations for almost a century. Now, over 100 years after the death of Big Foot and his 146 Lakota, Wounded Knee II can be seen as a turning point in the restoration of Lakota values; the fundamentals of ancient beliefs are taking root once again.

PLATEAU AND BASIN

THE PLATEAU area stretches from central British Columbia, south and across the United States border, eastern Oregon and Washington, then across the majority of the northern half of Idaho and straddling the Continental Divide into northwestern Montana. It is laced by rivers – the names of several suggesting both their character and products, the Clearwater, Boulder, Salmon, Beaverhead and Cascade – and the Blue and Bitterroot Mountains which skirt the Columbia Plateau – the most dominant geographical feature of the area and through which runs the great Columbia River which, together with the Fraser in the north, is the lifeblood of the land and its people. The area, covering approximately two hundred thousand square miles, is one of great contrast and beauty being marked by forested mountains, deep valleys and canyons, clear rushing streams, open meadowlands and, to the south, bordering the northern rim of the Great Basin, windswept plains and desert regions dotted with sagebrush and rock.

The rivers are rich in fish resources, particularly salmon which migrate from the Pacific via tributaries of both the Fraser and Columbia; other fish also abound such as sturgeon, lamprey eel, whitefish and trout. The clear, cold waters, with their high oxygen content, support much life in comparison to the warmer and often murky rivers of the Great Plains. Whilst the area was largely devoid of buffalo, elk, deer and mountain sheep were common as well as otter and beaver.

The Plateau was dominated by two major linguistic groups: in the north, occupying the inland areas of present-day British Columbia,

This map shows approximate territories of tribes and language groups at about 1850, and somewhat earlier in the western and eastern edges of the Basin. After that, all tribes lost territory and some moved.

were the Salishan-speaking Shuswap, Lillooet, Thompson and Okanagan, while across the border into present-day Washington and Idaho lived the Kalispel, Coeur d'Alêne, Spokane, Colville, Sanpoil and Flathead. In the middle Columbia ranged the Sahaptin-speaking Klikitat, Yakima, Umatilla, Walla Walla, Palus, Nez Perce and Cayuse. Other linguistic stocks were also represented, such as the Kutenai in the northeast who spoke a language of their own, but now shown to be distantly related to Algonquian, and in the west – although their cultural traits tend to identify them more with the tribes of the Pacific coast – the Chinookans on the lower Columbia. Associated with this latter language was the foundation of the so-called

Key to tribes:
PLATEAU

1 Lillooet
2 Shuswap
3 Thompson
4 Nicola
5 Okanagan
6 Lakes
7 Kutenai
8 Kalispel
9 Sanpoil
10 Columbia Salish
11 Yakima
12 Spokane
13 Palus
14 Coeur d'Alène
15 Flathead
16 Nez Perce
17 Walla Walla
18 Cayuse
19 Umatilla

20 Klikitat
21 Wishram
22 Tenino
23 Molala
24 Klamath
25 Modoc

BASIN

26 Eastern Shoshoni
27 Northern Shoshoni and
   Bannock
28 Northern Paiute
29 Washoe
30 Western Shoshoni
31 Ute
32 Southern Paiute
33 Owens Valley Paiute
34 Kawaiisu

Chinook jargon, the Indian trade language of the Columbia River region, its use extending to the Pacific coast and reaching from California up to Alaska.

While gathering and hunting were important to the Plateau people, their principal subsistence depended on the salmon which were speared, netted, gorge-hooked or trapped, the latter method being by the use of weirs constructed of willows and boulders across the smaller streams. The spearing was a way of obtaining quantities of large salmon and these were caught from specially built platforms which projected over the water, or from jutting ledges of rock. The platforms were generally built above the weirs which impeded the movement of the fish. One magnificent painting by the Canadian artist, Paul Kane, vividly illustrates the various techniques used by the Spokane in the vicinity of the Kettle Falls on the Columbia River in what is now northeast Washington State. Clearly, in 1846, when the sketches used for the painting were made, the Indians highly valued this bountiful area; sadly, they lost it a century and a quarter later with the building of the Grand Coulee Dam across the Columbia whose backwater (as has happened with several other dammed rivers in the United States) has flooded forever this ancient Indian site.

The spears depicted by Kane, which were identical to a type used by the Nez Perce further south, consisted of a three-pronged gig attached to a shaft some 8ft (2.5m.) in length. Through each prong, which was made of a flexible wood such as hackberry, were pointed bone pins, these projected inward and away from the end of the prongs. The spear was not thrown, instead it was jabbed down into the water, the spread of the three prongs adding to its efficiency; it was a favorite style for night fishing, the light of pitch torches being used to attract the salmon. Another type of spear which had a detachable head was also used by the Nez Perce: here, the point was of heavy bone (cut from the thickest part of an elk leg bone) with a socket of elderberry wood, the whole being bound firmly together and attached to the shaft some 11in. (30cm.) from the head. When the salmon was speared, the head loosened from the shaft; fish, head and shaft were now easily pulled in by an attached braided cord. Whilst much of the fish caught was eaten fresh, a great deal was dried on scaffolds and smoked for winter use.

The Nez Perce, as with many other tribes on the Plateau, attended the great Dalles Rendezvous which was held every fall on the Columbia River where it cuts through the Cascade Mountain range.[1] For several environmental and historical reasons, The Dalles became one of the most important centres for a lively trade throughout the summer, reaching its peak in the fall. In the vicinity of The Dalles lived the Wishram and Wasco, both of whom spoke Chinookan dialects, and were identified as noted middlemen between the Plateau and Pacific coast tribes; they hosted many groups who came to their villages during the fall trading fair.

In order to obtain the goods they required, each tribe tended to specialize in producing or acquiring materials which they knew would trade well at The Dalles. Thus, the Nez Perce,

Above: Nez Perce warrior on horseback. He wears a Plains style eagle feathered warbonnet. The large tipi in the background is of canvas; it is unlined and hence suggests a temporary encampment.

several bands of which hunted on the Montana and Wyoming Plains to the east, brought along buffalo robes; others, such as the Klamath, specialized in camas bulbs, a widely used sweet and nutritious vegetal food; dentalium and other shells were brought in from the Pacific coast by the Wishram and Wasco. Although the Rendezvous appears to have been established long before white contact, according to the explorers Lewis and Clark, who visited The Dalles in January 1806, 'the circumstance which forms the soul of this trade is the visit of the whites' (Lewis and Clark, Coues ed., 1893, vol.II:787). From such contacts, Plateau people obtained access to somewhat outdated 'British or American muskets, powder, ball, and shot, copper and brass kettles, brass tea-kettles and coffee-pots, blankets . . . scarlet and blue cloth . . . brass wire [and] knives' (ibid:788). Clearly, the Plateau people became increasingly dependent on European goods which ultimately became essentials rather than luxury items.

The habitations of the Plateau Indians varied in style and emphasis, at least four distinct types having been identified. Traditionally, the northern Plateau tribes such as the Shuswap, Thompson and Okanagan, used semi-subterranean earth lodges; occupied by one or two families, they were constructed by excavating the dry sandy ground to a depth of some 2 meters and were about 13ft (4m.) in diameter, although sizes varied considerably. Poles were then laid across which were covered with grass and earth to a depth of 4in. (10cm.) or so and the entrance was generally, but not always, from the top, via a simple ladder. Further to the south amongst the Nez Perce, similar habi-

tations tended to be used by women before and after childbirth, and during the menstrual period, whilst a smaller sudatory lodge was used by boys above fourteen years of age.

A favorite habitation, however, used by many tribes on the Plateau both in winter and summer, was the conical lodge, formed by stacking seven to nine poles around a tripod and then covering the frame with mats woven from cattail (Typha latifolia) or tule (Scirpus lacustris). Such habitations gave the appearance of the Plains tipi, although on average they were somewhat smaller. For winter living these lodges were covered with two to four layers of mats and generally sunk about 2ft (60cm.) into the ground with the earth stacked around. On occasions, such habitations could be very large; Lewis and Clark reported seeing an ancient circular house ring some 30ft (10m.) in diameter, the rimmed circumference being about 3ft (1m.) in height and the centre sunk more than 3ft into the ground.

There were also communal long houses: Lewis and Clark in describing their visit to Neeshnepahkeook or Cut-nose, a Nez Perce chief, refer to the entire village of some thirty-eight families occupying two large houses. 'At a little distance from us are two Chopunnish houses, one of which contains eight families, and the other, which is by much the largest we have ever seen, is inhabited by at least 30. It is rather a kind of shed built, like all the other huts, of straw and mats in the form of the roof of a house, 156 feet long and about 15 wide, closed at the ends, and having a number of doors on each side. The vast interior is without partitions, but the fire of each family is kindled in a row along the middle of the building, about ten feet apart' (ibid:vol.III:988-9). The upright supports of these lodges separated the ridge poles by several inches so that an aperture extended the whole length of the lodge, thus serving as a smoke vent.[2] Poles were then leaned on to the horizontal ridge poles and long mats attached to these in a shingle-fashion; earth was packed against the lower part of the mat which was generally protected from decay with a covering of dry grass. The mats were carefully selected. Those of cattail were simpler in construction than those made of tule. The former were not very effective in repelling rain, thus although generally of the same size (approximately 4 × 10ft (1.2 × 3m.), the more exposed surfaces were covered with tule mats. As a safeguard against the wind, more poles were often leaned up against the mats and during cold weather – especially with the smaller habitations – the interior was lined with skins.

The Okanagan and other tribes further north also utilized a similar long house, but it was, according to one observer, a temporary shelter made to accommodate people at gatherings and at the fishing places. They were favored when communities camped together because they required a lesser number of mats than the conical tents to accommodate the same number of people. It is probable that Lewis and Clark, therefore, were describing a temporary Nez Perce camp. This is consistent with Mylie Lawyer's observations, who related that the long house (which she referred to as the *Lah-pit-ahl Ain-neet*) was popular when large groups of people got together, 'a gathering place for social, religious and war ceremonials' (M.L. to C.T., Lapwai: 1969).

As mobility increased with the introduction of the horse, those tribes on the eastern side of the Plateau region such as the Pend d'Oreilles, Flathead, Colville and some of the Nez Perce bands, made forays to the Plains buffalo country. There they traded for buffalo hide tipis which tended to displace the mat covered conical tent, being far more convenient for hunting and trading expeditions.

Prior to the introduction of the horse during the early eighteenth century, the Plateau was settled with small and independent bands generally on, or near, the many rivers and streams which characterized this region. As has been outlined, in adapting to their environment, they had shaped out a pattern of living – undoubtedly established over a period of several thousand years – which pivoted on the extensive use of fish and other food resources, wide travel, mutual interdependence and trade, and a limited war complex.

Travel to the great trading fairs held at such places as The Dalles, Kettle Falls and Celilo Falls, was mainly by means of canoe, portaging passed dangerous rapids such as those on the Upper Clearwater. The style of canoe varied. In the north, tribes such as the Shuswap, Thompson, and Okanagan used the sharp-snouted 'sturgeon nose' type which was made of cedar bark; the same style (as in Kane's illustration, right) was also used by the more southerly

Above: Tum-se-ne-ho, or The Man without Blood, a Spokane chief, by Paul Kane (1847). He carries a combined bow case and quiver as well as a second bow, a custom common among the Spokane.

Coeur d'Alêne and Kutenai. Rafts of tule lodge mats, rolled into bundles lashed together and pointed at each end like canoes, were also used on occasions. Tribes to the eastern part of the Plateau area, such as the Kalispel and Pend d'Oreilles, were particularly well known as expert canoe people and whilst these crafts resembled in shape those of the northern Salishan tribes, they differed in having the ends cut off square. Teit has suggested that this style was due to Iroquois influence, some of whom, in the employment of fur traders, 'made bark canoes of the eastern or Iroquois shape on

Flathead Lake' (Teit, Boas ed., 1930:350).

The Nez Perce (south of the Pend d'Oreilles in the valleys of the Clearwater), seem to have favored the simple dug-out type of canoe which was made from a single log and hollowed out by fires; it was propelled by either paddles or poles and could vary between about 16 to 42ft (5–13m.) in length. The former importance of water travel to the Nez Perce may be indicated by the Crow name for these people, A-*pu-pe*, which means 'to paddle'. However, even as early as 1806, canoes were scarce in the Nez Perce camps which Lewis and Clark visited, and some large villages were 'entirely without them' (Spinden, 1908:223). The horse, it seems, was now the major mode of travel and as with the Plains Indian it brought great cultural changes to all the Plateau people. Lewis and Clark were greatly impressed by the number of horses owned by many of the tribes whom they came into contact with during their travels through the Plateau region and, compared to the Plains Indians at this time, their wealth in horses was immense. The explorers reported that fifty to one hundred horses per individual amongst the Nez Perce was quite common, and forty years later it was reported that as many as fifteen hundred horses might be owned by Cayuse and Nez Perce family units, whilst reports for the Crow – considered to be the wealthiest of the northwestern Plains tribes – gives seven per lodge in 1805 and fifteen in 1830 (Ewers, 1955:25).

The traditions of the Flathead and Nez Perce credit the Shoshoni as furnishing them with their first mounts; the Shoshoni in turn said that they obtained them from their kinsmen, the Comanche, who, as early as 1705, raided the horse-rich Spanish settlements in what is now present-day New Mexico. The subsequent horse trade was thus via a complex route from such places as Santa Fe, probably west of the Continental Divide to the Snake River and Shoshoni Rendezvous, whence to the country of the Nez Perce, Flathead, Pend d'Oreilles, Kutenai and Kalispel. Tribal traditions of this

Below: A study of the Kutenai Indians on the Columbia River by Paul Kane accurately showing the sharp, sturgeon-nose type canoe and temporary habitations traditionally used by Plateau groups.

last tribe – typical of many – records the first appearance of the animal: 'Some people saw the horse's tracks where it had passed over some sand. They called other people, and discussed what kind of animal had made the tracks, which were strange to them all. Some thought it might have been a horse, as they had heard about them. Other people lower down, near the river bank, saw the man approach on the horse at a lope. They observed that he was smoking, and that he seemed to be quite at his ease. They watched him enter the river and swim across on the horse. They gathered around and examined the animal with much curiosity' (Teit, Boas ed., 1930:352).

An amusing story related by the Okanagan refers to the initial efforts to ride this strange creature, the main fear it seems was falling off! 'The first horse [we] obtained was very gentle. The first person who mounted it rode with two long sticks, one in each hand, to steady himself. Another man led the horse slowly, and the rider shifted the sticks (as one does with walking sticks) as they went along' (ibid:250).

Much of the Plateau region was fine horse country, the natural barriers protecting the animal from wandering too far and also from would-be thieves, whilst the well watered valleys, such as the Wallowa and Grande Ronde,[3] provided nutritious forage and shelter in winter. The horse also fitted well into the established seasonal movements of the Plateau people. By careful and selective breeding, such tribes as the Nez Perce and their close relatives, the Cayuse, built up enormous horse herds. Eliminating the poorer stallions by castration, the Nez Perce became justly famous for the superior speed and endurance of their horses, amongst the most distinctive of which was the traditional war-horse, which came to be known as the Appaloosa.

It was Meriwether Lewis, in 1806, who first made a definite reference to what was almost certainly the forebear of the Appaloosa, describing a few of the Nez Perce horses as being marked with large spots of white, irregularly scattered and intermixed with the dark brown or other dark shade. Later, in 1820, Alexander Ross of the Hudson's Bay Company observed that the Nez Perce preferred entirely white horses which were painted for war 'drawing a variety of hieroglyphic devices, the head and neck were dappled with streaks of red and yellow; the mane dyed black, the tail red, clubbed up in a knot and tied short . . . and the rider as well as the horse was so besmeared with red, blue and yellow ochre, that no one could tell what the natural color of either was.' (Ross, 1855:307). At this time, however, next to white, those which were speckled or white and black were in most demand, being used by distinguished warriors in preference to any other and being valued at two or three times the worth of other horses. They were more than just handsomely marked, being generally larger and heavier than the average Plateau breed, sure footed and possessing great endurance; they matched well the varying Plateau country, capable of travelling with equal ease through

Below: *The Kettle Falls on the Columbia River, by Paul Kane (1847). The highest falls on the river, they were favorite salmon fishing places for the Spokane, Colville and Walla Walla of the region.*

heavy timbered or mountainous terrain. Whilst the Appaloosa became indelibly associated with the Nez Perce, it is possible that the name derives from Palus, a tribe closely associated with the Nez Perce and Cayuse, the latter breeding a distinctive type of pony.

With the acquisition of the horse into Plateau culture – probably around the first quarter of the eighteenth century – the basic mode of travel was considerably modified, resulting in increased interaction between more distant tribes such as those on the Plains to the east, in particular the Blackfeet and Crow. It also led to an expansion on the already long established seasonal activities, in particular the scope for trade, which was greatly enhanced by an ability to transport quickly and easily large amounts of trade commodities; not surprisingly, the horse itself also became a highly valued trade item.

Unlike the Plains, neither the dog nor the travois were popular on the Plateau as a means of transporting equipment and whilst the Plateau tribes became adept horsemen, most of the horse equipment which they used, such as pack and riding saddles, bridles, cinches, whips and ropes, were adopted along with the horse from the Shoshoni. Nevertheless, when the Plateau people made their own horse equipment, it displayed some distinctive features. Men's saddles, in common with those used by the Plains Indians, were generally of the pad-type with the four corners of the saddle embellished with quill or beadwork; women's saddles, on the other hand, had a high pommel and cantel, generally with a hook or spike at the front with hanging triangular shaped flaps beautifully ornamented with trade cloth and beads. The stirrups were made of bentwood covered with rawhide, those used by the Flathead, Pend d'Oreilles and Nez Perce women being particularly distinctive in having beaded pendants attached to the bottom. Wide cruppers and horse collars were also used, the latter again exhibiting heavily embellished flaps similar to those used on stirrups. This attractive horse equipment was also used by the Crow and has been particularly associated with that tribe (Wildschut, Ewers ed.,1959). However, the style may have been copied by them from the Plateau people, the roots of which can in turn be traced to the Spanish settlements of New Mexico and Texas. The Nez Perce women's horse equipment and mode of riding was sufficiently distinctive for the Presbyterian missionary, Henry H. Spalding, to observe that their saddles were an 'improvement upon our side saddle if we consult the ease of the woman' and the Nez Perce woman always used a blanket or robe which was 'thrown over the saddle covering the lower part of the person . . . in my opinion the more modest way of riding as also the more natural & comfortable' (Fletcher, 1930:3).

With the acquisition of the horse, tribes such as the Coeur d'Alêne, Spokane and Nez Perce began to visit the Plains for buffalo hunting and trading. The goods which passed from east to west were chiefly catlinite and pipes of the same material, clothing, buffalo skins and robes. Whilst both Plains and Plateau people tended to make the same items, there was an emphasis on *quality* goods, it being recognized that one group was more skilled than the other in the production of certain items. For example, whilst the Plateau made headdresses, they considered that the finest were made by the Sioux,[4] and the Crow robes – of the softest tan and embellished with beaded or quilled bands – were greatly sought after: 'Often a horse and, in addition, a well-made leather shirt, was paid for one of the best kind of robes' (Teit, Boas ed., 1930:114). Porcupine quillwork, beaded and quilled pipe-bags, moccasins, and parfleches were all items made in quantity and *quality* which the Plateau tribes desired from the Plains people. This trade had a profound impact on their clothing styles, particularly that which was worn for ceremonial and dress occasions.

Whilst the trade in horses from the Plateau to the Plains was a major activity – and even the rare Appaloosa was occasionally traded (Ewers, 1955:217) – the Plains Indians also desired such items as salmon oil, pemmican, cakes of camas and berries, hemp and hemp twine, shells, certain types of beads, pipes of green soapstone, eagle-tail feathers, mountain-sheep horn and horn spoons, and woven bags. One of the most coveted items, however, was the highly perfected Plateau bow which the Plains tribes considered was greatly superior to those of their own make. Amongst the finest were those made from mountain-sheep horn, being a particular speciality of the Nez Perce.

The traditional dress of the Plateau was of soft tanned skins from the antelope, elk or deer, generally without the hair. The men wore soft-soled moccasins, leggings and breechcloth, shirt and a robe, whilst the women wore moccasins, calf-length leggings, a long dress and a robe. The women's dress of the Coeur d'Alène was very similar to that worn by the Nez Perce. Two deerskins formed the body of the dress, a third was used for fringing and shaping. 'The upper parts of the skins were folded down on the outside of the dress, forming a kind of false yoke at back and front. They were sewed to the body of the dress throughout, or stitched here and there with thongs. Pendants and tassels were often attached to the edges of the fold. The hair of the tailpiece was clipped in lines, and the end of the tail generally, but not always, cut off. Usually the sleeve parts were left open underneath, but sometimes they were stitched or tied here and there with thongs. Generally three rows of inserted fringe or thongs extended around the skirt below the waist. Single rows were also placed on the back and front of the dress below the yoke, but only rarely . . . Often all or the lower part of the yoke piece was beaded or quilled in lines following the contour of the edge of the yoke, or the dress itself was beaded immediately below the yoke . . . Most

Below: Kutenai Indians probably c.1900. The woman utilizes a baby carrier typical of the Plateau region, the rounded top embellished with beadwork in combined geometrical and floral patterns.

dresses reached to the ankles, . . . Some had several lines of quillwork across the breast and back of the body and many had long fringes following the edge of the yoke' (Teit, Boas ed., 1930:70). The leggings were also of tanned hide; they reached to the knee and were generally fringed on the outer edges. Most could be opened at the sides and wrapped around the leg and then fastened with tie strings, one string going around the leg above the calf to hold the leggings in place. They were often heavily beaded on the lower part with a narrower band extending up the outside of the legging.

Although Teit has identified five moccasin types which were worn by the Coeur d'Alène and adjacent tribes (ibid:72), the most popular and traditional type with wide distribution on the Plateau was constructed so that both the sole and upper were of one single piece of deerskin with the main seam extending around the outside of the sole starting on the inner side near the big toe and terminating a few inches beyond the heel seam. Near the base of the heel seam were additional strips of buckskin to enable the moccasins to be easily removed and an extra single piece of hide was sewn around the top producing flaps which could tuck under or be attached to the leggings. The summer soft-soled moccasin fitted snugly to the foot, but those made for winter use were looser, not infrequently being made of tanned hide – deer, antelope or buffalo – with the hair left on the inside.

After sustained and extended contact with the Plains tribes towards the end of the nineteenth century, a two-piece rawhide soled moccasin became increasingly popular, particularly amongst the more eastern Plateau people such as the Kutenai, Flathead and Nez Perce, and ultimately it all but replaced the ancient soft-soled type. Lewis and Clark likened the costume of the Nez Perce to that of the Shoshoni, extending on the idea of not only a general similarity in clothing styles throughout the Plateau region, but also to the Great Basin. However, deeper analysis indicates that there were considerable differences. For example, in his studies of Nez Perce women's dresses, Wissler concluded that here were 'a number of distinct cuts for the contour of the yoke and the bottom of the skirt. Yet, there is very little variation within the tribe, . . . [each tribe] followed a definite form for the bottoms of their dresses, making it clear that they had a fixed mode, or style for the cut' (Wissler, 1915: 65-6).

Above: *Flathead boys in dance costume, c.1900, one (left) in a beaded waistcoat with a shield on his back, the others with horse and porcupine guard hair roaches of a style imported from the Plains.*

Below: *Flathead woman and girl, c.1900. The woman carries a cradle attached to the pommel of her saddle; both use (trade) metal-bitted bridles. The lavish horse regalia is typical of the region.*

Thompson

The Thompson Indians, speakers of a Salishan language, live in British Columbia in rugged country east of the Coast Range. When whites first arrived in 1858 and 1859 they were living in many villages along the Thompson, Fraser, and Nicola rivers. By 1900 they occupied some 70 villages ranging in size from only two or three families to over 100 inhabitants. Winter houses were large, semi-subterranean, earth covered structures; summer dwellings were mat-covered frameworks of poles. Hunting and trapping was important, for deer, small mammals, and birds especially, while fishing for salmon provided a substantial share of the diet. By 1900 much food was obtained from stores and the Thompson Indians also grew potatoes, peas, beans, maize, turnips, raised chickens and hogs, and kept cows. The materials shown here were collected in 1897-1904 by James A. Teit, a white man married to a Thompson woman, who was trained and supported in his anthropological research by Franz Boas.

1 Saddle bag, red and black cloth appliqué on fringed leather bag.
2 Beaver spear point of deer leg bone.
3 Coiled cedar-root carrying basket with imbricated pattern representing combs such as No. 17.
4 Cedar bark face towel used by girl during her puberty isolation.
5 Birch bark container with design in red ochre; used as berry basket, etc. for many years.
6 Tobacco pouch on shoulder strap, of red strouding embroidered in silk. 'Octopus pouch' type (because of eight tabs).
7 Pair of buckskin young man's moccasins with silk embroidered design of flowers and horse heads.
8 Adze for canoe making, etc. with handle of service berry wood; evidently a reconstruction of an obsolete type, re-using a stone used as skin pounder.

9 Deer figure made of rushes, shot at with special bow for four nights after a person's death.
10 Wooden spoon.
11 Rattle of deer hoofs.
12 Model head to illustrate warrior's face paint and hair dress.
13 Model head to illustrate woman's face paint and hair dress.
14 Riding saddle shaped like a pack saddle; antler cross pieces, braided bark cinch and stirrup straps;

used with deerskin cover.
15 Tobacco pouch of fawn or doe skin, beaded and fringed, worn tucked under belt or sash or carried on arm.
16 Woman's buckskin cap with bead and button decoration; style obsolete after about 1885.
17 Comb of wood.
18 Bone whistle used by boy or girl during puberty ceremony.
19 Sock of twined grass, worn inside moccasin.

20 Buckskin bag, design embroidered in silk thread.
21 Pair of horn tweezers for removing beard hairs, with incised design representing a butterfly.
22 Beaded tobacco pouch of Nawissatken, chief of the Nicola River band.
23 Tobacco pouch (octopus bag) on sash, ornamented with beads and Hudson's Bay Co. buttons in design of wild flowers and leaves. Bought from Neakyapamuxoa.

Two particularly fine women's dresses – almost certainly Nez Perce and probably amongst the earliest now extant from this tribe – were collected by the Presbyterian missionary, Henry H. Spalding, who sent them to his brother in Oberlin, Ohio in 1846. Each dress, Spalding said, was valued at three horses[5] and the dentalium shells which embellished one of them he described as 'very costly' . . . and the shells removed 'From a single dress were once taken to the mountains by a man who lives near, & sold in small parcels for $1600.00 sixteen hundred dollars. A young lady (Red one) in one of these dresses, upon a firey horse well equiped [sic] with saddle & crouper [sic], makes a fine appearance.' Spalding's description continues, referring to objects which were so typical of Nez Perce accoutrements of the period when natural materials were utilized to their best effect – both for service and decorative embellishment. The elk teeth on the other dress and the cradle which he also sent, were, he explained, from the 'Buck elk, two from an animal, after & before certain ages'.[6] He refers to the woven fiber bags for which the Nez Perce are justly famous: 'The bags are made of

the hemp of the country & used for packing roots, etc.' (Fletcher, 1930:3). Such bags were coveted trade items; in the older types, the warp and weft threads were of hemp (*Apocynum cannabium*) and the false embroidery material was of bear grass (*Xerophyllum tenax*) dyed in soft natural colours and combined in such a way as to produce attractive geometrical patterns across the surface of the bag.[7] A distinctive flat topped hat (commented on by Lewis and Clark in 1806 (Lewis and Clark, Coues ed., 1893, vol.III:1017), without a rim and utilizing similar techniques of weaving to that for the bags, was also made and worn by Nez Perce women; it has been described as the highest form of Nez Perce textile art and 'the gayest portion of their dress' (Spinden, 1908:220).

Whilst Plateau culture was profoundly affected by the horse and the extensive contacts which they subsequently made with the Plains tribes to the east, the tribal domains remained largely intact and Plateau intertribal warfare was minimal.[8] Less so with forays to the Plains, where for almost one hundred years the majority of the Plateau tribes were arrayed in war against the Blackfeet and Crow (although

Below: A Cayuse chief known by the whites as David Young, c.1900. Note the elaborate horse mask and matching martingale. Young wears a spectacular horned headdress and ermine fringed shirt.

Left: Oscar Mark, or The Little Vessel, c.1870, a Wasco Indian of Warm Springs, Oregon. He wears a perforated and fringed buckskin shirt with a broad pony beaded band across his shoulder.

at times there was an uneasy truce). The Kutenai, Flathead and some of the Northern Shoshoni, in particular, viewed the Blackfeet and Crow as intruders into the western Plains region which for centuries they had used as intertribal buffalo country. Tribal traditions collected by Wissler and Teit[9] from Blackfeet and Plateau in the early twentieth century, confirmed the report of the explorer, David Thompson, who, when travelling in the region of present-day Calgary, Alberta, observed: 'All these Plains, which are now the hunting ground of the above Indians (Blackfoot), were formerly in full possession of the Kootenaes, northward; the next the Saleesh and their allies, and the most southern the Snake Indians' (Henry and Thompson, Coues ed., 1897:330).

Armed with guns which they obtained from the Cree to the east, the Blackfeet forced the Kutenai, Flathead and Shoshoni to abandon their former hunting grounds and some of the bands who had previously lived east of the Rockies were all but exterminated; others retreated to the Plateau. The Shoshoni were so badly decimated that for more than half a century none were 'seen on the northwestern

Above: *A Cayuse woman called Kupt, with her young son in a typical laced Cayuse cradle. The hoop in the cradle could be raised to protect the child's head. Kupt wears a basketry hat and a beaded band.*

Below: *Edna Kash-Kash, a Cayuse woman, outside a rush-mat covered tipi, c.1900. Note the fine costume – a woven basketry hat, buckskin dress and trade blanket embellished with beadwork.*

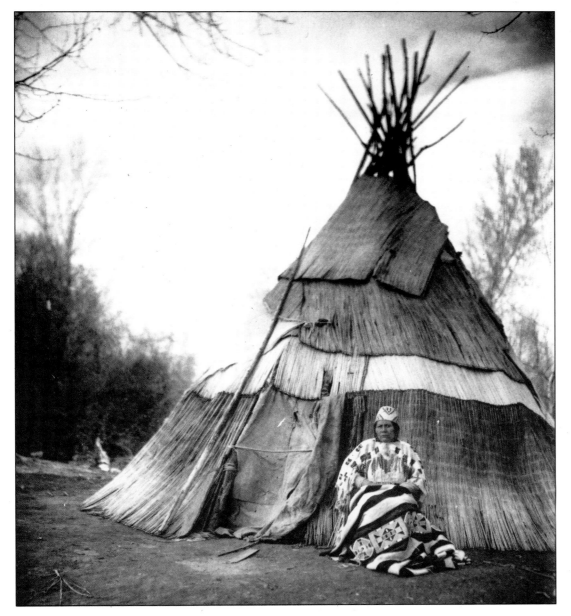

plains north of the Yellowstone' (Teit, Boas ed., 1930:126). This devastating experience had a positive and lasting effect; it greatly strengthened the interdependence ethos which was so much a part of the Plateau culture and added another – the war complex.

The Flathead invited the Coeur d'Alêne and other Salishan tribes to join them as partners when travelling to their former Plains hunting grounds, the result being a great war alignment of tribes (Plateau versus Plains). The latter were weaker in this respect because of the constant warring which occurred amongst the Plains people themselves (for example, the Crow and Blackfeet were almost constantly at war with one another). Thus, expeditions across the mountains were relatively commonplace, and parties of Coeur d'Alêne, Spokane, Kalispel, Pend d'Oreilles and Nez Perce hunted in territory now claimed by the Blackfeet and Crow. Initially, a rendezvous was made in Flathead country, then three or more large parties would travel to the Plains keeping in touch with one another during their travels. The worst enemy were the Blackfeet, but even with them the Plateau tribes would form a truce so that trading could take place for a few days. 'No one on either side was to quarrel, fight, or steal horses; but all were to be friends for the allotted number of days, and all were to play games and trade as they felt inclined . . . The conduct of the people during these periods of truce was in great contrast to their attitude at other times, when each side was always ready to attack or repel an attack. Sometimes . . . less than a day passed before one side made an attack on the other. The Blackfoot are said to have been the worst offenders' (ibid:114).

Some lasting friendships were, however, made particularly by the Nez Perce bands who commonly travelled to the Plains following the Lolo Trail[10] across the Rocky Mountains into present-day Montana and Wyoming, there to barter with a western branch of the Absaroka – the Mountain Crows. As early as 1806, Lewis and Clark referred to these contacts although they reported that of the seven groups of Nez Perce (whom they referred to as 'Chopunnish') only two travelled to the Missouri. In the 1860s, it seems to have been small bands such as those led by Looking Glass, who had the reputation of being a great wanderer, that forged and maintained these links.

The effect on these Nez Perce bands was that it led to the adoption of a number of Plains traits, particularly those of a material culture nature and it served in the second half of the nineteenth century to distinguish more clearly between two groups of Nez Perce, those strongly influenced by the missionaries and increasingly giving up the traditional religious, tribal customs and lifestyle and those who wished to maintain their independence and ethos. Henry Spalding, for example, instructed the Nez Perce 'to give up native dress before they could receive the rewards of salvation and the power of Christian spirits' and many native materials 'were abandoned or destroyed, mostly by burning'[11] (Shawley, 1974:259). Divisions increasingly became apparent; as the Nez Perce Agent, John Monteith, reported in August 1872: 'The tribe is about equally divided between Treaty and those who term themselves Non-Treaty Indians. The Non-Treaty portion with very few exceptions reside on the outside of the Reserve along the Snake River and its Tributaries. They never ask for assistance . . .' (Brown, 1967:36).

Although convenient from the white man's standpoint to regard the Nez Perce as one single body, this was entirely inconsistent with the traditional social organization of these people – the tribe consisted of bands, both Treaty and Non-Treaty, each with its own leader. Regardless of the appointment by Government officials of Lawyer as 'Head Chief of the Nez Perces Nation', the bands largely acted independently (ibid:31).

By the mid-nineteenth century, the Plateau country became increasingly subjected to white settlement and, in an attempt to avoid conflict, the Stevens Treaty of 1855, amongst others, defined Nez Perce territory. Agreement was reached with little dispute, the Treaty being signed by Lawyer, a highly respected leader and direct descendant of Chief Twisted Hair who had so well received Lewis and Clark half a century previously.[12] Forty-seven others also signed; the anticipated difficulties it appeared had thus been resolved, but sadly, not for long. Five years later, in 1860, a trader named Elias D. Pierce discovered traces of gold deposits on the Reservation and by the end of that year, Pierce had set up camp with some thirty-three recruits. The intention was to mine the following spring (ibid:30).

Anticipating a further influx of miners,

Below: A Umatilla woman called by the whites Nellie Salmon, c.1900. Her dress is heavily fringed with beads. The corn husk bag is probably of Nez Perce make and the leggings Sioux.

Above: A group of Umatilla, c.1900. The costumes are a mixture of traditional Plateau accoutrements – feathered headbands, basketry hat and bag – and Plains clothing such as the buffalo headdress.

another Treaty attempted to reduce the Reservation further. This time, an agreement could not be reached and the Lower Nez Perce – which included Looking Glass's band – walked out of the negotiations, refusing to sign. It was again left to Lawyer and others to negotiate and this time the lands of the Lower Nez Perce – largely the Non-Treaty faction – were ceded by Lawyer and the Band Chiefs closely associated with him. This included the Wallowa Valley, a traditional homeland of Tu-eka-kas or Old Joseph, as he was known to the whites: there were deep regrets and concern on both sides. As Agent Monteith observed in 1872: 'It is a great pity that the valley was ever opened for settlement. It is so high and cold that they can raise nothing but the hardiest of vegetables . . . It is a fine grass country and raising stock is all that can be done to any advantage. It is the only fishery the Nez Percés have and they go there from all directions . . . If there is any way in which the Wallowa Valley could be kept for the Indians I would recommend that it be done' (ibid:38).

This report was written some months after Old Joseph died, who on his deathbed charged his son never to relinquish the Wallowa and Grande Valleys. 'Always remember that your father never sold his country' (Brady, 1916:55). As *Hein-mot Too-ya-la-kekt*,[13] better known to the world as Joseph, later commented: 'I buried him in that beautiful valley of winding waters. I love that land more than all the rest of the world' (ibid.).

In 1872, Monteith had also reported that whilst at that time there were no white houses yet built in the Wallowa Valley, some were to be built 'this fall' . . . [Then] the question will have to be settled soon to those Indians living outside the Reserve . . .' (Brown, 1967:38).

In 1877, General Howard's[14] adjutant, Major H. Clay Wood, considered the legality of the 1863 Treaty and concluded: 'In my opinion the non-treaty Nez Perces cannot in law be regarded as bound by the treaty of 1863, and in so far as it attempts to deprive them of a right to occupancy of any land its provisions are null and void. The extinguishment of their title of occupancy contemplated by this treaty is imperfect and incomplete' (ibid:37). Nevertheless, as more whites, believing they were within their rights, moved into the valley, the situation became tense. One historian who considered the status of these incoming settlers was led to the conclusion that a number were 'human parasites of varying degrees of undesirability'; he quotes Major Wood's authoritative study of the Nez Perce problem, who had observed: 'I could fill page after page in portraying the number and nature of outrages the Indians and their families were subject to' (ibid:44-5).

In a final council meeting between Joseph and Howard, a show of military force finally caused capitulations: the Non-Treaty Nez Perce agreed to leave the Wallowa and Grande Ronde Valleys. Howard reported 'We have put all non treaty Indians on reservation by using force and persuasion without bloodshed.'

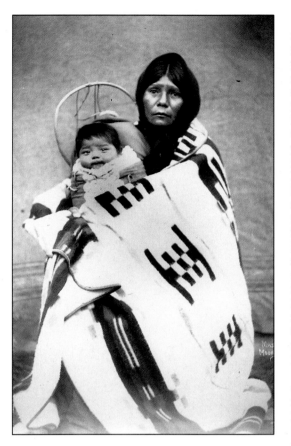

Above: *A Yakima woman and child, c.1900. The baby is in a typical hoop-protected and laced cradle; the woman wears a fine heavily woven blanket, almost certainly a trade item from farther west.*

Below: *Joseph Untush's family on the porch of their home, 1923. Although the time-honored techniques of fruit preservation have changed, traditional styles remain in the woven baskets.*

An unrealistic time limit of thirty days for the move to be completed added to the consternation and deep resentment of the Nez Perce, and young W*ahlitits*, whose father had been murdered by a white man some three years earlier, decided to seek revenge. As one historian put it, 'a taunt about Eagle Robe's death that was the match that lit the fuse' (ibid:65). On Wednesday, 13 June 1877, W*ahlitits* and two young companions killed Richard Devine: the next day they killed Henry J. Elfers, Robert Bland and Harry Becktoge. The trio were joined by seventeen others from White Bird's camp and, plied with stolen liquor, the rampage continued. Detailed analysis clearly demonstrates that the prominent leaders – Joseph, his brother O*llokot*, Looking Glass and T*oo-hool-hool-zote* – had no part in these incidents and that their attempts to deliver the culprits were foiled by unscrupulous volunteers. As Agent Monteith reported to General Howard, 'the fact is there is a certain class here who are afraid there will not be an Indian war' (ibid:66). In less than a week the die was cast and a war with the Non-Treaty Nez Perce was on.

The first major conflict, at White Bird Canyon on 17 June 1877, caused consternation in the ranks of Howard's force under Captain David Perry, when approximately seventy warriors 'quickly and completely routed a column consisting of four officers and ninety-nine men plus ten or eleven armed citizens. Not only did the Indians whip them soundly, but they wiped out one-third of the cavalrymen and chased the remainder for about thirteen miles' and in 'one salutary demonstration, the Nez Perce showed that not only would they fight but that they could fight with the skill, courage and determination that would have been creditable to the best troops in the Army' (ibid:139-40). Sobered

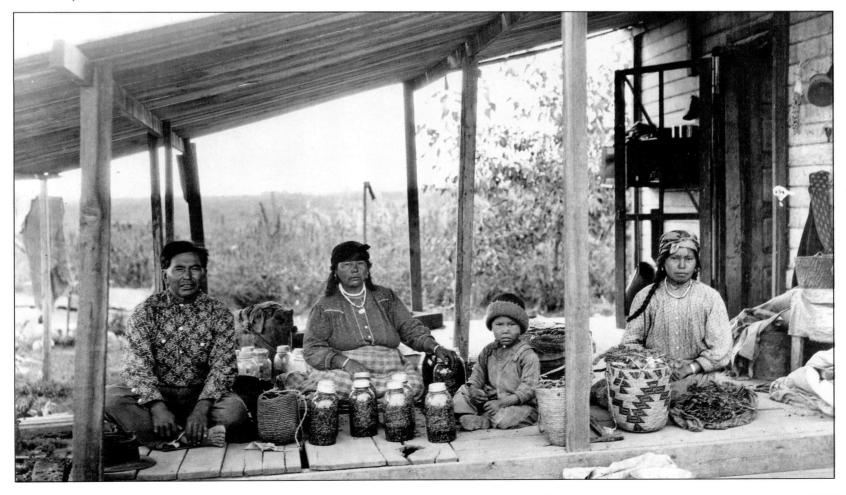

by this defeat, Howard now mustered a more than five hundred strong artillery-supported force. The chase of some two hundred and fifty Nez Perce warriors together with their families numbering about five hundred women and children was on . . . it took nearly four months and seventeen hundred miles across rugged terrain to stop them just forty miles short of their final intended destination, Sitting Bull's camps in Canada. Howard undoubtedly regretted penning the following: 'Other troops are being brought forward as fast as possible . . . [I need] authority for twenty five Indian scouts . . . Think we shall make short work of this', Howard to Division Headquarters 15 June 1877 (ibid:131).

Although supported with these further reinforcements, the Nez Perce again turned the tables on Howard; they encircled the troops and pushed on to the valley of the Clearwater and then dug in for protection. This time, however, on 11 July, assisted by the howitzers, four companies of cavalry, six of infantry and five of artillery acting as infantry, in total some four hundred and forty men exclusive of his staff, Howard, after twenty-four hours of siege, routed the Nez Perce; an enormous amount of property was abandoned and as one elderly Nez Perce woman related, 'many, many, had been wounded'. So harrowing was this attack, and probably anticipating what the future would hold, Joseph was prepared to surrender at this point, but differences of opinion existed in the Nez Perce camp in regard to a Treaty of Peace, with White Bird, Looking Glass and *Too-hool-hool-zote* voting to make for the buffalo country. The precedent of hanging had already been established for leaders who were involved in uprisings and this was a major fear amongst the Nez Perce, thus whilst at the Clearwater they lost so much which was vital to their subsistence, they refused to capitulate and picking up the one hundred and fifty mile long Lolo Trail, they headed through the Bitterroot Mountains toward Montana. Travelling through the Bitterroot Valley, exhausted but

Above: *Looking Glass, a Nez Perce chief, shown in a Crow camp, 1871. Looking Glass and his group of Nez Perce were firm friends of the Mountain Crow. He was killed at the Bear Paw Mountains in 1877.*

still defiant, they camped on the banks of the Big Hole River. There at dawn on 9 August, they were attacked by the two hundred-odd force under Colonel John Gibbon who, under orders from Howard – now lagging sadly behind somewhere on the Lolo Trail – had ridden out from Fort Missoula to head off the fleeing Nez Perce.

The Battle of the Big Hole on 9 August resulted in a terrible massacre of some eighty Nez Perce, fifty of whom were women and chil-

dren: 'Many women and children were killed before getting out of their beds. In one lodge there were five children. One soldier went into it and killed every one of them' (ibid:254). Andrew Garcia later related what his wife – who as a seventeen year old girl was in the Nez Perce camp – told him of her terrible ordeal: 'The bullets came through [my father's] Gray Eagle's lodge like hail and rain, and hit one of Hoot Owl's women in the head, killing her dead, and another bullet hit one of Hoot Owl's sons in the breast, so that he fell down and lay there. With this rain of bullets coming through the tepee and the noise of the soldiers' guns, with the warriors and white men's yells, . . . the scream and shrieks of the squaws and children . . . Then [we] all tried to get out of the tepee at once, . . . but the soldiers were there . . . Hoot Owl and his other woman and two of the small children were shot dead, and [my] father shot in the belly, . . . [my] sister . . . now fell dead with a bullet through her head . . .' *In-who-lise* was struck in the right shoulder and fell down near the creek bank: she recovered with a soldier standing over her and tried to get up by grabbing his leg – the surprised soldier pushed her back with the butt of his gun, hitting her in the mouth injuring her lips and teeth (Garcia, Stein ed., 1977:215).

Although the initial phase of the attack was successful, the tide of battle unexpectedly turned. One scholar of the Nez Perce has dramatically described that moment: 'Soon, at one end of the camp could be heard the voice of White Bird, and at the other, that of Looking Glass. In tones that stood out above the sounds of the fight like the notes of a bugle call, these two chiefs rallied their warriors and turned what had started as a rout into a desperate fight' (Brown, 1967:255). After the Nez Perce managed to regain their camp, Gibbon later recorded: 'Few of us will soon forget the wail of mingled grief, rage, and horror which came from the camp four or five hundred yards from us when the Indians returned to it and recognized their slaughtered warriors, women, and

Links with the Plains: Indian ponies (not Appaloosas)

Cheyenne/Lakota. Horns of prong horned antelope refer to swiftness and survival powers of one of the purest Plains animals

Cheyenne. Dragonfly symbolic of whirlwind and associated with the thunder and rain spirit. Protective

Cheyenne. Pony painted with motifs symbolic of wounds received, point of impact and bleeding emphasized

Blackfeet. Pony with figure of man on chest, symbolizing that a man was ridden down in battle by owner of the horse children' (ibid:258).[15] More than forty women and children and some twenty-six warriors were dead and others would die of their wounds – including *In-who-lise*'s father, Gray Eagle – to be buried on the Trail. But the Nez Perce would not give up, they pushed on for another thousand miles – Camas Meadow on 20 August where *Ollokot* and twenty-seven Nez Perce warriors stalled Howard's men by stampeding his horses and mules . . . 13 September, Canyon Creek, where Nez Perce marksmen stopped four hundred Seventh Cavalry troopers under Colonel Samuel Sturgis whilst the women and children escaped with the horses[16] . . . A respite at Cow Island, 23 September, where a raid on an Army cache, deposited because the Missouri was too low to get it to Fort Benton, provided much needed supplies[17] . . . and finally, 30 September, on to the Bearpaw Mountains, camping on Snake Creek, only forty miles from the Canadian border. With Howard – now dubbed by the Nez Perce as General Day After Tomorrow – and Sturgis judged to be some two or three days march away, the remnants of the Nez Perce clearly considered themselves safe: they were wrong.

On 18 September after receiving a report – which took five days to arrive – from General Howard and Colonel Sturgis that the Nez Perce had 'left them hopelessly in the rear' (ibid:378), Colonel Nelson Miles, together with some three hundred and fifty men, rode from Fort Keogh on the Yellowstone travelling northwest towards the Bearpaw Mountains arriving within a few miles of Snake Creek on 29 September. Early on Sunday 30 September, their movements shielded from the Nez Perce by a blinding snowstorm, they attacked the village; the result was a devastating repulse with some twenty per cent of Miles' force put out of action. As Captain Snyder later recorded: 'Our loss today Capt Hale & Lt Biddle & 23 enld [en-

Below: *This horse was traditionally associated with the Nez Perce, but it is possible that the name actually derives from Palus, a closely associated tribe also known for their horsebreeding skills. The characteristics of this animal were the distinctive speckled markings, together with great endurance and surefootedness; on average they were larger and heavier than the typical Indian pony.*

The Appaloosa

Keyhole shaped rawhide pendant symbolic of Morning Star. (Typical of regalia used by Crow women.)

Crow bridle, with Spanish bit and rawhide headstall, beaded and painted

Nez Perce cornhusk bag

Saddle: wooden framework covered with rawhide, with high pommel and cantle, both covered with soft buckskin with hide and cloth pendants embellished with beadwork in typical Crow patterns

Reins of partly braided, pliable rawhide

Crow horse collar, buckskin and red trade cloth embellished with beads

Blackfeet. Painted with symbols of former battles to arouse courage and enthusiasm for war

Wooden handled quirt

Stirrups shaped by heating then covered with rawhide. Spanish inspired

Nez Perce

Cornhusk bags are a well-known specialty of the Nez Perce. These are flat, flexible wallets made by twining without any loom or frame. The foundation warps and wefts are cords of Indian hemp bast or, less good, elderberry, willow, or other bark, twisted by rubbing across the thigh. The decoration is applied by false embroidery: as part of the weaving process a strand is wrapped around the weft each time it passes in front of the warp. The outside surface is completely covered, while the inside shows only loose ends of the false-embroidery cords. These decorative cords were originally of beargrass or ryegrass, but with the introduction of corn in the late nineteenth century the grasses were replaced by cords twisted from the pliable, slick inner parts of cornhusks. Colored designs were made by dyeing some of the false-embroidery cords with colors from minerals, barks, grasses, berries, green algae, or other natural materials. The designs are made up of geometric elements repeated in rows and columns in an all-over pattern, normally entirely different on the two sides of a bag (see No. 20 below). The designs have no meanings or significance, and the very varied patterns are only for esthetic effect. The bags were used to store and carry roots, berries and household items. They have been an important Nez Perce trade and export product at least since Lewis and Clark mentioned them in 1805. The designs on cornhusk bags are quite different from those painted on parfleches, which were formerly made of buffalo hide and used especially to store meat. These distensible containers were widely used by Plains tribes and in the eastern Plateau and Basin. Before Nez Perce weddings the groom's family might give parfleches filled with blankets, shawls, and calico to the bride's family, who reciprocated with the same number of cornhusk bags filled with dried roots. These artifacts are a small sample of those collected by Livingston Farrand on the Nez Perce Reservation in Idaho, 1902.

1–5 Cornhusk bags.
6 One of a pair of woman's leggings, of Cheyenne origin.
7–9 Cornhusk bags.
10–12 Parfleches – folded rawhide cases with painted geometric designs.
13–14 Cornhusk bags.
15 Parfleche.
16 Parfleche.
17 Comb.
18–24 Cornhusk bags.
25 Flat leather bag with beaded design like the parfleche designs.

listed] men killed and 4 Officers & 40 men wounded. Indians still hold their position' (ibid:389).

But one major objective had been achieved in that attack – the majority of the Nez Perce horse-herd was captured.

The next day, 1 October, under a flag of truce, Joseph attempted negotiations with General Miles; by now many of his relatives, friends and council members were dead or lost, including both Looking Glass and Joseph's brother, *Ollokot*, who had been killed the previous day. This left only the defiant White Bird and Joseph as the key leaders. Joseph stayed in Miles' camp overnight, the Nez Perce held Lt Jerome as a hostage; the next day, each man returned to his own camp, a stalemate had been reached.

According to one contemporary observer – Lieutenant Charles Erskine Scott Wood, Howard's acting aide-de-camp – the Nez Perce had literally honeycombed a portion of the site of their camp, and other transverse gulches, with subterranean dwelling places and communicating tunnels.[18] In addition, they were using their dead horses as fortifications as well as a source of food: 'Here they held their own, refusing all offers of surrender, and saying in effect: If you want us, come and take us' (Wood, 1884:141).

With the loss of most of the horse-herd, however, the possibility of yet another flight towards the Canadian border and freedom was out of the question.[19] Winter was now setting in and the freezing weather with rain and snow caused suffering on both sides. Howard and a small escort arrived on the evening of Thursday 4 October and the next day the terms of surrender were agreed, a message being conveyed by two Treaty Nez Perce who had daughters in Joseph's camp. There was little room for maneuver, Howard pointing out that his whole command was only two or three days behind him. This force, together with that of Miles', would have thus combined to a total of at least six hundred fighting men – to be arrayed against no more than one hundred able Nez Perce warriors, who had the added responsibility of protecting the women and children.[20] Promises were made of good treatment and Joseph asked if his people would be allowed to return to Idaho. 'He was told that he would, unless *higher authority* ordered otherwise'[21] (ibid). Joseph's final answer summed up the desperate experiences and now the plight of the remnant Nez Perce, its poignancy, eloquence and dignity being a remarkable tribute for all time to the people that he represented, for it was the end of an era:

'Tell General Howard I know his heart. What he told me before – I have it in my heart. I am tired of fighting. Our chiefs are killed. Looking-glass is dead. *Too-hul-hulsuit* is dead. The old men are all dead. It is the young men, now, who say 'yes' or 'no' [that is, vote in council]. He who led on the young men [Joseph's brother, *Ollicut*] is dead. It is cold, and we have no blankets. The little children are freezing to death. My people – some of them – have run away to the hills and have no blankets, no food. I want to have time to look for my children, and to see how many of them I can find; may be I shall find them among the dead. Hear me, my chiefs; my heart is sick and sad. From where the sun *now* stands, I will fight no more forever!'

(ibid)

The Nez Perce 'are among the most amiable men we have seen. Their character is placid and gentle, rarely moved to passion' . . . 'the Shoshonees are not only cheerful but even gay; . . .in their intercourse with strangers they are frank and communicative, in their dealings perfectly fair, . . . [nothing] has tempted them into a single act of dishonesty'.[22]

Left: *A Nez Perce boy called by the whites Joseph Ratunda, c.1900. His otter skin breastplate, hair roach and beaded moccasins show a strong Plains influence. Floral beadwork is typical Nez Perce.*

Below: *Hein-mot Too-ya-la-kekt, better known to history as Chief Joseph of the Nez Perce, 1901. The mottled feather in his hair is from the tail of a maturing golden eagle.*

Nez Perce Warrior, 1877

A Nez Perce warrior at the opening of the Nez Perce War that ended when the U.S. Army defeated the epic retreat toward the Canadian border led by Chief Joseph. The head-dress is of fur, ermine tails, and trimmed buffalo horns. The war shirt, sent to the Smithsonian in 1876, is of leather trimmed with yellow and red cloth, bands of porcupine quill-work and beads, horsehair tassels, and fur around the bottom. Used in the Nez Perce War were the buffalo horn cup once owned by Husis Owyeen, the bone war whistle owned by Peopeo Tholekt, and the Winchester carbine, Model 1866. The beaded moccasins came to the Smithsonian in 1876. A fine bow of mountain sheep horn (a Nez Perce specialty) is carried in a bow case attached to a quiver – an arrangement adopted from the Crow.

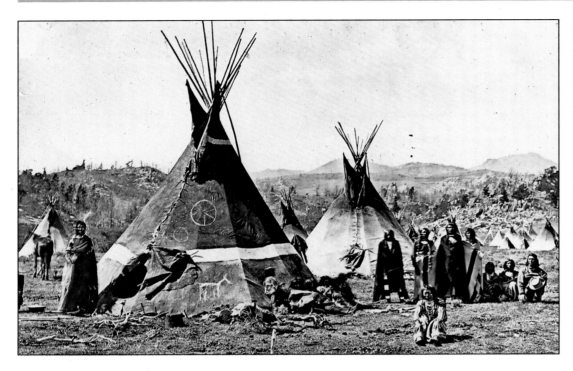

central and western Basin area. Here the environment varied from salt marshland to alpine herbland and the individual camp sites from large and well ventilated caves to small and open camps. Of particular interest is that more than eighty per cent of these sites were located between an elevation of about 5250 to 7550ft (1600-2300m.), only eleven per cent were located below 5250ft; for obvious reasons, the indigenous population generally avoided open desert with its lack of protective cover, intense heat and high aridity. Above 7550ft (2300m.) game was often unpredictable and limited, and winters severe. Clearly, the Basin people managed successfully to strike a balance between these environmental extremes.

Unlike the Plateau to the north where natural resources were generally predictable and abundant, leading to a subsistence economy which pivoted on intertribal trade, that of the Basin was largely characterized by a people whose lifestyle has led them to be described as 'superb resource generalists' (Harper, 1986:51). Roots and seeds were a major food resource;

Although there is no abrupt natural barrier change as one moves south from the Plateau to the Great Basin region, the declining influence of the two great rivers, the Columbia and Fraser, upon which so much of Plateau culture depended, becomes increasingly apparent. Lying as it does between the Rocky Mountains to the east and the Sierra Nevadas to the west, with only limited and widely varying precipitation – particularly to the west and south – the Great Basin with no rivers draining to the sea, includes the southern parts of Oregon and Idaho, all of Nevada and Utah, and the western halves of Wyoming and Colorado. It is a region characterized by mountains which tower above the flatlands, but the terrain varies markedly. In the central and southeast areas of this region, where the Colorado River has carved immense canyons whose towering walls exhibit richly coloured sedimentations, saltbush and sagebrush deserts dominate, whilst to the north and east in areas which are drained by the Snake and Green rivers, there are wide sweeping grasslands of varying composition and, at higher elevations, scattered open forests of conifers and alpine type herbland.

In this vast, diverse area covering some quarter of a million square miles, lived a predominantly Shoshonean-speaking people[23] whose territory once also extended to the Northern Plains and south almost into Mexico. In the northeast – at times overlapping with the Plateau Nez Perce and Flathead – were the Shoshoni and Bannock, to their west the Paviotso or Northern Paiute, whilst to the south of these tribes were the Western Shoshoni, Paiute and Ute. Unlike the Plateau people there was a great difference between the lifestyles of these various tribes, particularly after the acquisition of the horse by the more eastern Shoshoni and Ute, the latter using packhorses, although apparently not yet riding them, as early as 1650.

Recent archeological analysis of ancient camp sites in the more northern parts of the Great Basin – in the vicinity and to the west of the Great Salt Lake in Utah – gives some important insights into early Indian lifestyles, which are probably typical for much of the

Above: *The Shoshoni chief Washakie's lodge and encampment, Wind River Mountains, Wyoming, 1870. Note the wooden pins lacing up the cover at the front and pictographic symbols on his lodge.*

Below: *Interior of a Shoshoni lodge, 1878. The standing woman wears a striped Witney 'point' blanket. The baby is in a typical Shoshoni cradle; fine beaded saddle bags hang behind the figures.*

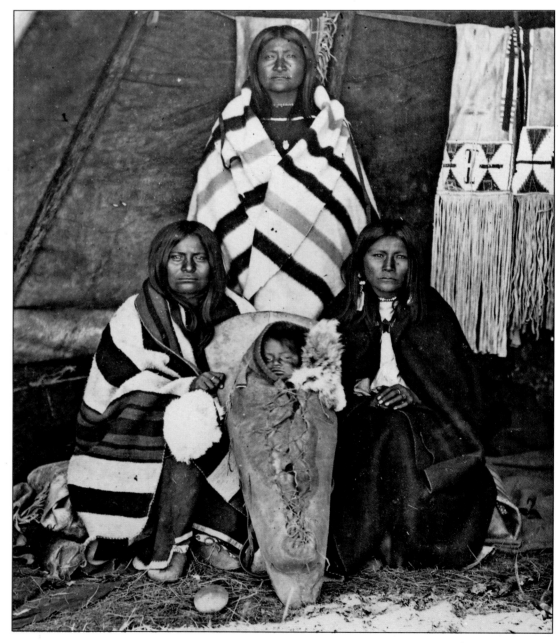

however, the prong-horned antelope was to be found scattered throughout the region and these, together with the more abundant jack-rabbit, were an important food resource, the annual family gatherings in the autumn enabling these animals to be captured by use of communal drives. In the east, the Northern Shoshoni and Bannock had the luxury of buffalo which, prior to c.1840, were to be found west of the continental divide. After this date, bereft of this resource locally, it was necessary for these tribes to travel annually to the Plains region – a hazardous venture in territory of gun-armed tribes – or accept the harsher alternatives of the more Central and Western Great Basin environment, where brush wickiups replaced the comfortable hide tipi for shelter, and a largely foraging economy that of hunting.

These central and western Shoshonean groups – largely occupying what is now Utah and Nevada – were, particularly in the mid-nineteenth century when first described by whites, referred to as 'Digger Indians', a derogatory term, drawing attention to their extensive

use of a pointed stick which was used to pry roots and wild vegetables from the ground. These people, variously designated as Gosiutes, Northern Paiute, Panamint, Kawaiisu, Chemehuevi (Southern Paiute) and Weber Utes[24] were loosely grouped according to the major type of food utilized, such as sunflower seed, root, pine nut, squirrel, sheep and even earth or dust eaters. A remarkably adaptable and practical people, they represented a culture sustained in the arid regions of the Great Basin for thousands of years, largely shut away from the outside world and little influenced by the Plateau or Plains people to the north and east. In order to survive, they utilized an immense range of plant and animal resources, some of the major root crops being camas, bitterroot, caraway, onion and Indian potato. Salad plants were miner's lettuce, sweet cicely, violets and certain brackens. Fruit, seed and nut crops which occurred in the foothill and riparian zones, were chokecherries, currants, oregon grapes, blue elderberries, amaranths, chenopods, sunflowers, acorns and pine nuts, the latter generally referred to as *piñon*, being amongst the most important for a large part of the region and a focus of great activity by groups in late summer and early autumn, particularly in the Central Great Basin.

Below: *The exterior of a Paiute rush covered dwelling, probably for winter use, c.1900. Note the cradle with the broad covering shade. The parallel lines on the band suggest a male child.*

Above: *Paiute couple, date not recorded but probably before 1880. The man wears a buckskin shirt with decorative shoulder flaps, the woman a trade cloth dress with a heavily beaded belt.*

Northern Paiute

Speakers of the Northern Paiute language once occupied some 70,000 square miles in Nevada and southeastern Oregon, as small semi-nomadic bands, not a unified tribe. The principal game animals were deer and mountain sheep. Small game also included hares, rabbits, marmots, and porcupines. Bird hunting was important, and special decoys were used to attract ducks to the hunter. In some areas fish were a major resource. Everywhere wild plants were basic – some 150 species were used. Piñon nuts were collected and processed with baskets, while special beaters were used to knock some kinds of seeds into a tray or conical basket. Seeds were usually cooked as a mush boiled with hot stones dropped into a basketry container. The reservation period for the Northern Paiutes began in the 1870s, but many people refused to move to the two or three areas set aside for them, and smaller reservations and colonies were established later. The Fallon and Pyramid Lake reservations are among those within the former N. Paiute territory. The government encouraged farming on the reservations, but with little success: the soils were unsuitable and water was lacking, especially when non-Indians began to divert streams. When the items shown here were collected by Robert H. Lowie in 1914/1915 many of the collecting and processing techniques and implements for seeds were still in use, although a decade later they were rare. In 1914 the only type of aboriginal clothing still in use was a basket hat for women.

1 Cradleboard of twined basketry with buckskin cover. Pyramid Lake Res.

2 Infant's cradle of twined willow rods. Fallon Res.

3, 4 Decoys for hunting ducks; duckskins over tule foundations. Pyramid Lake Res.

5 Twined basketry water jug, waterproofed with piñon pitch. Pyramid Lake Res.

6 Woman's dress, blue cotton printed cloth (model). S. Paiute, Moapa River Res., collected 1915.

7 Willow splints for making baskets. Pyramid Lake Res.

8 Twined basketry seed beater. Fallon Res.

9 Bent rod mush stirrer. Pyramid Lake Res.

10 Stone tobacco pipe smoked with straight wooden stem. Fallon Res.

11 Cane fire drill with sage wood hearth (model). Fallon Res.

12 Woman's dress of printed cotton cloth (model). S. Paiute, Shivwits Res., Utah, collected 1915.

13 Twined openwork basket for berries and nuts. Pyramid Lake Res.

14 Twined conical harvesting basket. Pyramid Lake Res.

15 Pair of men's sandals of twined tule (models). Fallon Res.

16 Man's cloth shirt (model). S. Paiute, Moapa River Res., collected 1915.

17 Two plain and two wrapped bone implements for team guessing game. Pyramid Lake Res.

18 Set of stick dice. Fallon Res.

The complex subsistence technology, developed in order to render the *piñon* crop both edible and suitable for storage, commenced with the collecting of the green cones with the aid of harvesting poles, which were then transported in large conical shaped woven baskets[25] for pit roasting which caused them to open; now piled up, the cones were beaten, or individual cones tapped, to release the seeds which were then lightly parched in a tray making the shells brittle – a combined flat metate and huller, together with winnowing, finally separated the seed and husk. The seeds were then given a final parching in trays: they could now be used in this raw state or ground into a meal from which a gruel was prepared. Alternatively, the meal was moulded into cakes which were then dried in the sun and in this form they were stored in lined ground pits for winter use, a vital step for survival given the unpredictable nature of the Great Basin, since studies have shown that 'good nut years are irregular: no definite cycle exists' (ibid:59). The Great Basin people, however, held the belief that a bumper crop occurred every seven years and in this respect they were correct, since it has been recently recognized that even in a single valley, local environmental factors were such that synchrony of production from one grove to another never occurred. The *piñon* subsistence complex also involved ceremonialism – prayers before the season, dances at the harvesting and special prayers of thanksgiving over the first seeds. Ceremonials of this sort are still (even in the late twentieth century) practiced, remaining 'as one of the key features of Native identity' (Fowler, 1986:65).

In addition to the communal antelope and rabbit hunts, there are descriptions of grasshopper drives. The first priest to visit the Western Shoshoni in the mid-nineteenth century, Pierre Jean De Smet, refers to an area which swarmed with grasshoppers and was often visited by the local Indians (probably the Gosiutes who lived some one hundred miles to the west of the Great Salt Lake). He relates a fascinating firsthand description: 'They begin by digging a hole, ten or twelve feet in diameter by four or five feet deep; then, armed with long branches . . . they surround a field of four or five acres, more or less, according to the number of persons who are engaged in it. They stand

Below: Wovoka, known by the whites as Jack Wilson, c.1895. Called the Paiute Messiah, he initiated the doctrine of the Ghost Dance: 'You must not fight . . . Do no harm to anyone . . . Do right always.'

Above: *Paiute women in close woven basketry hats gathering seed, Kaibab Plateau, c.1873. They bear large burden baskets and the close twill twined trays of the type used for winnowing pine nuts.*

Below: *Three Paiute women in traditional summer dress, wearing finely woven basketry skull caps and heavily buckskin fringed skirts. The woman at right appears to have a fur cape of rabbit skin.*

about twenty feet apart, and their whole work is to beat the ground so as to frighten up the grasshoppers and make them bound forward. They chase them toward the center by degrees – that is, into the hole prepared for their reception. Their number is so considerable that frequently three or four acres furnish grasshoppers sufficient to fill the reservoir or hole' (De Smet, Chittenden and Richardson eds, 1905, vol. III:1033).

The Gosiutes preserved some of these grasshoppers for future use by crushing them into a paste which they then dried; for more immediate needs they were either made into a soup or the largest selected for roasting at the campfire. In later years, white settlers would view the presence of such myriads of grasshoppers as bordering a plague, but to the indigenous population they were clearly seen as another natural subsistence resource, quite in keeping with the unstated but widely practiced ethos which characterized the Great Basin area – if it moves it can probably be eaten! There was, however, in all this an element of conservation and environmental manipulation; widespread, for example, was the avoidance of killing female animals during the gestation and rearing seasons and the Northern Paiute and Northern Shoshoni speared only male trout or salmon on the spawning beds or runs. Complex fish weirs were used to control migrating fish; the Washoe of the Pyramid Lake region cut the upper branches of browse plants to encourage deer herds to remain in the vicinity during the winter months and, at times, antelope were kept penned and killed as needed whilst some plant life was improved and conserved by selective harvesting and pruning.

The scarcity and unpredictable nature of food resources in the Great Basin region led to the development of a World View which put emphasis on respect for plants and animals so vital for survival in an often hostile environment. In the gathering of plants, for example, prayers were offered to the plant spirits and the Northern Paiute commonly buried a small stone or bead in the hole left vacant by a lifted root, whilst slain animals were often placed with their heads facing east or body parts, such as the eyes, glands and gall bladders, laid out or buried. Special terminology which may be used in an accompanying address reflected the respect shown for the animal and at the same time it was an appeal to the spirit powers that the food resource would be sustained. The power to cure disease frequently derived from the animal spirits, whilst more than three hundred plant species, burnt, crushed and powdered, were used medicinally. Great Basin mythology was also replete in references to plants and animals, the latter's adventures and misadventures explaining such things as the creating of the earth and its people, the formation of the seasons, food taboos and the establishment of social behaviour. Of particular interest, as recently pointed out by one anthropologist who has studied Great Basin culture in depth, is the naming of constellations after animals and associating these in turn with 'tales of their adventures and misadventures in the sky' (Fowler, 1986:96).

The Great Basin religion put strong emphasis on immortality. After death, the Western Shoshoni said the human spirit went to the land of the Coyote, who together with Wolf his

Below: A group of Washoes, members of a small tribe living around Lake Tahoe and speaking a language unrelated to others. These people wear Euro-American clothing but traditional hairstyles.

brother, had created the world; not until Wolf had revived and washed the spirit was its place correctly established. So strong was the belief in immortality that on occasions sutteeism was practiced; one 1861 eyewitness account refers to the killing of a Shoshoni woman in Carson Valley, Nevada, so that her spirit could accompany that of her husband to the land of the Coyote. Death and regeneration was a recurring theme in Great Basin religion. The anthropologist, Robert H. Lowie, for example, recorded the dream experiences of a Northern Shoshoni '... my body dropped, cold and dead. I looked at it for some time; it made no movement at all ... The Sun told me I would be restored to life ... I don't know how I returned. Suddenly I was back alive ... On another occasion, I went up to the clouds. The people I met there were nothing but skeletons ...' (Lowie, 1909:233). Another student of the Shoshoni reports that the predominate way supernatural messages were received was through 'unsought dreams' (Hultkrantz, 1986:44) and in this respect the experiences of the Paiute holy man, Tavibo, and later his son Wovoka, fit the Great Basin shamanistic pattern, but modified by Christian teachings.

The great communal drives for the antelope and jack-rabbit were also invariably associated with religious ceremony. Certain men were credited with the power to lure the game, their dance being accompanied by ritual and song: restrictions were associated with such rituals, for example, amongst the Paiute, women were excluded as were menstruating women amongst the Western Shoshoni, the belief being that the calling powers would thus be weakened.

The jack-rabbit was a source of both food and clothing to these interior Basin people and fine

Above: *Ute men, women and children, most in dance costume, c.1900. Dentalium shell ornaments, bone hair breastplates, beaded leggings and moccasins and roach-style headdresses are all in evidence.*

Below: *A Southern Paiute (Chemehuevi) woman weaving a basket. This tribe excelled at basketry, producing conical burden baskets and close coiled and twilled trays for sifting and winnowing.*

garments for winter use were fabricated from strips of the skins; but they were expensive, up to forty skins being required for a single robe. It was thus a garment owned only by the most prestigious and the majority sufficed with a few skins wrapping the feet and legs as protection against the harsh terrain. In summer, the men wore only a breechcloth and the women a double layered skirt woven from a fiber derived from sagebrush.

Except for the annual get-togethers, the majority of the year was spent by small family groups ranging tribal territory, and in addition to root and vegetable gathering, they snared and netted small animals, birds and fish. During spring and summer, housing consisted of temporary shelters or windbreaks made of reed mats and branches. A common form of pottery was a flat bottomed cylindrical shaped vessel with holes in the rim for suspension[26] and this, together with matting, stone metates, digging stick, twined and coiled basketry and open hooded baby carriers, made up the typical family household utensils. In winter, shelters were more substantial, some being subterranean with an opening through the mound-like roof which served as both door and smokehole; clusters of such habitations, when viewed at a distance, have been described as resembling a prairie dog town.

Such was the lifestyle which epitomized Great Basin culture: unchanged for thousands of years, a constant search for food and reduction of essentials to the minimum – an environment where survival of the fittest had a very real meaning.

Not all of this region, however, was so harsh and unremitting. To the east and north, as has already been described, the terrain changed and whilst in common with the Northern Paiute (Paviotso), Paiute, Washoe and Western Shoshoni there was still considerable depen-

Southern Paiute Elder, 1872

When Maj. J.W. Powell and his photographer John K. Hillers visited the Southern Paiute in 1872 and 1873 they saw a Kaibab Southern Paiute man sharpening a hafted chipped-stone knife while seated like this in front of a winter house with a pole foundation covered with grass, brush, and rushes. The girl behind him wears a beautifully tailored Plains-style buckskin dress made of two fawn skins and two separate pieces sewn into a yoke, which has a blue and white beaded design with two rows of perforated elk teeth below. The man wears hard-soled moccasins and fringed leggings with a painted design. The buckskin cap, tied underneath his chin, has hawk feathers attached. Powell brought garments very like these back to Washington for the Smithsonian collections.

125

dence on a foraging existence; the lifestyle of the Northern and Eastern Shoshoni, together with that of the Ute who between them ranged southern Idaho, western Wyoming, eastern Nevada and much of Colorado, differed to a marked degree, with a shift from bare essentials and now enhanced by intertribal trade which included Plains as well as Plateau tribes, access to buffalo country, a more complex social organization and ceremonial warfare and, from the early seventeenth century, contact with the Spanish Southwest which brought the greatest luxury of all – the horse.

The establishment of Spanish rule by Juan de Oñate in New Mexico in the period 1597-1610 led to the importation of several hundred horses to the region, within comparatively easy reach of Ute bands, particularly those in the vicinity of the San Juan river in present-day southern Utah and Colorado. These people soon acquired a knowledge of the horse and by the mid-seventeenth century used them, together with the dog, as pack animals. Ute tribal territory took in the majority of the Colorado Plateau which differed sharply from the interior Great Basin further west, having high average rainfall, giving well-watered valleys and grasslands; it was ideal pasture land for the horse and a resource rapidly exploited by the ped-

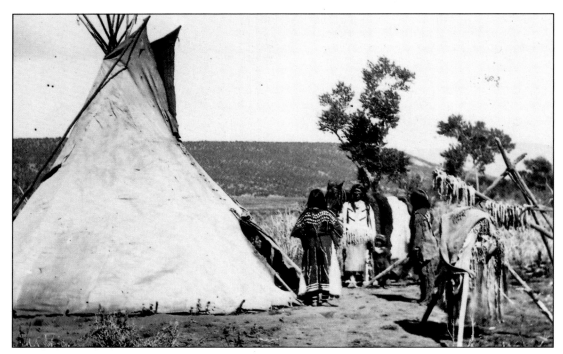

Below: A Ute warrior described as 'The messenger in full dress', c.1873. The broad bow is typical of the tribe, also the heavily fringed buckskin shirt and leggings. Note his beaded hair braids.

Above: A Ute camp on the eastern slope of the Wasatch Mountains, Utah, c.1873. The tipi was made of elk skin. At right are two conical pole frames and a sloping pole, supporting possessions and dried meat.

estrian Ute. The Pueblo revolt in 1680 and the establishment of missions by Father Eusebio Kino in Central Arizona amongst the Pima and Papago led to a further source of horses – acquired by both theft and trade – and by 1730 the horse had reached the Northern Shoshoni, who, rapidly adapting to an equestrian lifestyle, expanded their territory deep into the buffalo country of the Northern Plains and at least as far as the Belly River[27] in southern Saskatchewan. One group split off from the Eastern Shoshoni probably to be nearer the southern source of horses. Here, armed also with guns which they obtained from the French, they claimed the country from the Platte to New Mexico driving the Apaches south and, turning on their former allies the Utes, by 1755 had crossed the Arkansas. With both gun and horse they, together with the Kiowas, dominated the Southern Plains for more than a century; history knows them as the Comanches,[28] a Spanish rendering of a Ute word, *Cumanche*, 'enemies'. The Comanche never, however, completely severed their former Great Basin links and continued to visit back and forth, and some bands such as the Yamparika Comanche still had a taste for root vegetables, partially clinging to a Shoshoni foraging subsistence, but predominately now buffalo meat eaters, living in tipis – dashing and free.

By contrast, Shoshoni equestrian life on the Northern Plains was less successful. Archeological evidence suggests that as pedestrian hunters they at least made extensive excursions into Plains country 'before the birth of Christ' (Hultkrantz, 1968:59), and it was thus territory familiar to them; but the moving frontier of the horse from the west virtually coincided with that of the gun from the east and this, together with the devastating smallpox epidemic of 1781, gave the Shoshoni but transient equestrian residency. In less than a generation, under pressure from the well-armed Piegan who spearheaded Blackfeet[29] dominance of the Canadian Plains, the Shoshoni progressively retreated to the safety of the Rocky Mountains. For all their outward appearance, however, these Eastern Shoshoni retained much of their Great Basin culture – mythology, religion, forager economy, social organization and a widely intelligible language – and although it has been rigorously debated[30] there is much in one contemporary observation which attempted to distinguish between the Eastern and Western Shoshoneans: thus, when the former 'acquired a horse . . . he (became) a Shoshoni; if he found himself deprived of it, he was once again a Shoshoko (Walker or Digger)' (Trenholm and Carley, 1964:4).

Ironically, in just less than a century after the Shoshonean retreat from the Plains, it was to be reverberations from their peaceful Shoshoko kinsmen which led to the final collapse of the warlike spirit – epitomized by the Lakota – of the historic Plains Indian.

On New Year's Day 1889, during an eclipse of the sun, Wovoka, a Paiute holy man, ill with a high fever, had a vision; later, he related that

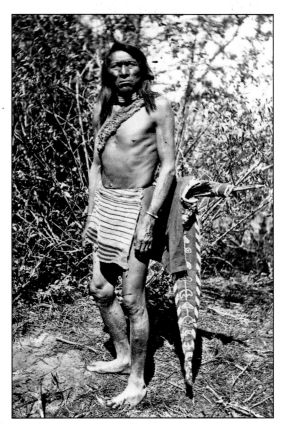

Right: A Ute warrior, Utah, c.1873. The otter skin band across the shoulder supports a combined bow case and quiver which has a long pointed drop heavily embellished with beadwork.

'When the sun died' he was taken up to heaven and saw God and all the people who had died a long time ago. Wovoka claimed that he was told by God that he must go back to earth and preach goodness, industry and peace to the Indians. If they followed his instructions they would be reunited with their relatives and friends who had died. A new world would be created where there would be no more death, sickness or old age (see Mooney,1896).

Much of Wovoka's experience reflected the Great Basin shamanistic pattern outlined earlier. It was, however, somewhat modified by Christian doctrine.

An important phase of the new faith was a dance for the Indians. It came to be known as the Spirit or Ghost dance, spreading to the Great Plains where each tribe put their own interpretation on Wovoka's teachings (see also Plains chapter, pp.98–9). In the case of the warlike and independent Lakota, it precipitated the tragedy of Wounded Knee and the death of Sitting Bull, both in 1890 – and inscribed forever in the annals of American Indian history the name of a gentle, Great Basin Paiute, whose vision reflected an immense and widespread yearning for a past life which was now rapidly disintegrating under the impact of the European-American.

References

1 This was some seventy-five miles southeast of a now particularly famous landmark – Mount St Helen's, Washington.
2 Mylie Lawyer, an elderly Nez Perce, direct descendant of Chief Lawyer and residing at Lapwai, said that during the Nez Perce wars of 1877 the makeshift shelters were of a single lean-to type (M.L. to C.T., 1969).
3 In present-day northeast Oregon.
4 (i) Teit reports that the Crows obtained these from the Sioux to trade to the Plateau people.
(ii) Mylie Lawyer had many items of Sioux make which were family heirlooms.
5 Spalding estimated that the dresses would sell for '$50 or $60 a piece' in the 'southern states'.
6 These milk teeth were highly prized by the Crow who used them to decorate their women's dresses: because of their rarity, imitation ones were made of bone.
7 More recently made bags are generally false embroidered with corn husk (hence the modern term 'corn husk bags'), colored with either soft toned native or the brighter (trade) aniline dyes and perhaps the addition of colored yarn. The end-product is, however, still highly attractive and the process is a time-consuming exercise. At Lapwai in 1969, Ida Blackeagle's daughter, Josephine, showed me a partially completed corn husk wallet. It measured about 7in. (18cm.) wide and she said that it took her mother 'about one hour' to do a one inch full width section. Such bags were not infrequently exchanged with the Crows for the rawhide parfleche.
8 Wissler, 1910:17, and Teit, Boas ed.,1930:304-5.
9 These tribal domains appear to have been established over a period of several thousand years. Unlike the Plains Indians, the Plateau people have no legends of ever living anywhere else.
10 An ancient Indian route across the Continental Divide from Idaho into Montana.
11 Mylie Lawyer reiterated this fact. The missionary/ school teacher, Kate McBeth, was said to have had an enormous bonfire (c.1875-6) to destroy 'leather materials'.
12 Lewis and Clark were very well received by the Nez Perce band led by Twisted Hair which formed the basis of particularly friendly relations between the Nez Perce and Americans in the years to come. Of interest is the fact that the explorers left American

flags at various places and sent one to Twisted Hair as a token of friendship (Lewis and Clark, Coues ed., 1893, vol.II:610). Research specifically on Nez Perce material culture in 1969 suggested that there was some preference by this tribe for the use of both stripes and stars in their 'decorative' work on such items as bags, shirts, women's dresses and horse equipment. The Nez Perce were greatly influenced by the flag design and incorporated it in their artwork as a mark of esteem to the explorers. At Yakima, the trader and collector Roger Ernesti showed me an unusual Nez Perce shirt which emphasized the star symbol. It had fringes of blue trade cloth, the white selvedge edge of each fringe being cut into a V shape. When the shirt was shaken, it gave the appearance of dancing stars.
13 Thunder Travelling to Loftier (Mountain) Heights.
14 Brig. General Oliver O. Howard, who was assigned to the northwestern command in 1876, was sometimes referred to as the Christian General (it was maintained by his men that he hated fighting on Sundays). Howard, who had distinguished himself in both the Civil War and on a mission to Cochise in 1872, was a man of strong humanitarian principles and largely in sympathy with the Non-Treaty Nez Perce.
15 Two years later, Garcia and In-who-lise returned to the Big Hole Battlefield – a site now scattered with human remains. They finally located the disturbed grave of Gray Eagle and reburied his bones. More than fifty years later, in 1930, Garcia returned to the site and found the lance head which he and In-who-lise had agreed to leave intact as a tribute to its former owner (Garcia, Stein ed., 1799:270).
16 Nez Perce sharpshooting was both effective and selective; cornered at the Clearwater, the elderly Otstotpoo advised not to bother with the common soldier, suggesting instead 'Shoot the commander!' (McWhorter, 1940:70). It was a technique employed time and again with great effect throughout the four month retreat.
17 This area is still remote and difficult for access. A visit by the writer to the Cow Island site in the summer of 1986 gave an opportunity to examine the deep rifle pits which are still to be found, dug during the Nez Perce–Seventh Infantry contingent skirmishes (under First Sergeant William Moelchert) on the night of 23 September 1877.
18 Some twenty years ago, it was still quite easy to

locate remnants of these fortifications and also the rectangular hospital area where the troops were buried. One surprising fact was the obvious close proximity of troops and Indians, perhaps no more than six hundred meters separated them.
19 Howard's mandate from General Sherman was a carte blanche to follow the Nez Perce wherever they went but not into Canada.
20 One of these children was Josiah Red Wolf (Heemeen Ilp Ilp), a boy of five at the time of the retreat. In 1969, I visited this ninety-seven-year-old veteran at the Sommerville Rest Home near Lapwai, Idaho (courtesy of Marcus Ware of Lewiston). Red Wolf was then the sole survivor of the 1877 war: it was a sobering and privileged experience to be in the company of a man associated with an historic event which took place almost a century earlier.
21 The emphasis is mine since this was a significant statement. Although it is clear that the officers of the day – Howard and Miles – made this promise in good faith, the complexities of politics prevented its implementation. After several years' exile in Indian Territory, Kansas, Joseph, together with some one hundred and fifty Nez Perce, were settled on a Reservation in Washington – some three hundred miles north of his beloved Wallowa Valley. He was granted but one visit to his father's grave in the summer of 1900 and died in Nespelem four years later – it is said, of a broken heart.
22 Lewis and Clark, Coues ed., 1893: 1017 and 556.
23 It should be noted that both the Shoshoni and Bannock languages belong to the Numic branch of the larger Uto-Aztecan linguistic stock.
24 Some of the designations were localized, for example, Brigham Young's term for the Weber Utes was Cumumbahs.
25 The Great Basin people excelled at basket-making; some were rendered waterproof and could be utilized for stone-boiling meat or vegetables.
26 A very widespread style which was used throughout the Great Basin and reached both the Plateau and Plains regions.
27 A Blackfeet term for the South Saskatchewan River just to the west of present-day Regina.
28 The Central Numic dialect spoken by the Northern Shoshoni is comprehensible to the Comanche.
29 The Blackfeet Confederacy consisted of the Siksika, Blood and Piegan.
30 See, for example, Hultkrantz (1968).

'For an unknown age before the white man first stumbled upon them in the sixteenth century, the Indians of California had dwelt in scattered bands, walled off from the rest of the aboriginal world by mountains and deserts.'

CALIFORNIA

FROM THE sub-sea level sands of Death Valley, the continent's lowest point, to the peaks of the Sierras, where Mount Whitney rises as the highest point of the lower forty-eight states, California is a land of contrasts. Its nearly 1,200 miles of coastline makes such a dramatic swing that Eureka, to the north, is the nation's most westward city outside of Alaska and Hawaii. Yet, San Diego, at the southern end of the state, is farther east than Reno, Nevada. This is the face of the present day California. Although modern names have been applied to the towns, rivers and regions of what was formerly aboriginal territory, the following paragraphs clearly emphasize the richness and variety of the land and why it was held in such esteem by the Indians of California.

Over millions of years, subterranean plates, volcanoes, glaciers, wind, and water have shaped the countryside that helped form such features as the great Valley, perhaps California's main topographic element. The Siskiyou Mountains are now a northern barrier that serves as a border between the Golden State and Oregon in an area where timber abounds, particularly in the northwest. Lava flows provide a surreal landscape in the northeast. Farther south, the Tehachapis, the Sierra, the San Bernadinos, and other ranges divide 'the so-called Valley of Southern California, a broad strip of broken country near the coast, from arid wastes of the Mojave and Colorado Deserts in the hinterland'.[1]

The Northern Rivers, the American, Feather, Indian, Pit, Sacramento, and Yuba, owe much to Mount Shasta's annual melting snows for replenishment of their southerly flow. The San Joaquin, which shares the name of the valley it waters, runs northward from its source in the mountains of present-day Fresno County, being joined by the Calaveras, Consumnes, Fresno, Kings, Mokelumne, Stanislaus, and Toulomne Rivers, as well as by a considerable number of other smaller streams.

The Klamath, Scott, and Trinity drain the seaward slopes of the Coast Range with the Eel, Mad, and Russian Rivers carrying water north of San Francisco Bay, the marvelous 'harbor of harbors' so cherished by Spain. To this port's south run the Salinas, Santa Clara, Santa Maria, and Santa Inez Rivers. Proceeding still southward, the Los Angeles, San Diego, San Gabriel, San Luis Rey, Santa Ana, Santa Margarita, and Ventura Rivers slow to a trickle much of the year or become dry beds until spring floods bring them back to life.

These various natural elements combine to form a half dozen life zones: Arctic, Canadian, Hudsonian, Transition, Upper Sonoran, and Lower Sonoran. The first areas exist, 'in the higher elevations of the Siskiyous, the Trinity Mountains, the Sierra, the San Bernardino and the San Jacinto ranges'. Next, the Santa Cruz Mountains, along with the upper portions of the Santa Lucias combine with 'all of the coast country north of San Francisco, the heavily watered northeastern counties and a long belt, between 2,500 and 5,000 feet high in the Sierra' to form the Transition zone. In turn, the foothills of the Sierras lie within the Upper Sonoran which also contain 'the lava plateaus of Modoc and Lassen Counties, the western slopes of the Sacramento Valley, the inner chains of the Coast Range and Valleys from Medocino County to San Francisco Bay, and all of the coastal region south of San Francisco' with the exception of those segments noted as part of the Transition zone. Finally, the Lower Sonoran consists of most of the Great Valley between Bakersfield and Red Bluff, 'all of the great arid desert regions southeast of the Sierra to the Nevada and Arizona lines, and several long narrow strips extending from the Salinas Valley south'.[2]

Each of the six environments support divergent flora and fauna. The high peaks of the Arctic-Alpine are treeless, but alpine buttercup, alpine shootingstar, blue and fragrant polemonium, Sierra primrose, and steershead can be found at these lofty elevations. The Sierra rosy finch makes its regular home here. Hummingbirds and the gray and white Clark nutcrackers

This map shows approximate territories of tribes and language groups in about 1800. After that, all tribes lost territory and some disappeared.

Key to tribes:

1	Tolowa	28	Maidu
2	Karok	29	Yana
3	Yurok	30	Konkow
4	Shasta	31	Nisenan
5	Hupa	32	Patwin
6	Chilula	33	Lake Miwok
7	Whilkut	34	Wappo
8	Wiyot	35	Coast Miwok
9	Chimariko	36	Miwok
10	Wintu	37	Northern Valley Yokuts
11	Mattole	38	Costanoan
12	Nongatl	39	Esselen
13	Sinkyone	40	Monache
14	Lassik	41	Foothill Yokuts
15	Wailaki	42	Southern Valley Yokuts
16	Cahto	43	Tubatulabal
17	Yuki	44	Salinan
18	Northern Pomo	45	Chumash
19	Northeastern Pomo	46	Kitanemuk
20	Eastern Pomo	47	Tataviam
21	Southeastern Pomo	48	Serrano
22	Central Pomo	49	Gabrielino
23	Southern Pomo	50	Luiseño
24	Kashaya	51	Cahuilla
25	Nomlaki	52	Cupeño
26	Achumawi	53	Diegueño
27	Atsugewi		

PACIFIC OCEAN

from chickadees to mountain quail. Moreover, coyote, muledeer, hawks, and some sparrows inhabit the Canadian zone, as well as are distributed throughout some other zones.

The Upper Sonoran zone encompasses a great chaparral belt that was once the home of the California grizzly and the nearly extinct California condor. Blue and scrub oaks, California buckeyes, digger pines, ceanothus, and species of manzanita and yucca grow along with several other shrubs. Anna hummingbird, bell sparrow, bush tit, California and stellar jay, California thrasher, dusky poorwill, house finch, mourning dove, valley quail, and yellow-billed magpie typify the feathered denizens of the zone. Land animals include antelope, brown-footed woodrat, brush rabbit, as well as the ring-tailed cat.

The Lower Sonoran zone offers its specialties, too. The Colorado Desert has bigelovia, a litany of cacti, California fan palm, echinocatus, mesquite, palo verde, and screwbean. In the Mojave Desert grow other specimens with the Joshua tree (*Yucca arborenscens*) standing out among the plant life. Fremont cottonwoods and valley oaks flourish in still different parts of the Lower Sonoran.

The zone has a fair share of nocturnal animals as well. All sorts of rodents, kit fox, chipmunk, opossum, jack rabbit, and, in times past, tule elk, share the land with desert tortoise, lizards, and snakes. In the air, blue grosbeak, cactus wren, hooded orioles, mockingbirds, phainopeplas, and Texas nighthawks are plentiful, while the long-legged roadrunner remains earthbound, depending as it does on speed of foot rather than the ability to fly as the key to survival.

With both an array of potential food sources and also numerous climatic advantages, California proved an attractive magnet for early hunter-gatherer peoples. While no one knows for certain when *homo sapiens* first trod on California soil, some evidence points to the arrival of humans over 20,000 years before the present.[3] Despite the lack of definitive evidence as to origins, with the passage of the ages, it is certain that distinct groups emerged with highly developed territorial and cultural traits. Of these, 'about one half of California was held by Penutian-speaking people', a collection of 'small families which linguists believe were related because their languages employ some of the same grammatical tricks'.[4] In general terms, the diverse 'tribes' followed a lifestyle which took on a more uniform pattern than usually evidenced elsewhere among North American Indians. One of the chief similarities revolved around the consumption of acorn-based foodstuffs. Over the centuries, the first people to live in California unlocked the secret of turning the bitter, tannic acid laden product of the oak into 'a rich, nutritional food' which, as a soup, porridge, or kind of bread, provided the mainstay of their diet.[5]

Two basic means allowed for this process to be accomplished. Either individuals pulverized and leached the nuts in sand or a basket or they could immerse or bury acorns in water or mud, and thereby not have to crush the nuts. Since the earth provided this source free for the taking, along with other plants and animals for sustenance, agriculture really did not evolve in early California.

Above: *A Karok, one of the most northerly tribes of California, in war costume of rod armor and helmet, with an animal-skin quiver under his arm.*
Photographed probably by John Daggett c.1898.

pass through as do the Sierra cony and white-tailed jack rabbit. Bighorn sheep also once ranged in this land.

At slightly lower reaches, the Hudsonian zone shares lodgepole pine as a mainstay of ground cover with the Canadian zone. White bark, foxtail, and silver pines grow higher up, mingling with mountain hemlock. Fowl and mammals, most importantly the alpine chipmunk, California pine grosbeak, mountain bluebird, Sierra cony, Sierra least weasel, Sierra marmot, white-crowned sparrow, and wolverine are found in the Hudsonian zone.

Besides lodgepole pine, the Canadian zone boasts yellow pine, Jeffrey pine, mountain pine, and red fir. Cancerroot, ceanothus, several species of corallorrhiza, dwarf manzanita, herbaceous vegetation, Sierra puffball, and snowplant carpet the floor. Blue-fronted jay, evening grosbeak, Sierra grouse, Sierra hermit thrush, Sierra junco, Townsend solitaire, water ouzel, and western chipping sparrow soar above. Various types of chipmunk share the zone with

mountain weasel, golden-mantle ground squirrel, Sierra chickaree, snowshoe rabbit, and yellow-haired porcupine.

In the Transition zone, however, lie most of California's great forests, the most impressive of which, the redwoods, often intermingle with broad-leafed maple, California laurel, Douglas fir, madrona, and tanbark oak. Other vegetation runs the gamut with several types of trees and many eatable plants being found to support the animal life and what was quite a complex food chain.

Black bear, bobcat, California ring-tailed cat, Columbian black-tailed deer, cougar, elk, fox, marten, mink weasel, mountain beaver, Pacific coon, and packrat once roamed in numbers. Many reptiles and amphibians find the range a suitable habitat, as do an assortment of birds

Moreover the people varied their diets by hunting, gathering, and fishing. They enjoyed resources which 'were bountiful in their variety rather than in their overwhelming abundance along special lines'. Thus, the fare contained venison, rabbit, gopher, lizard, snakes (including rattlers), ducks, and small birds, depending on local availability. These might be obtained by snares, throw stones, and such implements as could be fashioned from stone and other natural materials. Crayfish, molluscs, turtles, and an assortment of creatures from water and marsh might be procured in several ways with harpoons, nets, digging tools, and poison numbing among the means developed to take advantage of this type of bounty. Caterpillars, grasshoppers, maggots, and snails added to the possibilities for protein.

Despite the broad ranging approach to food, not everything was considered fit for meals, either because of religious beliefs or for practical reasons. For example, most northern groups would not eat dog, except the Yokuts, whose southern branch also 'relished the skunk, which when smoked to death in its hole was without offensive odor'. Conversely, these same connoisseurs of pole cats 'eschewed all reptiles, pronouncing them unclean'. Additionally, certain northern tribes rejected frogs, gopher snakes, and water snakes. Usually, the majority of groups refrained from grizzly bear

Below: *Indian men from several northern California groups in treaty at Round Valley, c.1858. The fourth white man from the left is probably Simmon P. Storms, first Indian agent of the Nome Cult Farm.*

Above: *An 1806 depiction by Georg von Langsdorf of the Spanish garrisoned Presidio of San Francisco. In the foreground is a native tule balsa, propelled by a pair of 'Ohlone' men.*

tication and diversity present among those people who made them. Examples from one of the best known practitioners of the art, the Pomo, who lived in a rather compact unit in the Russian River valley, underscore some of the points about the importance of basketry to California's past.[9] The Pomo produced baskets which gained 'the name, among Americans, of being the finest in California; according to many, in the world'.[10] Relying upon ten or twelve types of material, with five being commonly employed, the baskets often took on an intricate nature.[11] Willow normally served as the warp for both twined and coiled examples. For the woof, *Carex* (sedge root), *Cercis* (redbud bark), *Scripus* (bulrush root), and digger pine root were used, with the first named medium being the most important basic ingredient. In turn, red patterns relied upon the redbud (used most commonly with twined leaves). Dyed bulrush gave black patterns, usually for coil work. Finally, digger pine fibers, in the main, were the woof for course twined baskets. Thus, by 'convention and habit . . . practically all the basketry of the Pomo' consisted of these five materials.[12]

The Pomo, unlike most other California bas-

Above; *Little Ike, a Karok man, fishing for salmon with a plunge net from a fishing platform among the rocks at pame·kyá·ra·m on the Klamath River. Photographed before 1897.*

Right: *A Talowa woman shown wearing a fine basketry hat and clamshell bead necklaces and shell-decorated skirt. This photograph was taken by Edward Curtis (1868-1952) in the early 1920s.*

and coyote, mainly because these animals figured into many spiritual tenants. Sometimes brown bear was avoided, nor did 'birds of prey and carrion from the eagle down to the crow . . .' constitute common dishes.[6]

Thriving on the resources they found, California's Indian population rose, with estimates ranging from 133,500 to 350,000 inhabitants during the golden age prior to the arrival of the Spanish and others. Given even the higher figure, the average density represented only three people per square mile for those areas not considered an uninhabitable desert. These numbers would fall dramatically in the wake of later events so that 'the low point was reached between 1880 and 1900 with a recorded number of no more than 20,000 or perhaps 25,000 souls'.[7]

In their heyday though, these culturally and linguistically rich groups came into contact with each other in several ways. A major means of association resulted through the trade which occurred on an inter- and intra-tribal basis. Routes and complex exchange systems grew up where a wide assortment of commodities, tools, food, clothing, pottery, slaves, sea shells, and basketry changed hands between and among players from as far away as western Canada and the mainland of Mexico.[8]

Baskets came to be particularly prized and remain an important part of continuity between the past and the present. Serviceable, aesthetically pleasing pieces, the baskets of California's first residents served utilitarian purposes and also demonstrated the extraordinary artistic talents of their makers. These objects likewise bespoke of the level of sophis-

Hupa

The Hupa lived along the Trinity River in NW California, where they subsisted mainly on salmon and acorns. The men were wood workers, the women expert basket weavers. They shared with the neighboring Yurok and Karok the annual White Deerskin and Jumping dances, world-renewal and wealth display ceremonies each lasting ten days, and the Brush Dance to cure sick children. Hupa doctors were nearly all women. Dates of collecting are given below.

1 Drum-rattle for gambling songs. 1875.
2 Woman's hair ornaments. 1885.
3 Man's necklace, c.1928.
4 Young man's dance hat. Yurok (but collected from the Hupa). 1885.
5 Eagle feathers worn in White Deerskin and Brush dances. 1928.
6 Eagle feathers, as No. 5.
7 Headband of mink skin. 1944.
8 Headdress of buckskin and wolfskin. 1944.
9 Ornament for mouth of stuffed white deerskin for dance. 1929.
10 Eagle feather head ornament, used for White Deerskin and Brush dances.
1928.
11 Rattle belt for dance. Yurok (but collected from the Hupa). 1885.
12 Tobacco basket. 1899.
13 Pipe. 1885.
14 War bow. 1885.
15 Arrows. 1885.
16 Quiver. 1885.
17 Man's wand for Jumping Dance. Yurok (but collected from the Hupa). 1885.
18 Stone cooking vessel. 1885.
19 Stone sledge used for driving fish dam stakes. 1929.
20 Netting shuttle. 1889.
21 Nettle shuttle. 1875.
22 Stone pounder. 1928.
23 Woman's shell spoon. 1899.
24 Man's wooden spoon. 1908.
25-28 Men's elkhorn

spoons. 1875-99.
29 Shell beads for dance. 1928.
30 Elkhorn purse for dentalium money. 1890.
31 Dentalium money. 1875.
32 Elkhorn purse. 1883.
33 Spoon or trinket basket. 1899
34 Basket for boiling acorn mush. 1885.
35 Storage basket. 1890.

36 Acorn bread tray. 1899.
37 Salmon or meat tray. 1899.
38 Basket for acorn mush. 1899
39 Basket tray. 1899.
40 Basketry acorn flour scoop. 1899.
41 Man's apron for White Deerskin Dance, of civet skins. 1890.
42 Woman's dance skirt. 1885.
43 Woman's necklace. 1885.

44 Woman's dance apron. 1885.
45 Doctor's wand for Jumping Dance and curing. 1928.
46 Woman's hair ornaments. 1885.
47 Wicow's basketry cap. 1928.
48 Woman's basketry cap. 1885.
49 Woman's necklace. 1885.
50 Woman's hair ornaments. 1885.
51 Doctor's headdress, used in curing. Very old in 1944.

ket weavers who ordinarily worked in one or two techniques, employed upwards of a half dozen approaches. Not only did the Pomo use twining, the norm for the most northern reaches and for the Achomawi, Atsugewi, Modoc, Northern Wintu, and Shasta, but also they were adept at coiling, which generally dominated the remainder of the state. It seems the Pomo alternated between the two forms with equal ease and regularity.

When turning out coil pieces, the Pomo utilized both single rod and triple rod foundations. In the twined versions they perfected five weaves: plain, diagonal, lattice, three-strand twining, and three-strand braiding, beside incorporating a wealth of decoration and design elements.

While examples of Pomo basketry demonstrate some of the spectrum of this art so often associated with California's indigenous people, other indications of the cultural medley once represented by the state's Native American population might best be appreciated through a brief survey of several of the major groups who once carried out an array of lifestyles there. (For locations of the various groups mentioned in this survey see the accompanying map to this chapter on page 128.)

Starting to the far northwest, the Tolowa people speak an Athapascan dialect from whence their name came (a designation derived from the neighboring Yurok). Living in a dozen and a half or so towns, this group sometimes feuded among themselves but a

Above: *A Karok basketmaker, 1896. Of note, to her right, is a space-twined pack basket used for packing acorns, fish etc, and on her lap and beside her two partially twined baskets.*

Below: *A Hupa village on the Trinity River in 1898 or before. In the foreground are two houses of the traditional type, built of cedar planks, with three-pitch roofs covered with overlapping boards.*

Above: *Hupa participants in the Jumping Dance at the Yurok town of Pekwon, Klamath River, 1893. The men wear traditional buckskin headbands covered with woodpecker scalps, bordered with white deer belly fur.*

Below: *Hupa White Deerskin dance, 1891, a part of one of the two great World Renewal ceremonies performed by the Hupa, Yurok, and Karok-speaking peoples in northwestern California.*

number of villages might unite if an expedition was mounted against the nearby Yurok or Karok. Such exchanges may have been infrequent, however, since the Tolowa seemed to be middlemen in the trade of dentalium shells from Vancouver Island, a highly regarded commodity which served as currency in the region. Evidently the Yurok looked upon the Tolowa as being quite wealthy.

Beside being purveyors of dentalium, the Tolowa became skilled boatsman, constructing canoes from redwood trees. The made ropes and cords from a species of the iris, practiced twined basket-making techniques, and fabricated rattles from deer hooves for accompaniment to religious ceremonies, such as the girl's adolescence ceremony and dance. Other rituals included war dances, doctor-making dances, the Deerskin dance, and the so-called 'salmon dance' which was somewhat akin to a new year celebration which entailed 'the catching and eating of the first salmon of the season; after which fishing was open to all'.[13] Much later, in the last decades of the nineteenth century, they also added the Ghost Dance to their beliefs.

The Yurok and Karok flanked the Tolowa on the south and southeast respectively. The former group resided on the lower Klamath River and shared many traits in common with those around them as well as the inhabitants of the Pacific Northwest to Alaska. Living in more than fifty autonomous hamlets, the Yurok pursued fishing on the river and ocean along with hunting and gathering. They too made redwood canoes which could be bought for a pair of twelve-dentalium shell strings or ten large or sixty small woodpecker scalps. As can be deduced from this price structure, the Yurok had a sophisticated monetary system and, according to one source, they held wealth in high esteem. There was:

'Blood money, bride purchase, compensation to the year's mourners before a dance can be held ... Every injury, each privilege or wrong or trespass, is calculated and compensated. Without exactly adjusted payment, cessation of a feud is impossible except through utter extirpation of one party, marriage is not marriage but a public disgrace for generations, the ceremony necessary to the preservation of the order of the world is not held. The consequence is that the Yurok concerns his life above all else with property. When he has leisure, he thinks of money; if in need, he calls upon it'.[14]

Other standard costs provide an idea about relative value in the society. An eagle skin brought only one small shell while the 'dowry' for a bride could be as high as ten strands of shells of various lengths. This indicated the status of marriage since a fishing spot fetched only one to three strings, a house five, and a tract of land bearing acorns from one to five strings of shells. The last mentioned item, an acorn plot, indicates a concept of private land ownership. Indeed, in this individualistic culture, 'up to a mile or more from the river, all land of any value was privately owned; back of this, there were no claims, nor was their much hunting'.[15]

A number of other traits separated the Yurok from many other cultures. They observed inheritance practices, passing on much of their holdings to kinsmen. If an individual required ferrying across the water, the service customarily was granted free of charge. A shaman received considerable fees for services and those who entered the field might expect to make a considerable living. Class-consciousness existed to the degree that the Yurok made a definite distinction between rich and poor in their dealings.

Early Yurok clothing resembled that found throughout most of California. Young men regularly wore a folded deerskin wrapped around the waist while older men might go naked in warmer seasons. A buckskin fringed front piece and 'a broader apron or skirt ... brought around to meet the front piece' served as the standard garb for women. Women also wore basket caps as the rule. When weather dictated additional covering, a cape or blanket of two sewn-together deer hides provided protection. Wealthier women sported extensive ornamentation. For footgear, a plain one-piece, front-seamed moccasin sufficed, being used most commonly by women when traveling, obtaining firewood, or for dress occasions.[16]

This same physical description might be applied to the Karok, whose name comes from the adverb *karuk*, meaning 'upstream', their location in relationship to the Yurok. While outwardly very similar, the two groups differed in one major respect, their languages. The

Above: *Keintpoos, better known as Captain Jack, who served as a major leader among the Modoc in the siege of the Lava Beds, 1873. Taken by the U.S. Army, Jack was sentenced to death.*

Below: *Following the adage 'it takes diamond dust to polish a diamond', the U.S. Army employed Indian scouts (above) from the Warm Springs reservation to track down and pursue the Modoc.*

Yurok spoke an Algonquian tongue and the Karok belonged to the Hokan linguistic family.

Moreover, they could be distinguished from the culture found downstream in a number of other ways. For example, in the dance for adolescent girls, the men played a more prominent role than the males among the Yurok. Then, too, the Karok's 'world making' ceremonies were more defined. Finally, they prided themselves on the ability of their shaman, whom they claimed had no equal save among the Shasta and a few other groups located further over to the east.

This respect for the Shasta may have stemmed from a regular contact between the two peoples. Indeed, the nearby Shasta traded deerskins, obsidian, and sugar-pine nuts to the Karok for baskets, canoes, dentalia, seaweed, and tan-oak acorns.

Not all intercourse with outsiders stemmed from peaceful exchanges. The Karok raided periodically, the women sometimes accompanying the men, possibly to cook and carry provisions. The warriors occasionally donned a hide helmet or headband, along with armor of rods or elk skin as they set out to do battle.

It seems that the Shasta did not turn their aggressions toward the northeast where the Modoc made their home, ranging across the present-day Oregon and California state lines. Had the Karok attempted this, they would have met stiff residence since 'the Modoc ... probably possessed more tribal solidarity than the great majority of California Indians ...'[17] Although the Modoc have been included in the map on page 100 as a Plateau tribe, it is suggested here that the boundary between the

Above: *Joseppa Beatty, noted Central Pomo-speaking basket maker, with her husband and son on the Yokayo Rancheria, 1892. She works on a one-rod coiled basket, the rod seen projecting to her left.*

Below: *McCloud River Wintu men and boys, c.1872, at Colchoolooloo's Rancheria. The two men standing wear traditional netted down caps and demonstrate arrow release.*

Plateau and California was not, in the mid-nineteenth century, as fixed as this. As with many hunter-gatherers, their boundaries were not restricted. For this reason, and because of the importance of the events surrounding the resistance of Captain Jack and the Modoc Indians, the Modoc and their final flourish are considered in greater depth in this chapter.

For all this, the Modoc suffered greatly at the

hands of white encroachment. The steady increase in miners and settlers to their home eventually led to relocation on an Oregon reservation. In the mid-1860s, they began their short-lived, turbulent stay with the Klamath who spoke a Lutuami-based language, as did the Modoc. Friction increased between the two occupants of the reserve. The situation deteriorated even more with the killing of a Klamath shaman by one of the Modoc who would play a major part in subsequent events. Soon thereafter, some of the Modoc quit the confines of Oregon to head back to their former Lost River region in California under such leaders as John Schonchin and another key player variously known as Keintpoos, Kintpuash, or, more commonly, Captain Jack. It was Jack who had shot the Klamath healer thereby bringing about charges of murder. Under the circumstances, he saw the wisdom of returning to the traditional Modoc territory. This move, however, caused yet more conflict since 'just north of Tule Lake, white settlers had already moved in with their herds and had erected cabins'.[18]

Some four years passed with an uneasy attitude prevailing on both sides. Kintpuash, whose father had been killed by whites under Ben Wright, in 1852, could not be persuaded to rejoin the Klamath. Failing to dislodge Jack and his compatriots, local citizens turned to the U.S. army for assistance.

The local senior military officer in the area, Major John Green, attempted to speak to Captain Jack in September 1872 but to no avail. Within weeks, Green's superior, Brigadier General E. R. S. Canby decided to press the issue. He sent orders for the arrest of Captain

Wintu

The Wintu were hill people whose economy was based on the use of salmon, deer, and acorns. Objects shown are from an excellent collection made in 1872–5 by Livingston Stone while in charge of the U.S. salmon-hatching establishment on the McCloud River. At this time the Indians here were relatively undisturbed, although other Wintu had suffered greatly, from a malaria epidemic in the 1830s, from gold miners' pollution of their streams, from the intro-duction of cattle ranching, and from massacres and forced relocation to reservations. After the railroad arrived in 1875, the McCloud R. Wintu and others underwent rapid culture change with the increase in white settlement and with the introduction of several new Indian reli-gions. Stone got along well with the Wintu, and this collection is perhaps a more important re-sult of his work than was his failed attempt to use California salmon spawn for restocking sal-mon streams on the Atlantic coast. No other collection so well documents aboriginal Wintu arts and technology.

1 Twined storage basket.
2 Twined cooking basket, with lizard and rib design.
3 Twined cooking basket.
4 Twined storage basket.
5 Twined basket, probably a woman's hat.
6 Woman's hat, twined basketry, weft of natural and alder-dyed grass and fern stems.
7 Twined basket, probably a woman's hat.
8 Front part of woman's skirt, buckskin and twine strings, wrapped with vegetable fiber, pendants of pinenut seeds, tin and buttons.
9 Belt of human hair, worn by girl at puberty ceremony (a major ritual of the Wintu).
10 Fur head ornament for dances.
11 Fur strip used to tie hair on top of head.
12 Front part of skirt, type worn by women before the 1870s, of pinenut seed shells

threaded on buckskin strings.

13 Openwork twined baskets containing manzanita berries for flour, wrapped in grass.

14 Dance skirt of wild swan feathers with small squares of flicker quills.

15 Woven beadwork pouch for carrying shot or wild tobacco.

16 Feather head ornament, for dances.

17 Head ornament for dances

with small squares of flicker quills.

18 Head ornament for dances, feathers of great western horned owl and white-headed woodpecker.

19 Dance head ornament, a red wool knitted cap with feathers (including woodpecker scalp) and two rattlesnake rattles.

20 Twined basket.

21 Sinew-backed yew bow, buckskin wrap at grip, twisted sinew bowstring.

22 Arrows with glass and

obsidian points.

23 Carved wooden pipe for smoking wild tobacco.

24 Sling used for killing small game; buckskin pouch, twisted sinew cords.

25 Twined basket.

26 Drinking cup.

27 Twined basket.

28 Twined serving basket.

29 Shaman's basket.

30 Twined serving basket.

31 Twined serving basket.

32 Birdbone whistle used for dances.

Jack and two other important headmen, Black Jim and Scarface Charley. Miscalculating the effect of this directive, a detail set out in response to Canby's command. On the morning of 29 November 1872 Captain James Jackson, Lieutenant Frazier A. Boutelle, and Assistant Surgeon Henry McElderry rode with some three dozen or so enlisted men from Company B of the First U.S. Cavalry into the Modoc camp. Jack, asleep in camp along with most of the other villagers, awoke to find armed men in their presence. The would-be captors' arrival led to bloodshed. An exchange of fire left casualties on both sides. The Modoc fled. A war had begun.

In the confusion, Jack escaped as did many others of the band. Splitting into at least two different parties, the Modoc ultimately regrouped in the region south of Tule Lake, which had been called by some 'hell with the fire burnt out'. Here, 'in this wild expanse of black lava, that nature had piled into a gigantic fortress', the Modoc made their stand. They knew every fissure, cavern, and passageway. Patches of grass subsisted their cattle. Sagebrush and greasewood yielded fuel. Water came from Tule Lake.'[19] The weeks which passed before the U.S. government's forces arrived on the scene allowed the Modoc to prepare for the siege which ensued. Scarface Charley particularly would distinguish himself once the whites

Below: *Cecilia Joaquin, a Central Pomo speaker from the Sanel community at Hopland demonstrating the use of the seed beater to collect seeds in a close-twined burden basket, in the early 1920s.*

Above: *Traditional site of Pomo fish camp, Clear Lake, c.1900. The permanent house frames were covered each year with fresh tules, sometimes replaced after white contact by large sheets of canvas, as here.*

arrived to do battle.

Regulars and volunteers surrounded their foe. After their first attack on 17 January 1873, the troops found the Modoc to be tenacious freedom fighters. The opening engagement ended in a clear victory for the Lava Beds' defenders, despite the fact that they were outnumbered by an estimated seven to one. In defeat, the whites broke off to tend to their wounded and see to their dead.

Time passed. The Modoc held their own against cavalry, infantry, artillery, and militiamen from Oregon and California. New tactics seemed in order. Kaitchkona (also known as Toby Riddle), Captain Jack's cousin, and a few other courageous individuals visited the entrenched Modoc in an effort to reach some sort of settlement. In addition, a peace commission dispatched from Washington, D.C., arrived with hopes of bringing an end to hostilities. For six weeks they tried to entice Jack and his people to the bargaining table but their efforts produced no results. By this time, Canby had come from his headquarters in Salem, Oregon, to assume field command. He sought to end the whole affair, moving his units closer to the Modoc stronghold. Captain Jack finally met with the general. This exchange allowed the Modoc to state their case. They wanted the troops to withdraw; they requested their own reservation on the Lost River; and they sought protection 'from charges of murdering a number of settlers'.[20]

Nothing came of this conference. Then, on 11 April 1873, Canby again went to speak with Captain Jack. On Good Friday, Canby and other fellow commissioners resumed negotiations. In the midst of the talks Captain Jack pulled out a concealed weapon and fired point blank into Canby's face. The wounded officer attempted to flee. Another Modoc fell on Canby and finished him with a knife. Two of Canby's party, the Re-

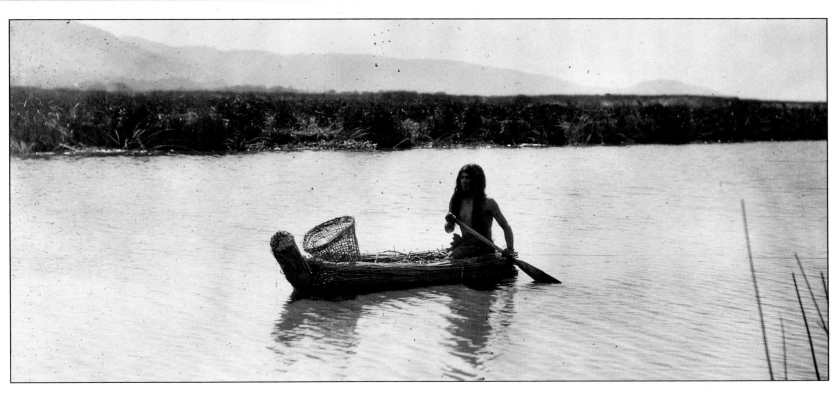

verend Eleazer Thomas and Oregon Superintendent of Indian Affairs, A. B. Meacham, went down in the killing frenzy. When the slaughter stopped, Canby and Thomas were dead and Meacham sustained wounds, not the least of which was the loss of his scalp.

Up to that point, the Modoc had gained considerable sympathy for their cause, with the military being painted as incompetent aggressors. Now, public opinion turned. Canby's successor redoubled efforts to dislodge the enemy. After considerable bloodshed and suffering, on 1 June 1873 the ill-fated Modoc survivors capitulated. A trial followed with Captain Jack and three others being given the death sentence. The remaining 153 Modoc received a different fate, relocation to Quapaw Indian Agency in present-day Oklahoma.

While this clash of cultures was well known, the Modoc were not the only Native Americans to suffer at the hands of Europeans and Euro-Americans. From 1769, when the Spanish arrived to establish their first settlements in Alta California, a long, unfortunate decline in the Indian population and territory began. The first long-term contact started in the south with those groups living in the north being the last to face the consequences of meeting the newcomers.[21] They would not be exempt forever though, for as Captain E. D. Townsend, assistant adjutant general for the Pacific Division, confided in an 1852 entry to his diary:

'If the tale of these poor wretches inhabiting the more Northern parts |of California|, could be impartially related, it would be a picture of cruelty, injustice and horror scarcely to be surpassed by that of the Peruvians in the time of Pizzaro. In their eager search for gold the whites have boldly penetrated and explored wilderness and mountains far beyond the reach of settlements. They have established themselves in many cases, in large communities so that Tribes of Indians were left between them and the settlements. Aggression would naturally be of fre-

Above: *Pomo fisherman in a tule boat on Clear Lake, space-twined collecting basket in the prow. Speakers of six distinct languages lived around this lake in over a dozen separate communities.*

Below: *Northeastern Pomo dancers at a Big Head dance (also called Bole-Maru or 1872 Ghost Dance), at Stony Creek, Colusa County (Big Head in the center, Charlie Watham on the left), in 1907.*

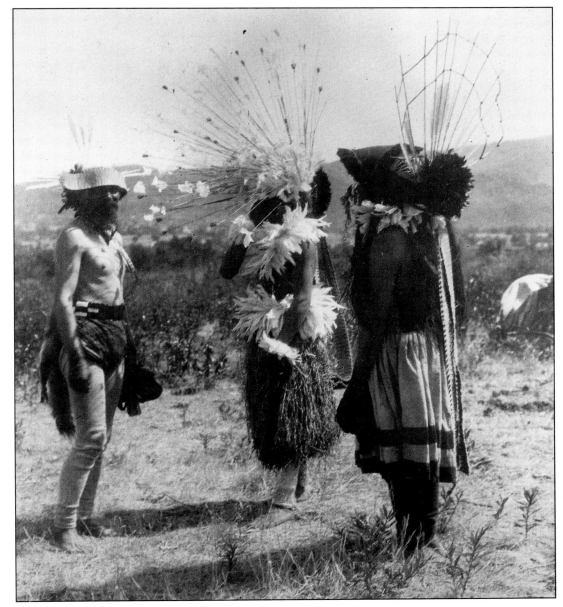

Pomoan

The Pomoan tribes are famous for fine basketry. Here is a selection from those collected by J.W. Hudson in the 1880s–90s to show the shapes, materials, techniques and designs associated with specific uses. Baskets were then beginning to be made for sale, as manufactured products replaced them in everyday Pomoan use. Below, tribe is given when known, with language: CP=Central Pomo; EP=Eastern P; NP=Northern P.; SP=Southern P.

1 Meal storage bowl, plain twined basketry. Tsetum, NP.
2 Burden basket. Yokiah, CP.
3 Flail for beating seeds off plant into burden basket; of willow shoots.
4 Jar of coiled basketry. Póma, NP.
5 Feast cup. Limma, CP.
6 Fishworm pan, spaced lattice twined willow shoots; bottom mended.
7 Feast tureen. Cokowa, CP.
8 Dowry basket, boat-shaped coiled, sedge and redbud on 1-rod foundation, decorated with quail feathers and beads. Póma, NP.
9 Feast dish, coiled, sedge and bulrush on 3-rod willow foundation, decorated with red woodpecker and quail feathers and clamshell beads. Yokaia, CP.
10 Jewel basket, decorated with clamshell beads, trade beads, and quail and woodpecker feathers.
11 Dish, coiled, sedge, bulrush and quail feathers. Yokiah, CP.
12 Jewel basket, 3-rod coiled, sedge, bulrush, quail and woodpecker head feathers, beads. Ano, NP.
13 Set of net-weaving tools, of mountain mahogany and manzanita wood.
14 Squirrel skin pouch for pipe and tobacco.
15 Arrows.
16 Sinew-backed cedar bow.
17 Sinew-backed ash bow.
18 Meal storage bowl, diagonally twined sedge and redbud over willow shoots, decorated with quail feathers. Póma, NP.
19 Jewel basket, 3-rod coiled, sedge, covered with woodpecker, meadowlark, and bluejay feathers and shell beads. Cikom, EP.
20 Marriage token. Yokiah, NP.
21 Condiment dish, perhaps by Mary Benson. Limma, CP.
22 Ornamented cup, 1-rod coiled, sedge, bulrush,

quail and woodpecker feathers, beads. Amo, NP.

23 Jewel basket, 3-rod coiled, sedge, bulrush, quail feathers, beads. Póma, NP.

24 Necklace of clamshell and magnesite beads.

25 Man's dance plume, worn on crown of head, of tail-feathers of Lewis woodpecker.

26 Man's dance forehead band, of flicker tail feathers.

27 Woman's dance forehead

band, of weasel skin with projecting pendants of beads and flicker feathers.

28 Woman's dance plume, worn on crown of head, of turkey tail feathers.

29 Jar, 1-rod coiled, sedge redbud. Póma, NP.

30 Small (child's?) boat basket, 1-rod coiled, sedge, redbud. Yokiah CP.

31 Meal cup, 1-rod coiled, sedge, bulrush. Yokiah, CP.

32 Dowry basket, exchanged with food at marriage.

Yokiah, CP.

33 Ornamented dish, 1-rod coiled, sedge, bulrush, beads. Codokai, NP.

34 Snail jar, plain twined, sedge, bulrush, redbud. Buldam, NP.

35 Basket hopper for mortar, plain twined, willow root, redbud. Póma, NP.

36 Basket jar, similar to type presented to bereaved at funeral; 3-rod coiled, sedge, bulrush, trade beads, shell beads. Yokiah, CP.

Coast Miwok Chief's Wife, 1833

Beside Bodega Bay a high-status woman offers guests acorn mush in a feast basket decorated with olivella shell beads and red head-feathers from scores of woodpeckers. Her downy feather robe, worn only by prominent women, is woven of ropes made by wrapping feathers around a doubled cord. Each robe required specific feathers from hundreds of birds (Canada and snow geese, mallards). The woman's ear ornaments have abalone shell pendants on strings of clamshell beads wrapped at the top with a pair of meadowlark scalps. She wears necklaces of clamshell and olivella beads, and a double apron of shredded tules. Two men paddle ashore in a tule balsa boat. Robe, basket, and ear ornaments are all examples collected by Gov. Gen. von Wrangell of the Russian American Fur Company in 1833.

quent occurrence on one side or the other, and the whites found it convenient to seize upon Indian lands, or to move them away for any cause, it was an easy matter to raise a quarrel in which the natives were made to appear in the wrong, and then an expedition would be fitted out against them which would butcher sometimes, thirty, fifty or a hundred men, women and children.'[22]

In these few terse sentences, Townsend summarized the fate of not only many California Indians but also that of numerous native peoples all over North America.

Before this tide swept away the old ways, however, the diversity of California's native cultures flourished. The northern peoples went about their daily lives. There were the Achumawi, Atsugawi, Chimariko, Pomo (the main bands of which were the Northwestern, Central, Southern, Southeastern, and Eastern bands), and Yana, who all shared Hokan as the base for their dialects, as did the Shasta, whereas the Hupa, Cahto, Lassik, Mattole, Nongatl, Sinkyone, Wailaki, and Whilkut had Athapascan as a base, just as was the case with the Tolowa. Another pair of people communicated in Yukian, the Yuki and Wappo, with a third practitioner of the language being a possible offshoot of the Wappo who were surrounded in a small enclave by the more numerous Eastern and Southeastern Pomo.

The remainder of the northern groups spoke in a root of Penutian. The Konkow, Lake Miwok, Maidu, Miwok, Nisenan, Nomlaki, Northern Valley and Southern Valley Yokuts, Patwin, and Wintu fell into this category, as did the Coast Miwok and Costanoan.[23] These last two peoples might be looked at in more detail to obtain a better sense of several representative traits found among many of the other inhabitants of this part of the state, along with some of the unique characteristics which set them off from others who once lived in California.

To begin with, the Coast Miwok and Costanoan territories surrounded San Francisco Bay, the former being found on the north and the latter to the south and east, and occasionally in Marin and the islands of the Bay. Besides similarities in language, they shared many attributes which provide a means for comparison and contrast.

Starting with the Costanoan, for whom considerable enthnographic information exists, some eight major subdivisions have been noted. Each of the groups had 'separate languages, as different from one another as Spanish and English'.[24] Evidently, they had no common name for themselves but 'the label Costanoan had its roots in Spanish history [the term being taken from *Costanos* or coast people] and has long since established itself as a recognized language family'.[25] More recently, 'Ohlone' has been applied to the Costanoan. Descendants of this stock tend to prefer the newer reference.

In those earlier times, when the people had

Right: A Nisenan boy wearing flicker feather headband, large abalone shell gorget at his neck and a belt covered with abalone pendants and beads worn as a bandolier, all objects of wealth. Photographed possibly by A.W. Chase, prior to 1876.

no commonly accepted single name, outer appearances nonetheless reflected their ties. Men and boys commonly went about naked while a grass or tule apron, which covered the front and back below the waist, constituted the clothing for women. When the weather dictated, capes or cloaks fashioned from deer, rabbit, water-fowl feathers, or sea-mammal skins provided protection.[26] Even mud occasionally served 'as insulation from the cold – a custom not recorded among their neighbors, the Coast Miwoks'.[27]

The Costanoans regularly walked barefooted

and without head coverings, except on ceremonial occasions. Painting and tattoos provided decoration and clan affiliation, the former practice being applied in patterns which made it appear as if the people wore striped tights. Pierced ears could be adorned with beads, feathers, flowers, or grass while pierced nasal septums might hold a small bone, although the custom was not universal and seemed only to apply to men. Both sexes often added necklaces of beads, feathers, and shells (abalone and olivella) to their wardrobe.

For shelter, poles bent into a conical shape

Maidu

These objects are a sample from a large early collection of traditional Maidu artifacts, which was assembled in 1899-1903 by Roland B. Dixon. Most of the types of objects shown here went out of use among the Maidu during the present century. This collection comes from three distinct groups or tribes, now called Maidu, Konkow and Nisenan, which were all known as Maidu in Dixon's time. In the following list the tribal origin is mentioned where it can be identified.

1 Headband of flicker feathers, worn by male dancers attached across the forehead. Konkow.
2 Cloak of hawk feathers attached to a net foundation. Konkow.
3 Rattle made of moth cocoons with small pebbles inserted.
4 Pair of split-stick rattles used to accompany ceremonial dances during the winter.
5 End-blown flute of elder wood, with four fingering holes.
6 Feather plume stick of bird scalps and the tips of quail feathers attached to a stick. Konkow.
7 A pair of tremblers, worn stuck horizontally in a ceremonial headdress, one on each side of the head. Konkow.
8 A feather bunch, made of half feathers inserted into a coiled rope of feathers. Konkow.
9 Stone found in a deer, worn around the neck by a deer hunter as a charm.
10 Wooden pipe used for smoking native tobacco. Nisenan.
11 Stone pipe, drilled by tedious tapping with an antler pick.
12 Flaked obsidian knife, considered to be a valuable and powerful object, worn by a shaman around his neck and used in curing.
13 Bow used in hunting and warfare. Made of yew, with a layer of deer sinew glued to the back to add strength. Konkow.
14 Deer arrows, two with obsidian points. Konkow.
15 Squirrel arrows, with long foreshafts. Arrows were painted in patterns unique to each owner. Konkow.
16 Quiver made of a wildcat skin turned inside out. Konkow.
17 Pair of snowshoes, used in the mountains where the snow is deep.
18 Feather bunch, made like No. 8, worn by a dancer

inside a crown of feathered rope. Konkow.

19 Coiled basket, used for cooking acorn mush or soup. Nisenan.

20 Coiled basket tray used for holding food, as a receptacle for sifting acorn meal, and as a cover for large conical baskets. Nisenan.

21 Hairbrush made of pine needles.

22 Coiled basket with arrow-feather design, used for cooking. Nisenan.

23 Four bones used in the popular hand game. Two players each have a marked and an unmarked bone, and the opposing side guesses which hands hold which kind of bone.

24 Coiled basket dipper. Nisenan.

25 Indian-made reduced-size model of a fish trap.

26 Cap of netted cord, used mainly as a foundation to which were pinned feather elements of an elaborate ceremonial headdress.

Konkow.

27 Tumpline of twine, passed across the forehead or chest to support a burden basket. Konkow.

28 Cocoon rattle for dances, similar to No. 3. Nisenan.

29 A full-size model of the sort of figure used at the annual mourning ceremony held in the autumn for five consecutive years after the death of a prominent man. Konkow (or perhaps Nisenan).

and covered in brush or tule sufficed. Occasionally, split redwood or redwood bark constituted the basic construction material. The building of balsas was another use for tule. Double-blade paddles propelled these light craft swiftly through the water.

These people produced other items as well. Baskets, frequently embellished with beads, feathers, and mother-of-pearl were typical. Wild onion or soaproot brushes, mollusc shell spoons, wooden stirring paddles, and various stone implements made many daily chores possible. Both self-bows and sinew-backed versions launched arrows with bone and stone tips.

As with other material necessities, the Costanoan depended on nearby natural resources for food. The ubiquitous acorn, available from several types of live oak, served as the basis for flour to make mush and a form of bread. Other seeds could be roasted and ground into meal too, with chia, digger pine, and holly-leaf cherry offering other forms of subsistence, and which, according to the early missionary, Francisco Palou, could be made into 'a sort of dumpling, ball-shaped and the size of an orange, which was very rich and savory, like toasted almonds'.[29] Strawberries, manzanita berries, and Christmas or the Toyon berry offered other treats in season. Roots, such as 'amhole' (soaproot or Chlorogalum), along with wild carrots, onions, and the herb chuchupate could be obtained too.

Besides vegetable matter, dog, grizzly bear, mole, mountain lion, mouse, rabbit, raccoon, skunk, and squirrel could be taken on land, with snares serving to catch the smaller creatures. The Costanoan likewise hunted deer and did so with deer's heads masks as disguises. They took seals too, although the means of hunting these mammals is uncertain. Quail, hawks, doves, ducks, and geese could be had with nets and traps, depending on the type of the bird. Nets also brought in sturgeon and salmon. Shellfish, most notably abalone, clams, and mussels, offered fine fare when gathered from December through April when they were safe to consume. Shark, swordfish, and other saltwater species may have been killed with spears or taken by hook and line. Occasionally, when a whale washed ashore, the Costanoans held a feast for this specially prized meat.

The Costanoan considered certain food taboo for new mothers who abstained from meat, fish, salt, and cold water for a number of days after giving birth. As young adolescents, females observed these same dietary restrictions. They held some sort of puberty rite as well, while males celebrated their entry into manhood by induction into what was known as a 'datura' society.

Once of age, a young man might take a wife. He and his relatives provided a gift to the bride's family. Then, the couple started their life together with no further formalities. When an infant arrived, the mother nursed for about twenty weeks, during which time the wife and husband refrained from sexual relations. Padre Palou commented on the fact that he saw many of the couples living 'in the most perfect union and peacefulness, loving their children dearly, as the children their parents'.[30] In the event two people chose to end a relationship, they simply separated. Evidently, the children remained

Above: A Nisenan girl wearing an abalone shell necklace and headband and belt decorated with abalone shell pendants, objects of great wealth. Photographed possibly by A.W. Chase before 1876.

with the wife. For a woman who lost a husband, mourning involved such practices as smearing the face with asphalt or black ashes and the cutting of hair. When laying the dead to rest, the women used a stone pestle to beat their breast and heads. The deceased's belongings would be destroyed or buried, while the body might be cremated but sometimes was buried, especially where a person was poor.

In the main, the Costanoan made contact

Below: A Chumash woman wearing a back skirt of painted deerskin ornamented with shells and fringe fronted apron and prized columella bead necklace, picking prickly pears.

with Europeans in the late eighteenth century and soon thereafter provided the population required for the establishment of several Spanish missions founded to the south of the Golden Gate.[31] Conversely, the Coast Miwok (sometimes spelled Mewuk and Meewoc) traced their association with foreign visitors to a much earlier time. Beginning in 1579, some of these inhabitants of land north of San Francisco set eyes upon Sir Francis Drake's crew who had come ashore to repair their ship. They made presents of arrow quivers, feathers, skins, and tobacco to the English and crowned Drake, treating him as a god. Descriptions by the British depicted them as tall, striking, and strong people who regularly traveled at the run. They parted their long hair in the middle or tied it behind in a bunch, the men wearing beards but scant clothing, other than a deerskin loin cloth on occasion.

The double apron favored by the Costanoan persisted among Coast Miwok women. Blankets or capes of rabbit fur and other small mammals resembled those of their southern and eastern neighbors. They likewise carried on the practices of tattooing, body painting, and adornment with feathers fashioned into belts and wristlets. Clamshell disk beads sometimes added to the display but usually this material served as currency.

For food, the Coast Miwok shared a similar diet as described for the Costanoan. They added greens such as miners lettuce, monkey flower, and watercress, and also may have consumed California buttercup and lupine either as greens or in seed form. Other seeds provided the basis for pinole or a mush. Wild cucumber or manroot and edible roots, most notably the bulbs of the wild hyacinth, found their way into the diet.

Coast Miwok diet taboos paralleled those of the Costanoan, but a new mother could have fresh fish and kelp. Sexual abstinence did not seem to last as long as the Costanoan, however, although fathers halted their fishing and hunting activities for a brief period and did not smoke during the same time of abstinence.

These people tended to be monogamous and expected fidelity. When a spouse died, her or his goods were to be buried with them, unless many children remained behind. In that case, shell money would be kept back for the use of the family. This was important since all transactions required payment.

While a monetary system existed, the concept of land ownership was foreign to the Coast Miwok. Nevertheless, they regarded food-producing sources and fishing rights as private property to be respected. So strong was this concept that the Coast Miwok marked their belongings with some sort of personal ownership symbol. They were far from totally materialistic people, however, and supported intricate religious beliefs centered around dance, doctoring, fasting, offerings, and prayer. Often they accompanied many of these ceremonies with music provided by bone whistles, bull-roarers, drums, flutes, and rattles. When not engaged in religious practices or providing food, shelter, or clothing, these first residents of present-day Marin County played games of skill and chance primarily aimed at adults, while children played with dolls and other toys.[32]

Leisure time for some other groups who

Yokuts Shaman's Dance, 1880

A shaman of the Tachi tribe of Southern Valley Yokuts performs a secular Watiyod (spring dance), to entertain onlookers and collect money. Spectators put small amounts of money in the basket beside the singer, who shares it equally with the dancer. The singer marks time with two split-stick clappers of elderberry wood. The shaman wears a skirt of strings of milkweed fiber with owl down twisted in and flicker feathers on the ends, and a separate belt woven with beads. In his ears are falcon feathers; his necklace is of shells and an abalone pendant. His body is painted black and white, and he holds two feather bunches. The fine shaman's headdress rests on a base of owl feathers. The central feathers are magpie, wrapped with red wool and mink fur, with a band of crow wing feathers below.

dwelled along the coast cannot be ascertained with the same certainty. This particularly proved the case with the Esselen people who lived just south of the Costanoan. In fact, little information remains on these people who 'were one of the least populous groups in California, exceedingly restricted in territory, the first to become entirely extinct, and in consequence are now as good as unknown . . .'[33] Soon after contact with the Spanish, the people became part of the mission complex at San Carlos, eventually disappearing as a distinct, independent stock. What little data still remains about them stems from some knowledge about their language which was a generalized Hokan derivative.

So, too, did the Esselen's nearby Hokan-speaking relatives, the Salinan, suffer reductions in numbers after the arrival of the Spanish. In the period before contact with outside forces, the Salinan subsisted on birds, fish, reptiles, and most mammals in their area 'with the single exception of the skunk, and possibly dog and coyote . . .'[34] A half dozen types of acorn, grasses, clover, berries, sunflower, pine nuts, chia, buckeye, and wild oats could be had in their territory.

They took much from the Yokuts way of life in their beliefs, customs, and industries since they frequently traded and carried on other forms of interaction with these people. While friendly with the Yokuts the Salinan usually considered the Costanoans as enemies. Final-

Above: A Diegueño platform granary used for storing mesquite beans, near Santa Isabel, San Diego County. Photographed by Henry W. Henshaw in 1892 or 1893.

Below: Four Diegueño men wearing traditional feather headdresses and black and white body paint; the two women in front wear calico skirts and plaid shawls, and one also has face paint (1880s).

ly, despite a common boundary to their south with the Chumash, the Salinan remained rather aloof from this fellow Hokan language group.

The Chumash far outnumbered the Salinan and ranged over a larger area. They, nonetheless, succumbed to the mission process which at first they willingly accepted. In fact, the Chumash may well have been the first natives of California to be 'discovered' by explorers flying the ensign of Spain. In 1542-3 Juan Rodríquez Cabrillo met the Chumash, who inhabited not only the coast but also some offshore islands making them 'more nearly maritime in their habits than any other California groups'.[35] Their canoes, tomol or tomolo, consisted of planks bound together with cords and then caulked in asphalt found readily around the beaches. Light and swift, the crafts could be powered by as few as two or three paddlers but at times larger versions could be propelled by eight men and carry an additional half dozen passengers.

Besides these plank canoes, the Chumash made another important product, spear-throwers. They could be used on land or at sea, in the latter instance making it possible to harpoon seals and otters. Although these products set the Chumash apart to a certain extent from other California Indians, they did draw upon other native groups for inspiration: from the Yokuts and the Shoshoneans of the southern part of the state for their basket making.

The Shoshoneans formed a corridor on the eastern side of the state which ran almost the entire lower two-thirds of California. Another spur jutted out to the west below today's Santa Barbara and above San Diego. The various sub-elements consisted of such peoples as the Kitanemuk, Tubatulabal, Serrano, Gabrielino, Luiseño, Cahuilla, and Cupeño. Another common name assigned to eastern bands located toward Arizona and Nevada (and considered in the Plateau and Basin chapter) was Pah-Ute or Paiute. On the eve of the American Civil War, some of these people crossed swords with the U.S. army under Major James Henry Carleton. For some time, friction continued but eventually subsided as these Mojave Desert based residents dwindled in numbers.[36]

The 'cousins' of the Paiute, living in what is now the greater Los Angeles area and extending down toward San Diego (the Gabrielino and Luiseño) did not clash openly with military forces of Spain, Mexico, or the United States, 'although they had oft-times distinguished themselves in warfare with other tribes'.[37] One of the weapons the Gabrielino devised when they did engage in combat was the war club, 'which ranged from a heavy stick to a shorter form with a definitely marked cylindrical end …'.[38] Additionally, they developed a curved stick, the *makana*, which they wielded with great effect against rabbits and birds as a sort of boomerang.

The Gabrielino were also innovative in that they had moveable stone mortars for the grinding of various plant foods rather than being restricted to bedrock mortar holes they could not be take along to enable relocation to another site when a village moved. The Luiseño also used moveable mortars alongside bedrock ones. The so-called portable variety actually constituted a large boulder of up to 200lb (90kg) which was hollowed out to form a recessed surface.

A small variation of the Luiseño mortar likewise found its way into the Diegueño society, one of the southernmost inhabitants of California, who, along with the Kamia, Yuma, Hal-chidhoma, and Mojave peoples living in an arc which ran to the east and then up the Colorado River, spoke Hokan dialects. Pottery makers as well as basket makers, the Diegueño employed other familiar aspects of California native culture, most significantly tule balsas which they paddled with double bladed oars. They made pipes of stone and pottery too, the former types presumably being set aside for religious purposes.[39] Gourd and turtle shell rattles provided accompaniment to ceremonies but the Diegueño had no drums, nor did any other southern California group for that matter. (See pp. 152–3 for examples of Diegueño artifacts.)

The Diegueño numbered among the first of California's Indians to be incorporated into the Spanish missions. While the impact of the experience took its toll, the intent was far more benign and humane that the conditions which resulted when the United States gained control of the region after concluding the Treaty of Guadalupe Hidalgo (1848), in the wake of the War with Mexico. The discovery of gold soon followed this transfer of title. With that event, pressure grew to remove the Native Americans to reservations, which:

'from their inception in 1853 until relatively recent times, is hardly a matter of pride. During the 1850s and 1860s, many of the officials placed in charge of Indian affairs were unfit for their posts. Too often, whenever a reservation contained valuable land, selfish whites were permitted to swoop in, and the Indians were driven on to rocky or sandy terrain'.[40]

In time, reactions against this deplorable situation led to reform movements. One champion of the California Indians' cause, Helen Hunt Jackson, wrote two books which attempted to bring the plight of these people to a sympathetic audience. Her publications, A *Century of Dishonor* and *Ramona*, released in 1881 and 1884 respectively, caused ripples to be felt in Washington, as did writings of Mary Hunter Austin and Marah Ellis Ryan, both of whom followed Helen Hunt Jackson's literary tradition most effectively.[41]

Redress came slowly. The Dawes Act of 1887 attempted to reverse the disintegration which escalated in the nineteenth century. Reduced to less than six dozen reservations, with as few as seventy people living on some in the 1960s, the battle to regain lost land went to the courts and Congress. One Federal commission awarded $29 million in exchange for the estimated 64 million acres which once sustained the state's Amerind population. Unfortunately, 'These legal victories came rather late … and have scarcely proved useful in salvaging tribal integrity.'[42] In fact, a mass exodus to cities, particularly Los Angeles and its environs, has depleted reservations even more than before such financial settlements took place.[43] In the urban environment, California Indians tend to be outnumbered by all others, including Indians from groups which originated outside of the state. Thus, the first people to tread this territory struggle to maintain an identity in the face of overwhelming odds. They confront the possible fate of Ishi, 'the last of the wild Indians' of California, whose passing ended an era.[44] Such a loss would effect not only the people of the many cultures who once thrived in California but also diminish us all.[45]

References

1 Federal Writers' Project, 1943: 9.
2 All information and quotations about the various environmental zones are taken from ibid.: 23.
3 Joseph and Kerry Kona Chartkoff, 1984, shed additional light on this topic.
4 Wissler, 1966: 202. The other main language families once extant in California were the Algonquian, Hokan (including the Isoman), Lutuamian, Shoshonean (also called Uto-Aztecan), and Yukian; Heizer and Whipple, 1971: 111. According to another source, some twenty-two linguistic families had existed at one time or another in the state, speaking 'no less than 135 regional dialects'; Rolle and Gaines, 1979: 21.
5 Wissler, 1966: 203.
6 The section on food came from Heizer and Whipple, 1971: 297-300.
7 Cook, 1976: 1, 199.
8 Davis, 1974, discusses this subject in some detail.
9 The group itself deserves more attention than just for its basket work. Some of their world views, for example, are of great interest, as indicated in Clark and Williams, 1954.
10 A. L. Kroeber, 1970: 244. To place work by California native basket makers in context, refer to Mason, 1976.
11 Merrill, 1980, explores this topic more fully.
12 Heizer and Whipple, 1971: 319.
13 Ibid.: 53.
14 A. L. Kroeber, 1970: 2.
15 Ibid.: 34.
16 Ibid.: 76.
17 Ibid.: 319.
18 Thompson, 1971-5. This publication provides a fine overview of this conflict and is recommended reading.
19 Utley, 1984: 171.
20 Members of the Potomac Corral of the Westerners,

1966: 196.
21 For more on this topic consult Cook, 1976a. Also refer to Heizer ed., 1974.
22 Edwards ed., 1970: 56.
23 It should be noted that gold discoveries in the acorn bearing domain inhabited by the Miwok and Yokuts led to friction between the native people and the encroaching white miners. While space prohibits further discussion of this topic, the reader should consult Crampton ed., 1975, for an excellent account of this turbulent time.
24 Lang, 1979: 3. Generally speaking, this synopsis of the Costanoan and Coast Miwok was taken from this source as found on pp.1-56.
25 Ibid.: 7.
26 An early Franciscan missionary noted many of the Costanoan men were bald and bearded and made 'a habit of pulling out the hair of their eyebrows by the roots …'. The same source also mentioned observing capes of beaver skins and pelican feathers for the men and 'plaited tules' skirts for the women, 'for very few skins of animals are seen among them'; Bolton ed., 1926: 121.
27 Lang, 1979: 11.
28 Heizer and Treganza, 1972, provides more details about sources of materials for stone implement making.
29 Fray Francisco Palou, 'The Founding of the Presidio and Mission of Our Father St Francis', George E. Dane, trans XIV, *California Historical Society Quarterly* (June, 1953): 109.
30 Ibid.: 110. Palou was not the only missionary to provide important commentary about early California Indians. Many of the other padres did so, one important example of this type of information being found in Geiger and Meighan, 1976.
31 The northern Costanoans could be found at Missions San Francisco Assis, San Jose, Santa Clara,

and Santa Cruz and the southern Costanoans made up the main numbers at San Juan Bautista, Soledad, and San Carlos. Here, as elsewhere throughout New Spain, the mission, a key colonial institution sanctioned by the Spanish sovereigns to deal with the native people, 'had three fundamental purposes. They desired to convert him, to civilize him, and to exploit him', Bolton, in Bannon ed., 1974: 190. For more on certain aspects of native activities at these combined religious and civil complexes, see Webb, 1952.
32 To provide an overview and some context in this area, the reader should consult Cullin, 1975.
33 A. L. Kroeber, 1970: 544.
34 Ibid.: 547.
35 Ibid.: 550
36 Casebier's two monographs, *Carleton's Pah-Ute Campaign* and *The Battle at Camp Cady* (both published by the author in Norco, California, during 1972) provide details on this short-lived military operation.
37 Reid, 1926: 49.
38 A. L. Kroeber, 1970: 632.
39 The people in this region tended to manipulate both stone and bone by inlaying the basic materials with various patterns and designs. Burnett, 1944, delves into this subject at some length.
40 Rolle and Gaines, 1976: 24.
41 Tuska and Pickasski, 1983: 12-14, 190-91, 303-4, provides basic details about the work of these three authors.
42 Rolle and Gaines, 1976: 27.
43 Wax, 1971: 36, 216-17, 222, shares some useful statistics for more recent times.
44 Theodora Kroeber, 1976, traces this fascinating, bittersweet story.
45 For further reading, Heizer, ed., 1978, remains a must.

Diegueño

These objects were collected by Constance Goddard Du Bois in 1903, 1904, and 1905 from various Indian communities (named below when known) in southern California near the Mexican border, whose members spoke a single Yuman language. The people of some of these communities were and are known as Kamia, Ipai, Tipai, or Kumeyaay. They are descendants of the groups of 'Mission Indians' who were gathered with considerable resistance into the first Franciscan mission in Alta California, established in 1769 at San Diego – hence the name Diegueño. The missions were secularized in 1834, initiating the long Diegueño struggle to preserve their lands and livelihoods. In pre-mission times the Diegueño depended for subsistence on acorns and mesquite beans, flour made from various seeds, on berries, fruits, and other vegetable foods, and on deer, rodents, and birds hunted by the men (rodents supplying the most meat). A little corn and beans were grown on newly-flooded lands. Important in ritual and shamanistic practices was a vision-producing drink of toloache root. Some shamans cured with herbal remedies as well. Girls' puberty rites were important in many Diegueño communities. A particularly important ceremony commemorated deceased members of a clan, with feasting, the distribution of gifts to non-relatives, dancing with images of the deceased, and at dawn burning of the images, regalia, and new goods. Shamanistic tricks and contests were a part of this ceremony.

1 Cooking pot; old type.
2 Two-mouthed jar.
3 Pottery jar. Manzanita.
4 Two-mouthed jar.
5 Pottery dish. Campo.
6 Tool to smooth pottery.
7 Pottery pipe, used with rabbit bone stem; model of old type made at La Jolla.
8 Throwing stick to hunt rabbits.
9 Woman's stick game.
10 Half of girl's skirt, of elder bark fastened with milkweed cord; worn with another such in front or behind; model of an obsolete style. Mesa Grande.
11 Woman's basketry cap. Campo.
12 Blanket or robe of twined rabbit-skin cords. San Felipe.
13 Twined openwork basket.
14 Brush of yucca fibers for sweeping off metate (grindstone). San Felipe.
15 Pottery paint dish.
16 Pottery dish.
17 Woman's carrying bag of milkweed cords. San Felipe.
18 Pair of yucca fiber sandals. Manzanita.
19 Horsehair halter. Campo.
20 Man's carrying basket. La Jolla.
21 Net cape with pendant eagle feathers used in (obsolete) eagle dance.
22 Stick game. Mesa Grande.
23 Wand used by shaman to throw a 'pain' into an enemy, and also for curing; in the wooden handle is an archeological stone Elko Eared projectile point made c.1500 BC.

THE NORTHWEST COAST

THE NORTHWEST Coast offers a mild climate with a wide array of food resources. Several distinctive cultures developed on the Northwest Coast from the Columbia River through coastal British Columbia to the top of the Alaskan panhandle. The cultures are very similar in some ways and remarkably diverse in others. People from all regions developed a rich ceremonial and spiritual life. They invested tremendous creative energy in artistic expression, including songs, dances, legends and spectacular, philosophically powerful art work.

There are several different languages indigenous to the Northwest Coast, each with its own subdivisions or dialects. Since there were no large political units outside of the individual village, the cultures are conveniently grouped today according to language. The southern portion of the Coast, including the mainland and lower Vancouver Island, is the homeland of the Coast Salish. The Nuu-chah-nulth people live on the west coast of Vancouver Island and were formerly called the Nootka, a name originally

Below: *Interior of a Tlingit chief's house in the village of Klukwan, c.1895. The painted and carved screen known as the 'rain wall' (rear) epitomizes the high symbolic content of Tlingit art.*

given them by Captain Cook. They are closely related to the Makah on the tip of the Olympic Peninsula in Washington state, and the national boundary that separates them is a relatively recent development in the history of the Northwest Coast. The Southern Kwakiutl villages are in northeastern portions of Vancouver Island and the adjacent mainland. Branches of the Northern Kwakiutl, who speak different dialects and have some different cultural characteristics from the Southern Kwakiutl peoples, live in the central portion of the British Columbia coastline. The language of the neighboring Bella Coola people is related to that of the Salish; they originally moved to central British Columbia from the south and adopted some cultural traits of central groups. Along the coastline and the lower Nass and Skeena Rivers to the north are the villages of the Tsimshian. The Queen Charlotte Islands are the homeland of the Haida Indians, whose large seaworthy cedar canoes kept them from being isolated. A few centuries ago a group of the Haida moved northward and settled what is now the southern portion of Prince of Wales Island in Alaska. They are now known as the Kaigani Haida but have maintained communication with their relatives on the Charlottes: here, too, the national boundary is both recent and arbitrary. Tlingit Indians live along the panhandle of southeast Alaska; some also moved into inland British Columbia. Because this chapter focuses on the eighteenth and nineteenth centuries, past tense will be used; but it should be emphasized that Northwest Coast Indians still live on the coast today and are culturally and politically active.

Northwest Coast peoples enjoyed a relatively favorable natural environment compared to most other places in North America. While the entire region can get harsh winds and rain, only the portion in the north regularly gets freezing winters and heavy snowfalls. The yearly salmon runs offer a fairly reliable food resource; and there are a variety of other fish, shellfish, sea mammals and plants, roots and berries to supplement the diet and compensate for poor salmon seasons. However, the native peoples were able to take advantage of these resources only because they developed very specialized knowledge and highly efficient tools for both harvesting and processing.[1] People stored food they harvested in the summer for consumption in the winter. Thus, like agriculturalists, they did not have to travel after food in the winter and could establish permanent villages.

Because of this environment, the region supported a relatively dense population compared

This map shows approximate territories of tribes and language groups in the early nineteenth century. After that, all tribes lost territory.

Key to tribes:

1 Eyak	**16** Makah
2 Tlingit	**17** Southern Coast Salish
3 Haida	**18** Quileute
4 Nishga	**19** Chemakum
5 Gitksan	**20** Southwestern Coast Salish
6 Tsimshian	**21** Kwalhioqua
7 Haisla	**22** Chinookans
8 Haihais	**23** Clatskanie
9 Bella Bella	**24** Tillamook
10 Bella Coola	**25** Alseans
11 Oowekeeno	**26** Siuslawans
12 Kwakiutl	**27** Kalapuyans
13 Northern Coast Salish	**28** Coosans
14 Nootkans (Nuu-chah-nulth)	**29** Athapaskans
15 Central Coast Salish	**30** Takelma

to other places on the continent north of Mexico. While population estimates are always speculative, it has been suggested that there were over 46,700 Indians in coastal British Columbia in 1835.[2] Undoubtedly the population there was greater before white diseases were introduced. In 1880 the native population of southeast Alaska was estimated at about 12,000, and again, the population was undoubtedly smaller than it had been before the arrival of Europeans.[3]

Traditionally people lived in numerous villages along the coastline and inland rivers. Often large extended families lived together in communal longhouses spread in a row along the beach. The villages were permanent settlements inhabited for generations or longer. People made excursions from them for hunting and fishing, trading, social activities and military raids. The village was the major political unit, and people identified first and foremost with the leadership in their village.

The villages were always located along waterways, either the coastline or rivers closely connected to the coast. From the sea came food, but also materials that were used in manufacturing clothes and tools – skins from sea mammals, as well as bones, bladders, and sinew. The great temperate rainforests were also vital to the cultures. Trees, especially cedar, provided the materials for large communal houses, sturdy canoes, and a variety of utilitarian and ceremonial items.[4] Women used the inner bark of the cedar and the roots of cedar and spruce to weave highly functional baskets, capes, mats, and cordage. Some of these baskets were woven so tightly that they could hold water.[5]

In addition to the food it yielded, the ocean was tremendously important for transportation. The coastline of the region is rocky and irregular, and land transportation was much less practical than travel by canoe. Again, it was the Indians' technological skill that made it possible for them to take advantage of this opportunity. They built large canoes, spreading them to a functional width with steam. In this method, water is placed in the bottom of the dugout log and hot rocks are dropped into it to create the steam. The sides of the canoe must be well balanced in width to create a stable and seaworthy vessel, and the entire process takes considerable work and skill. The canoes were vital for hunting and fishing, and also for trade and social exchange between villages up and down the coast. People from southeast Alaska may have traveled down the coast as far south as California for trade. In some Haida oral traditions there are stories of voyages to Hawaii, although these have yet to be corroborated by any archeological record.

The Northwest Coast region was probably inhabited very shortly after the ice sheets from the last Ice Age uncovered the coast line – some 9000 to 13,000 years ago. The land and water fluctuated for some time before reaching the configuration we know today. At first the human populations were nomadic, but as the flora and fauna came to resemble that of the present, they developed the food-storing technologies that make permanent villages feasible. Archeological finds suggest that the cultural characteristics known in recent times were already highly developed at least fifteen

PACIFIC OCEAN

hundred years ago and probably somewhat earlier.[6] Indians on the Northwest Coast traded with other coastal groups and with inland peoples prior to the arrival of Europeans,· so they were by no means isolated. Substantial contact between Indians and Europeans began to occur in the last quarter of the eighteenth century. Thus, that time is often known as the beginning of the historic era, but Northwest Coast Indians had a vibrant history and kept oral historical records long before the arrival of the Europeans.

On all parts of the Northwest Coast, family ties were extremely important. People identified closely with extended families and with

lineages, and in many places rank and political leadership were hereditary. Each lineage owned certain privileges. These ranged from the right to perform specific dances to the right to use resources in a certain geographic area. In most places on the coast there were various levels of social status, including people of high rank, people of lower rank, and slaves who were captured in battle or purchased through trade.[7]

Among the Tlingit, Haida and Tsimshian on the northern coast, the society was matrilineal, and children inherited through their mother. Thus, a leader might be succeeded by his sister's son rather than by his own son, and boys were often trained by their maternal uncles. In

the northern groups with matrilineal descent, social divisions based on kinship were especially important. For instance, the Tlingit divided themselves into two basic hereditary groups, known as moieties. One was known as the Raven, while the other was called the Wolf (or occasionally the Eagle). Everyone in society belonged to the Raven or Wolf moiety, and people could only marry someone from the opposite moiety. Thus, since the society was matrilineal, children always had the same moiety affiliation as their mother and a different one from their father. Each moiety was subdivided into smaller groups, which anthropologists often call clans or sibs. The Raven moiety had some twenty-seven clans.[8] Within each village, there would be a leader for every clan that lived there. Many clans had branches in more than one village, but leadership always remained local. Social organization among the Haida and Tsimshian was similar, with some clans also among the Northern Kwakiutl.[9]

Among the groups on the lower coast – the Southern Kwakiutl, Nuu-chah-nulth, Bella Coola and Coast Salish groups – inheritance came from both parents. Family ties and local kinship group relationships were still considered extremely important. As in the north, kinship families had recognized leaders who gave guidance about such matters as resource use and marriages.[10]

In all parts of the coast, ties between different kinship groups were politically and economically essential. These ties were solidified through trade, and often – as in Europe – marriages helped promote political and economic relationships between different kinship groups or different villages.[11]

Ceremonial gatherings also served to develop and reinforce these ties. There were many different types of ceremonial gatherings up and down the coast. Today they are often all re-

Above: *Interior of a Tlingit dwelling, Sitka, Alaska. Clothing and metal utensils evidence white contact but the open interior of the plank house is typical of many dwellings.*

Below: *A Tlingit village in Alaska, c.1883. The siting of houses in this permanent village is typical, located on low benches slightly above the high water mark of sea or flood-level of rivers.*

ferred to by one term – potlatch – which is a word from the Chinook trade jargon meaning 'to give'.[12] Actually, though, there was tremendous diversity in the nature and purpose of the ceremonies. They were very complex institutions combining social, cultural, spiritual, political and economic elements. Because of the diversity on the coast and the complexity of the celebrations themselves, it is difficult to discuss them without reducing them to a much too simplistic level.

In brief, potlatches were sponsored by a host who had saved food and material goods for the express purpose of the occasion. Guests were invited from other kin groups and other villages, and the celebrations could continue for days or considerably longer. During the potlatch, the host displayed and emphasized certain rights or prerogatives. For instance, these privileges might include the right to take the name, political title or other hereditary prerogatives of a relative who had recently died. In some potlatches parents or other relatives would confer certain prerogatives on their children. The prerogatives were expressed at the potlatch through dances, songs, oration and display of art.[13]

The guests from other lineages and other villages watched these claims to rights, acting as witnesses. The host fed them amply from the food he had stored, and gave them gifts from the material possessions he had accumulated for the purpose. When the witnesses accepted the food and gifts, it was understood that they affirmed the host's right to claim the privileges displayed during the potlatch. In effect, the witnesses were paid for publicly acknowledging these rights and for keeping the memory of the potlatch alive. People passed on stories of potlatches they had attended, creating a communal memory of the event and of the affirmation of the host's right to the privileges he displayed there. This system of witnessing, of communal memory and of oral tradition functioned very efficiently as a way of keeping records, and made a written language unnecessary.

Thus the potlatches were extremely important for validating rank and leadership. They were also vital for passing the rich cultural heritage from generation to generation, for during ceremonies children saw the songs, dances and art work that referred to the history and legends of their families and their people. The potlatches served an economic role, for they kept goods circulating in several ways. A leader saving for a potlatch would often loan goods, receiving goods of their value back with interest as the time of the celebration grew near. That leader then distributed goods to his guests in payment for their witnessing role. In return, high ranking guests would aspire to reciprocate with their own potlatch, matching or exceeding the gifts of the former host. In preparing for that event, they would loan some of their goods. Thus, the potlatch system supported a cycle of exchange of material wealth. The host of a potlatch might be almost bereft of material possessions at the end of the gathering, but his wealth measured in honor would be greater.

Ceremonies took place in the winter months, when families were living on food they had stored during the summer and autumn. Freed from the necessity of traveling for food, they were able to take the time for large social gatherings. Thus the rhythm of life moved with the seasons, with different economic, social and cultural activities in different times of the year.

Whatever the season, Northwest Coast peoples surrounded themselves with artistic expression. There was no firm demarcation between 'art' and 'daily life', as tends to exist in Western cultures today. Northwest Coast arts were functional arts, adapted to perform a task or convey a message. The purpose of the art went far beyond aesthetics, and it was intended for much more than contemplation. Northwest Coast peoples decorated tools and utensils they used in daily life, and they created spectacular and dramatic masterpieces to display crests or for use in dances. Men carved wood, bone and antler and sometimes also worked in stone. Women wove with plant and animal fibers, decorating their vessels, mats and blankets with careful designs. While most adults developed skills in making articles for daily uses, it took specialized training to create monumental and ceremonial art. Thus, carvers of totem poles, masks and similar art works apprenticed with master carvers to learn the skills. They earned high reputations for their

Below: *Sitka Jake, a Tlingit, wearing Chilkat dance headdress and blanket, the latter woven by women from cedar bark and mountain goats' wool from designs drawn by men on a special pattern board.*

Tlingit

The Tlingit are a nationality, not a unified political body, living on the strip of mainland and hundreds of islands just offshore, along the panhandle of southeastern Alaska. There are three main groups of Tlingit tribes or local communities, each consisting of nearby villages occupied by several matrilineal clans. Clans had territorial rights, and each one owned several crests which leading members displayed on totem poles in front of lineage-owned houses, and on many objects. Social ranks and the right to display crests were validated in potlatches, where property was distributed by the hosts to guests. Dance and feast regalia included the famous Chilkat blankets, and button blankets with designs outlined in imported mother-of-pearl buttons, often also with fine appliqué designs representing clan crests. For the objects in both spreads, the tribe of origin is given where known, along with the date when the object was collected (or when it entered the museum).

1 Rope of twisted cedar bark worn as a belt in dancing. Hutsnuwu, 1881.
2 Wooden hat with carved beaver and potlatch rings c.1883.
3 Dance cape, of leather with painted design of bear, wool tassels, deer hoofs on fringe. 1903.
4 Carved wooden box, for holding food. Chilkat, 1882.
5 Shaman's wooden rattle, representing oyster catcher. Hoonah, 1884.
6 Classic ancient style bi-pointed fighting knife, hammered from trade iron, eyes inlaid with abalone. Sitka, before 1870.
7 Northern style dagger, with bone handle carved to represent bear. Hutsnuwu, 1881.
8 Pair of small canoe paddles. 1876.
9 Dance frontlet, carved and painted wood representing a bear. Haida, Skidegate, 1883.
10 Frontlet, portrait of a

favorite daughter of a Haida chief. Haida, Skidegate, before 1903.

11 Food bowl, kerfed and bent wood, painted. Sitka. 1884.

12 Wooden spoon with carved handle.

13 Leather pouch containing set of gambling sticks. Chilkat, 1882.

14 Twined basket with cover. 1893.

15 Twined basket with cover. Sitka. 1882.

16 Chilkat blanket, twined, of mountain goat wool. 1893.

17 Dance headband of twined cedar bark, dyed red, with abalone ornament. Stikine. 1905.

18 Carved horn comb. Sitka, 1884.

19 Carved wood food box. Sitka, 1884.

20 Wooden food dish in shape of seal. Hutsnuwu, 1881.

21 Ladle of mountain sheep horn. Sitka, 1874.

22 Carved wooden spoon.

Hutsnuwu, 1881.

23 Rope of twisted cedar bark, worn as belt in dancing. Hutsnuwu, 1881.

24 Twined basketry hat. Chilkat, 1903.

25 Wooden food dish, ends carved and painted. 1874.

26 Carved wooden dish for a child. Stikine, 1876.

27 Silver bracelet engraved with raven. Sitka, 1875.

28 Silver bracelet engraved with whale. Sitka, 1875.

29 Carved wooden berry spoon. Stikine, 1875.

proficiency, and leaders commissioned art from these masters. In the Tlingit region, usually art was commissioned from an artist who belonged to the opposite moiety from the patron.[14]

Northwest Coast Indian art is well known today internationally. Most people associate the term either with the highly structured linear art of the northern regions of the coast, or with the dramatic and colorful dance masks of the Southern Kwakiutl. In fact, there is tremendous diversity in artistic expression up and down the coast, and it would be much more accurate to refer to Northwest Coast Indian arts in the plural. Regional artistic styles developed, and in some cases specific styles can be traced to individual villages. There are certain characteristics common throughout the coast, and others that differ regionally.

There were three principal forms of art made

Above: Tlingit men and boys in dance costume, 1895. Their clothing is mainly fabricated from trade cloth adorned with beads, bone or mother-of-pearl buttons in traditional patterns.

on the coast: two-dimensional design in the way of painting or light engraving; three-dimensional sculpture, usually woodcarving; and the production of baskets, mats, woven hats, and textiles. Two-dimensional design appears on a wide variety of articles. Pigment for paints was made from minerals such as red ochre and copper mixed in a medium of fish roe; later artists adopted commercial pigments bought through trade. House fronts and canoes sometimes had motifs painted on them. Large storage chests were often painted, or both painted and engraved. Woven hats sometimes also had painted motifs, showing collaboration between female and male artists. Wood food bowls and grease dishes often had two-dimensional design engraved on their surface, and utensils such as berry spoons were also frequently painted or engraved. Ceremonial items such as masks were also painted. Two-dimensional design was practiced long before Europeans arrived on the Northwest Coast. Archeological finds suggest that the technical, highly formalized styles found on the northern part of the coast were developing there at least a thousand years ago.

Three dimensional sculpture also included a wide range of articles, from wood carving tools to feast dishes and ceremonial masks – and, on some parts of the coast, the totem poles for which the region is famous. The tradition of

Left: Eight Tlingit men, three of them in treasured Chilkat blankets, the group at left in headdresses (with carved wooden frontlets) embellished with sea-lion whiskers and whole ermine skins.

sculpture extends back centuries and possibly millennia. Very expressive stone sculptures have been found in many regions of the coast dating back at least three thousand years.[15] Almost certainly these same artists were practicing in wood as well, but wood deteriorates more quickly than stone and is less likely to be preserved in archeological sites.

Female artists made woven and coiled baskets, woven mats, hats, capes and textiles. After trade with Europeans started, they also practiced beadwork and appliqué, and outlined designs on commercial wool dance blankets by sewing rows of decorative pearl buttons. Until recently, these art forms unfortunately received less attention in the literature about Northwest Coast Indian arts, but they, too, required substantial skill and creativity. Like wood, basketry does not last well in archeological sites except under unique circumstances, but there are still enough indications to suggest that Northwest Coast people have made baskets for thousands of years.

Each of these three primary art forms differed regionally on the coast. The two-dimensional design made by northern artists – the Haida, Tsimshian and Tlingit – was quite different from that made by artists to the south – the Southern Kwakiutl, Nuu-chah-nulth, Bella Coola and Salish. Northern Kwakiutl villages, in a central position between these regions, produced some works resembling northern styles

and others suggesting a southern influence. The two-dimensional art practiced by the Haida, Tsimshian and Tlingit artists follows the same very technical set of conventions. It is very difficult to tell two-dimensional art from these peoples apart unless there is documentation, or unless the work also has sculptural qualities. The very complex art style is known today as 'Northern formline'.[16] Stated much too simply, artists depicted animals by using a series of standard conventions and combining them in fairly uniform ways. Basic outlines are defined by 'formlines' which are curvilinear; right angles are rare. The formlines vary greatly in width, giving the designs a dynamic sense of fluidity and motion. The lines converge and diverge to form certain shapes that recur again and again. Thus, a somewhat oval shape, called today an 'ovoid', usually depicts eyes and joints in limbs or appendages. U-forms often indicate ears, snouts, and wing feathers, and the fins and flukes of sea mammals and fish. There were very standard ways that artists combined the formlines to create these elements, and there were also standard ways in which artists placed the design within the shape of the field they had to decorate. Individual expression writ

Below: Tlingit in ceremonial costume at a potlatch in Klukwan, Alaska. The man to the left wears an elaborately painted hide tunic over a trade shirt. Some of the men have metal nose rings.

large was not the goal; but individual artists had personal styles that were all the more creative because of their subtlety.

Two-dimensional design in the more southern groups, by contrast, followed fewer standard conventions. Thus there is considerably more variety in style. It is usually not difficult to distinguish Southern Kwakiutl, Nuu-chah-nulth and Salish two-dimensional design from each other. Each of these groups had their own aesthetic and artistic goals. Unfortunately there is not much information about Southern Kwakiutl art in the eighteenth century. In the nineteenth century these artists experimented with elements from northern painting, varying them significantly to create a style that is distinctly Southern Kwakiutl. The early works from the Nuu-chah-nulth, found in archeological sites and collected by late eighteenth-century European explorers, suggest a tradition emphasizing rows or bands of geometric elements and liberal use of circles and dots. Some of the curves suggest more northern elements. In the mid-nineteenth century, some Nuu-chah-nulth artists also began incorporating more northern elements into their art work. The lines and shapes in Coast Salish two-dimensional design have much in common with the northern graphic art, although again there are fewer standard conventions, more wide-ranging variation between designs, and a highly developed aesthetic unique to Salish artists. It is

Tlingit

Tlingit economy in the past was a maritime one, as it still is largely today. Five species of salmon are important, especially in the summer. Halibut are taken in the spring as, formerly, were seals and otters. Waterfowl were taken in spring and summer, and the dense forests behind the beaches furnished berries, roots and deer, bear, marten, mink, beaver, mountain sheep and mountain goat. Northern style art displayed on most Tlingit artifacts follows

rules governing the representation of animal and human forms that include wrapping essentially 2-dimensional designs around 3-dimensional objects, rearranging body parts in ways that sometimes made deciphering difficult, and connecting elements of designs with carefully planned form-lines. The scale of an object has little effect. Lines and forms are treated the same way whether carved or painted. Wood is the main material, with bone and ivory also used; shell inlays are common. Copper was used and valued aboriginally.

1 Cylindrical twined basket with cover. Sitka, 1882.
2 Woodworking adze, steel blade, bone handle; the straight adze type typical of southern area. Makah (not Tlingit), 1876.
3 Wooden box, painted, with fitted lid with opercula inlay. Sitka, 1884.
4 Stone maul. Sitka, 1884.
5 Wooden box, carved, with fitted lid with opercula inlay. Hutsnuwu, 1881.
6 Knife for woodcarving, 1901.
7 Woman's knife. Sitka, 1892.
8 Fish knife. Sitka, 1884.
9 Stone fish pounder, Sitka, 1874.
10, 11 Stone rubbers, perhaps for hide dressing, 1876.
12 Dress of white-tanned caribou skin. 1901.
13 Large labret, worn by woman. 1900.
14 Wooden fish masher. Baranof Is. (Sitka or Hutsnuwu).
15 Twined basket.
16 Twined basket. 1890.

17 Harpoon head and line. 1890s.

18 Buckskin shirt. Sitka, 1875.

19 Drum, hide stretched over a pine hoop. Sitka, 1875.

20 Shaman's necklace of incised ivory pendants. Sitka, 1884.

21 Bone snuff tube. Chilkat, 1882.

22 Stone carving of bear. Killisnoo, Hutsnuwu, 1903.

23 Graver's tool. 1901.

24 Awl in carved handle. Hoonah, 1881.

25 Wooden headdress for dancing. Hoonah, 1881.

26 Shaman's cape, painted, with rattles. Sitka. 1875.

27 Shaman's mask. Sitka, 1904.

28 Wooden tobacco pipe. Sitka, 1884.

29 Carved ivory charm. Sitka, 1882.

30 Copper mask, shell inlays, fur hair. Yakutat, 1926.

31 Dance helmet, carved from single block of wood, painted, with tufts of hair. Sitka, 1875.

32 Wooden collar and face mask, worn as armor; held in place by cord between teeth; notches for eyes. Sitka, 1874.

33 Body armor, of rods held together by twined cords. Hutsnuwu, 1882.

34 Knife; non-Indian steel blade, Tlingit-made handle. 1881.

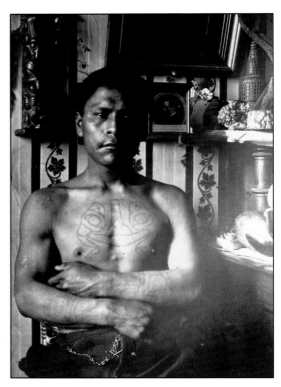

Left: Haida shaman and patient re-enacting a cure. The dress of the shamans varied according to the spirit possessing them, generally consisting of an apron or cloak covered with esoteric designs.

Right: Johnnie Kit Elswa, a Haida from Skidegate, Queen Charlotte Is., 1886. The tattoos allude to events in family history: on his chest a brown bear is represented, at each wrist a dogfish.

from plant fibers. The inner bark of the cedar, cedar root, spruce root and grasses were most often used. Twining was the technique most prevalent, although women from interior Salish villages also made coiled baskets. Dyed grasses and other dyed plant fibers were added during the manufacturing process to form decorative designs, which were usually geometric. Types of designs and forms of baskets varied somewhat from region to region. In the eighteenth century, the Nuu-chah-nulth wove a very distinctive conical-shaped hat with whaling scenes. Along with their close relatives the Makah, they were the only Northwest Coast peoples to hunt whales, and these whaling hats are unique to that region.[19]

Women in some groups – particularly Coast Salish and Tlingit – also wove blankets from animal wool. Salish women used hair from small domesticated dogs as well as wool of mountain goat, often mixed with plant fibers.[20] Tlingit women made the famous Chilkat dancing blankets of mountain goat wool and cedar bark. These blankets show elaborate figures in Northern formline design, taken skillfully from a pattern painted on a wooden board by a male

Below: Potlatch dancers, Klinkwan, Alaska, c.1900. Potlatches, complex ceremonies involving feasts and dances, were very important to Northwest Coast tribes such as the Tlingit, shown here.

possible that far back in antiquity there was once a much more uniform art style on the coast, and people in different regions chose to modify it in different directions.[17]

Sculptural styles differ substantially up and down the coast. In the north, where two-dimensional art is almost identical, sculptural styles vary considerably from language group to language group. The variations are even greater in the south, where each group has a particularly distinctive carving style and a unique genre of masks.[18]

Women up and down the coast were proficient at weaving baskets, mats, hats and capes

artist.[21] When commercial beads became available through trade, women also began using them for ceremonial items.

Ceremonial and monumental art played a variety of roles in traditional cultures. Like artistic style, these roles varied from region to region. In northern areas, much of the ceremonial art displayed crests identifying the lineage of the owner. Thus, a man wearing a mask of a bear would belong to the Bear sib or clan. In some ways, the crests served much as coats of arms in Europe. In other ways, they differed from coats of arms, for they also might refer to experiences that the wearer's ancestor – the

Above: *A Bella Coola village, c.1885, on the British Columbia coast. The village shows several painted house fronts along the beach and basket fish traps behind the foreground figures.*

person who founded the family – had had with an actual bear spirit.

In fact, much of the art refers to a primordial time when boundaries between human beings, spirits and animals were much more fluid than they are at present. During this time, animals could marry human beings, and sometimes spirits transformed themselves from animal form to human form. People who had experiences with animals and spirits in these ways could acquire the right to display an animal as a crest and to pass that crest on to descendants. Thus, a work of art that displays a crest may do more than signify genealogy. It may also speak of the history of the family and of the specific rights that family enjoys as a result of ancestral experiences. In effect, the art work makes visible all the invisible rights the family has – the rights to perform certain dances, sing certain songs, tell certain stories, and claim a specific ancestral history. These rights were carefully guarded, and it was inappropriate for any member of society to perform a dance or sing a song to which he or she was not entitled.

Crests were displayed in a variety of contexts. Masks were carved in the form of crests and worn in dances. Ceremonial frontlets with crest designs were worn on the forehead. Chilkat blankets were woven with crest designs, and basketry hats had crest designs painted on them. Sometimes house fronts were painted with crest designs. Probably the most well-known form of crest display is the totem pole, which has become a symbol for the Northwest Coast today. Contrary to popular belief, they were not carved all over the coast, and were most prevalent among the lower Tlingit, the Haida, the Tsimshian and the Kwakiutl peoples. There has been some debate as to whether totem poles existed prior to the arrival of European traders with their iron tools.

Almost all scholars agree today that totem poles were a well-established art form before Europeans arrived. However, it is also almost certainly true that the iron tools – as well as the ceremonial activities that were supported by the fur trade – increased the number of totem poles being carved.

There were many types of totem poles, varying in size depending on their function. When a high-ranking person died, often his successor, or other members of his family, raised a pole in his honor. The pole would display crest figures pertinent to his ancestry. Other poles, known as frontal poles, stood against the front of house displaying crests of a family living in it. Interior house posts, which were shorter than most memorial poles and frontal poles, supported the beams of the house. In some regions of the coast, especially among the Haida, human remains were placed in grave boxes at the top of mortuary poles. Mortuary poles tended to be relatively short, with one or two primary crest figures displayed. In places on the coast where people were buried, carved figures were often placed to mark the grave. Freestanding carvings of human beings, known as welcome figures, were sometimes placed on village beaches, especially in the lower half of the Northwest Coast, to welcome visitors.[22]

Totem pole raisings were accompanied by a potlatch. The guests who came acted as witnesses affirming that the family raising the pole had the right to do so. The potlatch accompanying a memorial pole would honor the person who had recently died, and would create a

Right: *Traditionally the heavy cedar timbers of a Northwest Coast indoor house frame as well as center gable post were carved and painted. From such features the heraldic or totem pole evolved. Widely distributed along the northern part of the coast, the freestanding pole in front of the house seems to have been quite a recent innovation, its heyday being between c.1850 and 1900. Majestic, dignified and imposing in their design, each figure on the pole referred to the crest of the owner and his family or incidents in their history.*

Haida Heraldic or Totem Pole

Watchman figures wearing so-called potlatch rings which referred to wealth and prestige

Mammal (probably a bear) holding two smaller animals

Carving was enhanced by limited painting, natural pigments being used: black was obtained from coal and charcoal, red from alder bark or iron ore

Mammal (probably a bear) holding a small human figure

Raven with small human figure on the front

Haida

Haida territory is the Queen Charlotte Islands in British Columbia and a small part of Alaska immediately to the north. The traditional social organization is matrilineal, with lineage ownership of the large plank houses. There was no overall Haida political organization; regional groups of villages are recognized. Totemic crests were associated with the lineages and with individuals within them. Most were animals and birds, but some referred to natural phenomena such as clouds, rainbow, evening sky. This was a highly ranked class society, with ceremonies intimately related to individual status. These rituals included feasts, potlatches, and dance performances, during which prestige and status were achieved and maintained by the display and distribution of objects of wealth. Guests were served special foods in fine dishes and bowls. Dance regalia was varied and elaborate, including masks and headdresses, and specialized musical instruments such as drums, rattles, and whistles. Elaborate, carefully controlled artistic decoration was emphasized, and nearly every artifact was decorated, usually with zoomorphic designs. Specialists in carving and painting were highly respected. The art style is widely appreciated not only on the Northwest Coast, and is currently practiced by many fine artists. Objects illustrated in these two spreads (except as otherwise noted) were collected between 1875 and 1884 by Judge James G. Swan of Washington Territory at the localities mentioned.

1 Dance cape; wool blanket with mother-of-pearl buttons and appliquéd red flannel design of a killer whale with attached dorsal fins. Skidegate.

2 Dance mask, representing a sparrow hawk.

3 Dance mask, representing an old woman with labret in lower lip. Cumshewa.

4 Dance headdress, worn by a woman.

5 Spherical rattle, of painted wood, two pieces tied together. Skidegate.

6 Dance mask of painted wood, copper inlays, represents a bear, with collar of cedar bark and wood pendants.

7 Carved and painted figurine. Sitka.

8 Headdress for crow dance. Skidegate.

9 Carved wooden tobacco pipe. Sitka.

10 Head ornament for dance, representing killer whale, painted wood head with movable flukes, connected by cloth to painted wood tail. Skidegate.

11 Food dish, of wood kerfed and then steamed and bent. Skidegate.

12 Double whistle of wood, for dances. Skidegate.

13 Dance rattle, carved and painted wood, represents raven with man and frog on back, sparrow-hawk on breast. Masset.

14 Large wooden whistle representing mountain demon's call. Skidegate.

Haida

The Haida in aboriginal times depended chiefly on fish (particularly halibut, sockeye and salmon) and shellfish, and then on sea mammals (seals, porpoises, sea lions, sea otters), plant products (especially berries, also roots, seaweed, and hemlock and spruce inner bark), and land animals (deer, caribou, beaver, bear) and birds. Everyone collected shellfish and birds' eggs and hunted birds. Women gathered roots and berries, seaweed, and materials for basketry. They prepared, cooked, and preserved all foods, tanned animal skins, made all the clothing and basketry. Men fished and hunted both sea and land animals, built houses, made the large canoes, and did all the wood carving and painting. Basketry hats were woven by women and the painted designs on them were applied by men. Haida art is similar in style to that of Tlingit, Tsimshian, and Bella Bella, but carving in argillite is a Haida specialty; some basketry patterns are distinct from those of their neighbors.

1 Fine carved slate (argillite) box made for sale, top design a killer whale, added heads in front (bear), and ends (wolf).
2 Carved argillite panel. Collected by Wilkes Expedition, 1841.
3 Carved argillite, made for sale, representing a platter with a fish.
4 Dance cape, dark blue blanket with red appliqué design representing killer whales. Skidegate.
5 Carved panels of wood with bone inlays, with European (perhaps Russian) motifs, made for sale. Collected by Wilkes Expedition, 1841.
6 Feast dish of wood, carved and painted ends, opercula inlay on rim. Collected by J.J. McLean, 1882. Hutsnuwu, Tlingit.
7 Bowl of mountain sheep horn. Collected by J.J. McLean, 1884, Sitka.
8 Chief's bow and arrow, used in dances, obtained

168

from Capt. Skedans, chief of Kloo.

9 Twined basketry hat with painted design. Masset.

10 Bowl of mountain sheep horn, shaped by steaming then carved and inlaid with abalone shell.

11 Bowl of mountain sheep horn. Ft Simpson.

12 Dance hat, of blue-painted wood with copper inlays and eight twined basketry potlatch rings.

13 Dance skirt trimmed with Chinese coins, edged with quillwork and fringed with puffin beaks. Skidegate.

14 Twined basketry hat, of fine spruce root fibers, a virtuoso imitation of a Panama hat. Skidegate.

15 Dance headdress, painted wood, representing duck on top of killer whale. Skidegate.

16 Food dish of mountain goat horn.

17 Food dish of mountain goat horn, carved to represent a duck.

Skidegate.

18 Iron sealing harpoon head attached to line, with wooded sheath. Collected by J.L. Gould, 1884.

19 Wooden food dish, representing a seal. Collected by Lt L. Curtis 1881.

20 Close-twined spruce root basket. Collected by Lt G.T. Emmons, c.1892.

21 Yew wood sealing club, carved to represent a sea lion. Masset.

Haida Canoes

Stern raised high above water facilitates sea-going travel.

Sharp pointed paddles for propulsion; also formidable weapons

Canoes were hollowed from single trunk by means of controlled burning and use of adze and chisel

Heraldic design: the thunderbird, omnipotent victor of the heavens and helpful spirit to man

Heraldic design: the killer whale, spirit and lord of the seas who dominated the underworld

Built for sea-going travel, hence projecting bows raised high above the water

Above: *As sea-faring, island people, the Haida were highly dependent upon canoes for their daily activities. Made from the trunks of the red cedar, Haida canoes were considered among the finest available.*

communal memory that that person had been so honored. Totem poles were commissioned from master carvers who had apprenticed to learn their skills and who had earned reputations as fine artists. Between the cost of the pole itself and the potlatch ceremonies surrounding the pole raising, each pole represented a considerable expense.

The art that displays crests also displays con-

Below: *The southern Kwakiutl village of Koskimo, Quatsino Sound, Vancouver Is., c.1880. Note the houses made of hand-hewn cedar planks, various shapes of canoes, and fishing gear on the beach.*

siderable wealth. Wealth on the Northwest Coast was measured by rights as well as by material possessions. Thus, art work displaying a crest suggested a much broader complex of entitlements belonging to the family that owned the crest. Not all art on the Northwest Coast displayed crests in this way, but other forms also spoke of rights and entitlements. Ceremonial masks also were worn in very pres-

tigious dances that were inherited. People gained the right to participate in the dances and to claim the less visible wealth of their inheritance by going through initiations. The dances formed a part of this initiation. Examples of art associated with these dances are the dramatic masks used in ceremonies among the southern Kwakiutl and the Nuu-chah-nulth.[23]

The Southern Kwakiutl are particularly well known for their Tseyka dances or winter ceremonies, known popularly as the Hamatsa dances. These dances, too, refer to ancestral experiences with spirits. The Hamatsa, or initiate, re-experiences the adventures of an ancestor who encountered the supernatural cannibal spirit Bakhbakwalanooksiwey. This spirit was attended by a number of fierce birds capable of eating human beings. The ancestor escaped and brought back to his family the right to perform dances he had learned from the encounter.[24]

During the winter ceremonies, the boundaries between human beings and spirits were temporarily transgressed, as were the boundaries between present and past and the boundaries between initiate and ancestor. The initiate relived the experiences of the first ancestor in his encounter with Bakhbakwalanooksiwey. After a period of isolation, he returned to the village during the winter ceremonies in a wild state, and was tamed and restored to his former human state in a set of specific dances. Gradually the boundaries between human being and spirit, between present and past, and between initiate and ancestor were re-established.

During some of these dances, dancers wear large masks representing the cannibal birds that attended Bakhbakwalanooksiwey. These dramatic masks were carved of wood with great strands of red cedar bark draping from them. The masks have movable beaks that the dancer opened and closed by working a network of strings. The cedar bark strands hung thick, obscuring the dancer's body and hiding his hands as he moved the strings. The clap of the beak added both sound and motion to the dance.

The Tseyka ceremonies spoke of special privilege limited to people who inherited the right to those entitlements and who had gone through a specific initiation to gain the right to

display them. The art work helped re-enact – or to re-experience – the ancestral experiences that conferred the privileges to the descendants. A ceremony with similar function took place among the Nuu-chah-nulth and the Makah peoples. They called it the Klookwana or the Klookwalli, respectively. In this ceremony, initiates were removed by supernatural wolves, and villagers participated in dances to help bring them back. These efforts eventually succeeded and the initiates returned to dance specific dances they had inherited. The dances were performed in set orders. In some of these dances, dancers wore carved masks represent-

Above: *Kwakiutl winter ceremony speech of the leader Hō-letite, c.1894. His blanket is probably of red trade cloth with pattern insert of black,and bone and mother-of-pearl buttons adorning edges.*

ing wolves. In others, headdresses made of flat painted boards were worn on the forehead. These represented profiles of the wolf, mythological lightening snake or thunderbird. Again, in the Klookwana or Klookwalli, boundaries between human being and spirit, present and past, initiate and ancestor are temporarily transgressed.[25]

Some Salish peoples – those living on the

Below: *Kwakiutl village, Fort Rupert, Vancouver Is., c.1888. Note the traditional windowless cedar plank dwellings, one with a painted front (left), and several carved totem poles.*

Kwakiutl

Kwakiutl is the language of about thirty named tribes (one of which is also called Kwakiutl) on northeast Vancouver Is. and the adjacent mainland. Today there are fifteen Kwakiutl reserves, each governed by an independent band council. All except two of the objects shown here were collected between 1897 and 1904 by George Hunt (of Tlingit and English parentage) who was raised in the Kwakiutl town of Fort Rupert, married a Kwakiutl, and was a full parti-

cipant in Kwakiutl society. For forty years he was a co-worker and colleague of Franz Boas, with whom he recorded and published massive amounts of information on Kwakiutl traditional culture, including the language, oral literature, fine art and material culture, and elaborate rituals which were the centerpiece of Kwakiutl life and are still important. Kwakiutl religious ceremonies involve dramatic performances, with masked dancers, singing, and oratory, often re-enacting myths owned and inherited within families.

1 Raven mask worn by hám-atsa dancer in Winter Cere-monial. Nakwoktak tribe.
2 Shining Dawn mask. Koskimo tribe.
3 Mask representing grizzly bear kneecap. Koskimo tribe.
4 Sun mask. Kwakiutl tribe.
5 Cedar bark neck ring worn in Winter Ceremonial by partly tamed hámatsa initiate.
6 Red cedar bark head ring worn by partly tamed hámatsa initiate. Kwakiutl

tribe.
7 Woman's cape of twined yellow cedar bark. Nakwoktak tribe.
8 Pair of nose ornaments. Kwakiutl tribe (collected by Boas).
9 Young woman's cedar bark pouch. Tsawatainuk tribe.
10 Twined basketry bag. Kwakiutl tribe.
11 Spoon of mountain goat horn. Kwakiutl tribe.
12 Wooden spoon. Kwakiutl tribe.
13 Axe, weapon of nutlmatl

or 'fool dancer', participant in hámatsa ceremony. Tsawatainuk tribe.

14 Rattle with hámatsa face. Koskimo tribe.

15 Club for killing halibut. Kwakiutl tribe.

16 Wedge for splitting wood. Kwakiutl tribe.

17 Woman's bucket. Kwakiutl tribe.

18 Drinking bucket for chief's wife. Koskimo tribe.

19 Feast dish for eating boiled berries or crab-apples. Koskimo tribe.

20 Chief's daughter's dish. Kwakiutl tribe.

21 Dagger of performer impersonating Dzoónokwa, a powerful supernatural giantess.

22 Girl's work box. Kwakiutl tribe.

23 Skull-shaped rattle. Koskimo tribe.

24 Wooden comb. Kwakiutl tribe.

25 Raven mask of hámatsa dancer. Tsawatainuk tribe.

26 Frog puppet used by performer in Winter

Ceremonial. Koskimo tribe.

27 Dish for serving soaked dried salmon. Koskimo tribe.

28 Model of 16ft feast dish associated with Dzoónokwa giantess at the Winter Ceremonial.

29 Mask for the Tlásulá, so-called Summer or Weasel Dance.

30 Wasp dancer mask. Tsawatainuk tribe.

31 Woodworking adze. Collected about 1881 by I. W. Powell.

Kwakiutl Basket Making, 1850

A woman and her grand-daughter sit working on the platform raised above the beach in front of a Kwakiutl village. A dugout canoe has been lifted up (at right) and fish dry on racks below. The house fronts of adzed planks with painted designs, and the totem poles (including one with a movable beak at the door) resemble those in the village of Alert Bay. Both people show skulls intentionally shaped, the results of pressure in infancy from bundles such as those on the baby whose cradle is rocked by the woman's toe. She wears abalone shell ear pendants and a blouse of calico trade cloth. Both have skirts of shredded cedar bark and robes twined from cedar inner bark and edged with sea otter fur. The bark strips for weaving the baskets are kept flexible in water in the wooden box.

Right: *Kwakiutl group gathered around blankets at a potlatch, photographed at Fort Rupert before 1895. Potlatch gatherings were banned by the Canadian government in 1884 as part of the federal Indian policy and remained illegal until 1951.*

Olympic Peninsula near the Makah – also participated in dances of this nature. Among the Salish living along the Puget Sound, other ceremonies took place that did not feature initiates. Nevertheless, they too spoke of the fluidity of boundaries. These ceremonies, known as Spirit Canoe ceremonies, were performed to cure people who were ill. Shamans, or people in the community invested with special powers to communicate with spirit helpers, enacted a canoe voyage into the world below the earth where the souls of the dead stayed. The ceremony was intended to cause the spirit helpers of the shamans to make the actual journey and bring back the soul of the ill person. During the ceremony, distinctive wooden boards and carved figures were used to help evoke power and to bridge the boundaries between human beings and spirits. Because of their potency, these art works were kept in hiding away from the village when they were not in use.[26]

Coast Salish art often referred to personal spirit helpers, even when on utilitarian objects. Particularly in British Columbia, a very distinctive mask style was also used. This mask, known as the Sxwayxwey mask, was used by individuals at very personal times in their lives: births, marriages, deaths, and at times when they took new names. Unlike other masks on the coast, these masks have blunt cylindrical eyes that extend from the surface of the mask. They also often use the technique of 'visual

punning', incorporating bird designs into the features of a larger mythical figure.[27]

This technique of visual punning is prevalent up and down the coast, so it deserves more mention here. In 'visual punning', portions of one animal double as portions of another animal. Thus, the wings of an eagle may also

Below: *Swinomish warriors launching a canoe. Made from the dug out trunk of a cedar tree it would be up to 50ft (15m.) long, curved projections at bow and stern giving great stability in rough seas.*

portray the pectoral fin of a whale, enabling an artist to suggest shared identity.[28] Again, this artistic technique implies that boundaries can be very fluid. Two presences can occupy the same place at the same time, just as the dancer can exist in present and past at the same time.

The discussion above has often talked about initiates who gained the right to perform certain dances and claim certain privileges through inheritance. Some ritualistic art was also used by another small sector of society, the shamans or spiritual healers. These people had special powers to transcend the contemporary boundaries between human beings and spirits and to communicate with spirits directly. They used those powers to help heal ill people and to foresee events. Each shaman had a personal spirit helper or a series of helpers, and his or her personal collection of art work that was used to call on the power of these helpers. The shamans and their art work were often buried away from villages because of the danger of their power.

The art and ceremonial expression on the Northwest Coast was integrally connected to all parts of life. Utilitarian objects and ceremonial objects alike were decorated. The art was functional art, often used in the place of a written language to convey genealogy and to preserve historical memory. Similarly, the ceremonies kept experiences of ancestors alive and also made hereditary privileges evident. Certain art work both represented and facilitated the power of shamans to cross the boundaries between human beings and spirits and to call on supernatural powers. The ceremonial life was extremely rich and varied on the Northwest Coast. Despite strong cultural oppression on the part of non-native peoples who opposed native ceremonialism in the nineteenth century, many ceremonies have survived and are practiced today.

The earliest record of contact between Northwest Coast Indians and Europeans occurred in 1741, when the Russian explorer Chirikov harbored his ship briefly in the area in southeast Alaska near present-day Sitka. The next recorded contact was in 1774, when the Spanish explorer Juan Perez reached the Queen Charlotte Islands and traded with Haida Indians there. Perez was followed by another Spanish expedition the following year, and by the English captain James Cook in 1778.[29]

The Indians on the Northwest Coast were well accustomed to trading with other indigenous groups, and were interested in the materials the Europeans brought. In the initial years of exchange with Europeans, iron – especially iron with a blade – was particularly in demand. In return, Indians traded food and furs, especially the thick fur of the sea otter.

Captain Cook's crew discovered that they could sell sea otter pelts for very high profits in China. This information became generally known in 1784 when the journals of that expedition were published, and investors began supporting trading voyages to the Northwest Coast. Very quickly, the Northwest Coast became a commercial center with Europe and the eastern United States, and the Indians on the Northwest Coast engaged in active trade in sea otter pelts. By 1820, these small sea mammals had practically disappeared.

The maritime fur trade affected native lives in a variety of ways. It was not without its incidents of violence: the sailing ships were always armed with cannon, and misunderstandings arising from cultural and language differences could lead to tragedy on both sides. Fur traders accidentally introduced diseases such as smallpox, and since native peoples

lacked natural immunities the diseases hit hard. Traders introduced firearms as well; it is still unclear whether these weapons increased deaths in intertribal warfare.

In a more positive light, the maritime fur trade introduced a great influx of material wealth into Northwest Coast societies in a short period of time. This new wealth helped support ceremonialism and cultural expression. There were probably more potlatches and more production of ceremonial art in the decades immediately following the advent of the maritime fur trade than there had been previously. The fur traders were for the most part transient. They did not appropriate native resources, and they had no wish to change Indian cultural or economic activities as long as Indians kept bringing furs. The trade may have disrupted social structures somewhat by making wealth accessible to a wider range of people. However, it did not attack native culture, and in some ways it supported it.[30]

This situation began to change as European and Euro-American settlers moved to the Northwest Coast. These settlers expected to be permanent residents, and they wanted land resources that belonged to Indians. These developments happened at different times in different parts of the Coast. Except for the Sitka region, where Russians had the settlement of New Archangel, Indians in southeast Alaska did not feel great pressure from non-natives until after Alaska was transferred to the United States in 1867. In southern British Columbia, pressure was felt somewhat earlier. In 1849 the British Government started encouraging the colonization of Vancouver Island in order to keep the United States from claiming it. In the 1850s, some treaties were made with Indians in British Columbia. After that time, reserves were established without treaties. The white settlers and their government appropriated lands that belonged to Indians and restricted their access to these lands. Gunboats patrolled the coast-

Above: *Culchillum, a Central Coast Salish, by Paul Kane (1847). His medicine cap appears fringed with ermine strips and quill wrappings, with two eagle feathers delicately attached to the top.*

Below: *The impact of the white man on Southern Coast Salish (Puyallup). Their lives were changed dramatically by the infiltration of non-Indians into their territory on the Northwest coast.*

line, ready to shell native villages if there were signs of insurrection. The first Governor, James Douglas, had recognized native title to land, but his successors denied Indians ever had title. Entering the 1990s Indian land settlement issues in British Columbia remain unresolved.[31].

In southeast Alaska the situation was much the same. No treaties were negotiated and no reserves were set aside except for one which was formed after a group of Tsimshian Indians from British Columbia followed the missionary William Duncan across the border in 1887. From 1867, when Alaska was transferred to the United States, to 1877, the U.S. army was stationed in southeast Alaska; in 1879 they were replaced by naval gunboats. In the 1870s, industrialists began moving into the region to establish canneries and mining concerns. Indians became wage laborers in these indus-

tries, working for relatively low pay and leaving villages to live in cannery or mining housing. Land issues in southeast Alaska were dealt with through a settlement in 1959 – following decades of pressure – and the state-wide Alaska Native Claims Settlement Act in 1971.

Along with the settlers, Christian missionaries came to the Northwest Coast. Russian Orthodox missionaries had been active among the Tlingit in New Archangel in southeast Alaska since the mid-nineteenth century, and in the last quarter of the century southeast Alaska also saw the arrival of Roman Catholic, Presbyterian and Friends missionaries. In British Columbia, starting in the mid-nineteenth century, missionaries from Roman Catholic, Anglican and Methodist denominations were represented. In addition to church services, missionaries ran schools for children and adults. Some, such as William Duncan,

established 'model villages' separated from existing villages, where Indians lived in European-style houses and agreed to abandon traditional forms of cultural expression such as the potlatch.[32]

Indians on the Northwest Coast had mixed reactions to missionaries. Many were interested in access to the missionary teachings – especially because missionaries could help them learn English and other skills that would equip them to survive in the new Euro-American society that was developing around them. As white settlers appropriated native lands and white industries took over native fishing streams and food resources, it became harder for Indians to continue entirely in their traditional economy, and it was increasingly important for them to be able to work as wage laborers.[33] Missionaries could help them acquire these skills and could prepare them for functioning in a society where white people were ready to exploit them. While missionaries are often condemned for their paternalistic, condescending and frequently dictatorial attitudes, they cared whether Indians survived and they believed at the time that their actions were helping the Indians.

However, missionaries and government officials did much more than teach English. They also held that traditional native culture was at the best that of 'heathens' and was at worst depraved. They waged an active campaign to stop Indians from practicing their own cultural expression and from passing on their heritage

Left: John Hunter, a Nuu-chah-nulth, in dance costume, c.1925. His heavy robe is hide, probably painted with (mainly) red and black pigments. Such fine carved and painted headdresses are rarely found in ethnographical collections.

Below: Effects of trade on the Nuu-chah-nulth. The main figure holds a trade gun, as does the man to his left who also wears a blanket which is probably not of indigenous manufacture.

Makah

The Makah lived in large plank houses in five semi-autonomous permanent villages on the tip of the Olympic Peninsula; today they mainly live at Neah Bay, one of these five. The village headmen and their immediate families occupied the top social rank and validated their positions by giving potlatches. Whaling was a particularly prestigious occupation, ritualized and hereditary. The large sea-going canoes were also used to hunt fur seals and for trading expeditions, and were exported to tribes to the south and east. Fishing for salmon and halibut provided an important part of the diet, but land mammals were little used. A major contribution to subsistence was made by women, who gathered shellfish, berries, and roots. Men engaged in complex woodworking technology. Carved food dishes were involved in conspicuous consumption by leading families. Women were versatile artists in basketry. All the objects shown here were collected by Judge James G. Swan between 1861 and 1884.

1 Braided grass tumpline, used for carrying loads on the back; the broad section ran across the forehead.
2 Model of whaling canoe, in the typical Makah shape, complete with harpoon and its inflated skin floats, and carved figures.
3 Halibut hook. (Halibut and salmon were fished especially in the summertime.)
4 Bow.
5 Arrows with brass points.
6 Two kelp fish lines with floats.
7 Knife used for splitting fish.
8 Dancer's rattle, made of scallop shells.
9 Braided grass tumpline, used for carrying loads on the back. As in 1, the broad section ran across the forehead.
10 Bow.
11 Wooden quiver and three arrows.
12 Twilled bag for spear heads and other gear.

13 Headdress for medicine dance, made from cedar bark, cut feathers, and red flannel.
14 Fancy work basket with foot and lid.
15 Large table mat, made for sale.
16 Large table mat, made for sale.
17 Woven rush bag.
18 Grass basket.
19 Carved stone with crest figures.
20 Bottle covered with coiled spruce root

basketry.
21 Carved wooden feast dish.
22 Wooden bowl in tortoise shape.
23 Small basketry table mat, made for sale.
24 Small basketry table mat, made for sale, as No. 23.
25 Short robe, twined, wefts of twisted downy bird skins.
26 Grass basket.
27 Straw basket made with three different tech-

niques.
28 Conical hat.
29 Plaited straw hat, copying non-Indian style.
30 Shaman's rattle, with carved weasel on top.
31 Shaman's rattle, with carved man's head and bird on top.
32 Fancy work basket with lid.
33 Bottle covered with fine coiled basketry.
34 Mat of checker woven cedar bark.

COURTESY STARK FOUNDATION, ORANGE, TEXAS

Left: *Interior of a Chinookan ceremonial lodge, by Paul Kane (1846). The spacious lodge is of hewn cedar planks; note the smoke-hole and cracks between the planks for good air circulation.*

native spirituality, native political systems and systems of hereditary rights – all of which seemed threatening to missionaries and government officials. The potlatch came to be viewed as the native custom that was preventing Indians from becoming 'civilised' as defined by missionaries and government officials, and they felt they had to destroy the potlatch if Indians were to become both Christians and citizens.[34]

Thus, in both British Columbia and southeast Alaska, missionaries and government officials launched an active campaign against native ceremonialism. In 1884, these efforts resulted in Canadian federal legislation outlawing potlatches. This law stayed on the books until 1951. Many Indians – and some white authorities – protested the legislation immediately, but to no avail. While it was not enforced regularly, the threat of prosecution – coupled with the other manifestations of cultural oppression the Indians faced – caused people to stop performing ceremonies in public. In some places on the coast, the ceremonies continued in clandestine fashion, always under the threat of prosecution. In other places, people gradually abandoned the ceremonies for the same reason.

In southeast Alaska, no legislation was passed outlawing potlatches. However, government officials and missionaries put strong pressure on Indians to stop potlatches, and many agreed to do so voluntarily.[35] Some felt that with white attitudes as they were they could not afford the prejudice that came from native cultural expression. When they were trying to find ways for their children to live with a reasonable amount of physical and psychological safety, they could not risk the prejudice they faced from whites when they expressed their culture openly. In 1904, many Tlingit leaders in southeast Alaska agreed at the governor's request to stop holding potlatches.[36]

In addition to appropriation of lands and extreme cultural oppression, white settlement brought another devastating blow to native societies and cultures. This was the introduction of diseases and of alcohol. These problems, which first developed during the maritime fur trade, increased exponentially with white settlement. As more whites came in to the region regularly, more diseases were introduced. Equally significant, native peoples from a number of villages throughout British Columbia began to gather at one city, and an epidemic that broke out in that city could be carried throughout the region.

to their children. They often forcibly removed children from their parents and communities, raising them in residential schools where they were punished for speaking their own language or celebrating their culture.

The potlatch was a particular target of missionaries and government officials both in British Columbia and in Southeast Alaska. They viewed it as a threat for a variety of reasons. Since they measured wealth only in material possessions, it seemed wasteful to give away summer earnings during winter ceremonies. Indian agents in British Columbia, who wanted Indians to become agriculturalists, would have greatly preferred to see the money spent buying farm equipment and seeds. Missionaries

charged that children were taken out of schools during potlatches, while employers complained the ceremonies made workers unreliable.

However, probably the most fundamental reason for opposition to the potlatch was the recognition that those ceremonies kept native culture alive. It was the expression of native ceremonialism that passed on native history and culture to young people. It was also the expression of native ceremonialism that affirmed

Below: *Interior of Chinookan lodge, by Paul Kane (1847), with central fire place. Meat is smoked on the heavy beam across the lodge, as are animal skins which are made waterproof by the smoking.*

COURTESY STARK FOUNDATION, ORANGE, TEXAS

This in fact occurred in 1862, when a ship from San Francisco accidentally brought smallpox to Victoria. When Indians camped outside the city contracted the disease, white residents drove them away. They returned to their home villages, inadvertently bringing the germ with them. The tragic epidemic wiped out at least one third of the total Indian population in British Columbia, and in some areas along the coast line villages were practically eradicated. In addition to smallpox, other diseases such as

Left: A Makah fisherman holding a whaling harpoon. These were generally made of yew and were about 18ft (6m.) in length. The cutting point was a mussel shell held by elkhorn.

During this period, except among the Kwakiutl and Salish peoples, very little ceremonial art was still being made. Some artists made works to sell to tourists and other non-native peoples. Some of these works remained technically excellent, especially the baskets being woven by women for white collectors. Because women had fewer opportunities to earn wages in the white economy, they could afford the time it took to make baskets, and this activity was also compatible with child care. However, with so few traditional contexts for ceremonial art and with more opportunities to work in white industries, fewer and fewer male artists could afford the time it took to become skilled carvers and painters. Also, with the population decline, there were fewer masters left with whom to apprentice. Predictably, this situation worsened as the twentieth century went on. By the 1960s, when art historian Bill Holm studied the Northern Formline style, he could not find a practicing artist from the Bella Coola region who had learned in traditional methods.[40]

Despite the extreme cultural oppression and social disruption, though, native peoples retained their sense of ethnic identity and their cultural values. Even when ceremonialism was suppressed, these values remained. Today, when civil rights and human rights are more widely acclaimed, Northwest Coast native peoples are reviving their traditional ceremonialism and are again practicing their cultural expression openly. Artists are active again making traditional forms of art, both to sell to collectors as fine art and to use in their own ceremonies. Indians are also very well organised politically and are still seeking redress of injustices of the past. They are also playing a strong role in environmentalism, for the preservation of their culture is integrally tied to the preservation of the forests in their traditional homelands of the Northwest Coast.

measles, influenza, tuberculosis, venereal disease and alcoholism had grave and disruptive effects on native societies.[37] In a short period of time, every native person almost certainly had friends and relatives who had died. Due to the social disruption, populations consolidated into a few villages in some places on the coast. The devastation made it easier for forces of cultural oppression to take their toll.

By the first decades of the twentieth century, the open expression of native ceremonialism had been effectively suppressed by white authorities. In British Columbia Indians could and were prosecuted for continuing their ceremonialism. This was particularly true of people from the Southern Kwakiutl region, who continued their ceremonialism more actively than most.[38] The cultural oppression, along with the other forms of devastation that Indian societies faced, led to fewer and fewer ceremonies. Thus, there were fewer contexts in which traditional art was used, and fewer ceremonial art works were made.

Starting in the 1870s, museums in North America and Europe became very interested in collecting Northwest Coast Indian art.[39] Curators believed erroneously that the cultures would not survive and wanted to make a scientific record while it was still possible to do so. They sent collectors to the Northwest Coast to make 'representative' collections of the cultures. Collectors purchased art from native peoples who no longer were using it in ceremonies and who needed the money. Frequently, too, collectors took art from graves without permission. In a few decades, vast quantities of ceremonial art and of totem poles were removed from the Northwest Coast.

References

1 For more discussion of this point, see Holm, 1983: 15–16. For more detailed information on native methods of harvesting resources in their environment, see Stewart, 1973, 1977, 1984.
2 Duff, 1964: 38–9.
3 Jackson: 62–9.
4 For more discussion see Stewart, 1984.
5 Lobb: 21.
6 For more discussion of archeology of the Northwest Coast, see Carlson ed., 1976; MacDonald and Inglis, 1976; Fladmark, 1986.
7 For a succinct discussion of social organization on the Northwest Coast, see Macnair et al., 1984: 15–24; Bancroft-Hunt and Forman, 1979: 25–49. The discussion that follows is based on these sources.
8 Bancroft-Hunt, 1979: 37.
9 For more discussion of Tlingit social organization, see Jonaitis, 1986: 34–9; Holmberg, 1985: 10–11; de Laguna, 1972: 212–13.
10 Macnair et al., 1984: 21.
11 Macnair et al., 1984: 22.
12 Macnair et al., 1984: 22.
13 For a succinct discussion of ceremonialism on the Northwest Coast, see Halpin, 1981: 6–15.
14 Brown, in Corey ed., 1987: 157–75.
15 Duff, 1975.
16 This style was analysed in depth by Bill Holm in

Holm, 1965. It was here that he defined the terminology 'Northern Formline'. A popularization of his technical discussion is provided in Stewart, 1979.
17 A clear and succinct discussion of these styles appears in Macnair et al., 1984: 25–42.
18 A succinct description of the various cultural styles is found in Macnair et al., 1984: 43–62.
19 These hats were discussed in Vaughan and Holm, 1982: 32–3.
20 For more detailed discussion of Salish weaving, see Gustafson, 1980.
21 For more discussion of Chilkat blankets, see Samuel, 1982.
22 Halpin, 1981: 16–23.
23 Halpin, 1981: 7–12; Holm, 1987: 84, 100.
24 Holm, 1987: 100; Macnair et al., 1984: 50–51, 96; Holm, 1983: 86–7. The discussion of the Tseyka is based on these works.
25 Holm, 1987: 84.
26 Holm, 1987: 48–9.
27 Macnair et al., 1984: 52–3, 62.
28 A classic example is the Haida wood bowl illustrated and described in Macnair et al., 1984: 46–7, 50. The bowl is in the collections of the Royal British Columbia Museum, Victoria, B.C.
29 For more discussion of the interactions between Northwest Coast Indians and European explorers

and maritime fur traders, see Gunther, 1972; Pethick, 1973; Cook, 1973.
30 For more discussion of the maritime fur trade, see Duff, 1964: 53-60; Fisher, 1977; Vaughan and Holm, 1983; Wyatt, 1984.
31 For a comprehensive discussion of government policies towards native lands in British Columbia, see Tennant, 1990. Policies are also discussed in Duff, 1964: 60–74; Fisher, 1977.
32 For more more discussion of missionaries, see Duff, 1964: 87–101; LaViolette, 1973; Fisher, 1977: 119–45; and Fisher in Veillette and White, 1977: 1–11.
33 For more discussion of native involvement in wage-labor industries, see Knight, 1978; and Wyatt in *Pacific Northwest Quarterly* 78 (1–2): 43–9.
34 For discussion of opposition to the potlatch, see LaViolette, 1973; Sewid-Smith, 1979; Hou, undated; Halliday, 1935. A book on the potlatch prohibition, written by Cole and Chaikin, is soon to be published by the University of Washington Press.
35 Hinckley, 1982: 249–53.
36 Hinckley, 1982: pp.251–3.
37 Duff, 1964: 40–44.
38 For a discussion of arrests made following a potlatch in 1921, see Sewid-Smith, 1979.
39 For more discussion of collecting, see Cole, 1985.
40 Holm, 1965: vii.

THE SUBARCTIC

THIS VAST AREA spans the whole continent of North America from the Labrador peninsula in the east (including Newfoundland) and dipping to the south of Hudson Bay then west to Alaska. It encompasses a total area of some two million square miles inhabited by perhaps no more than 60,000 Athapaskan or Algonquian-speaking people.

Although the climatic features in the Subarctic tend to be uniform over large areas, the terrain is varied. Most dominant, however, is open woodland tundra of scattered coniferous trees, which is bordered in the north by an Arctic-alpine tundra and to the south by boreal forest, or Parkland, consisting of broadleaf trees scattered on wide expanses of grassland.

Approximately west of the Churchill River on the Manitoba shore of Hudson Bay were the Athapaskan-speaking people, and to the east the Algonquians. For successful fishing and hunting, small groups of extended families who were united by a common dialect lived together and followed the movements of the game animals; only for a comparatively short period during the summer months did these various groups briefly rendezvous, hence expressing a form of tribal solidarity. The Athapaskan speakers included the Tanaina, Tanana, Kutchin, Han, Inland Tlingit, Tahltan, Hare and Mountain Indians in the northwest and the Yellowknife, Dogrib, Slavey, Beaver and Chipewyan in the east and to the south of the Great Bear and Great Slave lakes. The Algonquians, such as the Strongwoods Cree, Western Woods Cree and Rocky Cree, were east and south of the Slave and Athabasca rivers. A broad sweep eastwards beyond Lake Winnipeg in present-day Manitoba included the Swampy Cree, Northern Ojibwa, Saulteaux and West Main Cree whose territory bordered the shores of the Hudson and James Bays. East of these bays and north of the St Lawrence River were the East Cree, Attikamek, Naskapi and Montagnais, the territory of the two latter tribes extending to the Labrador Sea. Because of the extensive area encompassed by the Subarctic region, it has been further divided into smaller regions – the Yukon, Mackenzie, Central (bordering the south of the Hudson Bay) and Eastern on the Labrador peninsula, and whilst the overall lifestyle of the people was similar, none, for example, practiced agriculture; they were all hunters and fishermen and tribal cohesion was minimal. However, the type of dwelling used, the mode of transportation, subsistence patterns, care of the elderly and warfare patterns were often markedly different. The emphasis on local band affiliation was a characteristic feature of much of the Subarctic social organization. Such bands readily adapted to the annual migrations and seasonal foraging ranges. They had a high degree of continuity, but a fluidity of composition, and one scholar of the Chipewyan has recently pointed out the great value of such organization in maintaining identity in a variety of traditional and modern environments. For example, whilst the nomadic herds of caribou were generally predictable in their movements, any erratic or unusual changes could be accommodated by the spatial distribution of the bands facilitating a communication network which could 'report on the direction of movement, dispersal and concentration of the caribou'[1] (Smith, 1978:68).

The total population of the scattered bands, which constituted a loose-knit tribe, was generally small; that for the Montagnais-Naskapi, for example, was some four thousand in the mid-nineteenth century occupying a territorial range of at least four hundred thousand

This map shows approximate territories of tribes and language groups in about 1850, and somewhat earlier in a large region west of Hudson Bay. After that, many tribes lost territory and others moved.

Key to tribes:
1 Holikachuk
2 Ingalik
3 Kolchan
4 Tanaina
5 Koyukon
6 Kutchin
7 Tanana
8 Ahtna
9 Han
10 Tutchone
11 Hare
12 Mountain Indians
13 Tagish
14 Inland Tlingit
15 Kaska
16 Tahltan
17 Tsetsaut
18 Sekani
19 Slavey
20 Beaver
21 Carrier
22 Chilcotin
23 Dogrib
24 Yellowknife
25 Chipewyan
26 Western Woods Cree
27 West Main Cree
28 Northern Ojibwa
29 Lake Winnipeg Saulteaux
30 Naskapi
31 East Cree
32 Attikamek
33 Montagnais
34 Beothuk

square miles. The statistics for the Chipewyan are similar: thus, a population density of one person per one hundred square miles was not uncommon in both Athapaskan and Algonquian territory.

A marked social characteristic of the Subarctic people was the great emphasis placed on personal autonomy and this gave rise to largely non-aggressive behavior in interpersonal relationships, thus avoiding domination and respecting others' freedom of action. Parents extended such behavior toward their children which led to the development of independent personalities with a high degree of self-reliance and personal initiative, traits so essential for maintaining harmonious life in the small extended family bands. However, a built-in symbolic warning that the independence must not be carried too far was another Subarctic trait; its message was conveyed in tribal mythology which warned of the dangers of extreme isolation from communal life and referred to lone forest prowlers, such as the Cree and Saulteaux Windigo (cannibal) and the Kutchin's 'bush men'.

The immense self-reliance and personal initiative displayed by the Subarctic people was underlined by a remarkable episode related early in the history of the Canadian fur trade and reported on by Samuel Hearne in 1770, who led an expedition from the Hudson's Bay post of Fort Churchill in search of the Coppermine River east of the Great Slave Lake. On their return journey, they came across a Dogrib woman who had escaped from Cree captors; alone for some seven months, she had not only built herself a small shelter, made snares to trap hares (the so-called snowshoe rabbit), fabricated snowshoes and begun work on a fish-net in anticipation of the spring melt, but had decorated her fur clothing. Hearne, obviously greatly impressed by this resourceful, brave woman, reported: 'It is scarcely possible to conceive that a person in her forlorn situation could be so composed . . . all her clothing, besides being calculated for real service, shewed great taste, and exhibited no little variety of ornament . . . as to make the whole of her garb have a very pleasing . . . appearance' (Hearne, 1958:169).

Above: *Ingalik man holding a pick and scoop used in fishing, Anvik, Alaska, c.1923. These implements were used in winter fishing for cutting a hole in and clearing the ice.*

Hearne's journal also gives an interesting perspective relating to the woman's lot in Subarctic culture at the time of early contact. Befriended by the influential Chipewyan chief, Mattonabee, Hearne was lectured on his misfortunes which were due, the Chief said, to the lack of women in Hearne's party. Women, he emphasized, were 'made for labor'; one of them, he maintained, could carry or haul as much as two men. They could also pitch the tents and keep up the fires at night. Further, he pointed out, although they did everything, they could be maintained at a trifling expense and, with wry humor added, that as they also acted as cooks, the 'very licking of their fingers' in scarce times would be quite sufficient for their subsistence (ibid).

The most common form of habitation was

Hudson Bay

ATLANTIC OCEAN

the conical tent – the 'wigwam' of the Algonquian-speaking groups – resembling the Plains tipi and covered with moose or caribou hides on the tundra, and bark in the forest regions. On occasions, the Cree used domed-shaped lodges covered with sheets of birch bark whilst the Kutchin, who had limited access to birch bark, utilized similarly constructed domed dwellings, but covered with skins. In both conical and dome-shaped lodges, the fireplace was located at the centre; an exception to this was the East Cree *shabúktowan*, 'the house that you walk right through', which resembled two wigwams joined together with a fire at each end and a smoke hole above each (Skinner, Wissler ed., 1911:14). In constructing the conical lodge, two poles were laid on the ground in the form of a cross; these were bound together at their intersection and set upright, a third pole was then placed into the crotch and this too was lashed in. By drawing the tripod closer together at the base, the top was elevated and the sides made steeper. Other poles were then laid into the foundation to support the covering of skin or bark. In the latter case, the bark was in rolls about 3ft (1m.) wide and varying in length depending on its position on the conical frame. Once the bark was in place, more poles were laid upon it, thus anchoring the cover. Skin wigwams were similarly constructed, thus mark-

Above: *Ingalik caches at Shageluk, Lower Yukon River, Alaska. Caches, in which food was placed, stood adjacent to houses in the village; they were then mounted on high posts safe from predators.*

Below: *An Ingalik man removing fish from a trap, holding a wooden scoop. Behind him is an ice chisel and long wooden ice scoop. Large traps of this type were mainly used for ling.*

edly differing from the Plains tipi which was generally of a single sewn cover and devoid of any external anchoring poles.

Wigwams were clearly not primitive dwellings, as a cursory inspection may suggest: the sewing of the bark rolls, the varying lengths, the shingle-like overlapping and the painted ornamentation referring, in the case of the East Cree, to property marks, point to a well-constructed and habitable dwelling suited to the environment and the nomadic lifestyle of the people. Likewise, wigwam organization and etiquette was well developed, poles being tied across the interior some 6 to 8ft (1.8-2.4m.) from the ground from which moccasins and utensils could be hung and it was not uncommon also to hang fish on this cross-piece directly above the fire for slow curing, whilst the place of honor for guests was recognized as directly opposite the door.

Caribou and moose, the most important large food animals, were the Barren Ground caribou of the northern transitional forest and the adjacent tundra, whilst to the south and throughout the boreal forests were the wood-

Below: *Lower Ahtna Indians from the Copper River valley of SE Alaska, c.1902. The clothing is decorated with bone buttons and beadwork on the carrying straps. Note moss for the diaper (right).*

land caribou, moose and a few woods buffalo.

The Chipewyan technique of hunting caribou was to drive them into the mouth of a chute consisting of bush or poles set some 50 to 65ft (15-20m.) apart, which led to a circular pound, up to a third of a mile in diameter; this pound enclosed a complex maze of bush hedging between which snares were set. Entangled caribou were despatched with spears whilst the remaining loose ones were shot with arrows.

In contrast, the enormous moose did not move in herds and a different technique had to be adopted, a method which was based on the close observation of the behavioral characteristics of the animal. In order to catch the scent of any following predator, a moose generally doubles back after feeding, resting at a spot downwind of its earlier trail. Responding to this behavioral characteristic, the Indian hunter avoids following the trail of the moose, but instead makes semi-circular loops downwind; when the moose's trail loops back, the hunter can accurately locate it. During the rutting season, moose could be attracted by use of a birch bark calling horn and in late winter immobilized by drawing them into deep snow, where they could be speared.

The main meat diet of the caribou and moose was supplemented by that from smaller animals such as beaver, hare, rabbit, muskrat

and squirrel, which could be trapped with deadfalls or snares. The Subarctic areas required large quantities of food to support families, it being estimated that at least four pounds of flesh could be consumed daily by each adult. It was essential that a high proportion of this flesh was fat in order to ensure the necessary calorie and fatty acid intake, thus the *type* of flesh eaten was important. Rabbits for example, were little valued by some groups as sustaining food, since most of the year they had limited body fat, a common native adage being that one could 'starve to death on rabbits'! (Rogers and Smith, 1981:135). One Hudson's Bay Company trader has pointed out that to these Subarctic people, the beaver – and this would be particularly applicable to the Cree in whose territory the animal abounded – was to a large extent what the seal was to the Eskimo. The beaver, in contrast to the snowshoe rabbit, carries a large amount of fat upon its body; it was, the Indians claimed, 'just as necessary to their well-being in the cold of winter as was bacon and butter to the white men' (Godsell, 1935:114).

The availability of food resources varied with the season and in order to preserve a balanced diet a good deal of meat and fish was preserved. On occasions during the winter, sometimes flesh was frozen, but the most common

Ingalik

The Ingalik, speakers of an Athapaskan language, lived in the late 19th century mainly at Anvik on the lower Yukon River and Shageluk on a nearby tributary. They hunted caribou, moose, bear, beaver, and other mammals, and waterfowl, and depended heavily on fish which they caught throughout the year, including during the winter when they set traps beneath the ice. The fish wheel trap introduced near the end of the century greatly increased the summer take of salmon. Each winter village was centered on a large, semi-subterranean building where ceremonies were held, and men socialized and made and repaired weapons and implements. The Ingalik traditionally observed seven major ceremonies involving feasting, gift giving, and a wide variety of dramatic dances, many of them masked, such as the Mask Dance which was to increase the numbers of game animals. The objects shown here were collected pre-1905 by the Rev. John W. Chapman, missionary at Anvik since 1887 (except for No. 13).

1 Pair of maskettes used by messengers who invite guests to attend Silver Salmon Mask Dance.
2 Grouse mask for Mask Dance.
3 Fire drill; birch rod spun by cord with toggles on ends; it is pressed into the hearth by means of the mouthpiece with bone inset. Anvik.
4 Bear mask for Mask Dance. Shageluk.
5 Mask painted with ochre, for informal dance at Mask Dance. Anvik.
6 Rings with feathers held in each hand by a dancer wearing the mask described above (No. 5). Anvik.
7 Wand with carved wolf figure, used by a dance master at Partner's Potlatch. Anvik.
8 Stone ulu or woman's knife. Anvik.
9 Half-man mask for Mask Dance. Shageluk.
10, 11 Two masks caricaturing Holikachuk men, for Mask Dance. Shageluk.

12 Otter mask for Mask
   Dance.
13 Custom of masked dances
   was shared with
   neighboring peoples, as
   illustrated by this N. Alaska
   Coast Inuit mask used at
   Point Hope, c.1903.
14 Birch bark container for
   liquids, berries, etc. Anvik.
15 Wooden ladle used as
   spoon or cup. Anvik.
16 Pouch made of fish
   (perhaps lamprey) skin.
17 Man's leather pouch with
   quill decoration. From the

Holikachuk neighbors of the
Ingalik.
18 Fingerwoven wool belt.
   Anvik.
19 Storage bag of leather with
   bird skin inserts.
20 Woman's twined grass bag,
   for carrying or storage.
21 Saucer of feather-tempered
   pot used with whitefish or
   seal oil and moss wick as
   lamp for lighting; obsolete
   by 1904. Anvik.
22 Mask of Siren being, for
   Mask Dance.
23 Maskette used by

messenger inviting guests
to Otter Mask Dance.
24 Crow mask for Mask
   Dance. Shageluk.
25 Mask, Father of Mosquito,
   for Mask Dance. Shageluk.
26 Raven mask for Mask
   Dance. Shageluk.
27 Mask of Siren being, for
   Mask Dance. Shageluk.
28 Mask.
29 Mask, Mother of Mosquito,
   for Mask Dance. Shageluk.
30 Mask caricaturing a
   Holikachuk man, for Mask
   Dance.

methods were to smoke or sun dry. One observer described the manner of smoking moose meat for quick preservation during traveling, as being accomplished 'by drying up the juice of the flesh by the heat from the fire' (Skinner, 1911:29). The flesh was sliced up and placed on a scaffold formed of four upright sticks of green wood driven into the ground in the shape of a rectangle and at a height of about 3ft (1m.); longitudinal bars were then lashed on the long sides and these supported the green wood grill over which the thin strips were hung. A sizeable fire cured the meat within two to three hours – sufficient to preserve it for a few days – but the method required that the meat be constantly turned toward the fire and, if traveling for some time, it was necessary to repeat the process by stopping earlier in the day. An alternative technique, which gave more permanent preservation, was to smoke it on a frame built of three poles which were fastened together with cross bars near the top; the meat was hung on these bars and smoked for several days. Enormous quantities of fish were often preserved in a similar way, particularly by those groups such as the Kutchin, some of the Hare bands, Tanana and Tanaina; indeed, in the case of the latter, salmon was the very basis of their subsistence.

Hide tanning was a crucial part of Subarctic technology and, in the case of the Chipewyans, the caribou was a central component to their whole material culture complex and whilst the animal was hunted, skinned and butchered by men, the exhausting tanning process was carried out by women. Unlike the tanning of buffalo and moose hides, which were stretched or pegged out, Chipewyan women stretched the 'green' hide over a log and defleshed the inner side with a bone tool with a serrated edge. The hide was then soaked in water for several days, which loosened the hair so that it could be more easily removed with a bone beamer. The brain from a caribou skull was removed and mixed with water to produce a soup-like substance which was worked into the hide by alternately soaking and rubbing. It was necessary to carry out this step in the process with great care, ensuring that all the hide was thoroughly soaked, because it was at this stage that the chemical reaction led to the preservation of the hide and prevented subsequent deterioration. The hide was then stretched out to dry, often aided by freezing, and then soaked in water to wash out the unreacted tanning solution. It was then made pliable during the final period of drying by pulling it over a pole and working it by hand. An attractive brown color could be imparted to the hide by smoking it on a tripod over a hardwood fire which was smothered with moss; the process had the added advantage of partially waterproofing the hide – due to resin impregnation – and repelling mosquitoes and flies.

Although there were some differences in the above process (some groups, such as the Dogrib for example, used urine to remove fat surplus in the hide (Hatt, 1969:18)), the basic technique was the same throughout the Subarctic region – defleshing, perhaps dehairing, tanning with fatty substances, and rigorous mechanical handling, during the final drying sequences.

Whilst there were considerable variations within the Subarctic region in naming of sea-

Above: *Lower Ahtna Indians, the daughters of Chief Stickwan, c.1902, probably near the Lower Tonsina or Taral. They demonstrate the use of tumplines in the carrying of camp equipment.*

Below: *View of a Beaver encampment in the Peace River area, c.1920, showing an arrangment of lean-to dwellings typical of the Athapaskan groups. The tipis are a Plains influence.*

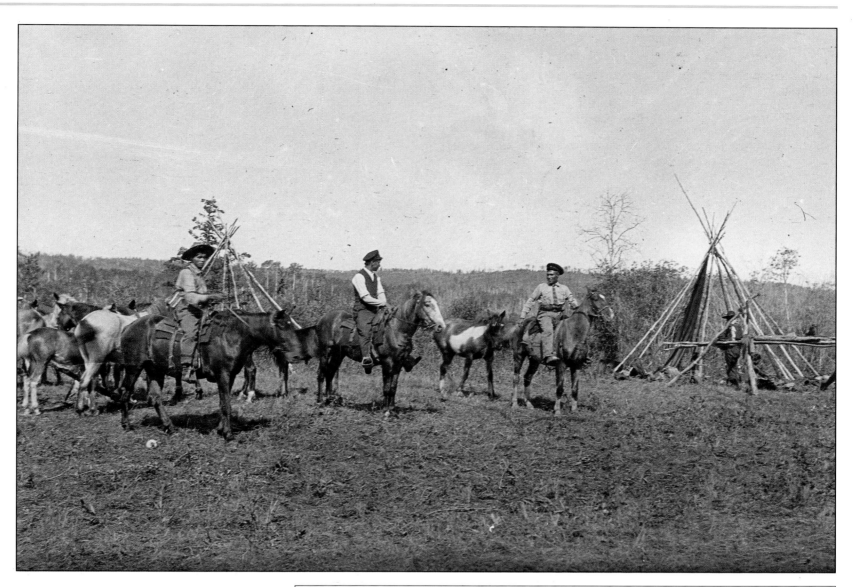

Above: *A group of Beaver hunters, c.1920. Although a late scene, it underlines the recorded fact that nomadism still persisted among these people even after the fur trade changed patterns of movement.*

sons and months, the annual cycle is fairly typical, putting emphasis on important seasonal events – the budding, blooming, leafing and fruiting of vegetation, moulting, migrating and pairing of animals and birds and the freezing of the rivers. The entry for January in the table refers to the winter as the 'old fellow' which caused the pine needles to drop, forming a covering on the snow just as pine boughs were laid on the floor of a wigwam to be used as bedding, an action referred to as 'spreading the brush' (Skinner, Wissler ed., 1911:48).

The Cree divided the year into eight seasons with twelve months or moons, producing a clearly defined annual cycle which is illustrated in the table below.

Group activities related to seasonal changes were determined by the relative abundance of fish or big game in a particular area. For example, in the case of the Tanana on the downstream sections of the major rivers which had heavy concentrations of salmon, there was an emphasis on fishing for their subsistence and they were the least mobile with a comparatively high population density. In contrast, those Tanana on the headwaters of the same rivers – perhaps less than two hundred miles away – put emphasis on hunting caribou, supplemented in July and August by the trapping of

SEASON		MOONS	
Cree	English	Cree	English
Sigun	Spring before open water	Migisupizun	Eagle month (March)
		Miskipizun	Gray goose month (April)
Miluskamin	Spring, after the water is open and before summer	Aligipizun	Frog month (May)
Nipin	Early summer	Sagipukawipizun	The month leaves come out (June)
Megwanipiu	Middle summer	Opaskwuwipizun	The moon when ducks begin to moult (July)
		Opunhopizun	The moon young ducks begin to fly (August)
Tukwagun	Early autumn	Weweopizun	Wavy or snow goose month (September)
Migiskau	Late autumn	Opinahamowipizun	The moon the birds fly south (October)
Pichipipun	Early winter, just before the frost	Kaskatinopizun	The moon the rivers begin to freeze (November)
Megwapipun	Late winter	Papiwatiginashispizun	The moon in which the young fellow spreads the brush (December)
		Gishepapiwatekimumpizun	The moon when the old fellow spreads the brush (January)
		Cepizun	Old month (February)

(AFTER SKINNER, WISSLER ED., 1911:48)

Kutchin

The Kutchin in the early nineteenth century lived in nine or ten regional bands on both sides of the present Alaska-Canada border, separated from the Arctic Ocean by a narrow strip of Inuit territory. Important as food were salmon, char and herring that were caught in weirs and with fishhooks, gill nets and spears. Small mammals, mountain sheep, moose and bear were hunted. The most prestigious hunting was for caribou, driven into surrounds or corrals, shot with bows and arrows, and speared while they swam. They provided food, bones to make tools and weapons, and skins for the fine, white-tanned leather used for clothing before about 1870. Both men and women wore a pullover shirt and trousers, the latter often with attached moose skin moccasins. Many of the objects shown here were collected before Kutchin technology was much affected by their participation in the fur trade, and by other outside influences. Dates of collecting are given, and (where known) the band of origin.

1 A man's caribou skin shirt, decorated with porcupine quills. Yukon Flats (or Birch Creek) band, 1866.
2 Man's caribou skin shirt, decorated with porcupine quills, pony beads, seeds, and red ochre. Yukon Flats (or Birch Creek) band, 1866.
3 Summer trousers with attached moccasins, made of caribou skin and beadwork. Yukon Flats (or Birch Creek) band, c.1860.
4 Pair of snowshoes, of the Loucheux type. Such snowshoes became standard across the western Subarctic. Probably Arctic Red River band, before 1905.
5 Man's caribou skin shirt, decorated with dentalia and

pony beads. Yukon Flats (or Birch Creek) band, c.1860.

6 Woman's shoulder band used to support a baby carried in a blanket; made of caribou skin faced with black velvet, beaded; before 1905.

7 Summer mittens on cord. Peel River band, c.1860.

8 Man's caribou skin shirt, beaded. This fine shirt was acquired by E. W. Nelson from an Innoko River Kutchin man trading at St Michael, whom he photographed wearing it one summer between 1877 and 1881.

9 Trousers that were worn with the above shirt.

10 Pair of mittens on a cord (to run through sleeves of shirt to prevent loss), collected with above shirt and trousers.

11 Pair of moccasins, Yukon Flats band, c.1866.

12 Model of one-man birch bark hunting canoe with spear; before 1905.

13 Knife. Yukon Flats (or Birch Creek) band, c.1860.

14 Ladle of mountain sheep horn; Han (not Kutchin) from Yukon River headwaters, c.1866.

whitefish. Such groups were amongst the most mobile following the caribou herds and had lower population densities. The general pattern was the same throughout the Subarctic region. Life was comparatively sedentary during the summer months when local bands rendezvoused along the shores of the rivers and lakes, an environment which afforded some protection from the great swarms of mosquitoes and blackflies. This was a time when social and family ties were reinforced and plans made for the coming winter. By early autumn, the gatherings dispersed, each band departing by canoe; at this time, the big game were in prime condition – the hides were at their best and the animals had an abundance of fat. Hunting was now a major activity and each band moved to its winter locality taking in meat and fish provision for the long winter months. The trapping of fur bearing animals took place in November and December when the furs were of the best quality. The pelts and hides were processed during the severest months of January and February when outside activities were virtually impossible due to intense cold and extended hours of darkness.

It was during these enforced periods of inactivity that the story makers recounted legends and perpetuated the tribal oral literature, whilst Montagnais-Naskapi hunters or shamans might assess their prospects, interpret dreams or organize discussion through the rituals of scapulimancy where moose, caribou or hare shoulder blade bones were held over a fire: the heat cracks, blackened spots and breaks were then interpreted in direct proportion to the ingeniousness of the practitioner. The custom was ancient, and has been sustained. It was reported on by the Jesuit missionary Paul Le Jeune who wintered with a

Above: *A Cree Indian from the Fort Edmonton area, by Paul Kane (1846). He wears a fine shirt which is embellished with heavy bands of pony beadwork across the shoulders and down the arms.*

Left: *Otisskun, or 'The Horn', a Cree warrior, by Paul Kane (1846). He wears a war cap; the headdress consists of a cap covered with white ermine fur, surmounted by horns.*

group of Montagnais in 1633-4 (Rogers and Leacock, 1981:184-6) and it was *filmed* by Hugh Brody in Pien Penashue's camp of Eastern Montagnais on the Goose Bay, Newfoundland, during the autumn of 1989 (Brody, 1990).

In addition to the tales of lone spirit woodland prowlers – the cannibals and bush men – it was also said that the spirits crossed the skies. In describing his travels with two Swampy Cree companions, one experienced observer reported that on witnessing the Aurora Borealis one remarked 'The *Choepi* [Ghosts] are having a good time to-night! . . . Look how the spirits of our departed friends are dancing . . . we call that *Pahkuk-kar-nemichik* – "The Dance of the Spirits!"' (Godsell, 1938:101).

In dealing with the supernatural, the East Cree, in common with most groups in the Subarctic, gave recognition to the enormous dependence on the products of the chase: this manifested itself in the form of sacrifices to propitiate the animals which they had to kill in order to survive. A widespread ethos recognized that a close bond existed between animals and human beings. Every animal was considered to have a spirit whose favor had to be sought, otherwise it could exert its influence to stop its species being killed by the hunters. Thus, the bones of beaver were carefully cleaned and cast into running water, whilst the heads of geese and ducks, the teeth of caribou and moose, the claws and skull of the bear, were cleaned and saved, serving not only as talismens and tallies, but also and, primarily, as an offering to the spirit of the respective animal. Bears, in particular, were highly honored, their skulls being carefully cleaned, dried and painted with stripes or dots[2] in red vermilion. They were then placed in trees out of respect to the animal.

At close quarters, the bear was a formidable opponent; nevertheless, because the bow was not considered powerful enough, they were

Above: *Cree hunting camp. The hide (or bark) covered conical wigwams have extra protective poles on the outside, a commonly used technique where the cover was of several pieces of material.*

hunted with club and knife. Crees reported that both the black and polar bears were particularly vulnerable when standing like a man, as they found difficulty in turning on the right side, thus an agile hunter was able to run in close and stab them in the heart. The creature was often likened to man and it was thought that they understood all that was said to them; as the hunter approached, he apologized and explained that the lack of food was the only motive for killing him and begged that the bear spirits would not be angry. At times, the bear was the winner, but the Cree explained that under these circumstances the animal could show compassion, such as in the case of a hunter who on attacking a bear was 'horribly scarred and mangled' but was finally set free when he pleaded with it for mercy (Skinner, Wissler ed., 1911:73).

In addition, the Subarctic people appealed to the powers of nature to help them with their great struggle for existence.[3] The winds were considered to be four brothers, the oldest and the most powerful being the north wind which brought the cold and had the power to punish evil doers. The other directions also had their distinctive characteristics and attributions (see table below).

For fast and effective travel, snowshoes were vital during the winter months; the style of snowshoe varied, generally being described by reference to the frame shape. As a generalization, broad oval, sometimes almost circular frames, were typical of the Montagnais-Naskapi, whilst the narrow elongated shape was used further west. Virtually all such snowshoes were of a wooden frame which was netted with rawhide thong generally referred to as 'babiche', which universally took the place of vegetable cordage, almost absent in these regions. Finely cut rawhide strips were made into snares and netted game bags, whilst the heavier strips were used for burden straps, tow-lines and sometimes even extensive fencing when driving caribou into the pound. The snowshoes were not uncommonly embellished with tufts of colored trade wool which enabled them to be located in deep snow, whilst the babiche netting was colored, generally red and black, and patterns produced by additional lacing at the toe and heel sections.

In this vast area, clothing tended to become increasingly elaborate from south to north. Widespread was the use of leggings or trousers with attached fur- or grass-lined moccasins and a semi-tailored dress or hide shirt. Some of the finest, both everyday and ceremonial, clothing from such tribes as the Kutchin and Dogrib, now resides in the Royal Scottish Museum, Edinburgh, having been collected by the Hudson's Bay Chief Trader, Bernard Rogan Ross, in 1859 and 1860. Collected just prior to the white man's all-pervading influence, they provide invaluable basic data for any Subarctic material culture studies (Kerr, 1953:32-5). In the case of the Dogrib clothing, the woman's costume consists of a smoked caribou skin dress sewn with sinew and decorated with red and white porcupine quills and red flannel, with a red and white quilled belt; tube-like leggings are also made of smoked caribou skin sewn with sinew, as are the separate straight center front seam-'T' back seam moccasins (Type 2(Ab), Webber, 1989:28). The man's costume is similarly constructed, which may have a slight hint of white influence, exhibiting as it does a curious military collar.

Similar everyday clothing for the East Cree was described by the explorer Alexander Mackenzie three-quarters of a century earlier, whilst Skinner describes a fine hooded coat worn by hunters which was made of caribou skin and retaining the hair 'somewhat resembling Eskimo parkas'. Of particular interest is that they were painted *inside* by outlining on the skin, the eyes and mouth of the animal, symbolically stating that the power of the living animal – its speed, endurance or cunning – was possessed by the garment and could be transmitted to the wearer (Skinner, Wissler ed., 1911:15-17).

Ceremonial regalia was an elaboration of everyday clothing, generally embellished with porcupine quillwork, dentalium shells or painted. The quillwork was later combined with trade beads which ultimately virtually displaced the indigenous quillwork. Several garments are particularly distinctive within these areas. The Naskapi, for example, were well known for use of clothing which was painted in

WIND		ATTRIBUTION
English	**Cree**	
West	*Nikapi-hun-nizeo*	'A favorable person, good and generous to mankind. This is the best hunting wind'
East	*Wapanung-nizeo*	'A stingy fellow, he starves the people, and will give them nothing to eat'
South	*Shawanung-nizeo*	'Gives food in summer, and has charge of it. He gives the berries'
		(AFTER SKINNER, 1911)

Carrier

The Carrier of British Columbia were much influenced by their proximity to the rank-conscious, potlatching Bella Coola and Gitskan, by the 19th-century fur trade, gold mining and Catholic missionizing, and by 20th-century lumbering. Anthropologist Julian Steward documented their material culture during his field research among the Stuart Lake Carrier in 1940. The names of his sources, carefully noted at the time, are also included here.

1 Recent fish net made with fine commercial cord, made by Sophie (Mrs Sam) Basil.
2 Pair of snowshoes with single strap harness, upturned toes. Models by Keon Sagalon.
3 Snow walking stick, with sinew netted hoop, burned spiral design. Model by Louie Billy Price.
4 Recent hide flesher of moose leg bone with notched blade. Made by Mrs Puis.
5 Old scoop to remove ice from fishing holes; sinew cords. From Louie Billy Price.
6 Old shuttle for making fish net. From Mrs Stevens.
7 Man's moose skin shirt, sewn with thread (rather than sinew). Model by Mrs Alec McKinnon.
8 Man's moose skin leggings, sewn with thread. Model by Mrs Stevens.
9 Old moose skin mittens, sewn with thread. From Mrs George Todd.
10 Moose skin high-top soft-sole moccasins, sewn with thread. Model by Mrs Isadore Louis.
11 Moose skin quiver. Model by Mrs Edward Thomas.
12 Old harpoon head for beaver, of steel, three barbs. From Mrs Jimmy Stevens.
13 Canoe paddle for lake travel, burned design on handle. Model, about ¾ size, by J. B. Patrick.
14 Recent birch bark container with wood strip rim, made by Mrs Isadore Louis.

15 Old pack net of moose rawhide, used by women. From Mrs D. Todd.

16 Beaver harpoon point made from moose leg bone, two barbs. Model.

17 Buzzer toy of moose joint on sinew cords, wooden handles. Model by Pierre Sagalon.

18 Shinny stick of poplar wood. Reduced size model by Louie Billy

Price.

19 Recent shinny ball, moose skin sewn with red and blue thread. Made by Mrs Sam Sekani.

20 Recent dog's back pack, double sack of moose skin. Made by Mrs George Todd.

21 Shuttle cock, a ball of spruce bark. Model by Pierre Sagalon.

22 Snow shovel of poplar wood. Model by Daniel Michel.

23 Recent moose skin carrying bag, with lace closure. Made by Mrs Isadore Louis.

24 Recent birch bark basket with wooden rim, cloth handle.

25 Hoop of twigs wrapped with willow bark, at which darts are thrown in popular team game. Model by Mrs Edward Thomas.

intricate patterns with tools of bone or wood, the main colors being red and yellow, but pigments were also mixed to obtain varying hues. Extended parallel lines were produced by the use of a multiple prong tool whilst fine lines were drawn with a curved paint stick; many of the designs were geometrical, but the so-called double curve motif was also commonly used. The work reached its fullest development on men's robes and summer coats, one specimen in the museum collections dating as early as 1740 (National Museum of Canada, Ottawa. Cat. No. III-B-588). This particular piece is made of soft caribou hide with fringed edges which were once wrapped with red porcupine quills. It is embellished with scores of double curve motifs in addition to straight lines, triangular figures and dots in a three-fold division, which one scholar has suggested symbolize the three cosmic zones which only a shaman, wearing the robe, could actually penetrate. Recent research has led to the speculation that such robes represented a religious microcosm and that, in donning the robe, the wearer entered into contact with the spirit world, abolishing time and entering into a primordial state. It is contended that his symbolic rebirth achieved with the robe 'was synonymous with the return of the sun, the renewal of the world, the rebirth of his people and, almost certainly the return of the caribou' (Webber, 1983:69).

Some of the earliest depictions of the magnificent prestige garments worn by the Athapaskan-speaking Kutchin to the northwest were made by Alexander Murray in his *Journal of the Yukon*, 1847-48. The distinctive pointed tailored shirts or tunics were often tailored in a complex pattern of many separate pieces of skin,

although the main body was generally made up of large pieces, front and back. The same style had also been traditionally worn by the Chipewyans who inhabited the country to the southeast. Indeed, the name Chipewyan, it has been suggested, was derived from the Cree name for this tribe, *Chepau-Wayanuk*, meaning 'pointed skins'[4] (Godsell, 1938:246; Duncan, 1989:46).

Prior to the introduction of beads, such garments were embellished with bands of porcupine quillwork, perhaps 2 to 2½in. (5-6cm.) in width, which extended across the chest and over the shoulders; similar bands were sometimes attached to the cuffs. There were variations in the quill techniques employed; in some instances the quills were held to the surface by two rows of stitches, the thread of sinew being caught into the surface of the skin between each fold of the quills. Alternatively, a markedly different appearance was obtained by a variation in the technique of folding the quills so that the quills crossed diagonally, producing a double sawtooth-like pattern. Five to six lanes of such work produced the full width bands, with patterns consisting of triangles, simple crosses, and bands predominately in red, white and blue. In addition, the lower edges were generally embellished with a buckskin fringe completely wrapped with quills near the point of attachment, for some 2½in. (6cm.), and then changing to alternate wrapped and unwrapped sections for another 2½in or so, finally terminating to a free fringe. The whole –

Below: Northern Ojibwa camp, date uncertain but probably around 1900. The woman (right) heats water in a metal trade kettle. Note headscarves worn as protection against swarms of mosquitoes.

sewn band and wrapped fringe – greatly enhanced the overall appearance of this prestigious and valuable garment.

An alternative quill technique was a type of surface weaving where quills were applied direct to the hide. First described by Orchard for the Tlingit (Orchard, 1916:36-7), but now rather firmly associated with the Alaskan Tanaina, the quills are laid lengthwise side by side on the hide surface. Spot stitches are concealed beneath the ends of the quills and at regular intervals a stitch is made across the surface of the quills; initially caught into the skin and under the quill on the outside edge of the decorative band, it then runs over the next quill and into the hide, running under the third quill, and so on across the entire width of the band and acting as a type of weft. At the commencement of the second row of stitches, the surface of the *first* quill is crossed, then under the second, over the third, under the fourth, over the fifth, repeating the sequence to the opposite edge. Additional quills were spliced in by bending the end of the previous quill together with the new one under the nearest spot stitch (ibid:fig.22).

A variant of this technique was to use a weft sinew such that, except for the outside quills, each rectangular exposed portion of quill was surrounded by a sinew thread. Whilst patterns were predominately made up of stripes, the techniques did lend themselves to the production of curvilinear motifs and, particularly in the older specimens, the colors were a distinctive yellow/orange, black/brown and natural white.

Such bands were also utilized to embellish mukluks (combined moccasins and leggings),

Cree Snowshoes

Thin rawhide lacing

Babiche: heavier rawhide lacing cut from moosehide gives strength to center

Colored wool tassels, decorative, and functional where shoes lost in deep snow

Frame, cross pieces of seasoned birch wood

Above: *The invention of the snowshoe in the Old World and its subsequent widespread use in North America enabled the development of cultures in areas where travel in deep snow would otherwise be impossible. This 'snowshoe' complex gave rise to an ever-broadening exploitation of land resources. A wide variety of snowshoe styles existed matching terrain and snow density. In the west they were long and narrow, as here; among the more eastern Montagnais-Naskapi they were much broader, some oval, others almost round. They were generally named according to form shape, Beaver tail, Bear paw and Swallowtail being some common terms.*

knife sheaths and mittens.[5] In the two latter cases, the quills were applied directly to the object, but for larger items – such as leggings and tunics – it was not unusual to work the quills on to a separate band and then sew them to the garment.

Separate woven quilled bands were, and still are, very much a speciality of the Slave and to a lesser extent, the Dogrib, who lived in the vicinity of the Great Slave Lake, North West Territories. Unlike the Tanaina work just described, this was done on a wooden bow loom. The warp threads were attached at each end of a green sapling, the tension bending the sapling into a bow shape so giving ample space below the threads for the work to be carried out unimpeded. A weft thread is now attached to the outer warp and then made to pass over and under the warp to the other side and back again; flattened quills are at the same time woven between the warp and weft threads. As the work proceeds, and each time a row is completed, the quills are pushed together so that the cross threads are hidden. Geometrical designs are produced by adding colored quills at various intervals. When the work is finished, the protruding underside ends of the quills are cut off for easy attachment of the band to an object. The finished piece has the appearance of fine cylindrical elements creating an impression that the quills themselves have been cut into short lengths and then woven in – as one could do with beads of a similar size and shape. The patterns produced in such work are wholly geometrical, commonly consisting of a series of repeated diamonds outlined in red, green, blue and orange quills. A notable feature of such work is the delicacy and repetition of the design patterns, in marked contrast to loom quillwork of some of the more southerly Algonquians such as the Cree and Métis (people of mixed Indian and French-Canadian blood) of the Red River area, where the patterns are bolder, design motifs are not quite so repetitive and larger quills are used.

A further feature of Slave woven quillwork is the occasional employment of moosehair in conjunction with the quills. Here, a number of hairs – perhaps four or five and equal to the width of a quill – are introduced in place of a quill so building up the stepped diamond patterns (Turner, 1955:38-9). Although commonly used as belts, bands of such quillwork were also attached to moosehide jackets, game bags and gun cases. This type of quilling required great skill and patience, and was much coveted, as Hudson's Bay Company factor Bernard Ross reported in 1862: 'The quantity done in a day by a skillful operative is about 2½ inches of belt size – and one of these articles is completed in about a fortnight, when it would be bartered for about 8 £-worth of goods' (Hail and Duncan, 1989:144).

The impact of trade goods on the Subarctic tribes was considerable. When Alexander Hunter Murray, a senior clerk of the Hudson's Bay Company, established Fort Yukon on the Porcupine River in 1847,[6] he made reference to the great importance of beads for trading to the

Left: *Montagnais-Naskapi winter camp, c.1910, showing the most common form of dwelling used in the region: 20 to 30 poles were used to form a conical framework covered with rolls of birch bark.*

Naskapi Hunter, 1880

A Naskapi hunter arrives home dragging a beaver he has killed. The ceremonial game carrying string, passed through the animal's nostrils, is designed to show respect for the game; red cords were used for beaver. The hunter wears a winter coat of tanned caribou skin with the fur side in, caribou skin leggings, and smoked deerskin mittens. His muzzle-loader is wrapped against the weather; he has a powder horn and a beaded shot pouch. His wife, smoking a stone pipe, has her hair wrapped around wooden blocks and wears a cloth cap and beaded cloth leggings. Her overdress is of caribou skin. The painted skin garments were brought to the Smithsonian the next year. The conical wigwams are covered with skins and canvas. A toboggan rests against one, with the front painted with a magical pattern.

Kutchin Indians, remarking 'Without *beads* and plenty of them you can do little or no good here . . . To trade here successfully, there ought to be for one year's outfit four boxes of common white beads, one box of red (same size) and one box of fancy' (Murray, Burpee ed., 1910:94). Beads were clearly a sign of wealth and prestige. 'I may here remark that all the chiefs hereabouts are young men, . . . none are considered a chief until they have 200 skins worth of beads . . . There is one man of the upper band who has between 90 and 100 skins in martens and beaver which he is keeping *all* for beads on our return' (ibid: 90 and 93). Murray further reported a competition with the Russian traders and expressed concern at the time it took to get suitable goods to the distant trading posts – perhaps up to *seven* years after the request. He also refers to the high value placed by the local Indians on the dentalium shells[7] and requests more for trading: 'They are most valuable, every Indian wears them, as nose and ear ornaments, for hair bands, etc.' (ibid:94)

Beads and dentalium shells were greatly favored by the Kutchin and Murray was impressed by the large quantities which they procured to embellish their clothing. His on-the-spot pen and ink sketches illustrate their early and extensive use as well as giving a wealth of ethnological detail which, although lacking some of the finer points relating to bead motifs, are found to be largely reliable when compared to actual specimens. The beaded bands which were attached to the garments resembled the earlier woven quillwork, the string of beads following the long axis of the band. Just as in the lanes of quillwork, patterns too were not uncommonly made up of striped rectangular figures, similar to quillwork; colors differed however, blue, red, as well as black and white dominated and preferences changed, sometimes remarkably quickly.[8] Actual examination of specimens reveals the use of large round-ended cylindrical shaped beads about 4 to 5mm.

in length and diameter to be common on mid-century and earlier pieces, whilst the slightly smaller and more rounded variety (generally referred to as 'pony beads' – see references to these in captions throughout the book), were more popular less than a quarter of a century later, possibly reflecting a change in trade patterns.

The coveted dentalium shell, whilst popular in the form of necklaces and carrying straps, was also combined with black or blue pony beads and sewn to the tunic or dress, generally following the contours of the shoulder cape. Whilst large areas could be covered comparatively quickly by the use of these shells, they were an exceedingly expensive embellishment. Murray, reporting from Fort Yukon in 1847, states 'these are traded in this country 6 and 8 for a beaver or 3 martens, a box of these shells here would be worth over *two thousand pounds*' (ibid:71-2).

By the 1850s, a smaller type of bead was gaining popularity in the Subarctic region. Generally referred to as a 'seed' bead, which ranged approximately 1 to 2mm. in diameter and came in a wide variety of colors, it was frequently used in combination with red and black cloth to embellish a wide variety of objects, considerably extending on the earlier artwork, which had largely been restricted due to the scarcity of natural materials.

About the same time, silk and cotton threads were being introduced, particularly in the Lake Winnipeg region, with outlets at such Hudson's Bay Trading Posts as Norway House, located on the northern shore of that great lake. Embroidering with such threads was particularly popular with the Cree, Saulteaux and Métis people of that region and, on a smaller scale, to the

Below: *Montagnais-Naskapi encampment, c.1883. Note the 'at ready' canoes adjacent to the lodge. Light and maneuverable, the 'crooked' canoe was well suited to the fast flowing rivers of the region.*

north and west, amongst the Chipewyan, Slave and Dogrib, who wrapped horsehair[9] fillers with colored threads, or used silk and colored ribbons or tape largely as decoration around the edge of moccasin vamps.

As was discussed earlier, whilst some of the pony beadwork patterns can sometimes be related to those found in the earlier quillwork, this is not the case with embroidery or seed beadwork, the dominant motifs being floral and most highly developed in the Great Slave Lake-Mackenzie River region amongst those tribes – particularly Chipewyan, Slave and Dogrib – who had firm contacts with the Hudson's Bay Company Trading Posts such as Fort Chipewyan on Lake Athabasca, and Forts Resolution, Rae and Providence, on the Great Slave Lake. The new media allowed greater freedom in the development of design motifs which had previously been largely confined to the geometrical in porcupine quillwork. Further, there were considerable outside influences, not least the missionaries, who after establishing a religious community on the Red River amongst the Plains Cree and Chippewa (Ojibwa) in 1818, expanded north to Lake Athabasca and the Great Slave Lake in 1849. It is almost certain that floral vestments, altar cloths and church paintings became the inspiration for these new design motifs. Certainly in the case of the church paintings, one Mother Superior reported: 'The native women, who enjoy silk thread, bead and quill embroidery . . . came to copy these designs from the Cathedral'[10] (Duncan, 1989:59).

Initial efforts at producing floral patterns could result in attractive but stiff designs but, in largely dispensing with a beaded background, which tended to crowd the decorative field, the motifs expand into dynamic semi-realistic, generally stemmed, patterns, which became the characteristic of much Athapaskan beadwork produced in the latter years of the nineteenth and early twentieth centuries. This

Cree

These objects were collected by the anthropologist Alanson Skinner in 1908 and 1909 in Ontario and Quebec from speakers of three different dialects of the Cree language. The Cree at Eastmain and Rupert House speak East Cree, those at Moose Factory speak Moose Cree, and those at Fort Albany speak East Swampy Cree and the rest are West Main Cree. When Skinner was conducting his research among them, they were hunters and fur trappers, living off forest products (primarily game and fish) and food obtained from the Hudson's Bay Company posts in exchange for furs. They lived in conical or domed wigwams covered with canvas, wore Euro-American clothes (hunters often used native moccasins), and hunted with guns. Travel was by birch bark canoes in summer, dog sled and snowshoes in winter. Crafts included woodworking, tanning, beadwork, and making rabbitskin blankets in a netting technique. Long missionized, the Cree were Catholics or Anglicans, though some native rituals persisted.

1 Beaming tool, for dehairing skin. Ft Albany.
2 Netting needle.
3 Wooden spoon for eating boiled caribou blood mixed with moss. Rupert Hse.
4 Toy snow shovel (full size 4–5ft long). Rupert Hse.
5 Boy's sling. Rupert Hse.
6 Crooked knife for carving; from Tom Bain, Moose Factory.
7 Old style crooked knife of beaver incisors. Eastmain.
8 Shot pouch of beaded cloth. Ft Albany.
9 Leather work bag embroidered with silk thread. Eastmain.
10 Beaded pouch for ammunition caps. Ft Albany.
11 Sealskin shot pouch. Eastmain.
12 Wooden ladle. Ft Albany.
13 Wooden ladle. Ft Albany.
14 Ladle, shape used to dip out boiled fish. Rupert Hse.
15 Spoon for boiled caribou blood mixed with moss. Rupert Hse.
16 Woman's bag made of

200

caribou fetus skin. Eastmain.

17 Pipe bowl made of red stone found on shore; 'beaver size' (trade value, one beaver pelt). Rupert Hse.

18 Birch bark container with cloth top. Moose Factory.

19 Birch bark porridge bowl. Ft Albany.

20 Model of wooden eating tray of type left in food cache at forest camp. Rupert Hse.

21 Model of net used to catch beaver. Rupert Hse.

22 Painted bear skull, hung up in forest for success in taking bears. Eastmain.

23, 24 Two lower lips of black bears; hunting charm or trophy. Rupert Hse.

25 Young bear's scapula, kept as charm and hunting trophy. Eastmain.

26 Caribou teeth charm.

27 Bone charm in bag tied to 23.

28 Stuffed goose head kept as charm or hunting trophy. Rupert Hse.

29 Beaded shot pouch. Ft Albany.

30 Beaded pouch for ammunition. Ft Albany.

31 Model of bow drill for making fire. Moose Factory.

32 Model of old style fish hook. Rupert Hse.

33 Rattling beater used with conjuror's drum. From 'Old Swallow', conjuror at Rupert Hse.

34 Woman's bag of summer caribou leg skin. Rupert Hse.

35 Child's rattle. Rupert Hse.

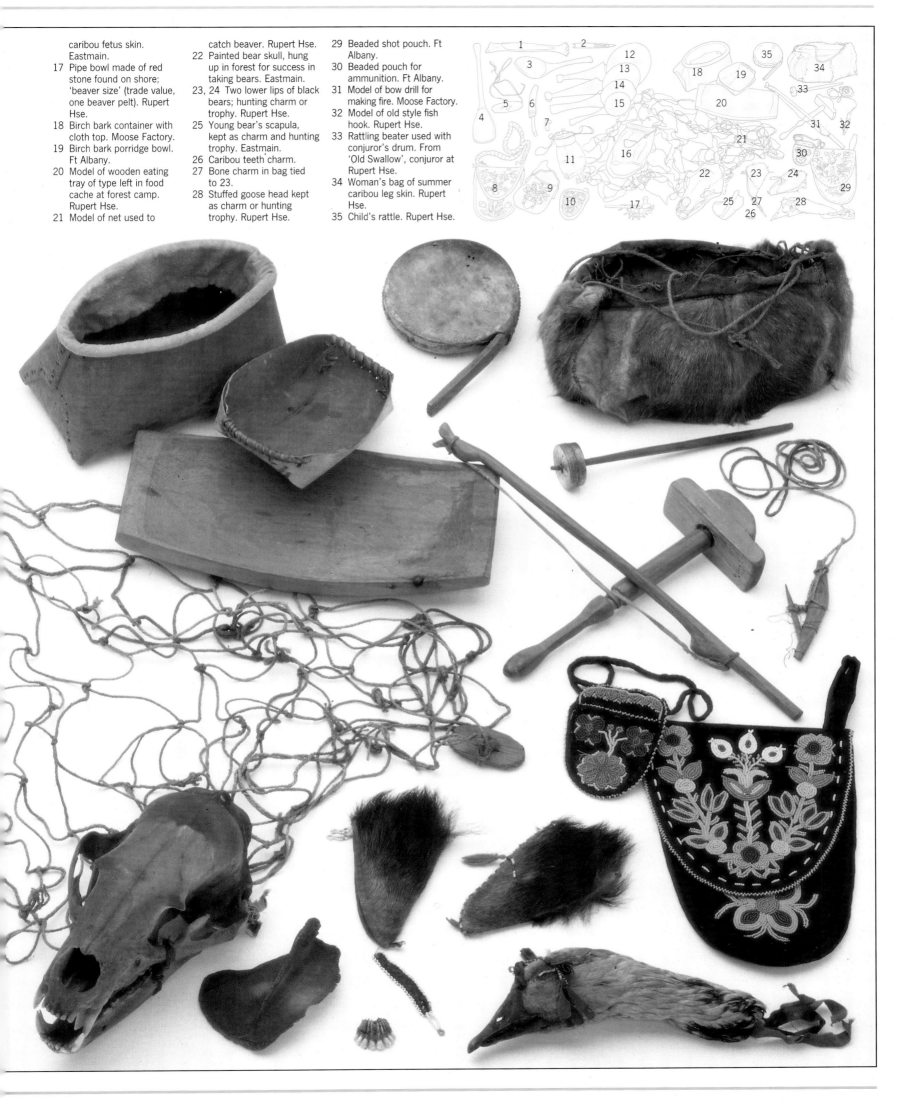

ready adoption of European technology epitomized the flexibility of Athapaskan society, developed over the centuries in order to survive in a frequently hostile and often unpredictable environment and where the natural materials required for ornamentation were difficult to obtain and use. It also became a source of revenue for the often impoverished families whose womenfolk turned their hands to the production of wall pockets, dog blankets, pouches, moccasins, mittens, gauntlets, jackets and even shelf valances, all magnificently embellished with beads and to a lesser extent, thread embroidery.[11] Much of the raw materials were supplied by 'The Bay' which,

since its foundation and Royal Charter from Charles II in 1670, encouraged the Indian people of the Subarctic to hunt and trap such creatures as the beaver, mink, ermine, fox, wolf, bear and otter, often with brutal metal traps supplied by 'The Company': all this to satisfy

Below: A *view of a Montagnais-Naskapi encampment on Grand Lake, Labrador, c.1891. Note the bark and hide/cloth covered conical lodges, the bearskin frame and the strips of wood which have been prepared for canoe building. Their lodges would have an opening for smoke just above the fireplace. The canoes near the dwellings underline the vital importance of mobility to the Indians.*

the demands of the European markets for exotic animal pelts. Clearly, by seemingly reconciling the ancient beliefs where animals were treated with respect and killed only for survival, Indian people expanded their hunting activities, thus obtaining some relief from the harsh Subarctic environment – expressed in utterances by the people themselves such as the Chipewyan eternal cry, 'Dow-diddla! dow-diddla!', 'It is hard! it is hard!' and the Montagnais' sentiment, 'We are poor, . . . and we live among the trees, but we have our children' (Godsell, 1938:250 and Hubbard, 1908:193).

But for this a price was to be paid because, as with the decimation of the immense buffalo herds on the Great Plains to the south in the last quarter of the nineteenth century, so too with the fur-bearing animals of these northlands. The immense number of animals which were slaughtered solely for their furs is illustrated by the Annual Reports of the fur companies. The returns of the North West Company,[12] c.1800, in a single season were:

Beaver	106,000
Bear	21,000
Fox	15,000
Kit Fox	40,000
Otter	46,000
Marten	32,000

Whilst trade values obviously varied, particularly when there was competition, the profits could be enormous. For example, when Alexander Murray set up a trading post in Kutchin territory in 1847 (as mentioned earlier), he reported that the Russian traders gave ten blue beads 'a little larger than a garden pea' for one beaver skin (Murray, Burpee ed., 1910:71). The slaughter continued, virtually unabated, for a century. Over a nine year period (1920-29), the average number of pelts returned per year by the Canadian provinces was:

Beaver	137,400
Red Fox	56,030
White Fox	39,688
Marten	43,480

The following year, however, saw a dramatic drop to less than fifty thousand in returns on the beaver, an animal generally considered emblematic of the fur trade, and which to several Subarctic tribes, as already mentioned, was as important to their territorial lifeway as the seal was to the Inuit. The enormous profits which could be made, as with the buffalo hunters some sixty years previously, caused the influx of white trappers who not infrequently employed hunting methods which gave scant regard for a basic woodland law, which decreed that female animals were left undisturbed during the breeding season. In this, they were encouraged by traders because, although the pelts at this time were poor in quality, they were still accepted by all 'except the Hudson's Bay Company' (Cory, 1935:66).

The Dogrib and Slaves north of the Peace River, incensed at the white trappers encroachment, retaliated by starting forest fires to drive out the white invaders. To the south and east, in traditional Chippewa and Montagnais-Naskapi territory, full bloods and Métis all reported the same tale: 'The beaver were going fast; in large areas they were already gone' (Grey Owl, 1935:48).

On the Subarctic-Woodland boundary north of Lake Nipissing, one Indian hunter in the winter of 1925-6 had 'twelve white men trapping or his family hunting territory . . . As the white newcomers trapped an area until it became barren, to protect themselves from exploitation, the Indians began to do the same' (Smith, 1990:80).[13]

European diseases, and in some cases poor diet, also weakened resistance. As with the Plains tribes, smallpox had decimated many of the northern tribes in 1791-2 and again in 1837-8, whilst the influenza epidemics, against which the indigenous populations had little resistance, caused havoc. Skinner (1911), for example, found that owing to the great mortality during the influenza epidemic which swept through Northern Quebec and Ontario in the winter of 1908-9, it was almost impossible to find anyone who was able to relate the myths and legends of the East Cree. Again, in 1917, it wiped out forty per cent of the Lake Nipigon Chippewa/Cree and, in the winter of 1927, most of the Prophet River band of Sekani.

By the 1930s, the great Subarctic was witnessing a fast vanishing frontier, with several parallels to events in the United States less than a half century before. It would, however, be too simplistic to suggest that in this case it was largely dominated by avarice because this exploitation needs to be appreciated in the context of the times. The Great Depression of the 1920s caused the influx of large numbers of white trappers and traders. Lured by dreams of wealth, they tried their hand at trapping, often with little regard for any form of conservation or humane killing. It was a desperate attempt to 'escape the joblessness and despair of the Great Depression' (Irving et al., 1985:23). Traditional techniques of trapping by the indigenous people rotated trapping areas; the experienced hunter specifically designed his trap set so that only particular animals were guided

to the trap and thus few unwanted and unnecessary catches were made.

By the beginning of the 1940s the economic effects of the Depression and World War were felt in the north; markets collapsed, and fur prices plummeted. Whilst a few white traders and trappers stayed, most left, almost as suddenly as they had appeared and the fur trade reverted to the Dene, Métis and other indigenous groups of the Subarctic. The change came only just in time and today (1990s) it is claimed that no commercially trapped fur bearing species is endangered or threatened with extinction and the animal depletions which occurred during the early part of the twentieth century have now been restored and the fur bearing animals are 'as abundant as they ever were' (ibid:48).

A new threat, however, confronts the Subarctic people as they now face the great anti-killing campaigns which stigmatize their very lifestyle. Living in a land which does not lend itself to agriculture and in a land where oil, gas and mining developments are enormously expensive, they have been hardest hit by such campaigns and they are becoming a serious threat to a long-standing and sound way of life which has adapted to and produced a balanced environment.[14] It has been suggested that the Subarctic people must assert their right to manage their ancestral lands and animals based not on imposed standards but on inherited principles.

Today this message has been sent forth to the people of Canada in English, French and, as an extract below illustrates, in an almost universal written language of the great Subarctic – Cree :

ᓄᐊᑦᐱᐊᕐᑐᓕᒪᐃᐦᐃᓕᐁᐃᐦᐃᐊᐃᐧᑲᐃᐅᓕᑦᒫ

(ibid:3)

References

1 Band communication clearly led to efficient exploitation strategies: whilst living in a severe environment, Smith points out the Chipewyan 'do not have myths and legends which emphasize starvation' (Smith, 1978:68).
2 Frank G. Speck has discussed the distribution and symbolism of dot ornamentation on both Inuit and Indian objects (Speck, 1925:151-72).
3 See epigraph to this chapter.
4 A close observer of the Chipewyans commented on the large number of caribou hides required to make a complete outfit for one hunter – ten to twelve – and 'an even larger number to supply him with lodge, lines, snares and nets' (Godsell, 1938:246-7).
5 Speyer, 1968:Abb.2 and 4
6 This was actually within Russian territory. As Burpee observes, Murray seemed to have deliberately invaded the ground of his rivals, but it was 'all in the game of the fur trade, and that game was a rough-and-tumble affair at the best'

(Murray, Burpee ed., 1910:5).
7 Petroff refers to the very high value placed on these shells in 1802: 'The price of one pair of these shells was a whole parka of squirrel skins' (ibid:71).
8 Duncan reports that a Hudson's Bay Company trade list refers to 'amber and crystal beads, both unsalable five years earlier, are listed as now acceptable' (Duncan, 1989:44).
9 Horsehair was another valuable trade item (Turner, 1955:64).
10 I am appreciative of discussions with Katherine Pettipas of the Manitoba Museum of Man and Nature, who first drew my attention to such influences in the summer of 1977.
11 The influence of some particularly active Métis women on such artwork was commented on by Agnes Cameron, a journalist who visited Fort Chipewyan in 1909. Of Mrs Loutit, a Métis lady of mixed Chipewyan, Cree and Scottish blood, Bell reported 'She weaves fantastic belts of beads and

sets the fashion for the whole North' (Cameron, 1912:321).
12 The most powerful of all the Hudson's Bay Company's rivals.
13 The great efforts of the English born, Archibald Belaney – better known as Grey Owl – in the 1930s to reintroduce the beaver and his emphasis on conservation were to earn him the title, 'Father of Canadian Conservation'.
14 The Canadian Director of Greenpeace recently observed: 'Greenpeace, of course, is opposed at a philosophical level to the inflicting of pain on any wildlife at all for any purpose. But . . . where you still have a semblance of the natural ecosystem and where you still have an abundance of the wildlife species . . . I don't see any reason not to attempt, at least, to retain some kind of balance between the original peoples there and the wildlife resources and the plant resources that they have depended on for so many centuries' (Bourque, 1986:11).

THE ARCTIC

THE ARCTIC conjures up romantic images of an untamed land of ice and snow, a land of mystery and grandeur. The Arctic is also seen as a harsh, unforgiving environment where any wrong choice is the difference between life and death. The Northwest Passage is one of many places where imagination and reality come together. Explorers have long tested themselves against the Arctic and continue to do so in the twentieth century. Nowadays, the Arctic is frequently envisioned as a refugium, one of the last pristine environments on the planet.

The Arctic is not a vast, uninhabited land. It is the homeland of three separate linguistic groups: the Aleut, the Yup'ik, and the Inuit-Inupiaq. In fact, not all of these groups live in the Arctic as defined by geographers. The Arctic is usually regarded as the region north of the treeline, the mean 10°C (50°F) July isotherm, and/or the line of continuous permafrost (Stager and McSkimming, 1984:27). Depending on the definition, some speakers of all these groups do not live in the Arctic. However, these people are regarded as the descendants of a common ancestral group, the Eskimo-Aleuts, and therefore they are all regarded as inhabitants of the Arctic by anthropologists.

Archeologists hypothesize that the Eskimo-Aleuts migrated across Bering Straits some 8-10,000 years ago (Turner,1988; Dumond, 1984). As they spread across the north the three linguistic groups evolved. First, Aleut separated from the Eskimo-Aleut stock and then Yup'ik and Inuit-Inupiaq split. Eventually these people colonized the area from Prince William Sound in southern Alaska to eastern Greenland. The peoples of the Arctic have many diverse cultures. They have never remained static and today they continue to change and adapt to new social, political and economic situations. (The title-page map shows a key to tribal territories of the Arctic; some groups or societies of the Arctic specifically mentioned in the text may be included in overall groups and will not be shown on the map.)

My breath, I have it here
My bones, I have them here
My flesh, I have it here
With it I seek you,
With it I find you,
But speak to me
Say something nice to me.
(Nineteenth-century Aleut love song, in Bergsland and Dirks, 1990:687)

In 1741 Aleut culture was changed irrevocably by the visit of two Russian ships. Captains Bering and Chirikov, on a voyage of discovery, became the first Europeans to visit the Aleutian Islands. Although Bering later died on the Commander Islands, following a shipwreck, many of his crew returned to Russia with a cargo of sea otter pelts. These pelts, highly prized by the Chinese Emperor and his court, were virtually unobtainable as sea otters had been hunted almost to extinction in the waters of the western Pacific. The discovery of a new land rich in sea otters led Russian fur traders, known as the *promyshlenniki*, to build boats and set sail for Alaska.

To the Aleuts, the visit of strangers in ships was an oddity but not a unique event. Steller, the naturalist on Bering's ship, noted the presence of iron among the Aleuts:

Two had, in the fashion of Russian peasants, a long iron knife of very poor workmanship, which may be their own and no European fabrication . . . From a distance, I observed very exactly the quality of this knife, when one of the Americans unsheathed it and cut a bladder in two with it, and I saw . . . that it did not resemble any European workmanship.

(Steller, 1988:103)

This iron may have come through trade from the northeast, or more likely from Japanese fishing boats blown off course and wrecked on the foggy islands (Black,1983). These contacts

Key to groups:
1 Siberian Eskimo (Siberian Yup'ik)
2 St Lawrence Island Eskimo
3 Nuaivak Eskimo
4 Aleut
5 Pacific Eskimo (Pacific Yup'ik)
6 Mainland Southwest Alaska Eskimo (Central Alaskan Yup'ik)
7 Bering Strait Inuit
8 Kotzebue Sound Inuit
9 Interior North Alaska Inuit
10 North Alaska Coast Inuit
11 Mackenzie Delta Inuit
12 Copper Inuit
13 Netsilik
14 Caribou Inuit
15 Sallirmiut (Sadlermiut)
16 Iglulik
17 Baffinland Inuit
18 Polar Eskimo
19 East Greenland Eskimo
20 West Greenland Eskimo
21 Labrador Coast Inuit
22 Inuit of Quebec

with strangers were rare and their impacts on Aleut society minimal.

In the early 1700s Aleut society was still expanding. The population for this period has been estimated at 12-15,000 (Lantis, 1984:163) spread throughout the entire 1200 mile Aleutian archipelago: a chain of active volcanic islands strung like a pearl necklace across the northern Pacific. The majority of Aleuts lived on the islands closest to the Alaskan mainland, but, even the Near Islands (those nearest Russia) were inhabited. Archeologists believe that the Aleutians were first occupied about 8,000 years ago with people reaching the Near Islands about 1,000 years ago (McCartney, 1984). This vast region can be divided into two based on dialect: Eastern and Western Aleut (Krauss, 1988:146). Within these regions

This map shows the approximate territories of tribes and language groups in about 1850 over most of the region, but somewhat earlier in northwest Alaska and coastal Labrador, and somewhat later for south Alaska and Greenland. After that, many groups lost territory and some disappeared.

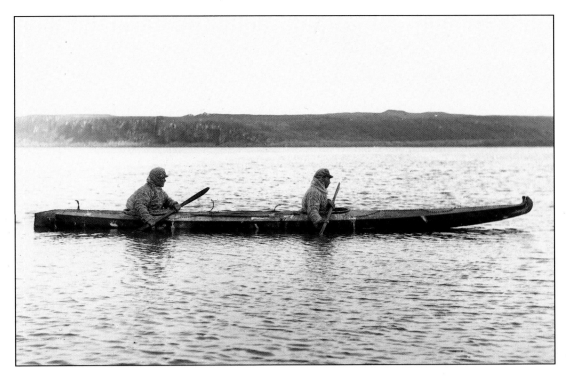

Above: *Aleut in two-hatch kayak (baidarka), St Paul Is., Pribilof Islands, c.1900. They tended to be of shallow draft and long in proportion to the beam, making them seem both light and fragile.*

there were many village-level societies each of which had their own territorial boundaries and their own leaders.

Relations between villages were generally cordial. Trade goods such as pine bark and birch bark were exchanged from the mainland to the treeless islands. Villagers visited each other for feasts and masked dances, usually held in December (Black,1980:89). However, relations were not always harmonious; murders, witchcraft and insults led to stealthy and deadly raids. Captives became slaves, and the raiders would quickly dismember those killed. Dismemberment dissipated the power contained within the deceased, preventing it from harming the attackers (Laughlin, 1980:103).

Aleut homes were dug into the ground to a depth of 5 to 6½ft (1.5-2m.). They were then roofed with whale bones and driftwood and covered with sod, '. . . when they have stood for some time they become overgrown with grass, so that a village has the appearance of a European church-yard full of graves' (Langsdorff, in Lantis, 1970:183). Some of these houses were single family dwellings, others were multi-family longhouses 40 to 65ft (12-20m.) long and 20 to 33ft (6-10m.) wide (Laughlin, 1980:50).

Houses were oriented along an east-west axis and the location of families within a house mirrored the importance of the east in Aleut cosmology where the east was viewed as the home of the creator (Black and Liapunova, 1988:57). The longhouses had a central passageway on either side of which were individual family compartments. All the families within a longhouse were related. The headman and his family occupied the easternmost compartment while the slaves lived at the western end. Entrance into these houses was through one or two holes in the roof; a notched log provided access to the floor.

These holes were the only means of entering and exiting houses. This left the occupants easy

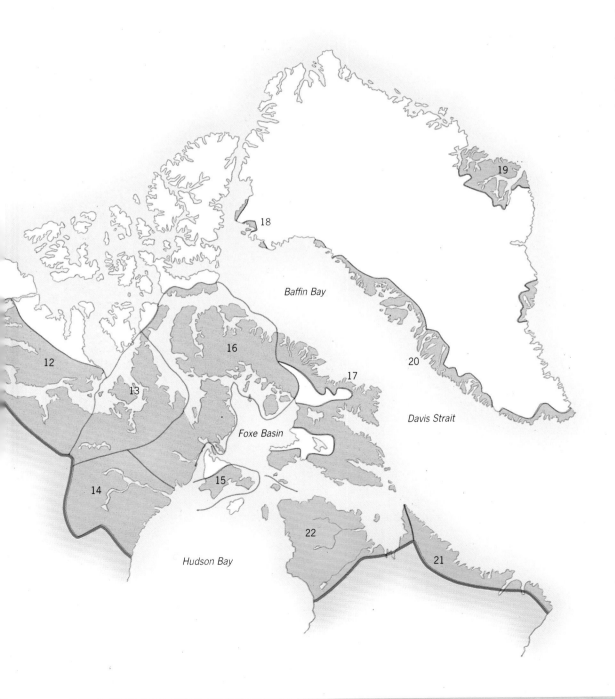

Baffin Bay

19

18

12

16

13

17

20

Foxe Basin

Davis Strait

15

14

22

Hudson Bay

21

prey for surprise attacks. The Aleuts employed three means to counteract this problem. Firstly, villages were usually located on isthmuses or narrow necks of land with dual sea access to provide a means of escape. Secondly, lookouts were posted to watch for unexpected and unwanted arrivals. Thirdly, secret compartments were excavated into house walls. During an attack, people could escape detection by taking shelter in these compartments.

Raids were rarely over territory. They were most often retaliatory feuds. The Aleuts had no need to fight over territory as the sea and land provided them with a bounty of resources. Starvation was almost unknown although March was often a lean time. There were very few land mammals on the Aleutians, but this lack of terrestrial fauna was compensated for by the variety of flora, marine fauna and bird life. The starchy roots of several plants were made into a thick gruel; the greens of fiddleheads, mountain sorrel, cress, cowslip and others were eaten and some herbs and roots were gathered for medicinal purposes. Berries including crow berries, salmon berries and cloud berries were both consumed fresh and stored for winter use. The beach grass (*Elymus mollis*) was used to produce the exceptionally fine baskets and mats made by Aleut women. Grasses were split into thin strands by fingernails and then twined. Baskets with over 1,000 stitches per square inch were made (Hudson, 1987:64). This quality of workmanship and attention to detail was characteristic of items created by Aleut women. Finally, monkshood was known to be poisonous and aconite was probably used for whaling. The gathering of these plants, with the exception of monkshood and some medicinal plants, was women's work. The women would store these seasonal plants for use throughout the year in pokes made from seals or seal lion stomachs (Collins, 1945).

Every spring flocks of waterfowl migrate to the Aleutians. Ducks, geese, swans, murres, puffins and many others lay eggs, raise their young and then fly south in the fall. The Aleuts gathered the eggs and hunted the different species adapting hunting methods to the habits of the birds. For example, puffins nest in burrows therefore the hunters placed snares over the entrance holes thereby strangling the puffins as they left their burrows in the morning. Another example was the hunting of albatross. 'The people sail out to catch them when the weather is quiet and foggy, because in such weather the birds cannot fly so well. The hunters move against them, since they know that the birds always fly up against the wind' (Merck, 1980:62).

The intertidal zone provided shellfish, octopus and seaweeds, foods that were gathered easily by women, children and the elderly. The availability of these resources gave widows a freedom to choose their own future rather than remarrying immediately as was the case among other northern peoples (Robert-Lamblin, 1982:199). They also saw people through the lean times when stores ran low and it was too rough to go out hunting.

Salmon were harvested throughout the summer and early autumn when they migrated up the short Aleutian rivers to spawn. Although many were caught and dried for winter use, the staples of the Aleut diet were the marine mam-

Above: *Oululuk, the chief village of the Aleut on Unalaska, with two-hole baidarka, by Louis Choris (1816-17). Even at this period white influence was evident, hence the Russian Orthodox church (left).*

mals, especially sea lions (Yesner, 1988). These mammals were hunted by men from their *baidarkas* (the Russian name for the Aleut kayak). Sea lions, seals and sea otters were hunted with darts thrown overhand using throwing boards. All men hunted these species. For a successful hunt a man prepared himself both physically and spiritually. Included in his hunting equipment were amulets to attract the animals and appease their spirits. 'Their preparation and place of preservation are kept secret, otherwise the amulets will lose their power. It is necessary to protect them from wetness; if an amulet becomes wet its owner will rot' (Jochelson, 1968:78).

Only a few men who had undergone special training would hunt whales. The hunt began on shore with the collection of the whaler's amulets, and the preparation of a special potion used to coat the dart and poison the whale. Some of the amulets used included hematite, feathers of a rosy finch and fluids from mummified bodies of dead hunters. The latter were considered extremely powerful amulets but the owner of such an amulet would lead a short life (Jochelson, 1968:78). When a whale was sighted a single hunter would set out to sea in his baidarka, then he would throw his dart into the whale and immediately return home, where he would enter an isolation hut and lie under a blanket for three days motionless. 'He behaved, . . . like a sick man and thus by sympathetic magic attempted to persuade the whale to be sick' (Laughlin, 1980:41). On the third day he would rise when the whale was seen to be dying. The people dispatched the whale and brought it to shore. It is not known how successful this method of hunting was. If the whale did not drift into your territory it might end up as the bounty of another village (Laughlin, 1980:41).

All these hunts were undertaken in the baidarka, a watercraft renowned for its speed and ability to withstand the rough waters of the Gulf of Alaska (Zimmerly, 1986:18). The Aleut baidarka was unique among kayaks as it had a bifurcated prow and a straight stern. These design elements are thought to have allowed the baidarka to ride over waves and counteract ' . . . the lift created when the bow meets waves'

(Heath, 1987:24) respectively. In the event of a sudden storm, Aleut would strap their baidarkas together thus creating a more stable craft.

Boys began learning kayaking skills from an early age. They had their tendons and ligaments stretched to allow them to sit in the baidarka for hours (Laughlin, 1980:28). They also played games mimicking hunting from a baidarka (Laughlin, 1980:2) and practiced with a baidarka in calm waters. Later, they would venture out in a two-hatched baidarka with an experienced hunter, often a maternal uncle. By late teens a boy would become a man by building his own baidarka. He was then considered to be ready for marriage.

Constructing a baidarka was extremely complex. First, driftwood was collected for the frame. Then the baidarka was crafted to the exact measurement of its owner. Many of the construction techniques were jealously guarded secrets passed from the father or uncle to the boy.

In some places, where the different pieces of the skeleton are fastened together, two flat bones are bound cross-ways over the joint inside, and this the chief assured me was of the greatest use in stormy weather. As the fastenings are apt to be loosened by the shock of the waves, these bones contribute essentially towards preventing such an inconvenience; but this art is not known to all, and is kept very much secret by those who possess it.

(Langsdorff, in Dyson, 1986:42)

Finally, women would cover the baidarka with the skins of sea lions. The women had to be careful that none of their hairs were caught in the seams or a sea lion, enraged by this female contamination, would bite a hole in it.

The Russian interest in the Aleuts is as much due to the versatility of the baidarka as to the presence of the sea otters in the region. When the promyshlenniki first visited the Aleutians they hunted by themselves. The Aleuts were regarded simply as useful trading partners. Then the Russians realized the potential of the baidarka for sea otter hunting. They began exploiting Aleut hunters, forcing villages to hunt by capturing hostages who were returned at the end of the hunting season (Pierce, 1988:121).

In the early 1760s the eastern Aleuts tried to rebel but they were crushed. In one incident,

Above: *Study of inhabitants of the Aleutian Islands, by Louis Choris (1816-17). Contact with traders, explorers and missionaries is already evident in these early portraits.*

the Russian Soloviev lined up a dozen men from Kashega and fired his musket at point-blank range to see how many Aleuts one bullet would kill. The answer was nine (Laughlin, 1980:129). The Aleut recognized their inability to succeed against the guns of the Russians. Introduced diseases further reduced their numbers and by 1799 only an eighth of the pre-contact population remained (Laughlin, 1980:130).

The Russian American Company (RAC) was

Below: *Karluk fishing/cannery village on Kodiak Is., Alaska, c.1900. Aleut fisherman brought fish to the cannery which at this time was manned by seasonal Chinese workers from San Francisco.*

established in 1799 and granted monopoly trading rights by the Russian crown. For most Aleuts this charter meant they became vassals of the company. The RAC was allowed to employ half the able-bodied men of a village and need only pay them a fifth of the wages of a Russian (Hansen, 1982:67) although often even these provisions were ignored by the company. This led to complaints by the Aleuts to the crown and a revision of the RAC charter in 1821. The change allowed the company to employ half the able-bodied men of a village for a period no longer than three years (Laughlin, 1980:130). By the 1800s Aleuts had been settled on the Commander and Pribilof Islands (the breeding grounds of the northern fur seal) by the RAC and Aleut hunters were located in Sitka and at the company's post, Fort Ross, on the California coast. One song in particular captures the loneliness of an Aleut hunter a long way from home.

Oh, what is it going to be?
What is he going to say?

Not expecting to be like this,
I entered again the end of it.

My islands, my dear islands there east!
Above them the clouds will be light in
the morning.

Over there it will be like that, too, in the
morning.
If I live on like this, endless, unceasing.

This boredom, this grief!.
   (Bergsland and Dirks, 1990:697)

Under the 1821 revision to its charter the RAC had to provide schooling, health services, churches and missionaries. The schools provided instruction not only in reading and writing but also in trades including shipbuilding, carpentry and metal working. Many of the students attending these schools were the offspring of Russian-Aleut unions, known as creoles. These unions led to a new class of people. At the top were the Russians, followed by the creoles and at the bottom the Aleuts. Health care was rudimentary; however, it did include a massive vaccination program following the devastating smallpox epidemic of 1838 (Black, 1980:103).

Most Aleuts were converted to the Russian Orthodox church by lay preachers who also built small churches. In 1824 the first missionary, Father Veniaminov, arrived in the Aleutians. This priest, beloved by his Alaskan parishioners, later became the Metropolitan of the church and is now Saint Innokenti. Another of the early priests was the creole Father Netsvetov, who had been educated in Russia (Black, in Netsvetov, 1980:xv). Why did the Aleuts

Aleut

These objects illustrate Aleut emphasis on sea hunting from kayaks, the use of intestines for waterproof clothing and bags, and specialization in very fine basketry twined of split dune grass. Russian influence, which began with the arrival of fur hunters in the 1740s, is evident in some of the forms and decoration. When known, the island of origin is given below. The dates are when the piece was collected or when it was received in the museum.

1 Twined dune-grass basket with false embroidery design, for carrying fish. Atka, 1882.
2 Twined openwork basket with colored thread decoration, 1903.
3 Fine twined basket with tight cover, decorated with blue, red, and yellow silk threads; probably made for sale. Attu, 1927.
4 Cigar case of very fine twined basketry with false embroidery design, a popular Aleut specialty, made for sale. Attu, 1874.
5 Model kayak, in typical two-hatch form, with paddlers wearing bentwood hats. Collected by Wilkes Expedition, 1841.
6 Conical hat of thin bentwood with polychrome painted abstract design, sea lion whiskers at back. 1868.
7 Cap of black leather, with white fur and red threads, in the shape of a Russian hat. Unalaska Island, 1868.
8 Thin wood hat with painted design of bird. Kayaligmiut (Yup'ik not Aleut), 1879.
9 Cigar case of fine twined dune grass, with false embroidery of wool thread, made for sale. 1921.
10 Basket with wool thread design near rim. Attu, 1894.
11 Twined openwork basket for carrying fish. Atka, 1879.
12 Twined basket with fitted cover, false embroidery design. Atka, 1879.
13 Woman's work basket, with fitted cover, of twined dune grass with colored wool thread design. Attu, 1920.

14 Table mat, twined dune grass, made for sale. Atka, 1879.

15 High top boots, dark and light colored leather, trimmed with fur and red and green wool. Attu, 1890s.

16 Bird spear, wood with multiple bone points. 1890s.

17 Throwing board, used to propel harpoon or spear while seated in a kayak; ivory hook and groove for butt end of spear which is on top, hole and notches for fingers of throwing hand. Painted red on top side, black on bottom Unalaska Island, 1892.

18 Work bag of sea lion intestine. Atka, 1879.

19 Bag of sea lion intestine, with decorative bands. Collected by Wilkes Expedition, 1841.

20 Large bag made of sea lion intestine.

Collected by Wilkes Expedition, 1841.

21 Waterproof overdress, of intestine. 1896.

22 Sealskin trousers. Atka, 1879.

23 Small twined pouch with colored thread decoration. 1921.

24 Table mat, twined dune grass, made for sale. Atka, 1879.

25 Pair of boots (mukluks) with fine appliqué design. Attu, 1890s.

Above: *An Aleut man, by Louis Choris (1816–17). He wears a hooded gut shirt and a hat with a painted eye shade of thin wood bent into shape, stitched at the back to produce a deep, inverted scoop.*

embrace Christianity so readily? Part of the answer may lie in the church's ability to provide hope and succour. another part may lie in the god-parenting of Aleuts by Russians creating kin and economic ties of benefit to both groups (Black, 1984:94; Kan, 1988:506).

By 1867 Aleut society had adapted to the Russian presence. The population showed signs of recovery, many Aleut children received some schooling, and everyone belonged to the Russian Orthodox faith. However, the Opium Wars had caused the sea otter market to collapse and RAC efforts to diversify the Alaskan economy had proved unsuccessful (Black, 1988:80). Also, Russian America was a very long

way from Moscow. Therefore, the Russian empire accepted an American offer to purchase Alaska for $7.2 million in gold.

Once again, without warning, life changed for the Aleut. The RAC was gone, the schools were closed, as were the health clinics, and many educated creoles chose to move to Russia. All that remained of the Russian presence was the church whose ministers were permitted to stay. The Aleuts were still vassals but they had lost power. The Russians had needed the Aleuts and the relationship had become symbiotic. The days of the sea otter hunt were gone and the Aleuts no longer had access to the trade goods on which they depended. The Aleutian Islands became a far flung and forgotten corner of the USA. Not until 1885, eighteen years after the departure of the RAC, was a mission with a school established (Morgan, 1980:114).

Gradually, Americans began to discover their new colony. A San Francisco concern purchased the assets of the RAC and renamed it the Alaska Commercial Company (ACC; Van-Stone, 1967:57). The ACC, interested in profits, concentrated on the lucrative Pribilof Island seal industry. The Americans expanded both the seal and sea otter hunts removing all quotas implemented by the RAC to protect these populations. By the 1880s the seal population exhibited signs of overhunting and the sea otter population was on the verge of extinction. In 1911 an international treaty curtailed the hunting of sea otter and placed strict quotas on the seal hunt.

Foxes were indigenous to a few of the Aleutian Islands and some had been introduced by the Russians. Independent American trappers and traders began leasing entire islands from the Government in 1880. With no predators and abundant waterfowl the foxes prospered and so

Below: *Aleut settlement, Karluk, Alaska, c.1900. To the left is a Russian Orthodox church and graveyard (the Russians brought their own religion to Alaska at least a century earlier); some semi-subterranean Aleut dwellings are seen (foreground).*

Above: *An Aleut woman, by Louis Choris (1816–17). There is considerable evidence of white contact in her dress, of trade cloth, and the cross, no doubt due to Russian Orthodox missionaries.*

did some of the independents. However, the collapse of the fur market in 1941 spelt the end of this industry. This boom and bust economy characterized other industries on the Aleutians prior to the Second World War. A gold mine brought a flurry of activity from 1886 to 1908. A cod salting station was built in 1876 and was soon followed by salmon canneries, and the establishment of a Norwegian shore based whaling station. This station operated from 1907 until 1939 taking an average 100 whales per season (Morgan, 1980:119).

The beginnings of the Second World War saw a collapse in the never stable economy of the Aleutian Islands.

St Lawrence Is. Eskimo, 1930

A man and his wife prepare the framework of a small umiak before fitting on the cover of split walrus hide. He has a typical Siberian and St Lawrence Island haircut, and wears ear pendants and charms on a necklace. On his belt are beads, a tobacco pouch and a sheath knife. His parka is made of caribou skin tanned and dyed red, with a dog skin collar. His trousers are of seal skin with the fur side out, and his boots have fine skin and fur appliquéd bands. The woman has tattooed patterns on her face and arms, and wears a charm on her armlet. Her parka, worn with one shoulder freed for her work, is of dark caribou fawn skin with white caribou skin insets and fringes of white Siberian dog skin. Her boots are of red-dyed sealskin with the fur side in. Near the house is a food storage rack.

Only the mind
will make a person
continue on,
only his will to follow
those who are successful,
Will bring him finally to his goal.
Great wealth will not bring him all that
*   way*
only his will to follow those who are
*   successful.*

Whoever has very little
must aspire to do
as others around him who are more
*   successful do.*

He must try to imitate, follow, and
*   listen*
to those he wants to be like, and only
in this way can he succeed in life.
(Leo Moses, in Woodbury, 1984a:69)

Speakers of Yup'ik languages have lived for centuries on both sides of the Bering Strait. Across this narrow waterway they traded, visited and occasionally fought. Items traded from Siberia to Alaska included iron, tobacco and the skins of domestic reindeer. The mottled variated domestic reindeer skins were especially valued by the Yup'ik of southwestern Alaska as they were more colorful than the coats of the wild Alaskan caribou. Tobacco, another prized commodity, almost circumnavigated the globe from its homeland in eastern North America to Alaska. Despite these ties, the differences between Yup'ik-speaking groups are vast. There are five separate Yup'ik languages: Sireniski, Central Siberian Yup'ik, Naukanski (Siberian Eskimo), Central Alaskan Yup'ik (Mainland Southwest Alaskan Eskimo) and Pacific Yup'ik (Pacific Eskimo) (Woodbury, 1984a). In fact, the Siberian Yup'ik (Siberian Eskimo) are more similar to their Maritime Chukchi neighbors than to their American relatives (Hughes, 1984:249). This diversity extends from language to economy, social organization, belief systems and contact history. Here, only one language group will be discussed, the Central Alaskan Yup'ik, who inhabit the mainland of southwestern Alaska.

The pre-contact social organization of the Yup'ik centered on the family as did the Aleut although it was not as hierarchial, nor were slaves kept. Village societies maintained territories large enough to support their needs. The Yukon-Kuskokwim Delta teems with wildlife although much of it – the birds, anadromous fish and caribou – is migratory. This abundance enabled the Yup'ik to live in permanent villages located along river banks. During the spring, summer and fall they would travel into the country to intercept migrating wildlife. Each village consisted of many single family homes and one or two *qasgiq*, or communal men's house. Single family dwellings belonged to the women and were their domain. This is where

they would sew, cook, and raise their children. At around the age of six a boy would move from his mother's home to the qasgiq. This large dwelling had an important place in the lives of the men for it was where they ate, worked, played, held ceremonies, took sweat baths and slept. The transition to the qasgiq signalled the beginning of a boy's training for manhood.

'It was good for us to hear the admonitions of those in the qasgiq who did the speaking there, though we did not always think so. Poor me! Sometimes I thought they could see right through into me, into my life, when they spoke. It was chilling, I tingled all over. How could they know me so well . . . Their instructions on how to live come up again, and again . . . It is true, the qasgiq is a place of instruction, the only place where the necessary instruction can be given in full.'
(Joseph Eriday of Chevak, 1978, as told to Anthony C. Woodbury, in Fitzhugh and Kaplan, 1982:210)

Below: *Mainland SW Alaska Eskimos at a settlement on the Kuskokwim River, Alaska, c.1880. Their winter clothing, probably ground squirrel, beaver or muskrat skins, fits loosely and lacks the tailoring of some of the more northern groups.*

These instructions were extremely important. It was not enough for the youth to gain technical skills; they had to learn their place on the universe. In Yup'ik cosmology the universe consisted of many different layers held in a delicate balance. The ill-considered actions of people could offend the spirits thus upsetting this balance. The result could be illness, poor hunting or stormy weather. Therefore, a necessary part of growing up was learning correct behavior. For example, the relatives of a dead person could not use any sharp tools in case they accidentally cut the deceased's spirit. If a spirit was cut, 'it would become very angry and bring sickness or death to the people' (Nelson, 1899:312). While boys learnt in the communal men's houser, girls learnt from their mothers and female relatives.

The Yup'ik also believed in two different worlds: the visible and the invisible. These two worlds occupied the same physical space although the spirits of the latter were seldom visible to the occupants of the former. The boundary between these worlds was permeable and at times of transition such as birth, death or puberty it was most transparent. At these times accordance with proper ritual was crucial or *tunghat*, generally malevolent spirits, could be released and would harm the people.

All objects, animate and inanimate, had

spirits or *yuas* of human form. In the past all animals had the ability to transmute at will.

> After a while she saw a fierce old wolf coming over the rise on the bank of the lake. His red tongue hung out. When he came down he went over to the girl and prodded her on her side with his nose. Then he stood up beside her and was transformed into a big husky man in his prime. He wore nothing but a cape of wolfskin.
> (From *Adventures of a Young Girl*, told by Ella Lewis, in Tennant and Bitar, 1981:173)

By the time of contact animals had lost this power.

Occasionally, a hunter would still glimpse a human face in the eye of an animal he was pursuing and know that he had seen its yua. He would then carve a mask of his vision and at the next festival he would sing of his encounter while dancing with the mask. Shamans had similar experiences with tunghat which only they could see. The following dance was witnessed by Lt Zagoskin in the early 1840s:

> But now the skylight opens, and quickly, in a flash, a dancer slides down a strap and with a quick leap is on the stage; two pairs of women take their places beside him. He is wearing a mask representing a fantastic raven's head, and there he goes jumping about on the stage, calling

Above: *St Lawrence Island Eskimo children, 1888. Girls wore long hair, boys had tops of their heads shaved, both of which aped the adult style. The parkas are of reindeer skin with the hair side turned in.*

like a raven; the drums sound their rhythmic beat, the singers strike up a song. The dancer at one time represents a raven perching and hopping like bird; at another time he represents the familiar actions of a man who is unsuccessful in everything. The content of the dance is explained in the words of the song and may briefly be described as follows. A shaman is living in his trail camp. He is hungry, and he notices that wherever he goes a raven goes with him and gets in his way. If the game he is pursuing is a deer, the raven from some place or other caws, startles the deer, and makes it impossible to creep up within a bowshot of it. If the man sets a noose for hare or partridge, the raven tangles it or runs off with it. If he sets a fish-trap for imagnat, there too the raven finds a way to do him harm. 'Who are you?' cries the shaman at last. The spirit in the form of the raven smiles and answers: 'Your evil fate.'

(Michael, 1967:227)

Shamans were holistic healers, treating their patients' physical, psychological and spiritual symptoms. Gifted individuals, they could devine the cause of ill health or poor hunting.

When the infractions of people upset the universe the shaman would fly to the spirit world and mediate with the spirits in an effort to restore the balance.

Shamans and elders were responsible for the yearly ceremonial cycle. There were four major annual festivals: the Asking Festival (*Petugtaq*), the Feast of the Dead (*Merr'aq*), the Bladder Festival (*Nakaciuq*) and the Inviting-in Festival (*Kelek/Itruka'ar*). The Asking Festival was an intra-village event where kin relationships, particularly cross-cousin ties, were reinforced through the exchange of requested gifts. The Feast of the Dead ensured that the deceased would have food, drink and clothing in the after world. At the Bladder Festival the bladders of all seals caught during the year were inflated, painted and hung in the qasgiq. The souls of the seals lived in the bladders and for several days they were offered food, song and dances. Finally, the bladders and the souls were returned to the water. If the seals had been treated with respect they would allow themselves to be recaptured. The final festival of the year was the Inviting-in Feast. For this ceremony, held when food was scarcest, the people invited the spirits to share in what they had left. By inviting the spirits and reminding them of their past assistance, the people hoped to ensure successful hunting for the coming year.

Other festivals were held at different intervals. One of these was the Great Feast of the Dead. At this festival, often held ten years after the death, gifts were given away to honor the deceased. During the festival the spirit of the deceased was believed to enter its namesake. Many gifts and clothing were given to the namesake and were therefore also given to the deceased.

Once this festival had been held, it was no longer necessary to remember the individuals at the annual Feast of the Dead.

My children, where are you?
  Ai-ya-ya-yai.
Come back to us, our children,
We are lonely and sad.
  Ai-ya-ya-yai.
For our children are gone,
While those of our friends remain
  Ai-ya-ya-yai.
Come back, nephew, come back, we
  miss you;
  Ai-ya-ya-yai.
Come back to us our lost ones,
We have presents for you,
  Ai-ya-ya-yai.
  (Nelson, 1899:374-5)

The importance of the spirit world was not confined to rules of behavior and ceremonies, it permeated all aspects of Yup'ik life. Hunting equipment was exquisitely fashioned to please the yua of the prey, thus persuading it to give itself to the hunter. By carving bears, wolves and otters on to his weapons, the hunter appropriated the qualities of these predators. These disparate concepts, spiritual appeasement and appropriation of spiritual power were also incorporated into the clothing sewn by women (Chaussonnet, 1988).

Very complex concepts were contained in symbols on clothing and tools. A hole in the palm of a thumbless hand symbolized the game that the tunghat allowed to escape from the skyworld for the consumption of people. One simple symbol, the circle and dot motif, represented the Yup'ik world view. Like the universe, it had several layers of meaning; it stood for the all-seeing eye, the world and the layers of the universe, and the passageway from one world into the next (Morrow, 1984; Mather, 1985; Fienup-Riordan, 1988).

The first direct contact the Central Alaskan Yup'ik had with Europeans was with the Russians. This contact began following the establishment of the RAC's trading monopoly in 1799. The Russians explored southern Alaska and realized that beaver were available on the mainland. As the sea otter populations declined Russian interest in the beaver increased. The RAC constructed several trading posts on the mainland in the early 1800s. By 1845 Russian Orthodox missionaries had established themselves at most of these posts (Shalkop, 1987). The Yup'ik, however, maintained their independence from the RAC and some even resisted conversion to Christianity (Kan, 1988:513).

Following the sale of Alaska to the United States the RAC was replaced by the Alaska Commercial Company with very little impact on the population except an increase in quantity and variety of trade goods (VanStone, 1984:154). However, Yup'ik desire for trading goods led to a gradual change in their economy. Individuals who spent more time

Below: *Mainland SW Alaska Eskimos before store houses at Togiak, Alaska, c.1877. These were of split logs with curved roofs of cut sod and straw, here with stabilizing poles which act as battens.*

trapping beavers had proportionally less time available for subsistence hunting. Eventually, this led to a dependence on the trading posts (VanStone, 1984). In many communities, however, the subsistence economy with its seasonal hunting and gathering cycle was hardly disturbed at all.

The Russian Orthodox church continued to play an important role in Yup'ik life. Missionaries of other faiths attempted to convert the Yup'ik but were mostly unsuccessful. The work of a powerful Inuit minister led to the founding of a successful Moravian mission in Bethel in 1885 (VanStone, 1967:38).

The 'rich man's route' to the Klondike gold rush was up the Yukon River by paddle steamer from Saint Michael, Alaska. However, no gold was found in the Yup'ik territory and so the thousands of miners pouring into the Yukon Territory from 1896 to 1899 had almost no impact on the local population (VanStone, 1984).

In 1883 the first salmon cannery opened and was quickly followed by others (VanStone, 1967:67). At first these canneries employed Euro-American and Philippino workers, but by the 1920s many of the workers were native Alaskans. Seasonal job opportunities in the canneries created out-migration from some of the more northern and interior communities into Bristol Bay. These canneries and the trapping industry were the main employers of Yup'ik prior to the Second World War (VanStone, 1984).

Other than Christianity and clapboard above ground homes Yup'ik culture prior to the war was similar to the pre-contact culture. The last masked dance ceremonies were performed in the 1930s. Recently, this tradition as well as others have been undergoing a revival.

Speakers of Inuit-Inupiaq live in four countries – the U.S.S.R., the United States of America, Canada, and Greenland (formerly part of Denmark). Despite the thousands of miles, Inuit-Inupiaq is regarded by linguists as a single language with many separate dialects (Woodbury, 1984b; Krauss, 1988). The cohesiveness of the language stems from a recent migration from northern Alaska to Greenland in about AD 1000. Northern Canada and Greenland were inhabited as early as 2500 BC, however this population was overpowered and assimilated by the later migrants who adopted their culture and language.

The patient fur-clad man poised over a seal breathing hole. The smiling baby peeking out from its mother's parka. A howling wind sweeping over dogs and an igloo. A man paddling a kayak. These images form the stereotype of the Inuit – a smiling, friendly people eking out a marginal existence in a harsh environment. This stereotype ignores the diversity and complexity of Inuit societies. The Nuvugmiut (a subgroup of the North Alaska Coast Inuit) of northern Alaska were whale hunters and lived in semi-subterranean log houses in large permanent villages. They rarely used kayaks and only made snowhouses if caught on the land in a snowstorm. Their society was highly structured with special status accorded to the umialik, owner of a whale hunting boat. In contrast, the Padlirmiut (a subgroup of the Caribou Inuit) lived a nomadic lifestyle on the west coast of Hudson Bay. In spring they hunted seals basking on the ice, however, the rest of the year was spent in the interior hunting caribou and musk oxen. Padlirmiut society was strongly egalitarian; knowledgeable individuals were asked for advice but each person was free to reach his or her own decisions.

British explorers' descriptions of the Central Inuit, the people of the Canadian Arctic, are the origin of the Eskimo stereotype (Brody, 1987). There are many divisions within the Central Inuit; one of these is the Iglulik Inuit. The Iglulik Inuit consist of four societies: the Tununirusirmiut (of northern Baffin Island), the Tununirmiut (of northern Baffin Island), the Iglulingmiut (of northern Foxe Basin) and the Aivilingmiut (of the northwest coast of Hudson Bay) (Mary-Rousselière, 1984:432). In this section the culture and contact history of one of the Iglulik societies – the Aivilingmiut – will be considered in more detail.

While reading about the Aivilingmiut it is necessary to realize that generalizations are being made. There are myriad ecological niches across the north, each one providing Inuit with the challenge of discovering its complexities and designing hunting strategies to exploit its resources. Inuit oral history contains accounts

of individuals or groups who migrated into new regions and starved because they were unfamiliar with local conditions. In one incident, a murderer and his extended family (Tununirusirmiut) fled their home in order to escape revenge. They found an uninhabited island with abundant marine life and decided to settle. All winter they waited for the ice to freeze solid. It never did and eventually they all starved to death except one woman. In this region the local population (Iglulingmiut) had learnt to hunt on the shifting ice flows and thin elastic ice (only a few centimeters thick). The migrants, ignorant of this technique, eventually starved to death, surrounded by a sea of plenty (Mary-Rousselière, 1954).

Inuit-Inupiaq, in common with Aleut and Yup'ik, is an agglutinative language. For instance, the name Aivilingmiut is composed of aivik (walrus), -lik (place), and -miut (people of); it means, people of the place of walrus. The Aivilingmiut were renowned for their walrus hunting and their concommitantly strong dog teams. These teams enabled people to travel long distances to hunt, to visit relatives and later, to visit trading posts. Long voyages occurred in spring when the days were lengthening and warming, migratory birds were returning to their breeding grounds and basking seals provided relatively easy prey.

As the summer approached the hunters would move to the floe edge for walrus hunting. Walrus were harpooned either from the floe edge or from kayaks. The prow of the kayak was narrow so that the hunter could aim it between the tusks of an enraged walrus, thus preventing the walrus from ripping the skin of the kayak and drowning its occupant (G. Quluat pers.comm.). Once caught, the walrus was butchered and most of it cached for future use. Some parts were eaten immediately, either raw or cooked over a bone and oil fire. The Inuit diet is almost entirely meat. Meat contains all the nutrients required for life as long as both the fat and meat are consumed and a significant por-

Below: *Bering Strait Inuit man using a bow drill to make an ivory cribbage board, c.1902. This group produced a great deal of artwork, especially wooden and ivory sculptures to sell to sailors.*

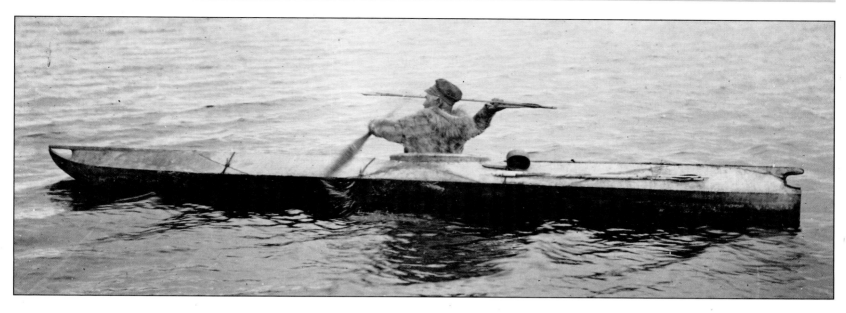

Above: *Bering Strait Inuit in a one-holed kayak throwing a harpoon with an atlatl, c.1888. The atlatl added an extra joint to the throwing arm and gave greater projection to the harpoon.*

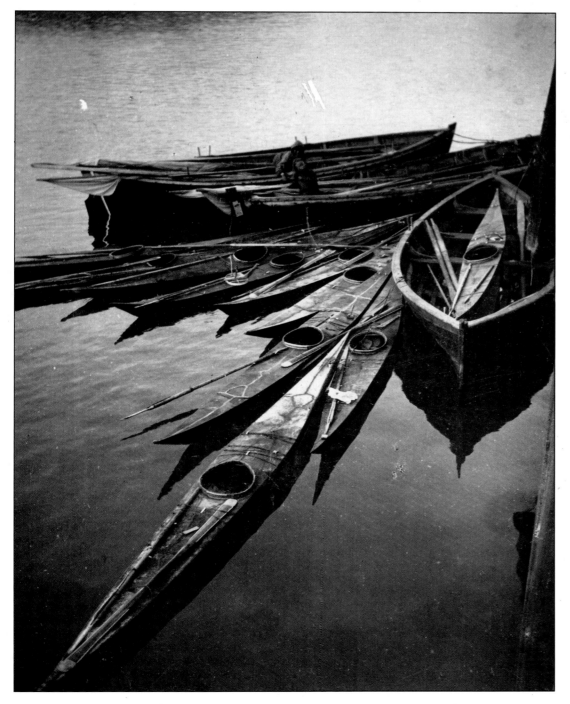

Below: *West Greenland Eskimo kayaks and umiaks. The subsistence of these people almost entirely depended on marine animals such as the ringed harp, spotted and hooded seal, walrus and whale.*

tion of the meat is eaten raw (Stefansson, 1946).

In autumn, people would split into smaller groups, often no larger than one or two families and travel to their summer hunting grounds. These families had areas they visited habitually (Damas, 1963) and, while there was no individual ownership of land, if others wished to hunt in these areas it was only polite to ask permission (R. Inuksuk pers.comm.). Autumn hunting varied. Generally, older men stayed on the coast hunting walrus, seals and whales until the sea ice formed. Younger men often hunted caribou in the interior (Mathiassen, 1928:24).

Caribou were hunted in many different ways. In some cases hunters would sneak up on the caribou raising their hands above their heads as if antlers. In other cases stone hunting blinds were built beside caribou trails. Yet another method required the participation of the entire family. A series of inukshuit (means: look like people) of stone were built along a caribou trail. Caribou mistook these cairns for people and were channeled into either a river or narrow valley. This method of corralling allowed people to take many caribou in a short time. The caribou provided not only sustenance but also bone and antler for tools, and fur for clothing. Caribou taken in September and October were preferred for clothing. Those taken later in the year, when the caribou had longer hair, were used for bedding.

When the sea froze (usually in the middle of September, Mathiassen, 1928:24) the older men and their families would also go caribou hunting. At this time of the year, Arctic char were caught using leisters at stone weirs. Some were dried and could easily be carried when the family moved camp. Others were cached and collected later by dog team.

In January/February the Aivilingmiut congregated in large villages of snowhouses. Snow is a versatile building material; not only is it plastic but it is also a good insulator. When traveling the Aivilingmiut built simple one-room snowhouses. In winter villages the houses could last several months. These complex houses had entrance passages and side chambers for clothes and meat storage. Sometimes houses were connected so that people could visit without going outside (cf. Rasmussen, 1929:46).

In winter, when the weather was bad, the people would live on their cached supplies. However, they took advantage of calm days to

Central Inuit

The Central Inuit, north and west of Hudson Bay, share the Inuktitut language and are culturally quite similar. The Copper Inuit and Netsilik hunted seals on the ice in the winter and caribou in the summer. The Sallirmiut (extinct by 1904), Iglulik, and Baffinland Inuit depended on large sea mammals. The Caribou Inuit lived off caribou supplemented by fish. The most important collections of artifacts (some are shown here) are those made by George Comer, under the direction of Franz Boas, while he was captain of a New England whaling vessel spending winters among these Inuit between 1895 and 1908. Inuit groups had been in intermittant contact with European and American ship crews for several centuries, but their material culture was so well adapted to the extreme environment that it remained largely unchanged except for the use of metal, beads, a little cloth, and the adoption of tobacco and some European foods. Ig. = Iglulik; CI = Caribou Inuit; LCI = Labrador Coast.

1 Snow shovel. Ig.
2 Model of kayak, with two paddles. CI.
3 Line for dragging a seal, with bone toggle. Ig.
4 Ivory case for keeping needles. Ig.
5 Ivory case for needles and pins. Ig.
6 Ivory needle case. Ig.
7 Pipe. Hudson Bay. (Ig?)
8 Line for dragging a seal, with ivory toggle. Ig.
9 Ivory needlecase on cord. Ig.
10 Harpoon head attached to skin line. Tununa (Ig?).
11 Boy's hooded parka. Savage Is., LCI.
12 Bone knife for cutting snow for melting and to build igloo. CI.
13 Saw. Netsilik.
14 Scraper of chipped flint mounted in bone handle. Sallirmiut.
15 Knife, with blade of copper salvaged from lost Franklin Expedition ship. Netsilik.
16 Wooden throwing board (atlatl). CI.

17 Bone scraper. CI.
18 Large knife, steel blade mounted in native handle. Sallirmiut.
19 Pair of snow goggles in Iglulik style. CI.
20 Woman's parka, with short flap in front, long one behind. CI.
21 Child's suit. Savage Is., LCI.
22 Wooden tray with bone mounts. CI.
23 Box of bent whalebone. Netsilik.
24 Scoop for removing snow from sealing hole in ice. Netsilik.
25 Spoon, with bone handle, musk ox horn bowl. Netsilik.
26 Copper kettle, salvaged from lost Franklin Expedition ship. Netsilik.
27 Bucket of whalebone. Sallirmiut.
28 Dish of whalebone on wooden bottom. Hudson Bay. (CI?).
29 Woman's knife (ulu). CI.
30 Dipper of musk ox horn.
Netsilik.
31 Wooden dish. Hudson Bay (CI?).
32 Bailer. Netsilik.
33 Musk ox horn spoon. Kidlingnukniut, west of Back River (Netsilik?).
34 Large skin bag, fur side out. Southampton Is. (Ig?).
35 Hard leather box with metal trim. CI.
36, 37 Ivory combs. CI.
38, 39 Ivory combs. Ig.
40 Set of dominoes, bone. Savage Is., LCI.

Above: *Copper Inuit caribou hunters. Caribou were mainly hunted with bow and arrow, bows generally composite with sections joined together with sinew; wood, antler and musk-ox horn were used.*

Below: *Copper Inuit building a snow house, c.1915. Such domed houses were used from October to May. A distinguishing feature of the Copper Inuit house was the flat topped entrance, partly visible here.*

hunt seals at their breathing holes. Seals keep many breathing holes open and the Aivilingmiut practiced several methods to increase their chances of success. Usually a group of hunters would go out together and each stand at a breathing hole. Sometimes, the women and children would scare the seal away from its other breathing holes, forcing it to the hole where the hunter waited. At other times a boy would drive a dog team in a wide circle around the hole occupied by the hunter thereby frightening the seal towards it (Mathiassen, 1928:44).

Winter was also a time for socializing, telling stories and renewing friendships and alliances. A single family's home was too small for a community gathering: consequently a large snowhouse, an architectural marvel, sometimes over 23ft (7m.) in diameter was constructed. In this building drum dances and shamanic seances were held. At the dances people would sing their personal songs. The following is the song of a great hunter and modest man.

> It is a time of hunger,
> But I don't feel like hunting.
> I don't care for the advice of old people,
> I only care for dreaming, wishing, nothing else.
> I only care for gossip;
> I am fond of young caribou, the age they
>   start getting their antlers;
> Nobody is like me,
> I am too lazy, simply too lazy,
> I just can't bring myself to go and get
>   some meat.
>   (Arnatkoak, in Columbo, 1981:90)

Aivilingmiut beliefs were quite similar to those of the Yup'ik. When the weather was poor or game disappeared, the shaman would hold a seance to divine the cause. During seances such as these, shamans transformed into bears and visited Uiniyumayuittuq (literally 'one who does not want a husband'), from whose hands sprang all sea mammals and who therefore controlled them. The shaman would comb her

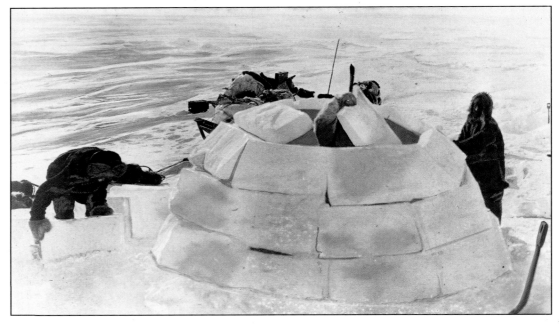

hair and ask forgiveness for the transgressions of the people.

> That woman down there beneath the
>   sea,
> She wants to hide the seals from us.
> These hunters in the dance-house,
> They cannot right matters.
> They cannot mend matters.
> Into the spirit world
> Will go I,
> Where no humans dwell.
> Set matters right will I.
> Set matters right will I.
>   (Houston, 1972:71)

Shamans were highly regarded individuals but they were not viewed as leaders. Likewise elders were respected and their opinions sought. Also, skilled individuals were consulted. A man who combined several of these functions was known as an *isumataq* (literally 'one who thinks'). He had the ability to command individuals and create new camps. This position was held through general acknowledgement not through coercion or heredity.

Aivilingmiut society was fairly flexible; people could come and go as they pleased. This flexibility was extremely important in an unpredictable environment. When an unexpected environmental crisis occurred and starvation appeared imminent camps dispersed. At these times a network additional to and reinforcing the kinship network was required. The Aivilingmiut maintained an elaborate alliance system that operated at many levels. Some of these alliances or fictive kin relationships were namesakes, joking partners, singing partners, trading partners, adoption, and spouse exchange partners (often incorrectly called wife exchange). 'The Eskimo ideal was to have a network, as extensive as possible, of kinship and fictive kinship relationships' (Mary-Rousselière, 1984:436). During normal times these partnerships were fun and made travel to new areas easy. In times of stress they carried the obligation of aid, usually provided as shelter and food. This obligation was often unrecognized by Euro-Americans when they participated in unequal spouse exchange alliances. In a spouse exchange the couples agreed to exchange partners for a short time. The result of this exchange was a mutual obligation for support in the future. It was also trans-generational; the offspring of the couples, whether related by blood or not, would regard each other as siblings (Guemple, 1961). This is a very different type of arrangement from that described by most Euro-Americans.

The earliest contact the Aivilingmiut had with Europeans was indirect. They were unaffected by the first British voyages in search of

Above: *Family group with dogs and loaded sled, Bering Strait Inuit, c.1880. Sleds were generally drawn by three dogs but this scene shows a particularly large sled with more dogs harnessed.*

Below: *Iglulik woman inside an igloo softening a skin by chewing. In the tanning process, fat and flesh were first removed, the skin dried. Softening could be by means of a stone scraper or by chewing.*

the Northwest Passage (1570s-1630s). In 1670 the British Crown granted the Hudson's Bay Company monopoly trading rights in Rupert's Land. The Company established forts in the 'bottom of the bay'. There were no beaver to the north and the Company was rarely interested in venturing into this area (they tried a whale fishery in Padlirmiut territory on the west coast of the Bay (1765-72; Ross, 1975) and sent the occasional exploratory expedition when their monopoly was challenged). By the early 1800s Inuit from the west coast of Hudson Bay were traveling to the Company post at Churchill to trade seals. As far as we know these were not Aivilingmiut, but, by 1821, when the first British explorers Parry and Lyon visited them, they already had iron knives and copper kettles (Parry, 1842; Lyon, 1824). Such possessions were most likely attained through trade with their southern neighbors.

Parry and Lyon were searching for the Northwest Passage by following the continental coast of North America. After two years' attempts to traverse Fury and Hecla Strait they returned to Britain and correctly reported that no viable route existed following the mainland. As a result, the Aivilingmiut remained undisturbed until 1860 when American whalers expanded their whaling into Hudson Bay. This led to a migration of Aivilingmiut southwards as they congregated around the whalers and took jobs working as crew members.

Inuit crews were not paid wages by the whalers, instead they received goods and food. If a hunter killed a whale he might be given a wooden whaling boat (Eber, 1989:102-3). Other rewards for service included shirts, guns, ammunition and knives. Women also worked for the whalers, scrubbing decks, cleaning clothes, and sewing winter clothing. Their remuneration included dresses, knives, scissors, needles and beads.

The whalers wintered over in Hudson Bay. As the sea ice formed they would allow the ship to be frozen in. A 'house' was built on the deck and became the venue for dances and theatricals. The Aivilingmiut built their villages beside the ship and went on board for meals and entertainment. During the winter the Aivilingmiut supplied the ship with fresh meat.

The presence of the whalers changed Aivilingmiut life in many ways. Guns and whale boats displaced the bow and arrow, and kayak (Mathiassen, 1928:92). Supplying the whalers

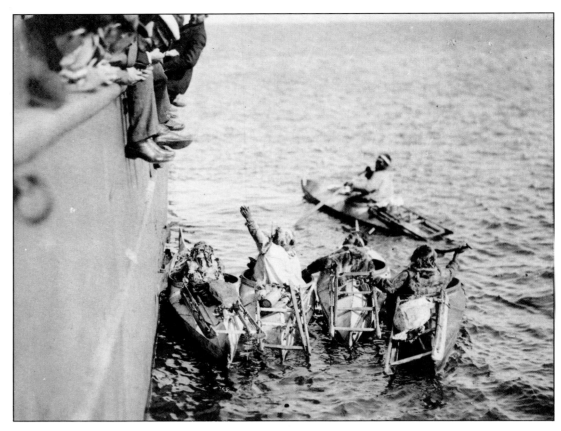

with fresh meat depleted local wildlife. The whalers introduced new foods including alcohol. Also, other Inuit groups, some former enemies of the Aivilingmiut, migrated into the region to work for the whalers. The tensions between these groups sometimes eruped into fist fights (Mathiassen, 1928:101).

As in all contact situations disease took its toll. Syphilis and tuberculosis were perhaps the most insidious, but even common diseases could have disastrous effects. In 1902 the Scottish whaler *Active* carried a sailor ill with dysentery into the region. This disease was so virulent that the Aivilingmiut of Lyon Inlet felt they had been bewitched by their neighbors (Rose, 1975:117). This same epidemic resulted in the virtual extinction of the aboriginal occupants of Southampton Island, the Sadlermiut (Sallirmuit). The deserted island was later repopulated by the Aivilingmiut (Comer, 1906).

Many of the impacts of whaling were negative, however; the Aivilingmiut and other Inuit who participated remember this period with fondness. It was a time of excitement, new

things and of great hunters. When the last whaling ship sailed away in 1915 never to reappear, the people were sad.

We wondered, but we never really knew why the whalers didn't come back. We were kind of regretful because we remembered how good their food had tasted and we remembered everybody getting together like a big family. When the whalers left, that big family feeling was gone.
(Leah Arnaujaq, in Eber, 1989:105).

Above: *Bering Strait Inuit trading with passengers aboard the steamer Roanoke, c.1900. They use traditional one-hole kayaks with frames across the top for transport of their wares.*

Below: *North Alaska Coast Inuit summer encampment showing both triangular and dome shaped dwellings. As caribou formed the staple diet of this group, the dwellings are probably covered with the skins of the animals.*

The Royal Canadian Mounted Police (RCMP) established their first eastern Arctic post in 1903 among the Aivilingmiut. Its purpose was to ensure Canadian sovereignty over the area and to collect duty from the American whalers. When the whalers left the RCMP remained to bring law and order to the north.

The Hudson's Bay Company, now interested in seals and white fox, moved in to fill the void

Above: *Four Mackenzie Delta Inuit with dogs and sled. Such sleds usually had bone or antler runners. They were commonly used for tundra land mammal hunting and for sealing at the floe edge.*

Below: *Men from Icy Cape, Arctic Ocean, Alaska, c.1880. Note the use of labrets — ornaments of bone and ivory — worn in holes pierced through the lips. Men's lips were pierced at puberty.*

left by the whalers. With the Company came the Catholic and Anglican missionaries. The Company, Royal Canadian Mounted Police and missionaries sought to change Inuit culture. The Company depended on the hunters to bring in furs and fostered a dependence on the goods already introduced by the whalers. They realigned, but did not radically alter Inuit subsistence economy. The missionaries sought to replace Inuit cosmology with Christianity. While they succeeded in converting the people and deposing the shamans, they were less successful in altering the people's fundamental beliefs about their world.

Finally, the RCMP were in the north as agents of the Canadian Government. It was their role to ensure that justice was done. Their imposition of an unknown legal system was confusing to a people who had their own system of customary law. Although the Company, RCMP and missions were paternalistic and autocratic institutions, they had relatively few representatives in the north. As a result of this lack of representation, their impact was limited. It was only after the Second World War that most Canadian Inuit groups became more exposed to southern Canadian education, and at last began to benefit from regular health services and social services.

'One observer . . . was moved by the beauty of the northern woodlands, familiar with its changing seasons, the material abundance and inspiration, giving . . . the poetry and spiritual essence of Chippewa culture.'

THE NORTHEAST

THE GEOGRAPHIC AREA here under discussion, conveniently referred to as the 'Northeast', stretches approximately from the northwestern shore of Lake Superior south to the confluence of the Ohio and Cumberland Rivers and then east to the Atlantic coast. Its northern border runs just south of the Lake of the Woods and the area extends as far south as the Virginia-North Carolina coastal plain. Newfoundland, once inhabited by the now extinct Beothuks, is included in the Subarctic chapter.

While it is useful to consider the concept of cultural areas in North America suggesting an internal homogeneity, it is important to stress that – and this particularly applies to the Northeast – there was great variation in lifestyle and, while dominated by Algonquian- and Iroquoian-speaking people, some Siouan in the west – *possibly* east as well – were also represented. Recognizing the difficulties of applying an all-embracing cultural description,

recent studies have subdivided the area into three further geographic regions, Coastal, Saint Lawrence Lowlands and Great Lakes-Riverine and, while even this tripartite division has its shortcomings, it more accurately delineates common lifestyles. For example, the Saint Lawrence Lowlands was the traditional home of the powerful and famous Iroquois Confederacy – the 'People of the Longhouse' – who shared similar cultural patterns which were based on fishing and horticulture, residence in mostly fortified villages, ritual sacrifice of prisoners, similar ceremonials and a matrilineal kinship system.

The major features within these three divisions of the Northeast are given in the table opposite on p.225, which also shows the major tribes of the Northeast and their associated linguistic grouping and main cultural patterns (with events which affected the tribes).

In terms of population, tribes or groups were

small, certainly no more than sixteen thousand for the Iroquois in the late seventeenth century, twenty thousand for the Huron prior to the smallpox epidemic during the winter of 1639-40 which reduced the population by one half, and some twenty-five thousand for the Chippewa in 1760. These, however, are but estimates since, in early days, only limited numbers of the various tribes actually came into contact with whites at any particular period, such as in the case of the Chippewa whose settlement pattern in the early historic period was that of many widely scattered and small bands. The fortunes of the Indian tribes, the changes in their lifestyles and population, can be illustrated by reference to one tribe – the Micmac – who were

This map shows approximate territories of tribes and language groups in the seventeenth century. After that, all tribes lost territory, some disappeared, some moved and a few new tribes arose.

Key to tribes:
1 Chippewa (Ojibwa)
2 Menominee
3 Winnebago
4 Illinois
5 Potawatomi
6 Sauk
7 Fox
8 Mascouten
9 Miami
10 Shawnee
11 Kickapoo
12 Algonquin
13 Nipissing
14 Huron
15 Ottawa
16 Petun
17 Neutral
18 Wenro
19 Erie
20 Seneca
21 Cayuga
22 Onondaga
23 Oneida
24 Mohawk
25 Mahican
26 Delaware
27 Susquehannock
28 Nanticoke and Neighboring Tribes
29 Va. Algonquians
30 Va. and NC Iroquoians
31 North Carolina Algonquians
32 St Lawrence Iroquoians
33 Western Abenaki
34 Eastern Abenaki
35 Maliseet-Passamaquoddy
36 Micmac
37 Southern New England and Eastern Long Island Algonquians

amongst the first to encounter Europeans.

It has been estimated that the population of these Algonquian-speaking people was about four thousand prior to white contact. Their territory was the area to the south and west of the Gulf of Saint Lawrence, the Gaspé Peninsula and the Maritime Provinces. This is a heavily forested region with many lakes and rivers and natural harbors along the extended coastline. By use of the canoe, scattered bands maintained strong ethnic identity between the seven districts traditionally observed by the Micmac.[1] Because the winters were so severe, only tobacco was cultivated and the subsistence was predominately one firmly based on an annual cycle of hunting and fishing. One of the most comprehensive reports on the Micmac which undoubtedly closely describes a lifestyle which had been established and little changed for centuries comes from the writings of the missionary, Pierre Biard (c. 1616). Describing those groups associated with Southern Nova Scotia, he refers to a two-phase type annual cycle now classified as 'diffuse' and 'compact' settlements.

In the first, which coincided with the winter season, the population was widely scattered throughout the seven districts; main activities at this time were beaver, otter, moose, caribou and bear hunting, which occupied the months of January to March. At the onset of spring, 'After the smelt comes the herring at the end of April; and at the same time bustards [Canada geese] . . . sturgeon, and salmon, and the great

Below: *A traditional Micmac wigwam of poles and branches bound with cedar bark fiber and covered with overlapping strips of birch bark and grass matting, photographed in 1873.*

(i) Coastal Zone. Atlantic Provinces of Canada and the seaboard of the United States to North Carolina. Separated from the interior by the Appalachian Mountains

Linguistic group	Major tribes	Cultural patterns/events
EASTERN ALGONQUIAN	Micmac Maliseet-Passamaquoddy Eastern Abenaki Lenni-Lenape (Delaware) Nanticoke Powhatan	The varying Eastern Algonquian languages appear to have constituted a continuum of variation along the coast. Population and dependence on agriculture increased southwards. Political organization varied from hunting bands in the north to rudimentary states in the south. These East Coast tribes were the first in the Northeast to come into close contact with Europeans. Because they lacked time to reorganize themselves under the impact of the Europeans, they were the most decimated or dispersed of all the tribes in the Northeast

(ii) Saint Lawrence Lowlands. Southern Ontario, Upper New York State and the majority of the Saint Lawrence and Susquehanna Valleys

Linguistic group	Major tribes	Cultural patterns/events
NORTHERN IROQUOIAN	Saint Lawrence Iroquoians Mohawk Oneida Onondaga Cayuga Seneca Tuscarora (after c.1720) Huron Erie Susquehannock	Practical intensive horticulture and fishing; often lived in fortified villages. Initially, they were sufficiently remote from the earliest centers of European contact that they were little affected and until 1760, after the fall of New France, the Iroquois maintained their autonomy. After this date, their homeland was increasingly depleted by white settlement

(iii) Great Lakes–Riverine. Adjacent to the Great Lakes of Superior, Michigan and Huron and west almost to the Mississippi

Linguistic group	Major tribes	Cultural patterns/events
CENTRAL ALGONQUIAN	Chippewa (Ojibwa) Ottawa Potawatomi Menominee Sauk & Fox Kickapoo Miami Illinois Shawnee	All these tribes depended on horticulture although the emphasis varied. Their kinship system was patrilineal. With European encroachment this area – through intertribal cooperation – became central to efforts opposing European domination, such as that of Pontiac in 1763 and Tecumseh in 1811

search through the Islets for [waterfowl] eggs... From the month of May up to the middle of September, they are free from all anxiety about their food; for the cod are upon the coast, and all kinds of fish and shellfish...' (Bock, Trigger ed., 1978:110).

At these abundant times, large groups – the 'compact settlements' – gathered at favorite camping sites along the coast or rivers. It was a time when friendships were renewed or made and, particularly, elements of tribal solidarity recognized. As Biard reported, it was principally at this time that 'they pay visits and hold their State Councils; I mean that several Sagamores [Chiefs] come together and consult ... about peace and war, treaties of friendship and treaties for the common good' (Biard, Thwaites

Above: *Group of Passamaquoddy with canoes. Virtually identical to the Maliseet, the combined group was adept at woodworking, the finest product being the light and maneuverable birch bark canoe.*

Left: *Jennie Bobb and her daughter Nellie Longhat, Western Delaware, 1910-15, in traditional Delaware women's finery, characterized by heavy necklaces, silver brooches, pony bead 'encrusted' moccasins.*

ed., J.R.3.1896-1901:89-91).

The French were greatly impressed by the Micmac and many found their way of life far more agreeable than that which they had experienced in their native land. French youths readily adapted to the Indian lifestyle and language, encouraged by the early French traders, who thus gained efficient interpreters and agents for the lucrative fur trade. The French found the Micmac a vigorous, handsome and healthy race, who were disdainful of those amongst the French who were squint or one-eyed, flat-nosed and hairy. The Micmac had few diseases; they knew nothing of fevers, gout or rheumatism and the French were impressed by their knowledge of plants, 'for wounds and other mischances' (Bishop, 1949:112). Thus, the Micmac formed strong friendships with the French[2] and they became increasingly dependent on trade goods, particularly such things as axes, metal knives and kettles. This improvement in their material possessions, however, was increasingly offset by rapid decreases in their population, due to smallpox and other diseases against which the indigenous populations had little resistance and their numbers, it has been estimated, decreased to some two thousand by the early eighteenth century.

The period 1610 to about 1760 saw an increasing dependence on the fur trade – mainly carried on with the French – and, whilst Acadia[3] was ceded to the English by the Treaty of Utrecht in 1713, the new owners found it impossible to gain control of the fur trade which had been monopolized by the French for so long; any attempted changes were fiercely opposed by the Micmac and not until 1779 did the difficulties that the English have with the Micmac actually cease.

The English trait of colonization was rapidly put into effect, the Micmac being confined to reservations and the old free hunting and fishing economy gone forever. The subsequent exploitation – further loss of lands, loss of water resources and the offer of only seasonal jobs at subsistence wages – is a shameful chapter in the settling of Acadia, but it did demonstrate the great resilience of the people. Adapting to the rapid changes, the men took to fabricating wooden craft items and baskets, whilst the women, utilizing some of their traditional knowledge and skills, together with those indirectly acquired from the Ursuline Nuns of Quebec, produced greatly prized souvenirs, which were embellished with quillwork, moosehair and beads. Thus, unlike the Beothuk of Newfoundland who were all but brutally exterminated by 1830, the Micmac population – much to the surprise of those whites who concerned themselves with Micmac welfare – actually progressively increased and by 1900 it again approached four thousand.

At least three basic central principles were shared by both the Algonquian and Iroquoian people who lived in this vast region. The first emphasized and defined the rights of the individual such that all actions of individuals were based on their own decisions and all group actions pivoted on the consensus of the participants. The second was that everybody shared, and in times of want the well-being of all was to be taken into account; charity and generosity were considered paramount principles by which all should abide. The third was that man was part of nature – not outside it – he was but part of the web of the natural world and the earth and woodlands could be neither owned nor exploited. One notable scholar, Cleland, managed to express this last principle particularly well:

> 'Thus a man is born and for a time becomes a cannibal, eating and taking energy from his fellow creatures; when his soul and shadow leave his body, Earth Mother takes it back to nourish the plants which in turn feed both animals and men. His debt is repaid, his spirit freed, and the cycle of life complete.'
> (Cleland, 1973:XIII)

These central principles were incorporated in the famed Confederacy of the League of the Iroquois, the founding of which is still celebrated today. According to Iroquois tradition, the League was founded by the prophet Deganawida[4] who had a vision of a great spruce tree which reached through the sky to communicate with the Master of Life. The tree was considered the sisterhood of all tribes whilst its roots represented the five Iroquoian tribes – Seneca, Cayuga, Onondaga, Oneida and Mohawk – who make up the Confederacy.[5] The names which each had for themselves give interesting insights relating to their location, activities and wealth (see table below).

The League was founded in about 1570 in response to the state of continual war which existed between the tribes of the region and had a double purpose: the establishment and enforcement of peace and the acquisition of strength to oppose any would-be intruders. An eagle perched at the top of the great spruce tree in Deganawida's vision was a symbolic reference to a state of vigilance against any enemy

Right: *Micmac man and woman, Nova Scotia, c.1865. Although not identified, the woman is probably Christianne Morris who was known for her great skill in producing exquisite bead- and quillwork.*

Tribe	Name for themselves
Seneca	'The great hill people'
Cayuga	'People at the mucky land'
Onondaga	'The people on the hills' (who took their name from their position on top of a mountain or hill)
Oneida	'The people of the standing stone'
Mohawk	'The possessors of the flint'
Tuscarora (after 1722)	'The hemp gatherers' or 'The shirt wearing people'

(AFTER LYFORD, 1945:9)

who might break the peace. The League was governed by a carefully worked out constitution, the laws and regulations of which were transmitted orally from one generation to another by selected leaders. At the time of its establishment, the centrally placed Onondagas were chosen as both the 'firekeepers' and 'wampum keepers' of the League. As 'firekeepers' of the League, it was the Onondagas' responsibility to call yearly councils at which the constitution and laws were rehearsed and differences resolved. At its foundation, the League took into account the established clan system which had been used by the five tribes from ancient times; each clan owned several personal names which served to define roles within the tribes, whilst the fifty chiefs who

Micmac

The Micmacs live in many settlements within the seven traditional districts of Nova Scotia and New Brunswick that they occupied in the 16th century and before. This is a region of heavy forests, a long indented coastline, and many rivers and lakes. The climate does not allow dependence on agriculture, and in aboriginal times tobacco was the only plant cultivated. The Micmacs subsisted on shellfish, herring, salmon and other fish, moose and caribou and birds' eggs, waterfowl, partridge, seal, beaver, rabbit, otter, and porcupine acquired for food and for hides, feathers, and quills. They traveled in fine large birch bark canoes, and on snowshoes. Birch bark was an important material for vessels and containers and for covering the conical wigwams in which they lived. In the French period from 1600 to 1760, fur trapping for trading transformed Micmac life. During the 19th century porpoises were hunted for their oil that was sold to traders. Toward the end of the 19th century the Micmacs were Catholic in religion and found employment especially in lumbering and in guiding sports hunters and fishermen. Trapping came to an end. About 1900 many Micmacs engaged in harvesting potatoes and blueberries. Elaborately beaded garments were worn by both men and women on special occasions. The items shown here were collected in 1913 and 1914 by G.A. Paul, a Maliseet-Penobscot Indian of Oldtown, Maine (except for a woman's cap collected about 1916 by his friend, the anthropologist F.G. Speck).

228

1 Wooden gauge for birch bark.
2 Twined spruce root basket with handle.
3 Birch bark box with wooden ends.
4 Bone dice for gambling game.
5 Burl bowl used to throw the bone dice.
6 Wooden counters for dice game; the shaped sticks are equal to four and five plain counters.
7 Pair of beaded garters; old when collected.

8 Beaded garter.
9 Baby's beaded cap.
10 Woman's peaked cap of red cloth, beaded with double-curve designs. Collected by F.G. Speck about 1916.
11 Man's cape of beaded red cloth (special occasions).
12 Blue cloth coat trimmed with red cloth and beads, worn by man for special tribal occasions.
13 Necklace, woven beadwork.
14 Toy moccasins.
15 Toy birch bark dish.
16 Wooden cooking spatula.

17, 18 Wooden gauges with spaced metal blades, for cutting splints for basketry.
19 Cowhorn rattle with incised designs.
20 Cowhorn rattle.
21 Head for lashing to end of a salmon spear; iron point and two wooden barbs to hold on the speared fish.
22 Man's hat of mooseskin with long hair from the animal's throat; worn with beaded flap at back.
23 Beaded armlets, old style.
24 Carved handle for knife.

Mohawk Warrior, 1750

A Mohawk warrior runs past a tree with a pictographic war record. He carries an English Brown Bess flint-lock and a metal tomahawk with scalplocks on the end. His powder horn is French, worn over a pouch woven of wool and beads like his belt and garters. His knife scabbard and black buckskin moccasins are decorated with porcupine quills. He wears a buck-skin breechclout and bead-edged leggings. Around his neck is a George I Indian medal. He is tattooed like the Mohawk in Benjamin West's 'Death of Wolfe', while his clothing, orna-ments, and weapons are very like those collected by George Townshend and shown in marble on two Mohawk supporters on the Westminster Abbey memorial to his son Lt Col. Roger Townshend, killed at Ticonderoga in 1759 while fighting with Mohawk allies against the French.

made up the 'Roll Call of Chiefs' were each elected from the appropriate clan members. Thus, the ancient social organization was maintained, giving stability and unification to the League, which would not have otherwise been obtained had the old social structure been discarded[6] (Tooker, Trigger ed., 1978:426-8).

The Iroquois clan system was matrilineal, emphasized by the custom of a child receiving a name belonging to the mother's clan. Of great interest is the power which the woman had in the selection of the clan chiefs: 'When one of these "federal" chiefs died, the clan mother (senior woman of the clan, that is, the "aged sensible" women recognized as such) in consultation with other women belonging to that clan in the same tribe chose the man who would assume that name and hence become successor to the deceased chief. Often she chose a man of her lineage (and of the lineage of the deceased chief), but if there was not a suitable man of this lineage, a man of another lineage in the clan might be chosen. If the clan did not have a suitable candidate, the name might be "loaned" to another clan, that is, the name give to a man belonging to another clan with the understanding that at his death the name would return to the clan that had loaned it' (ibid:425-6). Thus, although the League of the Iroquois had the appearance of a government consisting exclusively of males, each member of that governing body was in reality answerable to the women of his maternal family, which in fact consisted only of one female, the 'aged sensible' woman. There is little doubt that this power wielded by the women had its foundation in the Iroquoian subsistence patterns which were highly dependent on horticulture.

Maize, beans and squashes were the three major sources of nourishment to the Iroquois and these were regarded as sacred gifts from the Creator; called 'the three sisters', these foods played an important part in the ceremonials, particularly those associated with the spirit of gratitude. At the gathering and storing of these crops, the communities celebrated the completion of the cycle: 'The "three sisters" are happy because they are home again from their summer in the fields'[7] (Fenton, Trigger ed., 1978:301). A survey of Iroquois horticultural achievements, together with their knowledge of wild plants, leaves little doubt that as with their northern neighbors, the Huron, meat was of fairly limited importance to their subsistence. Up to seventeen distinct varieties of maize were produced, some sixty varieties of beans and some seven squashes. Additionally, they collected thirty-four wild fruits, eleven species of nuts, twelve types of edible roots, thirty-eight varieties of bark, stem and leaf products and six fungi. They also produced some twelve beverages and eleven infusions from parts of plants as occasional drinks, and whilst salt was little used, maple sap was very popular, being used to flavor corn meal, sweeten mush and as a beverage. Little wonder that culture statisticians have given the Indians of the Eastern Wood-

Right: A Mohawk girl, identified by her stage name, White Deer, wearing the neo-traditional special occasion costuming suitable for her performance as an 'equestrian wonder' at the 1901 Pan-American Exposition in Buffalo, New York.

Above: *Six chiefs of the Iroquois photographed on the Six Nations reserve, Ontario, Canada, September 1871. Most of the tribes sided with the British during the American Revolution and subsequently many moved to land along the Grand River in Ontario. These men hold the tribal wampum records, belts woven of white and purple beads with motifs symbolic of agreements and treaties between whites and other tribes. The gift of a wampum string held immense value for the Indians.*

lands 'a high rating in the ratio of food discoveries' when the Old and New World peoples are compared (Speck, 1945:38).

Iroquois villages were composed of bark-covered houses averaging perhaps 65ft (20m.) in length, 20ft (6m.) wide and 20ft high. The Iroquois referred to these as *ganonh'sees*, the 'longhouse', which, depending on its size, could accommodate between five and twenty families. There were only two doors, one at each end and lengthwise down the center ran a passageway 6½ to 10ft (2-3m.) in width, either side of which and raised 1½ft (50cm.) from the ground ran a platform which served as both seats and beds. Above this, perhaps 8ft (2.5m.) from the ground, was a second platform which could be used for storage and, if necessary, additional beds. The longhouse was divided into family apartments some 10ft (3m.) wide and either side of the passage, two families were served by a small fire set at intervals along the length of the house. In the roof were openings to allow for the escape of smoke and to give light to the interior; as necessary, openings could be shut off by use of a slab of roof bark. The longhouse was warm and weatherproof, but unlike the Plains tipi there was no direct control over the rising smoke. However, the large doors at each end undoubtedly produced a useful forced convection effect, expelling smoke through the roof apertures.

The longhouse was made from a basic framework of upright posts set into the ground and enclosing a rectangular floor area. Attached to the tops of the posts were flexible poles which were bent over to produce the roof frame. Slabs of bark about 5ft wide by 6½ft in length (1.5×2m.), preferably elm although basswood, ash, hemlock or cedar were also used, were then attached to the frame in an overlapping fashion with strips of the inner bark of hickory or basswood trees. As with the clearing of the fields the work was carried out by the men but longhouses were considered the property of the women.

Although similar houses were used by other tribes in the region – for example by the Huron to the north (who favored cedar rather than elm

bark) – the longhouse was the most conspicuous feature of Iroquois villages and each was a
microcosm of the whole community becoming
a symbol of identity, thus the common description for themselves – with some variations –
strongly conveyed the idea of them being 'The
People of the Longhouse'.

By the end of the eighteenth century, there
was a gradual abandonment of the longhouse
in favor of single family dwellings. However, the
longhouse has now become the council house
of the communities; whilst today the longhouse often resembles a modern building,
symbolically it states tribal unity and is the
center which perpetuates the teachings of the
Seneca prophet 'Handsome Lake' who, in 1799,
recognizing the social disorganization which
was occurring, urged return to the ancient
annual ceremonials of the Iroquois. The so-
called 'Longhouse Religion' has thus become a
'continued assertion of the integrity of an
Iroquois ethnic identity' (Wallace, Trigger
ed., 1978:442).

Early descriptions of Iroquois villages refer
to elaborate fortifications consisting of a stock-
ade and sometimes a moat. In illustrating his
attack on the Onondaga in 1615, the French explorer Samual Champlain shows massive pal-

Above: *The defeat of the Iroquois in 1609 at Lake
Champlain by a force of Huron, Montagnais, and
Ottawa with Champlain and his guns. Palm trees,
hammocks, and nakedness are the artist's inventions.*

Below: *Chiefs of the Iroquois Confederacy in the
Council House at the Six Nations Reserve, c.1910, the
Onondaga chief holding wampum strings. Flags above
represent the deer and turtle clans.*

isades which the Iroquois had constructed by driving two rows of tree trunks into the ground, inclining each pair so that they crossed some 16½ft (5m.) from the ground, the space between being filled with logs. The trunks were bound together at their point of crossing and horizontal beams were laid into the Vs, forming a narrow walkway protected on the outer side with bark slabs. Notched poles on the inner part of the palisade were used as rough ladders giving the defenders access to the protected walkway (Bishop, 1949:232). They were formidable forts and, even with the use of a cavalier,[8] the Onondaga held off the gun-armed French and their Huron allies for nearly a week until the attackers abandoned the action, much, it must be said, to Champlain's discredit in the eyes of both friend and enemy.[9]

Other than the supporting French, the raid on the Onondaga village was typical of inter-tribal warfare between Iroquoian speaking tribes. Indeed, such was the nature of the Iroquoian warfare pattern, it is unlikely that the Huron would have considered the Onondaga siege a failure because hostile encounters were not generally a struggle for hunting territory or land, but a test of a warrior's bravery, to take a scalp or two and perhaps prisoners for torture.

Prior to an expedition against the enemy and agreement having been reached in council, the Hurons traditionally had a war feast which was prepared by the women. The origin of the feast – and it also went some way to explain the warlike nature of the Iroquoians – was attributed in their mythology to a giant whom a number of Hurons had encountered on the shore of a large lake. When failing to reply politely to his greeting, one of the Hurons wounded the giant in its forehead. In punishment, the giant sowed the seeds of discord amongst the Huron, but before he disappeared into the earth he recom-

Below: *Caroline Parker, Seneca, sister of Gen. Ely Parker, c.1850, in a studio portrait wearing traditional costume she made herself, with elaborate beadwork on a wraparound broadcloth skirt.*

mended the war and *Ononharoia* feasts and the use of the war cry, *wiiiiii*. The feast was accompanied by singing and dancing by the young warriors who uttered abuse against the enemy with promises of victory and as they moved from one end of the longhouse to the other, 'under the pretext of doing it in jest, [they] would knock down others whom they did not like' (Trigger, 1969:46)

It was not unusual for several hundred Huron warriors to lay siege to an Iroquois village, generally the Seneca who lived closest to Huron territory. Such expeditions usually took place in the summer, when there was plenty of leaf cover and often had an air of an outing, as Champlain commented on the prelude to one Huron-Iroquois battle: 'This war had much of the character of an organized sport' (Bishop, 1949:147), the men travelling slowly towards enemy country, fishing and hunting along the way. On crossing Lake Ontario by canoe to the south shore, they would then hide, split up into smaller groups and then travel on foot to the Iroquois villages. Women and children were not infrequently captured before the village itself was put to siege. The principal weapon used in pre- or early contact times was the stone-headed or wooden ball-headed club. The latter was a formidable weapon at close range; commonly made of ironwood and up to 2ft in length (60cm.), it had a large knob or ball at the head, some 4½ to 10in. (12-15cm.) in diameter which was often carved with animal figures, perhaps emblematic of the owner's personal totem and protective power.[10] The ball-headed club was later superseded by the trade metal pipe tomahawk, and, likewise, the bow and arrow replaced by the gun, the latter having a particular impact on warfare tactics, for example the abandonment of wooden body armor (Trigger, 1969:47, illus.), and change in battle formation.[11]

In all cases, casualties were usually few in number, the young aspiring warriors laying emphasis on performing acts of daring. Generally, after a few injuries and deaths the attackers withdrew to their temporary forts which they commonly built near the enemy village. Pitched battles tended to be avoided and if reinforcements from other settlements were imminent the attackers left for home. The wounded were carried home in a makeshift basket sling, on the backs of their companions and, whilst it was a practical means of transport through the heavily wooded forest, it was appallingly uncomfortable for the injured. Champlain, who was himself wounded in the leg and knee by two Iroquois arrows, describes how the Huron men fabricated the frame of hickory or elm, attaching a seat with straps of hide or of the plaited inner bark of elm. The frame and burden were supported by a tumpline across the carrier's forehead and the wounded warrior sat on the seat, his legs under his chin and tightly bound in position. Champlain described his ordeal – undoubtedly an extremely unpleasant one experienced by many an immobilized Iroquoian warrior:

'It was impossible to move any more than a little child in its swaddling clothes... and this causes the wounded great and extreme pain. I can say this indeed from my own case, having been carried for

Seneca

The Senecas are one of the six tribes that formed the Iroquois League or Confederacy. Many have lived in Canada since 1784 when the League split into two duplicate political organizations, Canadian and American. The majority of the Senecas remained in New York where they lived on three reservations in the western part of the state. The Allegany and Cattaraugus Reservations are organized as the Seneca Nation, which seceded from the League in 1848. Senecas on the Tonawanda Reservation are not part of this Seneca Nation; rather, they maintain their political affiliation with the New York League. In other ways all Senecas are culturally very similar. A majority of the modern Senecas are Christians but a large minority are followers of the Longhouse religion that was founded by the Seneca prophet Handsome Lake between 1799 and 1815. On each of the Seneca reservations there is a longhouse, a ritual structure associated with this religion. The Tonawanda longhouse serves as headquarters. When the items shown here were collected (1905–10) on all three New York reservations, many Senecas were still farmers, growing corn, beans, and squash, the traditional Three Sisters referred to as 'our life supporters'. Several native types of implements were associated with the harvesting and processing of corn, while other traditional artifacts included the musical instruments used in Longhouse rituals. 'Traditional dress', worn only on special occasions, maintained the Iroquois styles of the early 19th century.

1 Large wooden bread bowl, used on lap to hold mealing stones and for other culinary purposes.
2 Wood splint basket for drying berries or green corn.
3 Hickory splint sieve for ground corn.
4 Fingerwoven man's belt of red wool and white beads.
5 Caribou skin kilt with embroidered floral design; part of man's formal dress.
6 Wooden cradleboard.
7 Burden strap (tumpline) of twined bark fiber.
8 Pack basket for harvested corn, with burden strap
9 Deer jaw for scraping green corn off cob.
10 Crooked knife for wood carving.
11 Washing basket for hulling boiled hominy.
12 Corn planting and berrying basket.
13 Woman's printed cotton cloth (long blouse) with beaded edges and silver brooches in four traditional Iroquois shapes.
14 Pair of woman's red flannel leggings with beaded designs.
15 Pouch or purse of cloth with floral design in raised beadwork.
16 Box turtle rattle used for Women's Dance.
17 Rattle of snapping turtle, with neck skin and head forming handle, carried by maskers in curative ritual.
18 Gourd rattle to accompany singers.
19 Cowhorn rattle used by singers for dances.

several days because I was unable to stand, chiefly on account of the arrow-wound I had received in my knee, for never did I find myself in such a hell as during this time; for the pain I suffered from the wound in my knee was nothing in comparison with what I endured tied and bound on the back of one of our savages. . .'

(Bishop, 1949:238)

Such journeys subjected the helpless incumbent to endless tossing, buffeting and whipping by the tree branches and half, sometimes complete, immersion in water as the bearer made his way through forest and streams, but it was greatly preferable to falling into the hands of Iroquois enemies.

Early explorers found much to admire in Iroquoian society; they describe, for example, the superb physique of the men and the beauty of the young women. There was surprisingly little internal conflict within the crowded villages and all were fond of laughter and jokes, applied good sense and justice in their affairs, showed great hospitality and, at times, great kindness. They had an acuteness of sense, great courage, endurance and were stoic to pain.

The Iroquoian treatment of prisoners was, however, another matter and many whites were stunned and appalled by what they saw. In Iroquoian war ethos, nothing was considered more desirable than to be credited with the capture of prisoners and more particularly the capture of an enemy warrior. On occasions, if several men claimed the capture of a particular prisoner, the prisoner himself would be requested to designate his official captor. In so doing, wily captured Iroquoians, who were well versed in the psychology of intertribal warfare, not infrequently named another who was less involved in his capture. In so doing, he struck a note of discord amongst his captors and sometimes, rather than allow the honor to go to the wrong man, he was helped to escape. Whilst women and children might be slain on the spot or taken back for adoption, male prisoners – unless there were too many of them – were taken back to the villages. On some occasions, men were formally adopted, receiving the name of a lost relative which 'served to dry the tears of the bereaved' (Trigger, 1969:49), but most often they were subjected to ritual torture which for some unexplained reason was part of Iroquois and Huron psychology and far less practiced by the Algonquian tribes.

The historian Francis Parkman has described in great detail the fate of one Iroquois prisoner who was captured by Hurons during the savage Iroquois-Huron war of 1648-50.[12] Saouandanancous was brought in by his Huron captors and adopted by an elderly chief who, having lost a son, had hoped that Saouandanancous might take his place; the prisoner's hands, however, had been seriously injured[13] and because of this, whilst treating him with courtesy and an outward show of genuine affection, he was condemned to die. He was put to death by fire so carefully applied that it took him over twelve hours to die. Astoundingly, his tormentors showed no signs of lack of self control and as each applied his particular torture they spoke to the prisoner in a kindly way. Equally extraordinary is that Saouandanancous demonstrated the courage and endurance expected of an Iro-

COURTESY STARK FOUNDATION, ORANGE, TEXAS

Above: Now-on-dhu-go, an Ottawa chief from Lake Michigan, Paul Kane (1845). The vermilion stripes on his face are symbolic; his hair appears to be tied at the front with a piece of red trade cloth.

quois warrior: during intervals between the torture he not only reported on Hurons who had been adopted into his tribe, but sang as well. When he finally expired, he was cut up and small pieces of his flesh distributed for eating.

In 1609, Champlain described a similar episode; after the battle at Ticonderoga, one of the dozen or so prisoners was selected for torture. The Huron harangued him with the cruelties which he and members of his tribe had practiced on them and that he should prepare himself to experience as much. They told him to sing 'if he had the heart' and Champlain reports that he did 'but it was a very sad song to hear' (Bishop, 1949:150).

Although it has been reported that on occasions the body of the dead man was burned as a sacrifice to the most powerful of the Huron supernaturals, Oki, 'the sky',[14] the ritually tortured prisoners were probably symbols of the tribe represented; as one anthropologist has recently explained it, the prisoners became a 'hate object on whom the frustrations of life and past wrongs could be expended' (Heidenreich, Trigger ed., 1978:386).

West and north of Huronia was the domain of an equally powerful, but politically considerably less coordinated, tribe – the Algonquian-speaking Chippewa – who occupied much of what is now the state of Wisconsin, southwest

Ontario and northeastern Minnesota. Unlike the Iroquois, who were too far south and so had largely to resort to elm bark for building their longhouses and fabrication of utensils and canoes, the Chippewa had easy access to a superior natural material – birch bark – and, in further contrast, depended far less on horticulture, the maize of their southern neighbors being largely replaced by superb wild 'rice' which grew in abundance in the countless streams and lakes so characteristic of the Mississippi headwaters region.

Wild 'rice' (Zizania aquatica) was not in actuality a true rice but an aquatic grass. Early explorers were greatly impressed by its nutritious value and it was an important component in the diet of the Western Great Lakes people, particularly the Chippewa and Menominee, whose tribal name was derived from the Chippewa for wild 'rice', manomini, it being the chief vegetal food for that tribe although for religious reasons they never attempted to cultivate it, seemingly as part of their unwillingness to 'wound their mother, the earth' (Hodge ed., 1907-10:843).

The rice was collected in late August or early September[15] with the people working in groups; certain areas were recognized as being the property of certain families and it was a right which was seldom disputed. Often the growth was so dense that the areas gave the appearance of enormous green meadows and the canoes needed to be poled through the torpid streams or shallow lakes, generally by a male member of the group, whilst the women gathered. Two sticks about 2ft (60cm.) long were used in the harvesting process; the women sat in the stern of the canoe and bent down the stalks (some could be over 20ft (6m.) high) with one stick and struck the kernel with the other; the process was continued until the canoe was full. On return to the temporary lake-shore camp, the 'rice' was laid out on sheets of birch bark for drying; it was then poured into a lined hole in the ground and pounded with long pestles, or curved sticks, to loosen the husks, perhaps several women participating in this part of the work. Finally, the 'rice' was win-nowed by pouring from one special large bark tray to another. The quality, size and taste dif-fered and it was recognized that certain areas produced particularly good crops, 'kernels there are small and better tasting than the ones around here' and the kernels on the La Pointe Reservation were 'finer than the ones at Red Lake' (Hilger, 1951:147). Nevertheless, whatever its type, as with the tapping for maple syrup in the spring it was an opportunity for group acti-vities and joyous gatherings.

The collecting of maple sugar was an activity of great importance as it was used in feasts and ceremonials and everyone was expected to eat all that was set before them. The sugar was used on fruits, vegetables, cereals and even fish. Although the collecting of maple sugar – which generally commenced in March – was a time of work, it was also one of pleasure and special wigwams were retained from year to year in certain areas. It was an opportunity for social and ceremonial gatherings and a chance to catch up on the previous year's tribal gossip.

The maple trees were tapped by making a gash in the trunk a meter or so above the ground. A cedar spike was then pounded into the tree at an angle and this allowed the sap to drip down into a birch bark bucket placed on the ground. The sap was then boiled and when it hung in strings from the stirring paddle it was

considered ready; it was then strained through a basswood-fiber matting and transferred to a granulating trough. It was worked as it cooled and the granulated sugar which resulted was pulverized into finer granules. Some of the sugar was packed into moulds to make little cakes, but most was put into *makuks* – special birch bark storage containers – and carried home for use throughout the rest of the year. In addition to its use as a highly nutritious food source, it was also mixed with water to make a refreshing drink. A small amount of the sugar was always offered to Manito[16] and this type of ceremonial – the offering of the first fruit or game – was observed with the first preparation of each seasonal food.

The vast woodland areas had an abundance of wild foods, such as cranberries, goose-berries, blueberries, black and red raspberries, cherries and grapes, hickory, hazel, beech and butternuts and also wild onions and potatoes, the former being particular favorites. Later in the summer when plants were fully developed, special attention was given to gathering herbs for medicine. The person gathering the herbs would offer tobacco to the four directions as well as to the sky and earth. Prayers were made in a low voice with promises that no more would be taken than was necessary, whilst hope was expressed that the mysterious powers would make their use successful. After gathering, the various plants were dried, each variety being separately stored. Whilst most of

Below: *Blackhawk and Winneshiek, Winnebago, before 1900. Both were prominent leaders, c.1870, among those Winnebago bands who resisted removal from traditional homelands in Wisconsin to Nebraska.*

Above: *A Kickapoo man, by Karl Bodmer (1833). At the time Maximilian met members of this tribe they had just been removed from their original homeland in Wisconsin to a reservation in Kansas.*

Below: *Winnebago woman tanning a deerskin, c.1880. The skin has been stretched on a vertical wooden frame and is being defleshed with a chisel-like tool. Note the two dwellings in the background.*

Secotan Luncheon, 1585

The North Carolina Algonquian village of Secotan, near Roanoke, was visited by the English artist John White in 1585; he made several very detailed watercolor drawings there. The man and woman sit, in typical postures, on a woven cattail mat, eating boiled hominy from a burl bowl. She holds a turkey feather fire fan, while corn and fish boil in a pottery vessel with pointed bottom. Beside the man is a clay pipe, kept in a leather pouch by his foot that resembles one collected near Jamestown about 25 years later. A gourd vessel in front has a corncob stopper. The woman is tattooed and wears a shell headband, while the man has the body painting of a warrior and wears a gorget of native copper, and skin and bead ear ornaments. Both wear buckskin garments, hers edged with shell beads.

Above: *The construction of a Chippewa birch bark canoe. Birch bark was the 'skin' of the elegant and graceful line canoe. The framework of the unfinished canoe shows the process of fabrication.*

Below: *Ne Shiw Shkak (Jack Davis) and Wis Ki gete (Rising Smoke), Potawatami. Fine ribbon appliqué decoration (at which this tribe excelled) is in evidence on the leggings worn by Rising Smoke.*

that which was three or more layers in thickness was suitable for peaked or domed winter wigwams, whilst two layers for the conical summer lodge would suffice.

The domed wigwam consisted of a framework made of flexible poles or saplings of ironwood or elm which were pushed into the ground and then bent over, producing a series of arches. Horizontal encircling poles were then lashed to the vertical poles with basswood fiber producing a net-like framework. The sheets of bark, perhaps over 6ft long and 3ft wide (about 2×1m.) wide, were then laid on a lining of woven cattail (*Typha latifolia*) mats, overlapping as one would shingle a roof; a smoke hole was left at the top, the fire was small and provided by several dry logs which radiated from the central hearth and as the logs burnt they were pushed inward. By careful selection of the wood, the flame could be made virtually smokeless. The permanent lodges generally had a platform about 1½ft extending part way around the interior, which served both as seats

the herbs were used as remedies for sore eyes, abdominal problems, skin and lung troubles, some were also used as hunting charms; powdered or in the form of fine roots, they were mixed with tobacco or red willow and smoked in a pipe. During the course of tracking the deer they occasionally sat down and smoked one of the herbs 'and it is said that before long the deer came toward them sniffing the air' (Densmore, 1929:129). For so many of these subsistence activities – the canoe to collect the wild 'rice' and the winnowing trays used to separate it, the *makuk* for collecting berries, the leak-proof containers for collecting the maple syrup and water, and the fabrication of their habitations – the Chippewa very much depended on one natural and remarkable material, *wigass*, or 'birch bark'; it was the very basis of their material culture.

Although the time varied in different localities, the Chippewa knew when to remove the bark without destroying the tree, but generally it was between the end of spring and early summer. The process of removing the bark was demonstrated by a Lac Courte (Wisconsin) Chippewa lady to Sister Inez Hilger: clutching her pocket knife in her right hand and 'with blade extending beyond her little finger [she] carefully cut the outer bark (only the outer bark is removed) from a place as high as she could reach, down to the root. In removing the bark she moved clockwise around the tree, loosening it carefully with both hands so as not to break it' (Hilger, 1951:133). It was later explained that when very large pieces of bark were needed, such as were used in making canoes, trees were felled and then all the bark stripped off. The bark was then rolled or folded and tied up with a basswood fiber and transported on the back of the gatherer; rolls or folded batches of birch bark were common in or close to the wigwams, ready for use. The actual thickness of the bark determined the use to which it could be put; that removed from the large trees could have up to nine separate layers and was suitable for making canoes. Some, however, was as thin and pliable as tissue paper, but so tough and durable that it was used for wrapping. Between these extremes were several other grades, mainly used for containers and trays;

art. One old woman used to act out her stories, running around the fire and acting while she talked' (Densmore, 1929:29).

Because the Great Lakes region was dotted with lakes and laced with streams and rivers, a great deal depended on transportation by canoe, the best being made of the versatile birch bark.[17] In common with most tribes inhabiting this area, the Chippewa were considered to be expert canoemen and builders, employing one of at least three styles although it is probable that the so-called 'high-ended' type was the old tribal form resembling that of the Algonquin further east. This particular type of canoe was still used by the Chippewa on Lake Nipigon in Ontario and also by the Menominee in Wisconsin in the nineteenth century. The artist and explorer George Catlin was particularly impressed with the Chippewa canoe, and the consummate skill with which it was fashioned, observing:

'The bark canoe of the Chippeways is, perhaps, the most beautiful and light model of all the water crafts that ever were invented. They are . . . so ingeniously shaped and sewed together, with roots of the tamarack, . . . that they . . . ride upon the water, as light as a cork.'

The skill required in handling these was not lost on Catlin:

and beds; many had a medicine pole, perhaps 20ft (6m.) high attached to the top of which was a small sacrifice to the mysterious and unfathomable potentials and powers of life and the universe – the Manito.

One observer, Frances Densmore, who spent over twenty years studying the life of the Chippewa, came to view these people with enormous respect. She was moved by the beauty of the northern woodlands, familiar with, its changing seasons, the material abundance and inspiration, giving, she concluded, the poetry and the spiritual essence of Chippewa culture. Densmore captured in words the warmth and beauty of the winter wigwam, where the 'winter

Above: Chippewa woman weaving a rush mat, typical summer occupation for older women. This appears to be a cedar bark mat of a natural golden brown, the patterns worked in dyed cedar strips.

evenings were social and pleasant. The fire burned brightly, but no work was done which placed a strain on the eyes. A favorite pastime was the making of birch-bark transparencies. The women made basswood cord or fish nets, and sometimes they made birch-bark makuks or dishes. The young men reclined in the wigwam and always had a drum conveniently near them. . . the winter was the time for story-telling, and many old women were experts in this

Below: An Ojibwa village near Sault Ste Marie, by Paul Kane (1846). The largest lodge, covered with sheets of silver birch at the top and matting near the bottom, suggests a makeshift encampment. Note child's cradle (center) with protective head bar.

'They gracefully lean and dodge about, under the skillful balance of an Indian, . . . but like everything wild, are timid and treacherous under the guidance of white man; and, if he be not an experienced equilibrist, he is sure to get two or three times soused, in his first endeavors at familiar acquaintance with them.'

(Catlin, 1841, Vol. 2:138)

Whilst the size of the canoe varied depending on its use, the typical model was just under 16ft (5m.) in length, 3ft (1m.) wide at the middle, and 1½ft (50cm.) deep. Such a canoe could carry about six adults. All measurements were based on the distances between various parts of the human body, although one basic unit employed by many good canoe makers was the 'hand spread' or span from the end of middle finger to the tip of the thumb. It took great skill to fabricate these crafts; the women generally prepared the ground, bark and pitch, whilst the men shaped the wood for the floor, ribs, stern and bow. The whole process was customarily supervised by a highly respected, skilled canoe maker, such expertise not uncommonly passing from father to son so that the traditional skills could indeed be maintained.

In one description of the fabrication of a birch bark canoe, it was reported that it took about a week to gather all the materials together and make the craft. All the material came from trees; the framework and lining was of lightweight cedar, the cords used to keep the frame and other parts together was of spruce root and the pitch for the seams was made from spruce gum, which was generally boiled to thicken it (that which was to be used on the

Above: *Grand medicine dance at Lac Courte Oreille Reservation, Wisconsin, 1899, one of the most important ceremonies of the Midewiwin (Medicine Lodge Society) of the Chippewa. This shows a candidate and mother within the framework lodge.*

Below: *Five Chippewa and Menominee drummers and two Chippewa dancers at a drum ceremony, c.1910, Menominee Reservation. Some Menominee ceremonies petitioned the spirits through the sacred drum which stands before the seated singers.*

Chippewa

The Chippewa in the U.S. (Wisc., Minn., Mich., N.Dak.) and southern Ontario, and the Ojibwa in western Ontario and Saskatchewan all spoke the Ojibwa language (many still do). In 1900 they were mainly forest dwellers, dependent on fishing, hunting, and wild foods (especially wild rice). The main religious ceremony was the medicine Dance of the Mide society. Except as noted, all the items here were collected by Frances Densmore between 1907 and 1930.

1 Birch bark bucket. White Earth Reservation, Minn.
2 Birch bark temporary dish. White Earth Res.
3 Man and woman dolls of slippery elm bark. Red Lake Res., Minn.
4 Man and woman dolls of cattail roots. Minn.
5 Wooden cradleboard with wrappings and ornaments; baby is museum-made plaster model.
6 Piece of cattail mat of type used for wigwam covers. Bois Fort Res.

7 Small cedar bark bag. Bois Fort Res.
8 Piece of cattail mat of type used for wigwam walls. White Earth Res.
9 Birch bark dish for wild rice. White Earth Res.
10 Game: deer bones, thimble, leather with holes, tied to iron pin for spearing them. White Earth Res.
11 Wooden spoon. White Earth Res.
12 Wooden spoon to stir maple sugar. White Earth Res.
13 Leaf patterns of birch bark

for beadwork designs.
14 Counting stick for gambling guessing game with bullets hidden in moccasins. Minn., 1891. (W. J. Hoffman coll.)
15 Piece of cedar bark mat of type used for floor mats. Bois Fort Res.
16 Wooden bowl for bear's head at Mide feast. White Earth Res.
17 Unfinished bag of slippery elm bark for holding wild rice. Minn.
18 Chief's cloth headband.

Leech Lake Res., Minn., 1891–2. (Hoffman coll.)
19 Child's toy: gray squirrel skin stuffed with wild rice. White Earth Res.
20 Piece of cattail mat of type used for floor mats. Bois Fort Res.
21 Cedar bark bag filled with wild rice, for storage.
22 Small model of snowshoes.
23 Needle for netting snowshoes.
24 Bone fish hooks.
25 Bow of oak, made in 1928 by Kawakatusk of Rainy

Lake Reserve. Ont., for the anthropologist J.M. Cooper.

26 Five arrows with bone points. Manitou Rapids Reserve, Ont. (Cooper coll.)

27 Skunk fur garter; part of costume of Keekweechiweepinank 'trying to throw' (Red Blanket) bought from him when he was an 1899 delegate to Washington.

28 Fur headband, and belt (?) of black velvet, white fur, and feathers. Part of Red Blanket's costume (see 27).

29 Red woollen breechclout. (As 28, Red Blanket's.)

30 Pair of beaded moccasins. (As 28, Red Blanket's.)

31 Ballheaded club from man named Odjibwe. White Earth Res.

32 Mide rattle. Red Lake Res.

33 Mide rattle. White Earth Res.

34 Two-headed drum, and drumstick wrapped with red braid, to accompany songs for moccasin game (see 14).

35 Buckskin coat, bands of weasel tails and woven beadwork across back. (As 28, Red Blanket's.)

36 Buckskin belt with woven beadwork. (As 28, Red Blanket's.)

37 Painted and beaded buckskin knife sheath. As 28.

38 Buckskin leggings with woven beadwork. As 28.

39 Stone pipe. As 28.

40 Woman's pipe.

41 Beaded cloth pouch. White Earth Res., 1891. (Hoffman coll.)

main seams being mixed with powdered charcoal which not only made the resin less brittle when it dried, but gave an ornamental appearance to the caulking). Often, the ground on which the canoe was to be fabricated was covered with a layer of sand so as to shape the canoe bottom, then long sheets of thick bark with the inner side of the bark to the outside were weighted down with a flat frame, which defined the approximate length and width of the canoe; large stones ensured that the frame and bark were held firmly in place. Seven or eight pairs of short poles were now driven into the ground, slightly inclined to the vertical, conforming to the shape of the lower frame and perhaps 3ft (1m.) or so apart at the middle; as the posts were positioned they eased the bark up at an angle and the canoe now began to take shape. The gunwales were now placed in lengthwise and the bark sewn in place with the spruce root; the gunwale gave shape and strength to the upper edges of the canoe and was prepared beforehand so as to have the correct shape and curve as were the sections of cedar for the bow and stern which were eased between the bark at each end. This was then trimmed, conforming to an approved outline. All the final sewing was carried out by the women, traditionally using a bone awl, the finer being done with split and soaked spruce root. Several women could probably complete the

required sewing on an average canoe in one day; some of the stitching was deliberately of uneven length, particularly at the ends, to reduce the likelihood of the bark splitting.

It was important that all overlapping edges of the bark were toward the stern of the canoe so as to ensure streamline flow around its contours, and that all the gores and laps were firmly stuck together with spruce gum. Ribs were now cut to length and shape and eased into place with a lining of thin strips of cedar placed between the ribs and the bark as the work proceeded; this protected the floor and sides of the canoe. Ribs, lining and bark were all kept moist, but the varying width cross pieces which permanently shaped the top of the canoe were sewn in dry.

The canoe was now left to dry for several days and, if necessary, pulled into correct shape by tying it between end stakes. It was then inverted and the seams sealed with the black spruce pitch.

Paddles were of birch or cedar, some 4ft (1.2m.) in length, approximately half being the blade which was 4½ or 6in. (12 or 15cm.) wide. Both men and women rowed, generally with the man seated in the prow and the woman in the stern; however, for fast travel up to four men might paddle at one time.

A good serviceable canoe would last a family perhaps a year; some men were known for

Below: *Household scene, Sauk & Fox, c.1900. The men are in front of winter lodges covered with rush mats, on either side of a summer work area under a brush-covered roof.*

Left: *A Sauk & Fox chief. His distinguishing turban/deertail headdress is surmounted by an eagle feather. A further sign of his high rank is the split bear and otter hide over his shoulder.*

making and supplying canoes and a typical price in the late nineteenth century would be a three point Hudson's Bay blanket.

There is little wonder that, given the great value of birch bark in the life of the woodland tribes, there are references to it as sacred material. The Abenaki, for example, named the birch *Gluskabe* which was one of their hero gods who, it is recorded, asked the tree 'to take care of the Indians' (Butler and Hadlock, 1957:49). A widespread mythological tale explains the migrations of birds back to the northern forests after the intense winters. The birds are caged in birch bark containers which are torn open by animal-men volunteers from the north, freeing the birds who fly north bringing the summer warmth and regrowth; symbolically, life emerges from the birch container, hence the patterns, produced by a scraping technique (sgraffito), of birds, plants and shrubs embellished on their outer surface.[18]

The spiritual life of the Western Lakes tribes, so eloquently captured in the writings of Frances Densmore on the Chippewa and referred to earlier, centered around the ceremonials of the *Midewiwin*,[19] or Grand Medicine Society, which has been particularly well documented for the Chippewa. The existence of the *Midewiwin* was not recorded by the Jesuit Relations (covering the period 1640 to 1700). However, it has been suggested that special efforts were made by the ritualists to conceal a religious rite which was in direct conflict with the missionary message.[20] The probable antiquity is suggested by its extensive distribution in the Western Great Lakes region, being practiced by the Potawatomi, Menominee, Winnebago, Sauk, Fox, and Kickapoo from 'early historic times' (Ritzenthaler, Trigger ed., 1978:755).

Whilst there were regional variations in the *Midewiwin* ceremony, the principles of ethical

Above: *Kiyo' Kaga, or Keokuk, a distinguished Sauk chief and able leader who was poisoned by one of his own band. In this early image (1847), he wears a necklace of bear claws on an otterskin collar.*

Below: *Sauk, Fox, Kansa delegation, Washington, 1867. Included here is Moses Keokuk, the son of Keokuk (above). Those present had just signed away their remaining land in Kansas for $1 an acre.*

Sauk and Fox

The Sauk and Fox tribes, speaking the same language and culturally very similar, have been close allies since 1733, although maintaining their distinct identities. Traditionally both hunted and trapped during the fall and winter while living in mat-covered lodges in hunting camps, and farmed corn, beans, and squash during the summer while living in large bark-covered lodges in river-bottom villages. Patrilineal clans owned their personal names and had various ritual functions. Within each of the two tribes there were two political organizations for war and peace, that had largely the same memberships but different leaders for the different functions. The Sauk and Fox were enemies of the Dakota and Chippewa and allies of the Iowa, Winnebago, and Potawatomi. During the colonial period they fought the French until 1737. Defeated by the U.S. Army in the Black Hawk War of 1832, the Sauk and Fox were moved from Iowa to Kansas in 1837 and 1842. Many of the Fox returned to Iowa during the 1850s, where they bought land that was later recognized as a reservation, the Mesquakie Settlement near Tama. The other Fox in Kansas joined the Sauk and moved with most of them to Indian Territory (now Oklahoma) in 1869, leaving a small band of Sauk in Kansas. The objects shown here were collected in 1901–3 by the ethnologist William Jones (himself a Fox from Indian Territory) among the Mesquakie (Fox) at Tama or, if so specified below, the Fox or Sauk in Indian Territory.

1 Woman's skirt with silk ribbon appliqué on red flannel; ceremonial.
2 Wooden hole-and-slot heddle for weaving beadwork.
3 Woman's dress, ribbon appliqué decoration. Sauk, Okla.
4 Woman's leggings with ribbon appliqué, beadwork, and buttons.
5 Wooden food paddle.
6 Black gourd warrior's rattle.
7 Bag with beaded design of underwater panther and 'TAMA'.
8 Bag of woven twine and blanket ravellings.
9 Feather fan.
10 Ball of native twine.
11 Braided hank of reed fiber for weaving bags.
12 Woven bag.
13 Pack saddle.
14 Man's fur turban.
15 Twined reed mat.
16 Woven bag, thunderbird design.
17 Twined bag.
18 Hide scraper for tanning.
19 Set of bone gambling dice.
20 Wooden bowl for tossing dice.
21 Young man's shirt with ribbon appliqué.
22 Boy's buckskin leggings. Fox. Okla.
23 Man's buckskin leggings. Fox. Okla.
24 Young man's beaded 'love bag'.
25 Bone spreader for roach headdress.
26 Boy's popgun toy.
27 Pair of woven beadwork garters. Fox. Okla.
28 Lacrosse stick. Okla.
29 Bundle of gambling sticks.

247

conduct, the desire for attainment of a long life, the interpretation of dreams and the phenomena of the natural world, permeated the activities of the Society. The basic ethics of the *Midewiwin* were that rectitude of conduct produced length of life and that evil conduct would eventually react on the offender. Stealing and lying and the use of alcohol were strictly forbidden, whilst respect towards women was emphasized. Male members of the *Midewiwin* were taught to be quiet in manner and moderate in speech and not hasty in action. As Densmore observed, 'this directed |my| attention to the gentle voices, the patience, and the courtesy of the old people who had been trained in the Midewiwin' (Densmore, 1929:87). The initiation ceremony was designed to inject a spirit power into the candidate, achieved by pointing a special medicine bag whereupon the candidate fell to the ground unconscious. The bags were made of animal or bird skins being distinctive of one of the four orders of degrees which could be attained in *Midewiwin* membership. The initiation of one candidate who was seated in the middle of the Grand Medicine Lodge, was described by one observer:

'The medicine men, four or five of them, came dancing in, carrying pouches. The pouches were made of the skins of beaver, otter, white martin or weasel – all elongated like snake skins. The dancers danced along the path of the wigwam and when they came near my uncle they threw their pouches at him. The "medicine" in them was so strong that he fell over and fainted. Each man then picked up his pouch and laid it on him, and he came to.'

(Hilger, 1951:69)

The *Midewiwin* medicine bags held a special small white shell called the *migis*;[21] this was considered the sacred symbol of the Society and traditionally associated with immortality. It was also the *migis* which transmitted the spirit power:

> *Here it is*
> *Here it is*
> *The weasel skin |medicine bag|*
> *Through it I shoot the white shells.*
>
> *It never fails*
> *The shell*
> *Goes toward them*
> *And they fall*

(Initiation songs of *Midewiwin* (Densmore, 1910:Songs Nos 52 and 63))

The ceremony was one of curing a sick individual or responding to a dream that directed application for membership should be made. The *Midewiwin* was generally an annual affair held in the late spring or early fall and lasted for up to five days, depending on the number of candidates. A possible reason for its popularity with the Chippewa is that they have been identified by one anthropologist as having an unusual preoccupation with health, a manifestation of this concern being the assortment of different roots and herbs which were used for medicinal purposes, gaining a knowledge of which was one major objective of the members of the *Midewiwin*.

A notable component associated with the Society was the use of bark rolls inscribed with pictographs, which referred to the instructions to be given to its members; they also recorded the songs and teachings of the *Midewiwin*. The rolls were some 2½ft in length by 1ft wide (75×30cm.), the pictographs being engraved with a bone stylus. To the uninitiated, they were

Below: *A Sauk summer lodge, covered with bark, photographed in Indian Territory in about 1884. An unusually large structure, it is probably the central council lodge of the village. Seated third from the left is the chief Pashipaho, otherwise known by the name 'Little Stabber'.*

virtually meaningless, but to those with the esoteric knowledge the figures were invaluable memory aids. The records were passed down through successive generations, the aged keepers initiating younger men as to the meaning of each pictograph. Such pictographic records in the Woodland region were by no means unique to the Chippewa alone, but because of their association with religious concepts of these people they have been extensively reported on (Hoffman, 1891: Mallery, 1893: Densmore, 1929).

Studies have shown that there were similarities between birch bark pictographs of all the Algonquian stock from the northeastern seaboard to west of the Great Lakes and the Abenaki in Maine even modified the ancient pictographic techniques when, in the late nineteenth century, they became 'engaged in civilized industries in which they have found it necessary to keep accounts' (Mallery, 1893:259). Extending on the nineteenth-century studies of Mallery, W.C. Sturtevant has recently demonstrated that Iroquois hieroglyphics[22] could convey extensive and sophisticated ideas to those familiar with the glyphs. Such pictographic work was perhaps the nearest approach to writing by the indigenous population of North America,[23] but the influx of Europeans caused its abandonment before further development took place.

'Had the whites delayed their coming for another century, . . . these Indians might have succeeded in establishing an enduring State based on the six foundation stones of the League – health, happiness, righteousness, justice, power, and strength of character'[24]

Above; *Wakusásse, a Fox warrior, painted by Karl Bodmer (1833). In this early portrait, the warrior wears a deer and porcupine hair roach embellished with feathers as a mark of success in battle. His face is painted with vermilion and brown ochre with what is possibly a lightning symbol.*

JOSLYN ART MUSEUM, OMAHA, NEBRASKA

Right: *Wah-com-mo (Fast Walker), a Fox warrior, in 1868. This tribe, who were closely associated with the Sauk, called themselves Meskwahki haki or Mesquaki, 'The Red Earths'. Wah-com-mo wears a grizzly claw necklace and carries an eagle feather fan and pipe tomahawk – traditional accoutrements used by high-ranking Sauk & Fox warriors.*

References

1 Cape Breton district, called *Onamag* by the Micmac, was – and still is – considered the residence of the head chief.
2 Although contacts with England may have occurred as early as 1497 when Sebastian Cabot was said to have taken three Micmac Indians to England, the rapport which the French developed contrasted markedly with the attitude of superiority which characterized most of the English colonists.
3 The early name for the areas of Nova Scotia and New Brunswick.
4 Deganawida was possibly of Huron descent. Closely associated with Deganawida was the Iroquois chief, Hiawatha, and the renowned woman chief of the Neutral Nation, Djigonsasen.
5 The Tuscarora joined in about 1720.
6 It has been suggested that the ideals underlying the founding of the League inspired the forming of the American Constitution because it is known that a number of the main writers of the Constitution were thoroughly familiar with the structure of the League.
7 Iroquois women's celebration song.
8 In this context, a moveable tower, overtopping the palisade.
9 This battle has been described as one of the most decisive in American history, it being suggested that had the Hurons and French won the land of the Iroquois, 'Iroquoia', would have been dominated by the French, displacing the Dutch, and the course of colonial history changed (Bishop, 1949:240).
10 One particularly fine Iroquoian ball-headed club is in the collections of Skokloster Castle, Sweden (Ryden, 1963:114-15). A similar club also with a lizard-like creature carved at the top of the handle is in the Museum of Mankind, London (King, 1982:85).
11 Champlain vividly describes the battle between the

Huron and Iroquois in which he participated in 1609 and demonstrates the useless protection which 'shields made of cotton thread woven together and wood' afforded against guns (Bishop, 1949:148).
12 War between Iroquois and Hurons dated from prior to colonial times; this particular conflict, however, finally destroyed the Huron Confederacy.
13 As soon as the Huron had an enemy in their power they tore out his finger-nails and bit or cut off the fingers which he used to draw the string of a bow. Whilst often causing serious infection, it rarely resulted in the prisoner dying before he reached the Huron settlements; indeed, he was well fed to ensure that he could 'better endure the tortures that awaited him' (Trigger, 1969:48).
14 Shamans and powerful warriors were also referred to as *Oki*. For a graphic 1616 description of a Huron *Oki*, see Bishop (1949:252).
15 This was just before the rice matured; if attempts were made to gather it later, a great deal was lost.
16 Manito, variants of which were manitto, manetto, manitoa and, more popularly as it has now been taken into the English language, manitou. It may be described as the 'mysterious and unknown potencies and powers of life and of the universe' (Hodge ed., 1907-10:800).
17 In comparison, although the Iroquois were great travelers, they were essentially landsmen, having only limited access to birch bark. Whilst they used canoes, these were fabricated of elm bark which has been described as 'a clumsy craft unsuited to long voyages, dangerous for crossing lakes, and suicide in white water' (Fenton, Trigger ed., 1978:303). The more northerly Huron (Wyandot), however, lived within easier range of birch bark country and mastered both technique of manufacture and use from their Algonquian

neighbors. (See particularly Adney and Chapelle, 1964:214-15 for more details on Iroquois styles of canoe, and their characteristics.)
18 With acknowledgement to Alika Webber (1978:57-61). The author wishes to emphasize here that there is no suggestion meant that such designs were necessarily universally read and understood; however, the roots of the symbolism could well be elucidated by tribal shamans in the mythological terms described.
19 In recording Chippewa language, vowels are indicated as: a, as pronounced in father; e, as in they; ĕ, as in met; i, as in marine; ĭ, as in mint; o, as in note; u, as in rule; û, as in but (acknowledgement to Densmore, 1929:10).
20 The diplomacy of the Algonquians was clearly not matched by the more volatile Iroquoians. It will be recalled that the missionaries' well-intentioned but zealous thrust amongst the Huron and Iroquois led to the martyrdom of several priests.
21 Hoffman states that the *migis* may consist of any white shell; a cowrie shell was used in one tradition (Hoffman, 1891:167) and Ritzenthaler, who observed the ceremony in the 1940s, also refers to a cowrie shell, *'mikiss'* (Ritzenthaler, Trigger ed., 1978:754).
22 American Indian Workshop, Vienna, April 1989.
23 It should be emphasized here that the reference is to peoples north of Mexico. For a discussion on writing in Mesoamerica, see Brotherston (1979:15-19). The Cree writing (referred to in the Subarctic chapter) was developed by the missionary James Evans in about 1840, whilst the mixed blood Cherokee, Sequoyah, developed an alphabet in 1821.
    Both developments, however, appear to have had their inspiration from European, rather than indigenous American, roots.
24 Observations on the League of the Iroquois, Palmer, 1949:102–3.

BIBLIOGRAPHY

Introduction

Fagan, B. M. 1987. *The Great Journey: The Peopling of Ancient America*. London: Thames and Hudson.
MacNeish, R. F. 1986. The Preceramic of Middle America. *Advances in World Archaeology*, vol.5, 93-130.
Martin P. S. 1973. The Discovery of America. *Science*, vol.179, 969-74.
Martin, P. S. and R. Klein 1974. *A Pleistocene Revolution*. Tucson: University of Arizona Press.
Turner, C. 1984. Advances in the Dental Search for Native American Origins. *Acta Anthropogenetica*, vol.8 (1&2), 23-78.
Williams, R. C. et al. 1985. Gm allotypes in Native Americans: Evidence for Three Distinct Migrations Across the Bering Land Bridge, *American Journal of Physical Anthropology*, vol.66, 1-19.

The Southeast

Note: This short list is intended to guide the reader to four invaluable sources of information on southeastern Indians.

Fagan, Brian M. 1991. *Ancient North America: The Archeology of a Continent*. New York: Thames and Hudson.
Hudson, Charles. 1976. *The Southeastern Indians*. Knoxville: University of Tennessee Press.
Smith, Marvin T. 1987. *Archeology of Aboriginal Culture Change in the Interior Southeast: Depopulation during the Early Historic Period*. (Ripley P. Bullen Monographs in Anthropology and History Number 6.) Gainesville: University Presses of Florida.
Swanton, John R. 1946. *The Indians of the Southeastern United States. Bureau of American Ethnology Bulletin 137*, Smithsonian Institution. Washington, D.C.: U.S. Government Printing Office. [Reprinted 1979 by Smithsonian Institution Press.]

The Southwest

Bahti, Tom 1968. *Southwestern Indian Tribes*. Flagstaff: KC Publication.
Baldwin, Gordon 1965. *The Warrior Apaches*. Globe: Dale Stewart King.
Ball, Eve 1970. *In the Days of Victorio*. Tucson: University of Arizona Press.
Bunzel, Ruth 1932. Introduction to Zuni Ceremonialism, Zuni Kachinas, Zuni Ritual Poetry, Zuni Prayers. *47th Annual Report of the Bureau of American Ethnology*. Washington D.C.: Government Printing Office.
Collier, John 1947. *Indians of the Americas*. New York: W.W. Norton and Company.
Dobyns, Henry F. and Robert C. Euler 1971. *The Havasupai People*. Phoenix: Indian Tribal Series.
Dutton, Bertha 1975. *Indians of the American Southwest*. Englewood Cliffs, New Jersey: Prentice-Hall.
Eggan, Fred 1950. *Social Organization of the Western Pueblos*. Chicago: University of Chicago Press.
Euler, Robert C. 1972. *The Paiute People*. Phoenix: Indian Tribal Series.
Goodwin, Grenville 1942. *The Social Organization of the Western Apache*. Chicago: University of Chicago Press.
Hewett, Edgar Lee and Bertha P. Dutton 1945. *The Pueblo Indian World*. Albuquerque: University of New Mexico Press.
Hoijer, Harry 1938. *Chiricahua and Mescalero Apache Texts*. Chicago: University of Chicago Press.
James, Harry C. 1956. *The Hopi Indians*. Caldwell, Idaho: The Caxton Press.
Johnston, Bernice 1970. *Speaking of Indians*. Tucson: University of Arizona Press.
Kluckhohn, Clyde and Dorothea Leighton 1962. *The Navajo*. Garden City, New York: Doubleday and Co.
Lumholtz, Carl 1902. *Unknown Mexico*. New York: Charles Scribner's Sons.
Lurie, Nancy O. and Stuart Levine eds 1968. *The American Indian Today*. Deland, Florida: Everett/Edwards.
Matthews, Washington 1897. *Navaho Legends*. New York: American Folklore Society.
Opler, Morris E. 1938. *Mescalero and Apache Texts*. New York: Memoirs of the American Folklore Society, vol.31.
Opler, Morris E. 1941. *An Apache Way of Life*. Chicago: University of Chicago Press.
Ortiz, Alfonso 1969. *The Tewa World*. Chicago: University of Chicago Press.
Ortiz, Alfonso ed. 1979. *Handbook of North American Indians*, vols 9 and 10, *Southwest*. Smithsonian Institution, Washington, D.C.
Parsons, Elsie Clews 1925. *The Pueblo of Jemez*. Andover, Mass: Phillips Academy.
Reichard, Gladys A. 1963. *Navajo Religion*. New York: Pantheon Books.
Smith, Anne 1965. *New Mexico Indians Today*. Santa Fe: Museum of New Mexico.
Sonnichsen, C. L. 1958. *The Mescalero Apaches*. Norman, Oklahoma: University of Oklahoma Press.
Spicer, Edward 1962. *Cycles of Conquest: The Impact of Spain, Mexico, and the United States on the Indians of the Southwest, 1533-1960*. Tucson: University of Arizona Press.
Spier, Leslie 1928. *Havasupai Ethnography*. New York: American Museum of Natural History.
Underhill, Ruth M. 1938. *Singing for Power*. Berkeley: University of California Press.
Weaver, Thomas ed. 1974. *Indians of Arizona. A Contemporary Perspective*. Tucson: University of Arizona Press.
White, Leslie A. 1935. *The Pueblo of Santo Domingo, New Mexico*. Memoirs of the American Anthropological Association, no.43.

The Plains

Bell, W. 1869. *New Tracks in North America*. London.
Bourke, Capt. John G. 1890. *Mackenzie's Last Fight With The Cheyennes*. Governor's Island, N.Y.H. (Reprint The Old Army Press, Bellevue. Nebraska. 1970.)
Brasser, Ted J. 1982. The Tipi as an Element in the Emergence of Historic Plains Indian Nomadism. In *Plain's Anthropologist*, vol. 27, no. 98. Lincoln, Nebraska.
Brasser, Ted J. 1987. By The Power of their Dreams, in *The Spirit Sings*. Toronto: McClelland and Stewart.
Butler, Colonel W. F. 1891. *The Great Lone Land*. London: Sampson Low, Marston & Company.
Carver, Jonathan 1976. *The Journals of Jonathan Carver and Related Documents 1766-1770*. Edited by John Parker. St. Paul, Minnesota: Minnesota Historical Society Press.
Catlin, George 1926. *The North American Indians*. 2 vols. Edinburgh:

John Grant.
Dempsey, Hugh A. 1972. *Crowfoot, Chief of the Blackfeet*. Norman, Oklahoma: University of Oklahoma Press.
Dodge, R. I. 1876. *Hunting Grounds of the Great West*. London: Chatto and Windus (reprinted 1976).
Hassrick, Royal B. 1964. *The Sioux. Life and Customs of a Warrior Society*. Norman, Oklahoma: University of Oklahoma Press.
Hughes, Thomas 1909. History of Blue Earth County, in *Minnesota Historical Society Collections*, vol.XII.
Johnson, Barry C. 1989.'A Captain of Chivalric Courage': Thomas H. French, 7th Cavalry. The Brand Book, vol.25. nos 1 & 2. 1987/88. London: The English Westerners' Society.
Kroeber, Alfred L. 1939 Cultural and Natural Areas of Native North America. *Publ. Amer. Archaeol. and Ethnol*. vol.38. University of California.
Laubin, Reginald and Gladys 1957. *The Indian Tipi*. 'Norman, Oklahoma: University of Oklahoma Press.
Lavender, David 1965. *The American West*. Harmondsworth, Middlesex: Penguin Books.
Lewis, Oscar 1942. The Effects of White Contact Upon Blackfoot Culture. Centennial Anniversary Publication, American Ethnological Society 1842-1942, University of Washington Press, Seattle.
Mackenzie, Charles 1889. *The Mississouri Indians. A Narrative of Four Trading Expeditions to the Mississouri 1804-1805-1806*, in Masson, 1889, vol.I.
Masson, L. R. ed. 1889. *Les Bourgeois de la Compagnie du Nord-Ouest*, vol.I.
McCann, Lloyd E. 1956. The Grattan Massacre. Reprint from *Nebraska History*, vol.XXXVII, no.1, March 1956.
McDonald, J. Douglas, A. L. McDonald, Bill Tallbull and Ted Risingsun 1989. The Cheyenne Outbreak Revisited: The Employment of Archaeological Methodology in the Substantiation of Oral History. *Plains Anthropologist*, vol.34, no.125: 265-9. Lincoln, Nebraska.
Miles, N. A. 1896. *Personal Recollections and Observations of General Nelson A. Miles*. Chicago and New York.
Neihardt, John G. 1932. *Black Elk Speaks*. New York: William Morrow.
Nye, Wilbur Sturtevant 1968. *Plains Indian Raiders*. Norman, Oklahoma: University of Oklahoma Press.
Pakes, Fraser J. 1989. *Making War Attractive*. The Brand Book, The English Westerners' Society, vol.26, no.2, London.
Smith, DeCost 1943. *Indian Experiences*. Caldwell, Idaho: The Caxton Printers.
Smith, Rex Alan 1975. *Moon of Popping Trees: The Tragedy at Wounded Knee and the End of the Indian Wars*. Lincoln: University of Nebraska Press.
Swanton, John R. 1952. *The Indian Tribes of North America*. Bulletin 45, Bureau of American Ethnology, Smithsonian Institution, Washington, D.C.
Taunton, Francis B. 1977. *Sufficient Reason?* Special Publication No.5, The English Westerners' Society, London.
Taunton, Francis B. 1986. *Custer's Field: 'A Scene of Sickening Ghastly Horror'*. In collaboration with Brian C. Pohanka. The Johnson-Taunton Military Press, London.
Taylor, Colin 1975. *The Warriors of the Plains*. London: Hamlyn.
Taylor, Colin 1980. *Ho, For The Great West!* Title Essay in The Silver Jubilee Publication of the English Westerners' Society, London. Edited by Barry C. Johnson.
Taylor, Colin 1981. *Crow Rendezvous: The Place of the River & Mountain Crow in the Material Culture Patterns of the Plateau & Central Plains circa 1800-1807*. American Indian Studies Series No.1, English Westerners' Society, London.
Taylor, Colin 1984. *Crow Rendezvous*, in *Crow Indian Art*. Edited by D. and R. Lessard. Mission, S. Dakota: Chandler Institute.
Thompson, David 1916. *David Thompson's Narrative of His Explorations in Western America, 1784-1812*. Edited by Joseph Burr Tyrell. The Champlain Society Publications, vol.12, Toronto.
Utley, Robert M. 1963. *The Last Days of the Sioux Nation*. New Haven: Yale University Press.
Utley, Robert M. 1967. *Frontiersmen in Blue: The United States Army and the Indian, 1848-1865*. New York: Macmillan.
Utley, Robert M. 1973. *Bluecoats and Redskins: The United States Army and the Indian 1866-1891*. London: Cassell.
Vestal, Stanley 1948. *Warpath and Council Fire*. Norman, Oklahoma: University of Oklahoma Press.
Vestal, Stanley 1957. *Sitting Bull: Champion of the Sioux*. Norman, Oklahoma: University of Oklahoma Press.
Wallace, Ernest and E. Adamson, Hoebel 1952. *The Comanches: Lords of the South Plains*. Norman, Oklahoma: University of Oklahoma Press.
Wissler, Clark 1904 Decorative Art of the Sioux Indians. *American Museum of Natural History*, vol.XVIII, New York.
Wissler, Clark and D. C. Duvall 1908. Mythology of the Blackfoot Indians. *Anthropological Papers of the American Museum of Natural History*, vol.II, New York.

Plateau and Basin

Brady, Cyrus Townsend 1916. *Northwestern Fights and Fighters*.New York: Doubleday, Page.
Brown, Mark H. 1967. *The Flight of the Nez Perce: A History of the Nez Perce War*. New York: Putnam's Sons.
D'Azevedo, Warren L. ed. 1986. *Great Basin*. Vol.11 of *Handbook of North American Indians*. Smithsonian Institution, Washington, D.C.
De Smet, Pierre Jean 1905. *Life, Letters, and Travels of Father Pierre-Jean De Smet*. Edited by Hiram M. Chittenden and Alfred T. Richardson. 4 vols. New York: F. P. Harper.
Ewers, John C. 1955 The Horse in Blackfoot Indian Culture. *Bureau of American Ethnology Bulletin 159*. Smithsonian Institution, Washington, D.C.
Fletcher, Robert S. 1930. The Spalding-Allen Indian Collection. Reprint from *The Oberlin Alumni Magazine*, Oberlin, Ohio.
Fowler, Catherine S. 1986. Subsistence, in *Handbook of North American Indians*, vol.11, *Great Basin*: 64-97.Edited by Warren L. Azevedo. Smithsonian Institution, Washington, D.C.
Garcia, Andrew 1977. *Tough Trip Through Paradise*. Edited by Bennett H. Stein. London: Abacus, Sphere Books.
Harper, Kimball T. 1986. Historical Environments, in *Handbook of North American Indians*, vol.11, *Great Basin*: 51-63. Edited by Warren L. Azevedo. Smithsonian Institution, Washington, D.C.
Henry, Alexander and David Thompson 1897. *New Light on the Early History of the Greater Northwest. The Manuscript Journals of Alexander Henry and David Thompson 1799-1814*. Edited by Elliott Coues. 3 vols. New York.
Hultkrantz, Åke 1968. Shoshoni Indians on the Plains: An Appraisal of the Documentary Evidence. Sonderdruck: Zeitschrift für Ethnologie, Band 93, Heft 1 u.2, Braunschweig.

Hultkrantz, Åke 1986. The Peril of Visions: Changes of Vision Patterns Among the Wind River Shoshoni, in *History of Religions*, vol.26, no.1. Chicago: University of Chicago Press.
Lewis, Meriwether and William Clark 1893. *The History of the Lewis and Clark Expedition*. Edited by Elliott Coues. 3 vols. New York: Dover (reprint).
Lowie, Robert H. 1909. *The Northern Shoshoni. Anthropological Papers*, vol.II, part 2. American Museum of Natural History, New York.
McWhorter, L. V. 1940. *Yellow Wolf: His Own Story*. Caldwell, Idaho: The Caxton Printers Ltd.
Mooney, James 1896. The Ghost-Dance Religion and the Sioux Outbreak of 1890. *14th Annual Report of the Bureau of American Ethnology to the Smithsonian Institution 1892-3*, Washington D.C. New York: Dover (reprint 1973).
Ross, Alexander 1855. *The Fur Hunters of the Far West: A Narrative of Adventure in the Oregon and Rocky Mountains*. 2 vols. London: Smith, Elder.
Shawley, Stephen Douglas 1974. *Nez Perce Dress: A Study in Culture Change*. University of Idaho.
Spinden, Herbert Joseph 1908. The Nez Percé Indians. *Memoirs of the American Anthropological Association*, vol.II, part 3. Millwood, New York: Kraus Reprint Co. (1974).
Teit, James A. 1930. The Salishan Tribes of the Western Plateaus. Edited by Franz Boas. Extract from *45th Annual Report of the Bureau of American Ethnology to the Smithsonian Institution*, Washington, D. C.
Trenholm, Virginia Cole and Maurine Carley 1964. *The Shoshonis: Sentinels of the Rockies*. Norman, Oklahoma: University of Oklahoma Press.
Wildschut, William 1959. *Crow Indian Beadwork*. Edited by J. C. Ewers. Museum of the American Indian, Heye Foundation, New York.
Wissler, Clark 1910. Material Culture of the Blackfoot Indians. *Anthropological Papers of the American Museum of Natural History*, vol.V, part 1, New York.
Wissler, Clark 1915. Costumes of the Plains Indians. *American Museum of Natural History*, vol.XVII, New York.
Wood, C. E. S. 1884. Chief Joseph, The Nez-Percé. *The Century Magazine*, VI. New York.

California

Bannon, Francis ed. 1974. *Bolton and the Spanish Borderlands*. Norman: University of Oklahoma Press.
Bolton, Herbert E. ed. 1976. *Historical Memoirs of New California by Fray Francisco Palou, O.F.M.* 4 vols. Berkeley: University of California Press.
Burnett, E. K. 1944. *Inlaid Stone and Bone Artifacts from Southern California*. New York: Museum of the American Indian, Heye Foundation.
Casebier, Dennis G. 1972a. *The Battle at Camp Cady*. Norco, CA: Dennis G. Casebier.
Casebier, Dennis G. 1972b. *Carleton's Pah-Ute Campaign*. Norco, CA: Dennis G. Casebier.
Chartkoff, Joseph L. and Kerry Kona Chartkoff 1984. *The Archeology of California*. Stanford: Stanford University Press.
Clark, Cora and Texa Bowen Williams 1954. *Pomo Indian Myths*. New York: Vantage Press.
Cook, Sherburn F. 1976a. *The Conflict Between the California Indians and White Civilization*. Berkeley: University of California Press.
Cook, Sherburn F. 1976. *The Population of the California Indians, 1769-1870*. Berkeley: University of California Press.
Crampton, C. Gregory ed. 1975. *The Mariposa Indian War 1850-1851. Diaries of Robert Eccleston: The California Gold Rush, Yosemite, High Sierra*. Salt Lake City: University of Utah Press.
Cullin, Stewart 1975. *Games of the North American Indians*. New York: Dover Publications, Inc.
Davis, James T. 1974. *Trade Routes and Economic Exchange Among the Indians of California*. Ramona, CA: Ballena Press.
Edwards, Malcolm ed. 1970. *The California Diary of E. D. Townsend*. N.P.: The Ward Ritchie Press.
Federal Writers' Project 1943. *California: A Guide to the Golden State*. New York: Mabel R. Gillis.
Geiger, Maynard and Clement W. Meighan 1976. *As the Padres Saw Them: California Indian Life and Customs as Reported by the Franciscan Missionaries 1813-1815*. Santa Barbara: Santa Barbara Missions Archives.
Heizer, R. F. and M. A. Whipple comp. and ed. 1971. *The California Indians: A Source Book*. Berkeley: University of California.
Heizer, Robert F. ed. 1974. *The Destruction of the California Indians*. Santa Barbara and Salt Lake City: Peregrine Smith, Inc.
Heizer, Robert F. ed. 1978. *Handbook of North American Indians*. Vol. VIII *California*. Washington, D.C.: Smithsonian Institution.
Heizer, Robert F. and Adan E. Treganza 1972. *Mines and Quarries of the Indians of California*. Ramona, CA: Ballena Press.
Kroeber, A. L. 1970. *Handbook of the Indians of California*. Berkeley: California Book Company Ltd.
Kroeber, Theodora 1961. *Ishi in Two Worlds*. Berkeley: University of California Press.
Lang, Kathryn M. 1979. *Golden Gate National Recreation Area: The Indian and Hispanic Heritage of a Modern Urban Park*. San Francisco: Golden Gate National Recreation Area, National Park Service.
Mason, Tufton 1976. *Aboriginal American Indian Basketry*. Santa Barbara: Peregrine Smith, Inc.
Members of the Potomac Corral of the Westerners 1966. *Great Western Indian Fights*. Lincoln: University of Nebraska Press.
Merrill, Ruth E. 1980. *Plants Used in Basketry by the California Indians*. Ramona, CA: Acoma Books.
Reid, Hugo 1926. *The Indians of Los Angeles County*. Los Angeles: privately printed.
Rolle, Andrew F. and John S. Gaines 1979. *The Golden State: A History of California*. Arlington Heights, IL: AHM Publishing Corporation.
Thompson, Erwin N. 1971. *Modoc War: Its Military History & Topography*. Sacramento: Argus Books.
Tuska, Jon and Vicki Pierkaski 1983. *Encyclopedia of Frontier and Western Fiction*. New York: McGraw-Hill.
Utley, Robert M. 1984. *The Indian Frontier of the American West 1846-1890*. Albuquerque: University of New Mexico Press.
Wax, Murray L. 1971. *Indian Americans Unity and Diversity*. Englewood Cliffs, NJ: Prentice-Hall.
Webb, Edith Buckland 1952. *Indian Life at the Old Missions*. Los Angeles: Warren F. Lewis.
Wissler, Clark 1966. *Indians of the United States*. Garden City, NY: Anchor Books.

The Northwest Coast

Bancroft-Hunt, Norman and Werner Forman 1979. *People of the Totem:*

The Indians of the Pacific Northwest. New York: Putnam's Sons.
Brown, Steve. From Taquan to Klukwan: Tracing the Work of an Early Tlingit Master Artist, p. 173, in Peter L. Corey, ed., Faces, Voices and Dreams: A Celebration of the Centennial of the Sheldon Jackson Museum. Seattle: Division of Alaska State Museums and Friends of the Alaska State Museum, 1987.
Carlson, Roy L. ed. 1976. Indian Art Traditions of the Northwest Coast. Burnaby: Simon Fraser University Archeology Press.
Cole, Douglas 1985. Captured Heritage: The Scramble for Northwest Coast Artifacts. Vancouver: Douglas & McIntyre.
Cole, Douglas and Ira Chaikin 1990. An Iron Hand upon the People: The Law against the Potlatch on the Northwest Coast. Vancouver: Douglas & McIntyre.
Cook, Warren L. 1973. Flood Tide of Empire: Spain and the Pacific Northwest, 1543-1819. New Haven: Yale University Press.
Duff, Wilson 1964. The Indian History of British Columbia, Volume 1: The Impact of the White Man. Anthropology in British Columbia, Memoir No.5. Victoria: Provincial Museum of British Columbia.
Duff, Wilson 1975. Images: Stone: B.C.: Thirty Centuries of Northwest Coast Indian Sculpture. Seattle: University of Washington Press.
Fisher, Robin 1977. Contact and Conflict: Indian-European Relations in British Columbia, 1774-1890. Vancouver: University of British Columbia Press.
Fisher, Robin 1977. Missions to the Indians of British Columbia, in John Veillette and Gary White, Early Indian Village Churches: Wooden Frontier Architecture in British Columbia. Vancouver: University of British Columbia Press, pp.1-11.
Fladmark, Knut 1986. British Columbia Prehistory. Ottawa: National Museum of Man.
Gunther, Erna 1972. Indian Life on the Northwest Coast of North America as seen by the Early Explorers and Fur Traders during the Last Decades of the Eighteenth Century. Chicago: University of Chicago Press.
Gustafson, Paula 1980. Salish Weaving. Vancouver: Douglas & McIntyre.
Halliday, W. M. 1935. Potlatch and Totem and the Recollections of an Indian Agent. Toronto: J. M. Dent.
Hinckley, Ted C. 1982. Alaskan John G. Brady: Missionary, Businessman, Judge, and Governor, 1878-1918. Ohio State University Press.
Holm, Bill 1965. Northwest Coast Indian Art: An Analysis of Form. Seattle: University of Washington Press.
Holm, Bill 1983. Smoky-Top: The Art and Times of Willie Seaweed. Seattle: University of Washington Press.
Holm, Bill 1987. Spirit and Ancestor: A Century of Northwest Coast Indian Art at the Burke Museum. Thomas Burke Memorial Washington State Museum Monograph 4. Seattle: Burke Museum and University of Washington Press.
Holmberg, Heinrich Johan 1985. Holberg's Ethnographic Sketches, edited by Marwin W. Falk and translated by Fritz Jaensch. Fairbanks, Alaska: University of Alaska Press.
Hou, Charles undated. To Potlatch or Not to Potlatch: An In-Depth Study of Culture-Conflict Between the B.C. Coastal Indian and the White Man. Vancouver: British Columbia Teachers' Federation.
Jackson, Sheldon. Alaska, and Missions on the North Pacific Coast. New York: Dodd, Mead.
Jonaitis, Aldona 1986. Art of the Northern Tlingit. Seattle: University of Washington Press.
Knight, Rolf 1978. Indians At Work: An Informal History of Native Indian Labour in British Columbia, 1858-1930. Vancouver: New Star Books.
Laguna, Frederica de 1972. Under Mt. Saint Alias. Washington, D.C.: U.S. Government Printing Office.
LaViolette, Forrest E. 1973. The Struggle for Survival: Indian Cultures and the Protestant Ethic in British Columbia. Toronto: University of Toronto Press.
Lobb, Allan 1990. Indian Baskets of The Pacific Northwest and Alaska. Portland: Graphic Arts Center Publishing Company.
MacDonald, George F. and Richard I. Inglis 1976. The Dig: An Archeological Reconstruction of a West Coast Village. Ottawa: National Museum of Man.
Macnair, Peter L. et al 1984. The Legacy: Tradition and Innovation in Northwest Coast Indian Art. Vancouver: Douglas & McIntyre.
Pethick, First Approaches to the Northwest Coast.
Samuel, Cheryl 1982. The Chilkat Dancing Blanket. Seattle: Pacific Search Press.
Sewid-Smith, Daisy 1979. Prosecution or Persecution. Nu-Yum-Baleess Society.
Stewart, Hilary 1973. Artifacts of the Northwest Coast. Vancouver: Hancock House Publishers.
Stewart, Hilary 1977. Indian Fishing: Early Methods on the Northwest Coast. Vancouver: Douglas & McIntyre.
Stewart, Hilary 1979. Looking at Indian Art of the Northwest Coast. Seattle: University of Washington Press.
Stewart, Hilary 1984. Cedar: Tree of Life to the Northwest Coast Indians. Vancouver: Douglas & McIntyre.
Tennant, Paul 1990. Aboriginal Peoples and Politics: The Indian Land Question in British Columbia, 1849-1989. Vancouver: University of British Columbia Press.
Vaughan, Thomas and Bill Holm 1982. Soft Gold: The Fur Trade and Cultural Exchange on the Northwest Coast. Portland: Oregon Historical Society.
Wyatt, Victoria 1984. Shapes of Their Thoughts: Reflections of Culture Contact on the Northwest Coast. New Haven: Yale Peabody Museum of Natural History and University of Oklahoma Press.
Wyatt, Victoria Alaskan Indian Wage Earners in the 19th Century: Economic Choices and Ethnic Identity of Southeast Alaska's Frontier. Pacific Northwest Quarterly 78(1-2):43-9.

The Subarctic

Boudreau, Norman J. ed. 1974. The Athapaskans: Strangers of the North. National Museum of Man, Ottawa.
Bourque, Jim 1986. This Land Is Our Life. Government of the Northwest Territories, Yellowknife, NWT.
Brasser, Ted J. 1976. Bo'jou, Neejee!. National Museum of Man, Ottawa.
Brody, Hugh 1990. Hunters and Bombers, in The Independent, 30 June 1990.
Cameron, Agnes D. 1912. The New North. New York: Appleton and Company.
Cory, Harper 1935. Grey Owl and the Beaver. London: Thomas Nelson.
Dickason, Olive Patricia 1972. Indian Arts in Canada. Department of Indian Affairs and Northern Development, Ottawa.
Dickson, Lovat 1973. Wilderness Man: The Strange Story of Grey Owl. Toronto: Macmillan.
Duncan, Kate C. 1989. Northern Athapaskan Art: A Beadwork Tradition. Seattle: University of Washington Press.
Duncan, Kate C. and Eunice Carney 1988. A Special Gift: The Kutchin Beadwork Tradition. Seattle: University of Washington Press.
Godsell, Philip H. 1935. Arctic Trader. London: Putnam.
Godsell, Philip H. 1938. Red Hunters of the Snows. London: Robert Hale.

Grey Owl (Wa-Sha-Quon-Asin) 1935. Pilgrims of the Wild. London, Lovat Dickson.
Hail, Barbara A. and Kate C. Duncan 1989. Out of the North: The Subarctic Collection of the Haffenreffer Museum of Anthrolpology. Brown University, Bristol, Rhode Island.
Hatt, Gudmund 1969. Arctic Skin Clothing in Eurasia and America: An Ethnographic Study. Arctic Anthropology, vol.V, no.2. University of Wisconsin Press.
Hearne, Samuel 1958. A Journey from Prince of Wales's Fort in Hudson's Bay to the Northern Ocean in the Years 1769, 1770, 1771, and 1772. Edited by R. Glover. Toronto: Macmillan.
Helm, June ed. 1981 Subarctic. Vol.6 of Handbook of North American Indians. Smithsonian Institution, Washington, D.C.
Honigmann, John J. 1981. Expressive Aspects of Subarctic Indian Culture, in Handbook of North American Indians, vol.6, Subarctic: 718-38. Edited by June Helm. Smithsonian Institution, Washington, D.C.
Hosley, Edward H. 1981. Intercultural Relations and Cultural Change in the Alaska Plateau, in Handbook of North American Indians, vol.6, Subarctic 546-55. Edited by June Helm. Smithsonian Institution, Washington, D.C.
Hubbard, Mrs Leonidas, Junior 1908. A Woman's Way Through Unknown Labrador. London: John Murray.
Irving, Susan et al. 1985 Trapline Lifeline/Sur La Piste Des Trappeurs. Prince of Wales Northern Heritage Centre. Northwest Territories Culture and Communications.
Kerr, Robert 1953. For the Royal Scottish Museum, in The Beaver: A Magazine of the North. Outfit 284, June 1953. Hudson's Bay Company, Winnipeg.
Murray, Alexander Hunter 1910. Journal of the Yukon 1847-48. Edited and annotated by L. J. Burpee. Publications of the Canadian Archives, no.4. Government Printing Bureau, Ottawa.
Orchard, William C. 1916. The Technique of Porcupine Quill Decoration Among the Indians of North America. Museum of the American Indian, Heye Foundation, New York (reprint 1971).
Rogers, Edward S. and Eleanor Leacock 1981. Montagnais-Naskapi, in Handbook of North American Indians, vol.6, Subarctic: 169-89. Edited by June Helm. Smithsonian Institution, Washington, D.C.
Rogers, Edward S. and James G. E. Smith 1981. Environment and Culture n the Shield and Mackenzie Borderlands, in Handbook of North American Indians, vol.6, Subarctic: 130-45. Edited by June Helm. Smithsonian Institution, Washington, D.C.
Skinner, Alanson 1911. Notes on the Eastern Cree and Northern Saulteaux. Edited by Clark Wissler. Anthropological Papers of the American Museum of Natural History, vol.IX (1912) New York.
Smith, Donald B. 1990. From the Land of Shadows: The Making of Grey Owl. Western Producer Prairie Books, Saskatoon, Saskatchewan.
Smith, James G. E. 1978. Economic Uncertainty in an 'Original Affluent Society': Caribou and Caribou Eater Chipewyan Adaptive Strategies. Arctic Anthropology, vol.XV, no.1., University of Wisconsin Press.
Smith, James G. E. 1981. Chipewyan, in Handbook of North American Indians, vol.6, Subarctic: 271-84. Edited by June Helm. Smithsonian Institution, Washington, D.C.
Speck, Frank G. 1925. Central Eskimo and Indian Dot Ornamentation. Indian Notes, vol.2, no. 3. Museum of the American Indian, Heye Foundation, New York.
Speck, Frank G. 1930. Mistassini Notes. Indian Notes, vol.7, no. 4. Museum of the American Indian, Heye Foundation, New York.
Speyer, Arthur 1968. Indianer Nordamerikas 1760-1860. Deutschen Ledermuseum-Deutsches Schuhmuseum, Offenbach.
Thompson, Judy 1983. Turn-of-the-Century Métis Decorative Art from the Frederick Bell Collection, in American Indian Art, Autumn 1983, Scottsdale, Arizona.
Thompson, Judy 1987. No Little Variety of Ornament: Northern Athapaskan Artistic Traditions, in The Spirit Sings. Toronto: McClelland and Stewart.
Turner, Geoffrey 1955. Hair Embroidery in Siberia and North America. Pitt Rivers Museum, University of Oxford, Oxford.
VanStone, James W. 1981. Athapaskan Clothing and Related Objects in the Collections of the Field Museum of Natural History. Fieldiana Anthropology, New Series no.4. Field Museum, Chicago.
Webber, Alika Podolinsky 1983. Ceremonial Robes of the Montagnais-Naskapi, in American Indian Art, Winter 1983, Scottsdale, Arizona.
Webber, Alika Podolinksy 1989. North American Indian and Eskimo Footwear: A Typology and Glossary. The Bata Shoe Museum Foundation, Toronto.

The Arctic

Bergsland, Knut and Moses L. Dirks, eds 1990. Aleut Tales and Narratives Collected by W. Jochelson. Fairbanks, Alaska: Alaska Native Language Center.
Black, Lydia T. 1980. Early History, in Morgan, Lael ed. Alaska Geographic – The Aleutians, vol.7(3): 82-105.
Black, Lydia T. 1983. Some Problems in the Interpretation of Aleut Prehistory. Arctic Anthropology, vol.20(1): 49-78.
Black, Lydia T. 1984. Atka: An Ethnohistory of the Western Aleutians. Kingston, Ontario: The Limestone Press.
Black, Lydia T. 1988. The Story of Russian America, in Fitzhugh, William W. and Aron Crowell. Crossroads of Continents: Cultures of Siberia and Alaska. Washington, D.C.: Smithsonian Institution Press, 70-82.
Black, Lydia T. and R. G. Liapunova 1988. Aleut: Islanders of the North Pacific, in Fitzhugh, William W. and Aron Crowell. Crossroads of Continents: Cultures of Siberia and Alaska. Washington, D.C.: Smithsonian Institution Press, 52-7.
Brody, Hugh 1987. Living Arctic: Hunters of the Canadian North. Vancouver: Douglas & McIntyre.
Chaussonnet, Valerie 1988. Needles and Animals: Women's Magic, in Fitzhugh, William W. and Aron Crowell. Crossroads of Continents: Cultures of Siberia and Alaska. Washington, D.C.: Smithsonian Institution Press, 209-26.
Collins, Henry B. Jr 1945 The Islands and their People, in Collins, Henry B. Jr., Austin B. Clark and Egbert H. Walker. The Aleutian Islands: Their People and Natural History. Washington, D.C.: Smithsonian Institution Press.
Colombo, John Robert ed. 1981 Poems of the Inuit. Ottawa: Oberon.
Comer, George 1906. Whaling in Hudson Bay, with notes on Southampton Island. Boas Anniversary Volume: Anthropological Papers Written in Honor of Franz Boas, New York: G. E. Stewart, 475-84.
Damas, David 1963. Igluligmiut Kinship and Local Groupings: A Structural Approach. Anthropological Series 64, National Museums of Canada Bulletin, 196.
Dumond, Don E. 1984. Prehistory: Summary, Handbook of North American Indians, vol.5, Arctic: 72-9. Edited by David Damas. Smithsonian Institution, Washington, D.C.
Dyson, George 1986. Baidarka. Edmonds, Washington: Alaska

Northwest Publishing Company.
Eber, Dorothy, H. 1989. When Whalers were up North: Inuit Memories from the Eastern Arctic. Kingston, Ontario: McGill-Queen's University Press.
Fienup-Riordan, Ann 1988. Eye of the Dance: Spiritual Life of the Bering Sea Eskimo, in Fitzhugh, William W. and Aron Crowell. Crossroads of Continents: Cultures of Siberia and Alaska. Washington, D.C.: Smithsonian Institution Press, 256-70.
Fitzhugh, William W. and Susan A. Kaplan 1982. Inua: Spirit World of the Bering Sea Eskimo. Washington: Smithsonian Institution Press.
Freuchen, Peter 1961. Peter Freuchen's Book of the Eskimos. Cleveland, Ohio: The World Publishing Company.
Guemple, D. Lee 1961. Inuit Spouse Exchange. Chicago: Department of Anthropology, University of Chicago.
Hansen, Craig A. 1982. Exploration and Development, in Henning, Robert A. ed. Alaska Geographic – Islands of the Seals: The Pribilofs, vol.9(3): 75-85.
Heath, John D. 1987. Baidarka Bow Variations, in Corey, Peter L. Faces, Voices and Dreams: A Celebration of the Centennial of the Sheldon Jackson Museum. Juneau, Alaska: Division of Alaska State Museums, 93-6.
Houston, James 1972. Songs of the Dream People: Chants and Images from the Indians and Eskimos of North America. Toronto: Longman Canada Ltd.
Hudson, Raymond L. 1987. Designs in Aleut Basketry, in Corey, Peter L. Faces, Voices and Dreams: A Celebration of the Centennial of the Sheldon Jackson Museum. Juneau, Alaska: Division of Alaska State Museums, 63-92.
Hughes, Charles C. 1984. Siberian Eskimo, in Handbook of North American Indians, vol.5, Arctic: 247-61. Edited by David Damas. Smithsonian Institution, Washington, D.C.
Jochelson, Waldemar 1968. History, Ethnology and Anthropology of the Aleut. Oosterhout, The Netherlands: Anthropological Publications.
Kan, Sergei 1988. The Russian Orthodox Church in Alaska, in Handbook of North American Indians, vol.4, History of Indian-White Relations: 506-21. Edited by Wilcomb E. Washburn. Smithsonian Institution, Washington, D.C.
Krauss, Michael E. 1988. Many Tongues – Ancient Tales, in Fitzhugh, William W. and Aron Crowell. Crossroads of Continents: Cultures of Siberia and Alaska. Washington, D.C.: Smithsonian Institution Press, 145-50.
Lantis, Margaret 1970. The Aleut Social System, 1750-1810, from Early Historical Sources, in Lantis, Margaret ed. Ethnohistory in Southwestern Alaska and the Southern Yukon: Method and Content. Lexington, Kentucky: University Press of Kentucky.
Lantis, Margaret 1984. Aleut, in Handbook of North American Indians, vol.5, Arctic: 161-84. Edited by David Damas. Smithsonian Institution, Washington, D.C.
Laughlin, William S. 1980. Aleuts: Survivors of the Bering Land Bridge. New York: Holt, Rinehart and Winston.
Lyon, George F. 1824. The Private Journal of Captain G. F. Lyon, of H.M.S. Hecla, during the recent voyage of discovery under Captain Parry... London: John Murray.
Mary-Rousselière 1954. Issingut: The starvation camp. Eskimo, vol.33(December): 9-13.
Mary-Rousselière, Guy 1984. Iglulik, in Handbook of North American Indians, vol.5, Arctic: 431-46. Edited by David Damas. Smithsonian Institution, Washington, D.C.
Mather, Elsie 1985. Cauyarnariuq. Bethel, Alaska: Lower Kuskokwim School District Bilingual-Bicultural Department.
Mathiassen, Therkel 1928. Material Culture of the Iglulik Eskimos. Report of the Fifth Thule Expedition 1921-24, vol.6(1). Copenhagen: Gyldendalske Boghandel.
McCartney, Allen P. 1984. Prehistory of the Aleutian Region, in Handbook of North American Indians, vol.5, Arctic 119-35. Edited by David Damas. Smithsonian Institution, Washington, D.C.
Merck, Carl Heinrich 1980. Siberia and Northwestern America 1788-1792: The Journal of Carl Heinrich Merck, Naturalist with the Russian Scientific Expedition led by Captains Joseph Billings and Gavrill Sarychev. Kingston, Ontario: The Limestone Press.
Michael, Henry N. ed. 1967. Lieutenant Zagoskin's Travels in Russian America, 1842-44: The First Ethnographic and Geographic Investigations on the Yukon and Kuskokwim Valleys of Alaska. Anthropology of the North: Translations from Russian Sources 7. Toronto: Published for the Arctic Institute of North America by the University of Toronto Press.
Morgan, Lael ed. 1980. Alaska Geographic – The Aleutians, vol.7(3).
Morrow, Phyllis 1984. It is Time for Drumming: A Study of Recent Research on Yup'ik Ceremonialism. Etudes/Inuit/Studies, vol.8:113-40.
Nelson, Edward W. 1899. The Eskimo about Bering Strait. Washington, D.C.: Smithsonian Institution Press.
Netsvetov, Iakov 1980. The Journals of Iakov Netsvetov: The Atkha Years, 1828-44, Kingston, Ontario: The Limestone Press.
Parry, William E. 1824. Journal of a second voyage for the discovery of a Northwest Passage from the Atlantic to the Pacific: Performed in the years 1921-22-23, in his Majesty's Ships Fury and Hecla, under the orders of Captain William Edward Parry, R.N., F.R.S., and Commander of the Expedition. London: John Murray.
Pierce, Richard A. 1988. Russian and Soviet Eskimo Indian Policies, in Handbook of North American Indians, vol.4, History of Indian-White Relations: 119-27. Edited by Wilcomb E. Washburn. Smithsonian Institution, Washington, D.C.
Rasmussen 1929. Intellectual Culture of the Iglulik Eskimos. Report of the Fifth Thule Expedition, 1921-24. vol.7(1). Copenhagen: Gyldendalske Boghandel.
Robert-Lamblin, Joelle 1982. Women's Role and Power within Traditional Aleut Society. Folk, vol.24; 197-202.
Ross, W. Gillies 1975. Whaling and Eskimos: Hudson Bay 1860-1915. Publications in Ethnology no.10. Ottawa: National Museums of Canada.
Shalkop, Antoinette 1987. The Russian Orthodox Church in Alaska, in Starr, S. Frederick ed. Russia's American Colony. Durham, North Carolina: Duke University Press, 196-217.
Stager, John K. and Robert J. McSkimming 1984. Physical Environment, in Handbook of North American Indians, vol.5, Arctic: 27-35. Edited by David Damas. Smithsonian Institution, Washington, D.C.
Stefansson, Vilhjalmur 1946. Not by Bread Alone. New York: MacMillan.
Steller, Georg Wilhelm 1988. Journal of a Voyage with Bering, 1741-1742. Stanford, California: Stanford University Press.
Tennant, Edward A. and Joseph N. Bitar, eds. Yupik Lore: Oral Traditions of an Eskimo People. Bethel, Alaska: Lower Kuskokwim School District.
Turner, Christy G. II 1988. Ancient People of the North Pacific Rim, in Fitzhugh, William W. and Aron Crowell. Crossroads of Continents: Cultures of Siberia and Alaska. Washington, D.C.: Smithsonian Institution Press, 111-16.
VanStone, James W. 1967. Eskimos of the Nushagak River: An Ethnographic History. Seattle, Washington: University of Washington Press.
VanStone, James W. 1984. Mainland Southwest Alaska Eskimo, in Handbook of North American Indians, vol.5, Arctic 224-42. Edited by David Damas, Smithsonian Institution, Washington, D.C.

Veniaminov, Ivan   1984. *Notes on the Islands of the Unalashka District*. Kingston, Ontario: The Limestone Press.
Woodbury, Anthony C. ed.   1984. *Cev'armiut Qanemciit Qulirait-Ilu: Eskimo Narratives and Tales from Chevak, Alaska*. Fairbanks, Alaska: Alaska Native Language Center.
Woodbury, Anthony C.   1984. Eskimo and Aleut Languages, in *Handbook of North American Indians*, vol.5, Arctic:49-65. Edited by David Damas. Smithsonian Institution, Washington, D.C.
Yesner, David R.   1988. Effects of Prehistoric Human Exploitation on Aleutian Sea Mammal Populations. *Arctic Anthropology*, vol.25(1): 28-43.
Zimmerly, David W.   1986. *Qajaq: Kayaks of Siberia and Alaska*. Juneau, Alaska: Division of State Museums.

The Northeast

Adney, Edwin Tappan and Howard I. Chapelle   1964. *The Bark Canoes and Skin Boats of North America*. Museum of History and Technology, Smithsonian Institution, Washington, D.C.
Bedford, June et al   1985. *Mohawk Micmac Maliseet . . . and other Indian Souvenir Art from Victorian Canada*. Canada House Cultural Centre Gallery, London.
Biard, Pierre. See J.R.
Bishop, Morris   1949. *Champlain: The Life of Fortitude*. London: MacDonald.
Bock, Philip K.   1978. Micmac, in *Handbook of North American Indians*, vol.15, Northeast: 109-122. Edited by Bruce G. Trigger. Smithsonian Institution, Washington D.C.
Brotherston, Gordon   1979. *Image of the New World: The American Continent Portrayed in Native Texts*. London: Thames and Hudson.
Butler, Eva L. and Wendell S. Hadlock   1957 *Uses of Birch-Bark in the Northeast*. The Robert Abbe Museum, Bar Harbor, Maine.
Catlin, Geo.   1841. *Letters and Notes on the Manners, Customs, and Condition of the North American Indians*. 2 vols. Egyptian Hall, Piccadilly, London.
Cleland, Charles E.   1973. *Art of the Great Lakes Indians*. Flint Institute of Arts, Flint, Michigan.
Densmore, Frances   1910 & 1913. *Chippewa Music. Parts I and II*. Bureau of American Ethnology Bulletins 45 and 53. Smithsonian Institution, Washington, D.C.
Densmore, Frances   1929 *Chippewa Customs*. Bureau of American Ethnology

Bulletin 86. Smithsonian Institution, Washington, D.C.
Fenton, William N.   1978. Northern Iroquoian Culture Patterns, in *Handbook of North American Indians*, vol.15, Northeast: 296-321. Edited by Bruce G. Trigger. Smithsonian Institution, Washington, D.C.
Hilger, Sister M. Inez   1951. *Chippewa Child Life and its Cultural Background*. Bureau of American Ethnology Bulletin 146. Smithsonian Institution, Washington, D.C.
Hodge, Frederick Webb ed.   1907-10. Handbook of American Indians North of Mexico. 2 vols. Bureau of American Ethnology Bulletin 30. Smithsonian Institution, Washington, D.C.
Hodge, G. Stuart   1973 *Art of the Great Lakes Indians* (Foreword). Flint Institute of Arts, Flint, Michigan.
Hoffman, Walter J.   1891 *The Midewiwin or 'Grand Medicine Society' of the Ojibwa. 7th Annual Report of the Bureau of American Ethnology for the Years 1885-6*, Washington, D.C.
J.R. = Thwaites, Reuben G. ed.   1896-1901 *The Jesuit Relations and Allied Documents: Travel and Explorations of the Jesuit Missionaries in New France, 1610-1791*. 73 vols. Burrows Brothers, Cleveland. (Reprint: Pageant, New York, 1959.)
Kenton, Edna ed.   1954 *Black Gown and Redskins: The adventures and explorations of the first missionaries among the North American Indians*. London, New York & Toronto: Longmans, Green.
King, J. C. H.   1982. *Thunderbird and Lightning*. London: British Museum Publications Ltd.
Lyford, Carrie A.   1945. *Iroquois Crafts*. United States Indian Service, Haskell Institute, Lawrence, Kansas.
Lyford, Carrie A.   1953. *Ojibwa Crafts*. Bureau of Indian Affairs. Haskell Institute, Lawrence, Kansas.
Mallery, Garrick   1893. *Picture Writing of the American Indians*. 2 vols. 10th *Annual Report of the Bureau of American Ethnology*. Government Printing Office, Washington, D.C.
Palmer, Rose A.   1949. *The North American Indians: An Account of the American Indians North of Mexico, Compiled from the Original Sources*. vol.4 of The Smithsonian Series. Edited by Charles Greeley Abbot. New York: The Series Publishers.
Parkman, Francis   1883. *La Salle and the Discovery of the Great West*. Boston: Little, Brown.
Pelletier, Gaby (ed.)   1977 *Micmac & Maliseet Decorative Traditions*. The

New Brunswick Museum, Saint John, NB.
Phillips, Ruth B.   1989. Souvenirs from North America: The Miniature as Image of Woodlands Indian Life, in *American Indian Art*, vol.14, no. 2, Scottsdale, Arizona.
Pohrt, Richard A.   1986. Pipe Tomahawks from Michigan and the Great Lakes Area, in *Bulletin of the Detroit Institute of Arts*, vol.62, no.1, Detroit, Michigan.
Quimby, George Irving   1960. *Indian Life in the Upper Great Lakes: 11,000 B.C. to A.D.1800*. Chicago: University of Chicago Press.
Ritzenthaler, Robert E.   1953 *The Potawatomi Indians of Wisconsin*. Milwaukee Public Museum Bulletin, vol.19, no.3, Milwaukee, Wisconsin.
Ritzenthaler, Robert E.   1978. Southwestern Chippewa, in *Handbook of North American Indians*, vol.15, Northeast: 743-59. Edited by Bruce G. Trigger. Smithsonian Institution, Washington, D.C.
Ritzenthaler, Robert E. and Frederick A. Peterson   1956. *The Mexican Kickapoo Indians*. Milwaukee Public Museum Publications in Anthropology, no.2, Milwaukee, Wisconsin.
Rydén, Stig   1963. *A 17-Century Indian Head Dress from Delaware*. Ethnos 2-4. The Ethnographical Museum of Sweden, Stockholm.
Speck, Frank Gouldsmith   1945. *The Iroquois: A Study in Cultural Evolution*. Cranbrook Institute of Science. Bull.23, Bloomfield Hills, Michigan.
Strong, William Duncan   1938. *The Indian Tribes of the Chicago Region*. Field Museum of Natural History, Anthropology Leaflet 24, Chicago.
Tooker, Elisabeth   1978. The League of the Iroquois: Its History, Politics, and Ritual, in *Handbook of North American Indians*, vol.15, Northeast: 418-41. Edited by Bruce G. Trigger. Smithsonian Institution, Washington, D.C.
Trigger, Bruce G.   1969. *The Huron: Farmers of the North*. New York: Holt, Rinehart and Winston.
Trigger, Bruce G. (ed)   1978. *Northeast*. Vol.15 of *Handbook of North American Indians*. Smithsonian Institution, Washington, D.C.
Turner, Geoffrey   1955. *Hair Embroidery in Siberia and North America*. Pitt Rivers Museum, University Press, Oxford.
Webber, Alika   1978. *Wigwamatew: Old Birch Bark Containers*, in *American Indian Art*, vol.4, no.1, Scottsdale, Arizona.
Whitehead, Ruth Holmes   1982. *Micmac Quillwork*. The Nova Scotia Museum, Halifax.

CATALOG

Catalog numbers for artifacts from American Museum of Natural History, New York (AMNH), and Smithsonian Institution, Washington, D.C. (SI)

Yuchi. AMNH. Book 50.
1. 5301, 2. 5837, 3. 5307, 4. 5309, 5. 5819, 6. 6186, 7. 5805, 8. 6183, 9. 5338, 10. 5308, 11. 5312, 12. 5313, 13. 5357, 14. 5361, 15. 5364, 16. 5339, 17. 5765, 18. 5370, 19. 5372, 20. 5814, 21. 5341, 22. 5808, 23. 5343, 24. 5303, 25. 5304, 26. 5825, 27. 5812, 28. 5824, 29. 5306, 30. 5821, 31. 5314-5315, 32. 5310, 33. 5836.
Seminole. AMNH. Book 50.I.
1. 2262, 2. 2247, 3. 5922, 4. 2353, 5. 2350, 6. 2298, 7. 2310, 8. 2307, 9. 2321, 10. 2258, 11. 2322, 12. 2254, 13. 2283, 14. 2265, 15. 3848, 16. 2358, 17. 2364, 18. 2323, 19. 2276, 20. 2275, 21. 2268, 22. 2253, 23. 2263, 24. 2338, 25. 2290, 26. 2291
Cherokee. Dept of Anthropology, SI.
1. 133005, 2. 133006, 3. 130488, 4. 135180, 5. 132998, 6. 281425, 7. 130489, 8. 133008, 9. 133007, 10. 130487, 11. 135185, 12. 130497, 13. 133021, 14. 133016, 15. 272972, 16. 272971, 17. 133010, 18. 63062, 19. 63061, 20. 383638, 21. 272976, 22. 135177, 23. 63082, 24. 135183, 25. 63075, 26. 281428, 27. 63069, 28. 209219, 29. 272979, 30. 63068, 31. 132979, 32. 63076, 33. 209217, 34. 130486, 35. 133019, 36. 63080, 37. 130487, 38. 135176, 39. 130487, 40. 132989, 41. 132977, 42. 6995, 43. 6996, 44. 281431.
Zuni. AMNH. 50.I (except as noted).
1. 9218, 2. 6712, 3. 9408, 4. 9232, 5. 9234, 6. 9125, 7. 8717, 8. 50/478, 9. 50/431, 10. 8738, 11. 8729, 12. 50/515, 13. 8759, 14. 50 2/261, 15. 9073, 16. 8872, 17. 9049, 18. 50/438, 19. 8962, 20. 9181, 21. 9066, 22. 9077, 23. 9163, 24. 9149, 25. 50/416, 26. 50/441, 27. 8923, 28. 50 2/344, 29. 50/512, 30. 9201, 31. 9233, 32. 9224.
Tarahumara. AMNH. Book 65.
1. 4600, 2. 1240, 3. 976, 4. 973, 5. 1228, 6. 980, 7. 986, 8. 891, 9. 1015, 10. 1020, 11. 1028, 12. 1223, 13. 1229, 14. 1246, 15. 1247, 16. 1255, 17. 827, 18. 1208, 19. 964, 20. 998, 21. 1183, 22. 897, 23. 3579, 24. 1249, 25. 1256, 26. 1187, 27. 1192.
Pima. Dept of Anthropology, SI.
1. 27828, 2. 217929, 3. 27830, 4. 218000, 5. 76073, 6. 174450, 7. 218134, 8. 218005, 9. 217978, 10. 217990, 11. 218000, 12. 217994, 13. 76021, 14. 27845, 15. 76022, 16. 217931, 17. 76051, 18. 218006, 19. 76049, 20. 218028, 21. 217931, 22. 218066, 23. 218043, 24. 218062, 25. 218075, 26. 218074, 27. 218041, 28. 76071, 29. 217907, 30. 217989, 31. 76035, 32. 76065, 33. 218037, 34. 218069, 35. 218053, 36. 218046, 37. 218067.
Western Apache. AMNH. Book 50.
1. 8667, 2. 8745, 3. 8844, 4. 8741, 5. 8919, 6. 8728, 7. 8913, 8. 8808, 9. 8819, 10. 8707, 11. 8772, 12. 8676, 13. 8876, 14. 8972, 15. 8669, 16. 8870, 17. 8688, 18. 8890, 19. 8690, 20. 8763, 21. 8767, 22. 8703, 23. 8694, 24. 8956.
Navajo. Dept of Anthropology, SI.
1. 9525, 2. 207780, 3. 166316, 4. 417754, 5. 417753, 6. 417727, 7. 417725, 8. 417726, 9. 417731, 10. 417723, 11. 417736, 12. 417741, 13. 417745, 14. 417743, 15. 74164, 16. 417749, 17. 417739, 18. 417739, 19. 417738, 20. 417737, 21. 9536, 22. 9549, 23. 9591, 24. 16490, 25. 16500, 26. 150448, 27. 9575, 28. 213093, 29. 175661, 30. 167429, 31. 129959, 32. 150445, 33. 76684, 34. 166614, 35. 165740, 36. 8404, 37. 166920, 38. 129572, 39. 178320, 40. 166924, 41. 129962.
Osage. Dept of Anthropology, SI.
1. 364532, 2. 364528, 3. 364519, 4. 364508, 5. 364506, 6. 364509, 7. 364520, 8. 364521, 10. 364518, 11. 364543, 12. 364517, 13. 364513, 14. 364524, 15. 364515, 16. 364537, 17. 364534, 18. 364541, 19. 364542, 20. 364533, 21. 364512, 22. 364522, 23. 364538, 24. 364540, 25. 364526, 26. 364525, 27. 364516, 28. 364507, 29. 364510, 30. 374523, 31. 364530, 32. 364528, 33. 364531, 34. 364529, 35. 364527, 36. 364528, 37. 364536.
Kiowa. Dept of Anthropology, SI.
1. 152261, 2. 165197, 3. 229863, 4. 229848, 5. 165219, 6. 229819, 7. 165224, 8. 229892, 9. 165257, 10. 165235, 11. 152841, 12. 165229, 13. 153013, 14. 152839, 15. 152854, 16. 152845.
Arapaho. AMNH. Book 50.
1. 1031, 2. 293, 3. 1032, 4. 657, 5. 584, 6. 314, 7. 1092, 8. 583, 9. 1033, 10. 942, 11. 581, 12. 941, 13. 381, 14. 1069, 15. 643, 16. 1048, 17. 585, 18. 1028, 19. 582, 20. 1075, 21. 345, 22. 951, 23. 953, 24. 388, 25. 1107, 26. 368A, 27. 360A, 28–30, 667, 31. 360C, 32. 1047, 33. 327. 34. 1089, 35. 973, 36. 871, 37. 935, 38. 614, 39. 1021, 40. 410.
Cheyenne. Dept of Anthropology, SI.
1. 6912, 2. 165851, 3. 166009, 4. 165991, 5. 165938, 6. 6913, 7. 165981, 8.

152813, 9. 165859, 10. 58615, 11. 166028, 12. 152815, 13. 290366, 14. 166018, 15. 152812, 16. 381669, 17. 165911, 18. 165831, 19. 8305, 20. 165925, 21. 165886, 22. 165988, 23. 360278, 24. 165837, 25. 165924, 26. 165919, 27. 153585, 28. 397807, 29. 165833, 30. 35641.
Crow AMNH. Books 50 and 50.I.
1. 50/6855, 2. 50–6861, 3. 50/6867. 4. 50/3889, 5. 50.1/4019, 6. 50.1/3981, 7. 50/6853A, 8. 50.1/3959, 9. 50/6868, 10. 50/6863, 11. 50/6849, 12. 50.1/4015, 13. 50.1/3999, 14. 50.1/3927, 15. 50.1/3928, 16. 50.1/3904, 17. 50.1/3998, 18. 50.1/3898, 19. 50.1/4003, 20. 50.1/3917, 21. 50/6832, 22. 50/6856, 23. 50.1/3558, 24. 50.1/3915, 25. 50/6850, 26. 50/6837, 27. 50.1/4018.
Hidatsa. AMNH. Book 50.I (except as noted).
1. 5352, 2. 5392, 3. 6023A, 4. 5436, 5. 5416, 6. 5346, 7. 5365, 8. 5416, 9. 5354, 10. 5482, 11. 5374, 12. 5422, 13. 7091, 14. 5431, 15. 5440, 16. 5461, 17. 50.2/1179, 18. 5464, 19. 5484, 20. 6037, 21. 5427, 22. 6040, 23. 7326, 24. 5356.
Thompson. AMNH. Book 16.
1. 1285, 2. 7987, 3. 9540, 4. 8637, 5. 1314, 6. 1304, 7. 4597, 8. 1293, 9. 8648, 10. 1329, 11. 1262, 12. 8013, 13. 8011, 14. 8710A, 15. 1298, 16. 1316, 17. 1283, 18. 8725, 19. 8615, 20. 6748, 21. 4570, 22. 9340, 23. 4568.
Nez Perce. AMNH. Book 50.
1. 3756, 2. 3757, 3. 3789, 4. 3787, 5. 3791, 6. 3784A, 7. 3731, 8. 3737, 9. 3736, 10. 3763, 11. 3764A, 12. 3799, 13. 3734, 14. 3730, 15. 3769, 16. 3764B, 17. 3743, 18. 3755, 19. 3735, 20. 3732, 21. 3733, 22. 3786, 23. 3792, 24. 3754, 25. 3751.
Northern Paiute. AMNH. Book 50.I.
1. 7915, 2. 7963, 3. 7934, 4. 7935, 5. 7920, 6. 8572, 7. 7910, 8. 7964, 9. 7981, 10. 7960, 11. 7961, 12. 8640, 13. 7906, 14. 7924, 15. 7965, 16. 8571, 17. 7921, 18. 7959.
Hupa. Dept of Anthropology, SI.
1. 21361, 2. 77183, 3. 411723, 4. 77191, 5. 341265, 6. 341267, 7. 383441, 8. 383442, 9. 342289, 10. 341272, 11. 77190, 12. 131171, 13. 77182, 14. 126512, 15. 126516, 126518, 16. 126517, 17. 126508, 18. 77172, 19. 342274, 20. 131151, 21. 21356, 22. 342272, 23. 131163, 24. 253074, 25. 21312, 26. 131145, 27. 21312, 28. 385630, 29. 341311, 30. 385631, 31. 21322, 32. 126521, 33. 131158, 34. 126537, 35. 385595, 36. 131144, 37. 131154, 38. 131152, 39. 131171, 40. 131156, 41. 385268, 42. 126502, 43. 77186, 44. 126506, 45. 341306, 46. 77183, 47. 341309, 48. 126548, 49. 77188, 50. 77183, 51. 383443.
Wintu. Dept of Anthropology, SI.
1. 19288, 2. 19287, 3. 19286, 4. 127,833A, 5. 19288, 6. 19292, 7. 19280, 8. 19309, 9. 13744, 10. 19273, 11. 19337, 12. 19307, 13. 19335, 14. 19310, 15. 19343, 16. 19274, 17. 19275, 18. 19272, 19. 19270, 20. 19282, 21. 19322, 22. 19346, 23. 19301, 24. 19318, 25. 127,833B, 26. 19298, 27. 19282, 28. 19349, 29. 19296, 30. 19283, 31. 19281, 32. 19268.
Pomoan. Dept of Anthropology, SI.
1. 203,290, 2. 203,321, 3. 203,268, 4. 203,359, 5. 203,462, 6. 203,265, 7. 203,447, 8. 203,420, 9. 203,456, 10. 203,487, 11. 203,350A, 12. 203,475, 13. 203,573, 14. 203,596, 15. 203,598, 16.203,601, 17. 203,600, 18. 203,311, 19. 203,471, 20. 203,492, 21. 203,408, 22. 203,406, 23. 203,485, 24. 203,605, 25. 203,586, 26. 203,583, 27. 203,584, 28. 203,585, 29. 203,381, 30. 203,514, 31. 203,347, 32. 203,320, 33. 203,405, 34. 203,284, 35. 203,299, 36. 203,498.
Maidu. AMNH. Book 50.
1. 275, 2. 3130, 3. 5243, 4. 5265, 5. 4034, 6. 274, 7. 279, 8. 3132, 9. 4015, 10. 1712, 11. 4028, 12. 4016, 13. 283, 14. 284, 15. 285, 16. 282, 17. 1660, 18. 277, 19. 1390, 20. 1382, 21. 5262, 22. 1373, 23. 4020, 24. 1374, 25. 5235, 26. 276, 27. 272, 28. 1595, 29. 4032.
Diegueño. AMNH. Book 50.
1. 4170, 2. 6101, 3. 4197, 4. 6102, 5. 4218, 6. 6105, 7. 6115, 8. 4105, 9. 4102, 10. 4082, 11. 4215, 12. 4080, 13. 4223, 14. 4088, 15. 4198, 16. 6106, 17. 4086, 18. 4100, 19. 4211, 20. 6123, 21. 5279, 22. 4104, 23. 4106.
Tlingit I and II. Dept of Anthropology, SI.
(I) 1. 60225, 2. 89035, 3. 2211278, 4. 67903, 5. 73856, 6. 9936, 7. 60188, 8. 21607, 9. 89051, 10. 221176, 11. 74410, 12. 7969, 13. 67899, 14. 168268, 15. 72442, 16. 168292, 17. 23484, 18. 74952, 19. 74411, 20. 60156A, 21. 16257, 22. 60146, 23. 60224, 24. 221177, 25. 16220, 26. 20858, 27. 19531, 28. 19530, 29. 20824.
(II) 72437, 2. 23376, 3. 75444, 4. 74375, 5. 60175, 6. 209878, 7. 153606, 8. 74362, 9. 16401, 10. 23414, 11. 23415, 12. 209551, 13. 204781, 14. 60182, 15. 168270?, 16. 203558, 17. 383131, 18. 20782, 19. 20732, 20. 64971, 21. 67867, 22. 221181, 23. 209883, 24. 60133, 25. 60218, 26. 20922, 27. 230062, 28. 74924, 29. 67879, 30. 332801, 31. 20785, 32. 16222, 33. 67914, 34. 424981.
Haida I and II. Dept of Anthropology, SI.

(I) 89198B, 2. 74751, 3. 89040, 4. 56460, 5. 89081, 6. 20866, 7. 13099, 8. 89089, 9. 20801, 10. 89143, 11. 89153, 12. 89070, 13. 88716, 14. 89063. (II) 88998, 2. 2416, 3. T-653, 4. 89197, 5. 2599, 6. 60168, 7. 74313, 8. 89096, 9. 20885B, 10. 20856, 11. 20613, 12. 20572, 13. 89187, 14. 89201, 15. 89041, 16. 88838, 17. 89162, 18. 73556, 19. 425001, 20. 168259, 21. 88824
Kwakiutl. AMNH. Book 16.
1. 8944, 2. 6887, 3. 8184, 4. 2344, 5. 4751, 6. 2352, 7. 8941, 8. 8078B, 9. 6905, 10. 2265, 11. 2279, 12. 2269, 13. 8548, 14. 8159, 15. 2150, 16. 9618, 17. 2244, 18. 8232, 19. 8214, 20. 2263, 21. 8561, 22. 2248A, 23. 6897, 24. 2300, 25. 8429, 26. 6812, 27. 8177, 28. 8951, 29. 2375, 30. 8534, 31. A^{1}193.
Makah. Dept of Anthropology, SI.
1. 1292, 2. 73740 (& T-14225), 3. 72649, 4. 72656, 5. 72657, 72655, 6. 72643, 72644, 7. 23372, 8. 4771, 9. 1292, 10. 72655, 11. 73567, 12. 72663, 13. 23377, 14. 23314, 15. 2331, 16. 2331, 17. 4746, 18. 9230, 19. 824, 20. 23309, 21. 1137, 22. 23374, 23. 23360, 24. 23360, 25. 1296, 26. 9224, 27. 23346, 28. 1039, 29. 23330, 30. 4120, 31. 4120, 32. 23327, 33. 13115, 34. 9232.
Ingalik. AMNH. Book 60.
1. 5076, 5077, 2. 5095, 3. 4932, 4. 5117, 5. 4954, 6. 4955, 7. 4945, 8. 4908, 9. 5118, 10. 5106, 11. 5105, 12. 5088, 13. 5844, 14. 4922, 15. 4984, 16. 5006, 17. 4937, 18. 4966, 19. 4925, 20. 4971, 21. 5007, 22. 5092A, 23. 5091, 24. 5113, 25. 5109, 26. 5115, 27. 5111, 28. 5122, 29. 5110, 30. 5102.
Kutchin. Dept of Anthropology, SI.
1. 2029, 2. 2030, 3. 882, 4. 234027, 5. 4971, 6. 238534, 7. 887, 8. 64278, 9. 64279, 10. 64280, 11. 7613, 12. 233471, 13. 898, 14. 7616.
Carrier. Dept of Anthropology, SI.
1. 381288, 2. 381298, 3. 381299, 4. 381279, 5. 381291, 6. 381345, 7. 381300, 8. 381301, 9. 381304, 10. 381303, 11. 381270, 12. 381276, 13. 381295, 14. 381260, 15. 381314, 16. 381277, 17. 381320, 18. 381323, 19. 381324, 20. 381313, 21–381329, 22. 381332, 23. 381309, 24. 381262, 25. 381328.
Cree. AMNH. Book 50.
1. 7457, 2. 7045, 3. 6977, 4. 6983, 5. 7057, 6. 6955, 7. 7053, 8. 7476, 9. 7055, 10. 7474, 11. 7049, 12. 7455, 13. 7456, 14. 6975, 15. 6978, 16. 7054, 17. 6996, 18. 6957, 19. 8097, 20. 6982, 21. 6993, 22. 7027, 23. 7019, 24. 7020, 25. 7029, 26. 7036, 27. XXXX, 28. 7039, 29. 7476, 30. 7473, 31. 6947, 32. 7009, 33. 7006, 34. 6990, 35. 7002.
Aleut. Dept of Anthropology, SI.
1. 65190, 2. 219270, 3. 337005, 4. 13513, 5. 2327, 6. 5772, 7. 6555, 8. 38717, 9. 316892, 10. 168296, 11. 65188, 12. 65198, 13. 313281, 14. 65209, 15. 383186, 16. 383206, 17. 168526, 18. 65251?, 19. 2134, 20. 2127, 21. 175828, 22. 65281, 23. 316888, 24. 65222, 25. 383187
Central Inuit. AMNH. Book 60.
1. 4355, 2. 4276, 3. 5510, 4. 5157, 5. 4300, 6. 5156, 7. 5523, 8. 5510, 9. 2783, 10. 4359, 11. 2886, 12. 2520, 13. 4544, 14. 4721, 15. 4550, 16. 2524, 17. 2634, 18. 2508, 19. 2584, 20. 2676, 21. 2883, 22. 2564, 23. 4691, 24. 5486, 25. 4614, 26. 4465, 27. 2450, 28. 5555, 29. 2649, 30. 4605, 31. 5784, 32. 5782, 33. 2878, 34. 6569, 35. 2544, 36. 2923, 37. 2922, 38. 2919, 39. 2914, 40. 1177.
Micmac. AMNH. Book 50.I (except as noted).
1. 7496, 2. 7478, 3. 7480, 4. 9728 & 9730, 5. 9732, 6. 9729, 7. 7461, 8. 7465, 9. 7471, 10. 50.2/587, 11. 9756, 12. 9765, 13. 7487, 14. 9757, 15. 7495, 16. 9777, 17. 9771, 18. 7484, 19. 7491, 20. 7490, 21. 9776, 22. 7454, 23. 7462, 24. 7486.
Seneca. AMNH. Book 50.
1. 6188F, 2. 6188E, 3. 6188D, 4. 1874, 5. 7321, 6. 5547. 7. 6229, 8. 6188B, 9. 5551, 10. 6231, 11. 6188C, 12. 6188A, 13. 1498, 14. 6237, 15. 6235, 16. 6888, 17. 6253, 18. 5553, 19. 6268.
Chippewa. Dept of Anthropology, SI.
1. 278121, 2. 278125, 3. 317212, 4. 317214, 5. 289081, 6. 283270, 7. 283273, 8. 278139, 9. 278123, 10. 278166, 11. 278158, 12. 278160, 13. 349690, 14. 153033, 15. 283272, 16. 278173, 17. 317211, 18. 154325, 19. 278176, 20. 283271, 21. 306985, 22. 349685, 23. 349687, 24. 349689, 25. 395417, 26. 395418, 27-30. 35-39. 201154, 31. 263532, 32. 278118, 33. 278119, 34. 278114, 40. 289083, 41. 153036.
Sauk and Fox. AMNH. Book 50.
1. 3543C, 2. 3539, 3. 7265, 4. 2235, 5. 2221, 6. 4881, 7. 3549, 8. 3550, 9. 4878, 10. 2204, 11. 3570, 12. 2216, 13. 2244, 14. 2234, 15. 5208, 16. 2220, 17. 4884, 18. 2205, 19. 2225, 20. 2223, 21. 2238, 22. 2279, 23. 2276, 24. 4888, 25. 4877, 26. 3508, 27. 2274, 28. 2253, 29. 3517.

INDEX

Page numbers in bold indicate illustrations. Important footnotes are indexed as, for example, 127n24

A

Achumawi 134, 145
Acoma 41
acorns 129
Adair, Col. William P. 31
Adena 10
agriculture 10
  Basin area 119, 122
  Southeast 13, 21-2, 25
  Southwest 37-8, 44, 46, 54-5, 58
Ahfitche, Governor 41
Ahtna 10
Ais 13
Aivilingmiut 216-17, 220, 220-22
Alabama 13, 25
Alaska Commercial Company 210, 215
Aleut 9-10, 204-7, 205, 210, 210
  artifacts 208-9
  and see Eskimo
Algonquian 227
  languages 7, 62-3, 100-101, 151n4, 182, 225
Alights on the Cloud 85
American Fur Company 76
American Horse 94
Anasazi 11, 37, 39
antelope 62-3, 119
Apache 9, 37, 39, 54, 54-5, 55
Apache Peaks Apache 54
  and see Apache
Apacheans see Apache
Apalachee 13
Appaloosa horses 103, 113
Arapaho 62, 66, 73, 76, 78, 78, 79, 80, 81, 81
  artifacts 82-3
Arapaho Spear Society 78
Archaic peoples 37
Arctic
  artifacts 206, 208-9
  ceremonies 214-15
  disease 222
  fishing industry 215, 217
  food sources 206, 213, 216-17, 220
  fur trade 210
  habitation 205-6, 212, 221, 222
  hunting techniques 206, 216-17, 220
  languages 7, 204, 212-13, 216
  and missionaries 207, 210, 215, 223
  population 205, 207
  religion 213-14, 220
  social organization 205-7, 210, 213, 216-17, 220-21
  trade 215, 222
Arikara 62-3, 66, 68, 73, 76, 98
Arivaipa Apache 54 and see Apache
arrows 9
  Apache 54
  Haida 168-9
  Hidatsa 96-7
  Konkow 146-7
  Pomo 142-3
  Tarahumara 48-9
  Wintu 138-9
  Yuma 47
art 11
  Northeast 227
  Northwest coast 157, 160-61, 164-5, 176, 181

Plains 67
  Southwest 44-5
  Subarctic 193, 196
Asilanapi 20
Asking Festival (Petugtaq) 214
Assiniboin 64, 67, 67, 73, 76
Atakapan 13
Athapaskan 6-7, 9
  languages 63, 134-5, 145, 182
atlatl 217
Atsidi Chon 58
Atsugewi 134, 145
Attikamek 182
Ayunini (Swimmer) 32

B

Baconrind, Tom (Washinha) 70
  regalia, special occasion dress 70-71
baidarkas 206, 206 and see boats
Bakhbakwalanooksiwey 171
balsas 130, 144, 148, 151 and see boats
Bannock 118, 127n23
Basin area
  agriculture 119, 122
  artifacts 120, 122, 124, 124
  clothing 123-4
  environment 118, 126
  fishing techniques 123
  food sources 118-19, 122-3
  habitation 124, 126
  languages 118, 151n4, 127n23
  religion 123
  social organization 124
  trade 126
Basketmakers 37
basketry
  Arctic 206, 208-9
  Basin 122, 124
  California 131, 131, 134, 134, 137, 138-9, 142-3, 146-7
  Northwest Coast 161, 164, 168-9, 174
  Plains 96-7
  Southeast 15, 17
  Southwest 50, 55
beads 197, 199
Bear Society 95
bears 192-3
Beatty, Joseppa 137
Beaver 182, 188
beavers 185, 189, 203
Belaney, Archibald (Grey Owl) 203n13
Bell, Dr William A. 79-81
Bella Coola 154-6, 165
beloved men 27
Beothuk 224
Beringia 6
Big Foot 99
Big Head 141
Big Head dance 141
Big Hole, Battle of the 112-13
Biloxi 13
birch bark 239, 245
Bird Rattler 65
bison see buffalo
Black Fox 98
Black Hills 88
Black Jim 140
Black Kettle 78, 81, 85
Blackfeet 62-8, 64, 65, 66, 72-3, 88, 108-9
Blackfeet Confederacy 66, 127n29
Blackfoot see Blackfeet
Blackhawk 237
Blackmore, William 73
Bladder Festival (Nakaciuq) 214
blowguns 16, 22

boats 141 and see baidarkas, balsas, canoes, kayaks, umiaks
Boas, Franz 106, 172, 218
Bobb, Jennie 226
Boudinot, Col. Elias C. 31
bows 9
  Aivilingmiut 220
  Haida 168-9
  Konkow 146-7
  Nez Perce 104
  Plateau 104
  Pomoan 142-3
  Spokane 104
  Tarahumara 48-9
  Ute 127
  Yuma 47
Brown, Margaret 31
Brulé 85
Brulé Lakota 76-8
buffalo 9, 63, 73, 119
Buffalo Bill Society 76
Buffalo Bill (William F. Cody) 94
Buffalo Society 95, 98
burial practices 10,16
busk festival 20, 30-32

C

caches 184
cacique 45
Caddo 13, 14, 63, 81
Cahitan 46
Cahokia 15
Cahto 145
Cahuilla 150
California
  artifacts 131, 131, 134, 134, 137, 138-9, 142-3, 146-7, 150
  clothing 136, 138-9, 144, 145, 146-7, 148
  environment 128-9
  fishing techniques 131, 148
  food sources 129-31
  habitation 134, 140, 145, 148
  languages 134-7, 145, 151n4
  population 131
  reservations 151
  settlers 137, 141, 145
  social organization 136, 148
  trade 131, 135
Calusa 13, 16-17
camas bulbs 101
Camas Meadow 113
Cameahwait 66
Canby, Brig. Gen. E. R. S. 137, 140-41
canoes
  Basin 120
  California 150
  Northeast 226, 239, 240-41, 244-5
  Northwest Coast 155, 170, 175
  Plateau 102, 102
  Southeast 24
  Subarctic 199, 202
  and see boats
Canyon Creek 113
Captain Jack (Keintpoos) 136, 137, 140-41
caribou 185, 217, 220, 220
Carrier, artifacts 194-5
Carrizo Apache 54 and see Apache
Carson, Col. Christopher 'Kit' 54, 55
carving 168-9 and see sculpture
Catawba 13, 13, 25, 31
Cayuga 225, 227
Cayuse 100, 102, 108, 109
Cedar Creek 94
ceremonies

Arctic 214-15
  Northeast 241
  Northwest 171, 171, 175-6, 181
  Plains 91
  and see dances
Chahta Imataha 21
Chakchiuma 13
Champlain, Samual 232-3, 236
Chapman, Rev. John W. 186
Chatot 13
Chemehuevi (Southern Paiute) 50, 58, 119, 124
Cherokee 11, 13, 25, 31, 32, 32-3, 33
  artifacts 34-5
Cheyenne 7, 62-3, 66, 68, 73, 76, 78, 81, 85
  artifacts 86-7
Chickasaw 13, 25, 81
chickee 30
Chilkat dancing blankets 157, 160, 164
Chimariko 145
China Lake 7
Chinook 100-101, 180
Chipewyan 182-3, 185, 188, 196, 199
Chippewa (Ojibwa) 10, 203, 224-5, 236-7, 239, 239-41, 240, 241, 244-5, 248-9
  artifacts 240-41
Chiricahua Apache 54 and see Apache
Chiricahua Cattle Company 54
Chitimacha 13, 14, 25
Chivaria, Juan 50
Choctaw 13, 15, 16, 21-2, 25
Chumash 148, 150
Cibecue Apache 54 and see Apache
Civil War 47, 55
clans, Creek 27
clothing
  Basin area 123-4
  California 136, 138-9, 144, 145, 146-7, 148
  Northwest Coast 166-9
  Plains 82-3, 92-3, 96-7
  Plateau Indians 104-5, 108, 114-15
  Southwest 48-9
  Subarctic 193, 196-9, 202
Clovis peoples 7-8
clowns 89, 92-3
Coast Miwok 145, 148, 150
  and see Miwok
Coast Mikok Woman, 1832 144
Coast Salish 154, 175, 176, and see Salish
Cochimi 46
Cochise 54
Cochiti 41, 41
Cocomaricopa 46
Cocopa 46, 47, 50
Cody, William F. (Buffalo Bill) 94
Coeur d'Alêne 100, 102, 109
Colville 100, 102
Comanche 62-3, 66, 73, 73, 76, 78, 81, 85, 126
Comer, George 218
compact settlements 226
Concho 46
Conquering Bear 76-7
cooking utensils 22
coontie plant 24
Copper Inuit 220 and see Inuit
Corn Dance (1950) 40
cornhusk bags 108, 114-15
Costanoan 145, 148
Cow Creek Seminole 25, 30
  and see Seminole
Cow Island 113
cradles 104, 109, 111, 118

Arctic 214-15
Northeast 241
Northwest 171, 171, 175-6, 181
Plains 91
and see dances
Crazy Horse 90-91, 95
Cree 66, 66, 182
  artifacts 200-201
  clothing 193
  embroidery 199
  and guns 64, 66
  lodges 184
  quillwork 197
  religion 192
  season names 189
  wind names 193
Creek 13, 20, 25, 32
Creek Confederacy 24-5, 27, 30
creoles 207
Crook, Brig. Gen. George 88-91, 94
Crow 66, 88, 108-9
  artifacts 92-3
  dances 88, 89
  and horses 102, 113
  language 63
  tipis 67, 77, 89
  Tobacco Society 90, 92
  trade 68
  and treaties 73, 76
  Washington delegation 90
Crow Dance 79
Crowfoot 99n16
Culbertson, Alexander 73
Culchillum 176
Cumumbah 127n24
Cupeño 150
Curly-Bear 65
Cusabo 13
Custer, Gen. George A. 86, 91
Cut-nose (Neeshnepahkeook) 101

D

Dakota 66
Dalles Rendezvous 101
dances
  Arapaho 79
  Big Head 141
  Blackfeet 64
  Cherokee 33
  Chippewa 241
  Creek 32
  Crow 88, 89
  Crow Dance 79
  Ghost Dancing 79, 98-9, 127
  Hamatsa 170-71
  Jumping Dance 135
  Pawnee War Dance, 1821 84
  Salmon dance 135
  Santa Clara Corn Dance, 1950 40
  Southern Kwakiutl 170-71
  White Deerskin 135
  and see ceremonies
datura societies 148
Davis, Jack (Ne Shiw Shkak) 239
de Leon, Ponce 14
de Soto, Hernando 14
Deganawida 227
Delaware 226
Densmore, Frances 242
dentalium shells 199
Desert peoples 37
Dieguêno 150, 151
  artifacts 150-51
Digger Indians 119
Dineh see Navajo
disease
  Arctic 222
  Cherokee theory 32-3
  Northeast 224, 226
  Northwest Coast 180-81
  Plains 73
  Southeast 13-14
  Southwest 39

Subarctic 203
Dixon, Roland B. 146
Dodge, Col. Henry 78
Dog Soldiers 78
Dogrib 182, 188, 193, 197, 199, 203
Dove Society 64
dreams 123
Du Bois, Constance Goddard 152
Dull Knife 94

E

eagles 44
East Cree 182, 192-3 and see Cree
Eastern Abenaki 225
Eastern Shoshoni 126-7
  and see Shoshoni
Eastern Sioux 68 and see Sioux
economic organization
  Plains 68, 72
  Southeast 21
  Southwest 39, 54-5
embroidery 199
environment
  Basin area 118, 126
  California 128-9
  Northwest Coast 155
  Plains 62-3
  Plateau 100
  Southeast 13
  Southwest 37
  Subarctic 182
Erie 225
Eskiminzin 54
Eskimo 9-10, 11, 211, 212, 213, 213, 214, 215, 217
  and see Aleut, Inuit
Eskimo-Aleut 6-7, 9-10, 204
Esselen 150
Estipah-Sikikini-Kots 63
Eudebe 46

F

face painting 46
Farrand, Livingston 115
Fast Walker (Wah-com-mo) 249
Feast of the Dead (Merr'aq) 214-15
Feathered Lance 85
Fields, Richard 31
figurines
  California 146-7
  Northwest Coast 166-7
fishing industry, Arctic 215
fishing techniques
  Arctic 217
  Basin area 123
  California 131, 148
  Plateau 101
  Southeast 22
  Subarctic 183, 184
Five Civilized Tribes 25
Flathead 63, 100, 102, 105, 109
Fleming, Lieut. Hugh B. 76
Florida 8, 24-5
food sources
  Arctic 206, 213, 216-17, 220
  Basin area 118-19, 122-3
  California 129-31
  Northeast 225-6, 231, 236-7
  Northwest Coast 155, 168
  Southeast 13, 22
  Subarctic 185, 188-9, 192
footwear
  Aleut 208-9
  Arapaho 82-3
  Crow 92-3
  Hidatsa 96-7
  Plateau Indians 104-5
  Tarahumara 48-9

formline art 161
Fort Apache Apache 54 **and see** Apache
Fort Atkinson Treaty 73, 76
Fort Benton 99n5
Fort Laramie Treaty 73, 76, 85, 88
Fort Robinson 95, 98
Fort Sumner 55, 58
Fort Wallace 78-9
Four Bears (Mató-Tópe) iii, 76
Fox 245, 249
funeral ceremonies 17, 20-21
fur trade
  Arctic 210
  and the military 76
  Northeast 226
  Northwest Coast 176
  Plains 72-3
  Subarctic 202-4

G

Gabrielino 150, 151
games 17, 26, 27, 146-7
ganonh'sees 231-2
Geronimo 54, 56
Ghost Dance 79, 98-9, 127
Gibbon, Col. John 89, 91, 112
Gluskabe 245
gold 88, 110, 215
Gosiutes 119, 122-3
governors (Puebloan) 45
granaries 150
Grand Medicine Society (Midewiwin) 241, 245, 248-9
grass-hoppers 122-3
Grattan, Lieut. John 76-7
Grattan Massacre 76-8
Gray Eagle 112-13
Great Peace alliance 78
Great Sioux Reservation 88, 98
Green Corn Festival 20, 30-32
Grey Owl (Archibald Belaney) 203n13
Gros Ventre 63, 66, 73, 76
guns 9, 64, 66, 68, 207

H

habitation
  Arctic 205-6, 220, 221, 222
  Basin area 124
  California 145, 148
  Plains 77
  Plateau 101-2
  Southeast 14, 15, 21, 22, 30, 32
  Southwest 58
  Subarctic 184-5, 188
  and see hogan dwellings, houses, igloos, lodges, longhouses, tipis, wigwams
Haida 120, 155-6, 161, 164, 166, 168
  artifacts 166-9
Halchidhoma 39, 46, 151
Hamatsa dances 170-71
Han 182
Handsome Lake 232
Hano 41
Hare 182, 188
harpoons 168-9, 181, 217
Harris, Ben P. 13
hats 164, 168-9, 208-9
Havasupai 46, 50, 50
Haylaema 17
Heemeen Ilp Ilp (Josiah Red Wolf) 127n20
Hein-mot Too-ya-la-kekt (Joseph) 111-12, 116, 116
Hidatsa 63, 66, 68
  artifacts 96-7
hide tanning 188

High Forehead 76-7
Hitchiti 13
Hodge, F. W. 42
Hō-letite 171
hogan dwellings 58 **and see** habitation
Hohokam 11, 37
Hokan languages 46, 136, 145, 151
hominy (tanfula) 22
Hopewell 10
Hopi 11, 39, 41, 44, 45, 45
horse trappings 67, 92-3, 96-7, 103-4, 105
horses
  introduction of 9, 102-4, 118, 126
  trade in 68
Houma 13
houses
  Arctic 212
  California 134, 140
  Northwest Coast 156, 165, 170, 171
  and see habitation
Howard, Brig.-Gen. Oliver O. 111-13, 116
Hudson, J. W. 142
Hudson's Bay Trading Company 73, 197, 199, 202, 222-3
Huichol 46
Hunká-Alowanpi Ceremony 91
Hunkpapa 88, 91
Hunt, George 172
Hunter, John 177
hunting techniques
  Arctic 206, 216-17, 220
  bears 192-3
  bison/buffalo 9, 63
  caribou 185, 217, 220, 220
  Plains 62-3
  Southeast 22
  moose 185
  Subarctic 185, 192-3
Hupa 134, 135, 145
Huron 225, 233, 236

I

igloos 221 **and see** habitation, snowhouses
Iglulik Inuit 216, 221
  artifacts 186-7
  and see Inuit
Iglulingmiut 216
Illinois 225
In-who-lise 112
incest 16-17
Ingalik 183, 184
Inland Tlingit 182 **and see** Tlingit
Inuit 216, 216, 217, 220, 221, 222, 223, 223
  artifacts 218-19
  and see Eskimo
Inuit-Inupiaq languages 204, 216
inukshuit 217
Inviting-In Festival (Kelek/Itruka'ar) 214
Iron Star 95
Iroquois 24, 225, 227, 231, 231-2, 236
Iroquois League Confederacy 224, 227, 231
Isleta 41
isumataq 220

J

jack-rabbit 123-4
Jackson, Helen Hunt 151
Jemez 41
jewelry 48-9, 58, 142-3, 144
Jicarilla Apache 39, 54 **and see** Apache

Jim, David 171
Joaquin, Cecilia 140
Jodrava 50
Johnnie Kit Elswa 164
Jones, William 246
Joseph (Hein-mot Too-ya-la-kekt) 111-12, 116, 116
Josiah Red Wolf (Heemeen Ilp Ilp) 127n20
Jova 46
Jumping Dance 135

K

Kaigani Haida 155
Kaitchkona (Toby Riddle) 140
Kalispel 100, 102-3, 109
Kamia 151
Kansa 245
Karluk 207
Karok 129, 131, 134, 135-6
Kash-Kash, Edna 109
Kaw 81
Kawaiisu 119
kayaks 205, 208-9, 216, 217, 222 **and see** boats
Keintpoos (Captain Jack) 136, 137, 140-41
Kelek/Itruka'ar (Inviting-In Festival) 214
Keokuk (Kiyo' Kaga) 245
Keokuk, Moses 245
Keresan 41, 45
Kettle Falls 101, 103
Keys 13
Kickapoo 225, 237, 245
Kicking Bird 85
Kill Spotted Horse 67
Kintpuash **see** Captain Jack
Kiowa 62-3, 66-7, 73, 76, 78, 81, 85
  artifacts 74-5
Kiowa-Apache 63, 66, 73, 76, 81
Kitanemuk 150
kivas 45
Kiyo' Kaga (Keokuk) 245
Klamath 101, 137
Klikitat 100
Klookwalli/Klookwana ceremony 171
Koasati 13, 25
Konkow 145
  artifacts 146-7
Kroeber, A. L. 42, 82
Kupt 109
Kutchin 182, 184, 188, 196, 199
  artifacts 190-91
Kutenai 63, 100, 102, 102, 104, 109
Kwakiutl 154, 170, 175
  artifacts 172-3
  and see Southern Kwakiutl
Kwakiutl Basket Making, 1850 174

L

labrets 223
Laguna 41
Lake Miwok 145 **and see** Miwok
Lakota 66, 78, 85, 88, 95
  political organization 98
  populations 62
  social organizations 98
  tipis 67
  and treaties 73, 76
Lame Deer 95
lances 48-9
land ownership 136
languages
  Algonquian 7, 62-3, 100-101, 151n4, 182, 225
  Arctic 7, 204, 212-13, 216
  Athapaskan 63, 134-5, 145, 182

Basin 118, 151n4, 127n23
California 134-7, 145, 151n4
  development of 7
  Hokan 46, 136, 145, 151
  Inuit-Inupiaq 204, 216
  Na-Dene 7, 9
  Northwest Coast 154-5
  Penutian 41, 129, 145
  Plains 62-3
  Plateau area 100-101
  rancheria groups 46
  Southeast 13, 25, 63
  Southwest 41
  Subarctic 182
  Uto-Aztecan 46, 63, 151n4
Lassik 145
Lawyer (Nez Perce chief) 110
Left Hand 78
Lenni-Lenape 225
Lieta 46
Lillooet 100
Lincecum, Gideon 21
Lipan Apache 54
Little Big Horn 88-91, 94
Little Ike 131
Little Raven (Ohnastie) 81, 99n13
Little Robe 81
Little Stabber (Pashipaho) 248
Little Tiger 27
Little Vessel, The (Oscar Mark) 108
lodges
  conical 101
  earth 70, 101
  Northeast 240, 244, 248
  Northwest Coast 184
  Plateau 101, 118
  Subarctic 184, 197, 199, 202
  and see habitation
Long Elk 90
Long Walk 58
Longhat, Nellie 226
Longhouse Religion 232
longhouses 101-102, 231-2, **and see** habitation
Looking Glass 109, 111-12, 112, 116
Lower Ahtna Indians 185, 188
Lowie, Robert H. 92, 120
Luiseño 150-51
Lumbee 13, 25
Lumholtz, Carl S. 48
Lutuamian languages 151n4

M

Maidu, artifacts 146-7
maize 10
Makah 154, 171, 181
  artifacts 178-9
Maliseet-Passamaquoddy 225
Man on a Cloud 85
Man without Blood (Tum-se-ne-ho) 102
Mandan 62-3, 66, 68, 73, 76, 76
maple sugar 237
Maricopa 50
Mark, Oscar (The Little Vessel) 108
masks 108, 166-7, 170-71, 175
Mató-Tópe (Four Bears) iii, 6
Mattole 145
Mayo 46, 46
Mazatzal Apache 54 **and see** Apache
Meadowcroft Rockshelter 8
medicinal plants 33, 237-8
medicine, Cherokee 32-3
medicine bags 248
Medicine Crow 90

Medicine Lodge Treaty 81
medicine lodges 80, 98
Menominee 225, 236-7, 245
Merr'aq (Feast of the Dead) 214
Mescalero Apache 54-5 **and see** Apache
Meskwahiki haki/Mesquaki (The Red Earths) 249
Métis 197, 199, 203
Mexico 8, 38-9
Miami 225
micco 27
Micmac 224-6, 227, 227
  artifacts 228-9
Midewiwin (Grand Medicine Society) 241, 245, 248-9
migis 248
Mikasuki 13
Mikasuki Seminole 21, 22, 24, 25, 25, 27 **and see** Seminole
Miles, Col. Nelson A. 94-5
Miniconjou Sioux 76, 88
  and see Sioux
missionaries
  Arctic 207, 210, 215, 223
  Northwest Coast 177, 180-81
  Plateau 109
  Subarctic 199
Mississippian Culture 10
Miwok 144 **and see** Coast Miwok
Mobile 13
Modoc 134, 136, 136-7, 140-41
Mogollon 37, 39
Mohave 46, 151
  Mohave Family, 1851, 51
Mojave **see** Mohave
moieties 45, 156
monetary systems 136, 148
Montagnais 182
Montagnais-Naskapi 182-3, 193, 197, 199, 202, 203
Mooney, James 32, 33, 34, 74
moose 185
mortars 22, 25, 151
Moundville 15-16
Mountain Crow 109 **and see** Crow
Mountain Indians 182
Mohawk 225, 227, 231
  Mohawk Warrior, 1750, 230
Murray, Alexander Hunter 197, 199, 203
musical instruments 48-9, 138-9, 146-7, 166-7, 241
Muskogee 13, 15, 25

N

Na-Dene languages 7, 9
  and see Athapaskan
Nakaciuq (Bladder Festival) 214
Nakota 66
Nambe 39, 41
Nanticoke 225
Naskapi 182, 193, 196
  Naskapi Hunter, 1880 198
Natchez 13, 17, 20-21, 25
nations, Apache 54
Naukanski 213
Navajo 9, 37, 39, 54-5, 58, 58-9, 59, 81
  artifacts 60-61
Ne Shiw Shkak (Jack Davis) 239
Neeshnepahkeook (Cut-nose) 101
Neighbours, Robert S. 78
Nez Perce 100-105, 101, 108-13, 112, 116, 116
  artifacts 114-15, 127n12

Nez Perce Warrior, 1877 117
Night Society 95
Nisenan 125, 145, 148
  artifacts 146-7
nomadism 58-9, 67
Nomlaki 145
Nongatl 145
Nootka **see** Nuu-chah-nulth
Northeast
  art 227
  artifacts 226, 239, 240-41, 244-5
  disease 224, 226
  ceremonies 241
  food sources 225-6, 231, 236-7
  fur trade 226
  habitation 239-40, 240, 244, 248
  population 224-6
  religion 227, 245, 248-9
  social organization 225-7, 231, 240
Northern Kwakiutl 154 **and see** Kwakiutl
Northern Ojibwa 182, 196 **and see** Ojibwa
Northern Paiute 119, 123
  artifacts 120-21
  and see Paiute
Northern Shoshoni 126 **and see** Shoshoni
Northern Wintu 134 **and see** Wintu
Northwest Coast
  art 157, 160-61, 164-5, 176, 181
  artifacts 155, 161, 164, 166-7, 168-9, 170, 174, 175
  ceremonies 171, 171, 175-6, 181
  clothing 166-9
  disease 180-181
  environment 155
  food sources 155, 168
  fur trade 176
  habitation 156, 165, 170, 171
  languages 154-5
  missionaries 177, 180-81
  population 155, 180-81, 183
  religion 165
  settlers 176-7, 180
  social organization 155-7, 166
  trade 155-6, 176
Now-on-dhu-go 236
Nuu-chah-nulth 154, 156, 161, 164, 171, 177
Nuvugmiut 216

O

Ofo 13
Oglala 85, 90, 91
Ohlone **see** Costanoan
Ohnastie (Little Raven) 81, 99n13
Ojibwa 240 **and see** Chippewa
Okanagan 100-103
Old Crow 90
Old Joseph (Tu-eka-kas) 110-11
Ollokot 111, 113, 116
Olsen-Chubbock site 9
Omaha 62, 67
Oneida 225, 227
Onondaga 225, 227, 232, 232-3
O'Odham (Pima) 37, 46, 46-7
Opata 38, 46
Oregon Trail 73
Osage 68, 69, 81
  artifacts 70-71

Osceola, Jim 30
Oto 77
Ottawa 225, 236
Oululuk 206
ovens 38
Ozette 10

P.

Padlirmiut 216
Pah-Ute see Paiute
Paiute 44, 58-9, 118, 122, 151
  and see Northern
    Paiute, Southern
    Paiute
Palmer, Edward 34
Palus 8, 100
Panamint 119
Papago (Tohono O'Odham)
  47
parfleches 114-15
Parker, Caroline 233
Parker, Quanah 85
  and Tonasa 73
Pashipaho (Little Stabber)
  248
Passamaquoddy 226
Patayan 37
Patwin 145
Paul, Benjamin 14
Paul, G. A. 228
Paviotso 118
Pawnee 63, 66, 70, 84
  Pawnee War Dance, 1821
    84
Pawnee Killer 78
Payne, John Howard 30
Pecos 41
Pend d'Oreilles 102, 109
Penutian languages 41, 129,
  145
Pesh-lakái-ilhini 58
Petugtaq (Asking Festival)
  214
pictographs 248-9
Picuris 41
Piega see Blackfeet
Pikimachay Cave 8
Pima (O'Odham) 37, 44, 46,
  46-7
  artifacts 52-3
Pima Bajo 46-7
Pinal Apache 54 and see
  Apache
Pinal Coyotero Apache 54
  and see Apache
pinole 48
piñon 119, 122
pipes see tobacco pipes
Plains Cree 63 and see
  Cree
Plains Indians
  art 67
  artifacts 96-7
  ceremonies 91
  clothing 81-3, 92-3, 96-7
  disease 73
  economic organization
    68, 72
  environment 62-3
  fur trade 72-3
  hunting techniques 62-3
  inter-tribal relations 78,
    81
  languages 62-3
  and Plateau Indians
    108-9
  political organization 98
  populations 62
  religions 67-9
  reservations 88, 98
  and settlers 72-3, 78
  social organization 66-7,
    72, 98
  tipis 65, 67, 77, 80, 89,
    99n1, 94
  trade 66, 68, 104, 109
Plains Ojibwa 63
Plateau Indians
  artifacts 102, 102

clothing 104-5, 108, 114-15
environment 100
fishing techniques 101
habitations 101-2, 101,
  109, 118
languages 100-101
and missionaries 109
and Plains Indians 108-9
reservations 110-11
and settlers 110-11
social organization 109-10
trade 101, 103-4, 109
Plenty Coups 90
Pojoaque 41
political organization
  Plains 98
  Southeast 16-17
  Southwest 39, 45
Pomo 131, 134, 137, 140, 141,
  145
Pomoan artifacts 142-3
populations
  Arctic 205, 207
  California 131
  Mississippian
    Culture 10
  Northeast 224-6
  Northwest Coast 155,
    180-81, 183
  Plains 62
  prehistoric 9
  Southeast 11, 13-14, 23
  Southwest 39, 46, 54
  Subarctic 182-3, 203, 205
Potawatomi 225, 239, 245
potlatches 157, 164, 165,
  170, 175, 180
pottery
  Basin area 124
  Plains 96-7
  Southeast 31
  Southwest 38, 45, 48-9
Powder Face 78
Powell, Maj. J. W. 125
Powhatan 225
Pretty Eagle 90
principales 45
puberty ceremonies 54, 148,
  213
Puebloans 37, 37-9, 38, 41,
  44-5, 54

Q

qasgiq 213
Quechan (Yuman) 7 and
  see Yuman
quillwork 196-7
quivers 127, 146-7

R

rafts 102
rancheria groups 46-7, 50
Ratunda, Joseph 116
Red Cloud 85, 94
Red Cloud Agency 95
Red Cloud War 88
Red Earths (Meskwahki
  haki/Mesquaki) 249
Red towns 25, 27
religion
  Arctic 213-14, 220
  Basin area 123
  Northeast 227, 245, 248-9
  Northwest Coast 165
  Plains 67-9
  Plateau 109-10
  Southwest 44-6, 54, 58-9
  Subarctic 192-3
Removal 25
Reno, Major Marcus 91, 94
reservations
  California 151
  Plains 88, 98
  Plateau 110-11
  Southwest 39
Riddle, Toby (Kaitchkona)
  140
Ridge, Rollin 31

Rising Smoke (Wis Ki Gete)
  239
River Pima 47 and see
  Pima
River Yuman 47, 50 and see
  Yuman
Rocky Cree 182 and see
  Cree
Romar Nose 78, 81
Royal Canadian Mounted
  Police 223
Russel., Frank 52
Russian American
  Company 207, 210, 215
Russians 206-7, 215

S

Sadlermiut (Sallirmuit) 222
Sahaptin 100
Saint Lawrence Iroquoians
  225 and see Iroquois
Saint Lawrence Island
  Eskimo, 1930 211
Salado 37
Salinan 150
Salish 161, 164, 171, 175 and
  see Coast Salish
Salishan languages 100
Sallirmiut (Sadlermiut) 222
Salmon dance 135
San Carlos Apache 54-5
  and see Apache
San Felipe 41
San Francisco 130
San Ildefonso 37, 41
San Juan 41
Sand Creek Massacre 78
Sand Papago 58
Sandia 41
sandpainting 58
Sanpoil 100
Sans Arc 88
Santa Ana 41
Santa Clara 41
  Santa Clara Corn Dance,
    1950 40
Santa Fe Trail 76
Santa Rosa Island 7
Santee 87
Santo Domingo 41
Saouandanancous 236
Sarcee 63, 66
Satank 81, 95
Santana 81, 85
Sauk 245 245, 248, 249
Sauk & Fox 225, 244
  artifacts 246-7
Saukamaopee 64-6, 72
Saulteaux 182, 199
scalping 72
scapulimancy 192
Scarface Charley 140
sculpture 160-61, 164 and
  see carving
sea otters 170, 204, 210
seal hunting 168-9, 210, 220
season names, Cree 189
Secotan Luncheon, 1585
  238
Seminole 7, 13, 23, 25, 25,
  30
  artifacts 28-9
  and see Mikasuki
    Seminole
  Seminole Ballgame, 1895
    26
Seneca 225, 227, 233
  artifacts 234-5
Sequoyah syllabary 32
Seri 38-9, 58-9
Serrano 150
settlers
  in California 137, 141, 145
  Northwest Coast 176-7,
    180
  and Plains Indians 72-3,
    78
  Plateau 110-11
  Subarctic 203

shabúktowan 184
shamans 149, 164, 175-6,
  214, 220
Shasta 134, 136, 145
Shawnee 225
Sheridan, Lieut. Gen. P. H.
  88
Shoshoni 63-7, 109, 118, 118,
  126-7, 150, 151n4
Shuswap 100-102
Silestine, Joe (Toshkachito)
  16
Sinagua 37
Sinkyone 145
Sioux 62-3, 68, 94
Sireniski 213
Sitka Jake 157
Sitting Bull 73, 88-91, 94,
  94-5, 98-9
Skinner, Alanson 28, 200
Slave 197, 199, 203
slave trade 24, 38
Slavey 182
sleds 221, 223
Slim Buttes 94
Smith, Billy 25
Smith, Fred 23
Snake Creek 113, 116
snowhouses 220 and see
  igloos
snowshoes 146-7, 193, 197
Sobaipuri 46-7
social organization
  Arctic 205-7, 210, 213,
    216-17, 220-21
  Basin area 124
  California 136, 148
  Northeast 225-7, 231, 240
  Northwest Coast 155-7,
    166
  Plains 66-7, 72, 98
  Plateau 109-10
  Southeast 15-17, 21, 23-5,
    27, 30
  Southwest 37-9, 41, 45-7,
    50, 54-5
  Subarctic 182-3
sofkie 24
Sonoran Catholicism 46
Southeast
  agriculture 13, 21-22
  artifacts 15, 17, 24, 31
  disease 13-14
  economic organization 21
  environment 13
  fishing techniques 22
  food sources 13, 22
  habitation 14, 15, 21, 22,
    30, 32
  hunting techniques 22
  languages 13, 25, 63
  political organization
    16-17
  population 11, 13-14, 23
  social organization 15-17,
    21, 23-5, 27, 30
Southern Athapascans see
  Apache
Southern Kwakiutl, 154, 156,
  161, 170-71 and see
    Kwakiutl
Southern Paiute
  (Chemehuevi) 50, 58,
  119, 124
  and see Paiute
Southern Paiute Elder,
  1872 125
Southwest
  agriculture 37-8, 44, 46,
    54-5, 58
  art 44-5
  artifacts 38, 45, 48-9, 50,
    55
  clothing 48-9
  disease 39
  economic organization
    39, 54-5
  environment 37
  habitation 54, 58
  languages 41

political organization 39,
  45
population 39, 46, 54
religion 44-6, 54, 58-9
reservations 39
social organization 37-9,
  41, 45-7, 50, 54-5
trade 38-9
Spanish, in the Southwest
  38-9
spear-throwers 150
spears 101, 208-9
Speck, Frank G. 18, 228
Spinden, H. J. 42
spinning 45
Spirit Canoe ceremonies
  175
Spirit Dance see Ghost
  Dance
Spokane 100, 102, 109
spouse exchange 221
square grounds 25, 30
Star That Travels 68
Stevens Treaty 110-11
Steward, Julian 94
Stidham, George W. 20
stomp grounds see square
  grounds
Stone, Livingston 128
store houses 215
Storms, Simmon P. 130
Strongwoods Cree 182 and
  see Cree
Subarctic
  art 193, 196
  artifacts 199, 202
  clothing 193, 196-9, 202
  disease 203
  environment 182
  fishing techniques 183,
    184
  food sources 185, 188-9,
    192
  fur trade 202-4
  habitation 184-5, 188, 197,
    199, 202
  hunting techniques 185,
    192-3
  languages 182
  and missionaries 199
  populations 182-3, 203,
    205
  religion 192-3
  settlers 203
  social organization 182-3
  trade 197-8
Sun Dance medicine lodge
  80
Susquehannock 225
sutteeism 17, 21, 123
Swampy Cree 182 and see
  Cree
Swan, Judge James G. 166,
  178
Swanton, J. R. 14
Swimmer (Ayinini) 32
Swinomish 175
Sxwayxwey mask 175

T

Taaiyalone Mesa 44
Tahltan 182
Tahono O'Odham (Papago)
  47
Tall Bull 78
Talowa 131
Tanaina 182, 188, 196
Tanana 182, 188-9, 192
tanfula (hominy) 22
Tanoan 41
Taos 38, 41
Tarahumara 39, 46
  artifacts 48-9
Tattooed Serpent 17, 20-21
tattooing 66, 68, 145, 164
Teit, James A. 106
Tekesta 13
Ten Bears 81
Tepehuan 46

Terry, Brig. Gen. Alfred H.
  88-9
Tesuque 41
Tewa 41, 45, 54
Thompson 100-102
  artifacts 106-7
throwing boards 208-9
Thunderbirds 67-8
Tillamook 9
Timucua 13
tipis
  Basin 126
  Plains 65, 67, 77, 80, 89,
    99n1, 94
  Plateau 101, 102, 109
  Southwest 54
  and see habitation
Tiwa 41
Tlingit 155-6, 156, 157, 160,
  161, 161, 164, 177, 182
  artifacts 158-9, 162-3
tobacco pipes 138-9, 146-7,
  166-7
Tobacco Society 90, 92
Tocabaga 13
Tohome 13
Tohono O'Odham (Papago)
  46-7
Tolowa 134-5, 145
Tonto Apache 54 and see
  Apache
Too-hool-hool-zote 111-12
tools 96-7
Toqua 16
Toshkachito (Joe Silestine)
  16
totem poles 160-61, 165,
  165, 170, 171
Towa 41
towns (Creek Confederacy)
  25, 27, 30
trade 10
  Arctic 215, 222
  Basin area 126
  California 131, 135
  Northwest Coast 155-6,
    176
  Plains 66, 68, 104, 109
  Plateau 101, 103-4, 109
  Southwest 38-9
  Subarctic 197-8
travois 66
treaties 99n7, 111
  Fort Atkinson 73, 76
  Fort Laramie 73, 76, 85,
    88
  Medicine Lodge 81
  Plains 73, 76
  Stevens Treaty 110-11
Tseyka ceremonies 171
Tshanny 15
Tsimshian 155-6, 161, 177
Tsolocha 33
Tu-eka-kas (Old Joseph)
  110-11
Tubatulabal 150
Tukabahchee 31
Tum-se-ne-ho (Man
  without Blood) 102
tunghat 213-14
Tunica 13, 25
Tununirmiut 216
Tununirusirmiut 216
Tuscarora 225, 227
Tutelo 13
Two Belly 90
Two Kettle 88

U

Uiniyumayuittuq 220
Umatilla 8, 100
umiaks 212, 217 and see
  boats
Untush, Joseph 111
Upland Yuman 39, 50, 58
  and see Yuman
Upper Piman 46 and see
  Piman
Ute 9, 44, 54, 58-9, 118, 124,

255

126, 126, 127
utensils 92-3, 96-7, 142-3, 166-9
Uto-Aztecan languages 46, 63, 151n4
Utse-tah-wah-ti-an-kah 69

W

Wagon Box Fight 88
Wah-com-mo (Fast Walker) 249
Wahlitits 111
Wailaki 145
Wakusásse 249
Walapai 46, 50
Walla Walla 100
Wallowa Valley 110-11
walrus hunting 216

Wappo 145
warfare 38, 72, 84, 233
Warihio 46
Wasco 101, 108
Washakie 118
Washin-ha (Tom Baconrind) 70
Washita 85, 91
Washoe 123, 123
Washram 101
Watham, Charlie 141
Watie, Saladin 31
weapons 138-9, 151 and see guns
weaving 46, 164, 240
Weber Ute 119 and see Ute
West Main Cree 182 and see Cree
Western Apache, artifacts

56-7 and see Apache
Western Woods Cree 182 and see Cree
whaling 206, 210, 222
whaling hats 164
Whilkut 145
White Antelope 78
White Bird 112
White Bird Canyon 111
White Deer 231
White Deerskin dance 135
White Horse 78
White Mountain Apache 54, 55 and see Apache
White towns 25, 27
Wichita 63, 81
wickiups 54 and see habitation
wife exchange see spouse

exchange
wigass 239
wigwams
  Northeast 239-40
  Subarctic 184-5
  and see habitation
wild rice 236-7
Willow Creek 94
Wilson, Gilbert L. 96
Wilson, Jack (Wovoka) 81, 98-9, 122, 127
wind, Cree names 193
Winnebago 237, 245
Winneshiek 237
Wintu 134, 137, 145
  artifacts 138-9
Wis Ki Gete (Rising Smoke) 239
Wolf Mountain 94-5

Wolf Plume 65
Wolf Sleeve 81
Wounded Knee 99
Wovoka (Jack Wilson) 81, 98-9, 122, 127
written language 32, 248-9
Wylyams, Frederick 79-81

Y

Yakima 110, 111
Yamasee 13
Yana 145
Yanktonai 88
Yaqui 39, 46
Yavapai 46, 50
Yellowknife 182
Yokuts 130, 145
  Yokuts Shaman's Dance,

1880 149
Young, David 108
yuas 214
Yuchi 13, 25
  artifacts 18-19
Yuki 145, 151n4
Yuman (Quechan) 7, 37, 46, 47, 47, 50, 151
  River 47, 50
  Upland 39, 50, 58
Yup'ik 204, 212-15
Yurok 9, 135-6

Z

Zia 41
Zuni 11, 41, 44, 45
  artifacts 42-3